ACTORS AND ROLES IN EU DISABILITY LAW

This open access book looks at the development and consolidation of EU disability law as a distinct field of enquiry. It provides novel approaches to studying EU disability law. In a departure from other books on the topic, it takes a contextual approach, both engaging with current debates and policies and providing rigorous legal analysis. In addition to looking at the 'how' of the field's development, it addresses the 'who' by charting the key stakeholders in the field. This is an insightful and innovative take on an increasingly significant field of EU law.

Volume 131 in the Series Modern Studies in European Law

Modern Studies in European Law

Recent titles in this series:

The EU and the Baltic Sea Area
Edited by Allan Rosas and Henrik Ringbom

The Evolving Governance of EU Competition Law in a Time of Disruptions: A Constitutional Perspective
Edited by Carlo Maria Colombo, Kathryn Wright and Mariolina Eliantonio

The European Integrated Border Management: Frontex, Human Rights, and International Responsibility
Giulia Raimondo

Private Autonomy in EU Internal Market Law: Parameters of its Protection and Limitation
Rufat Babayev

Free Movement and Welfare Access in the European Union: Re-Balancing Conflicting Interests in Citizenship Jurisprudence
Victoria Hooton

EU Trade and Investment Treaty-Making Post-Lisbon: Moving Beyond Mixity
Gesa Kübek

The Normative Foundations for EU Criminal Justice: Powers, Limits and Justifications
Jacob Öberg

EU Neighbourhood Law: Wider Europe and the Extended EU's Legal Space
Alessandro Petti

The Dynamics of Powers in the European Union
Edited by Christina Eckes, Päivi Leino-Sandberg and Anna W Ghavanin

The European Convention on Human Rights and Private Law: Comparative Perspectives from South-Eastern Europe
Edited by Mateja Durovic and Cristina Poncibò

Judging Composite Decision-Making: The Transformation of European Administrative Law
Filipe Brito Bastos

EU Diplomacy in Multilateral Fora
Edited by Christine Kaddous and Frank Hoffmeister

The Market Citizenship Illusion: Free Movement Rights for Atypical Workers
Alice Welsh

Actors and Roles in EU Disability Law
Edited by Delia Ferri and Eva S Krolla

For the complete list of titles in this series see www.bloomsbury.com/uk/series/modern-studies-in-european-law/

Actors and Roles in EU Disability Law

Edited by
Delia Ferri
and
Eva S Krolla

With a foreword by
Gráinne de Búrca

•HART•
OXFORD • LONDON • NEW YORK • NEW DELHI • SYDNEY

HART PUBLISHING

Bloomsbury Publishing Plc

Kemp House, Chawley Park, Cumnor Hill, Oxford, OX2 9PH, UK

1385 Broadway, New York, NY 10018, USA

Bloomsbury Publishing Ireland Limited, 29 Earlsfort Terrace, Dublin 2, D02 AY28, Ireland

HART PUBLISHING, the Hart/Stag logo, BLOOMSBURY and the Diana logo are trademarks of Bloomsbury Publishing Plc

First published in Great Britain 2025

A catalogue record for this book is available from the British Library.

A catalogue record for this book is available from the Library of Congress.

Library of Congress Control Number: 2025930453

ISBN: HB: 978-1-50998-427-5
ePDF: 978-1-50998-429-9
ePub: 978-1-50998-428-2

Typeset by Compuscript Ltd, Shannon

For product safety related questions contact productsafety@bloomsbury.com

To find out more about our authors and books visit www.hartpublishing.co.uk. Here you will find extracts, author information, details of forthcoming events and the option to sign up for our newsletters.

FOREWORD

This book, which is dedicated to an examination of various dimensions of European Union (EU) disability law – as the introduction in its reference to the 'looking glass' suggests – aims to present a different or unusual perspective on a field that has attracted considerable scholarly attention. And, indeed, the *leitmotif* running through the book is a productive one which brings many interesting aspects to light, namely 'the role of institutional and non-institutional actors' in promoting disability rights in the EU.

In that sense, although the chapters engage with many familiar topics and aspects of European disability law, analysing provisions of the UN Convention on the Rights of Persons with Disabilities and of the Employment Equality Directive, and discussing case law of the CJEU and national courts, they aim for the most part to do so using a somewhat different lens. To draw on the language of sociology, the book is not primarily focused on *structures* such as law, doctrine, legislation and cases, instead it focuses on the role and perspective of *agents* – the actors who work and mobilise in different ways to advance, shape, invoke, monitor and implement EU disability law.

Some of the actors discussed are institutional actors – such as the European Commission, Council of the EU and Parliament, the EU Fundamental Rights Agency – while others are transnational and domestic civil society actors, groups and individuals, such as the European Disability Forum, as well as employers and trade unions. The book analyses the role of such actors at various levels – for example the CRPD Committee at the international level, the European Commission, the Fundamental Rights Agency and the CJEU at the European level, and domestic courts and civil society actors at the national level.

Another way of putting it is that the book, as the editors themselves note in the introduction, is interested in examining the involvement of a multiplicity of actors in the 'participatory governance' of EU disability law. EU disability law in this collection of essays is presented as a dynamic amalgam that is created and shaped at different levels, and as the evolving output of many different instruments, institutions, structures, policies and processes. The editors and authors have also aimed to bring cross-disciplinary insights and different methods and approaches – some historical, some doctrinal, some empirical and some socio-legal – to bear on the subject. The book provides an overview of the evolution and development of disability law and policy in the EU over time, as well as 'deep dives' into the role of particular institutions and processes.

The field of EU disability rights is always a rich one to study, fascinating in its own right and in its achievements, but it is very interesting also as a case study of the development of EU law and policy in its interaction with international and domestic processes. In all, the emphasis in this collection on actors and agency, and on dynamism and development, together with the methodological pluralism of the various chapters, results in a very interesting and readable volume which brings a welcome fresh lens to the field of European disability law.

Gráinne de Búrca
Fiesole, 26 August 2024

ACKNOWLEDGEMENTS

This volume was conceived of within the remit of the project 'Protecting the Right to Culture of Persons with Disabilities and Enhancing Cultural Diversity through European Union Law: Exploring New Paths – DANCING', funded by the European Research Council and hosted at Maynooth University, Ireland. It presents some of the findings of this project and seeks to contribute to the emerging field of EU disability law. It includes contributions of fellow colleagues, most of whom have been 'critical' friends of DANCING since its inception. Despite some delays along the way, we thoroughly enjoyed developing this volume and the wonderful collaboration with all authors. We want to warmly thank them for having accepted our invitation to contribute, and for having supported the DANCING project in various ways. Most of all, we are grateful to all of them for their help in rethinking the emergence of EU disability law from different perspectives, as well as for their insights and patience during the editing journey. Special thanks go to our longstanding friend and wonderful colleague Dr. Charles E. O'Sullivan who, besides contributing with a chapter, provided a linguistic revision of some chapters in this volume. We are also grateful to the DANCING team for their help at different junctures of this book project. Last but not least, we wish to extend our sincere thanks to Sinead Moloney and Sasha Jawed and the whole team at Hart Publishing for their support and their patience in the process of delivering the manuscript.

Delia Ferri and Eva S Krolla
Maynooth, 26 August 2024

The DANCING project has received funding from the European Research Council (ERC) under the European Union's Horizon 2020 Research and Innovation programme (Grant Agreement No. 864182).

erc
European Research Council

DANCING

CONTENTS

LIST OF CONTRIBUTORS

Ollie Bartlett is Assistant Professor of Law at the School of Law and Criminology of Maynooth University (MU), Ireland. He conducts research in the areas of public health law and social rights. He is a member of the MU Assisting Living and Learning (ALL) Institute.

Bernardo Cortese is Professor of EU Law at the University of Padova, Italy. He has been a *référendaire* at the Court of Justice of the European Union. He considers himself a disabled person by association, being the proud father of a marvellous girl with important, long-term impairments, facing a lot of barriers hindering her full and effective participation in society on an equal basis with others.

Claudia Coveney is Lecturer in Sociology and Social Policy at the University of Leeds, United Kingdom. Her academic interests lie in understanding the opportunities that changing government structures offer to civil society and social movements, in particular movements of persons with disabilities. She is a member of the Centre for Disability Studies of the University of Leeds.

Bruno De Witte is Emeritus Professor of European Union Law at Maastricht University, The Netherlands and former Professor at the European University Institute (EUI), Florence, Italy. Previously, he was Co-Director of the Maastricht Centre for European Law and of the Academy of European Law at EUI.

Michael Doherty is Professor of Law at the School of Law and Criminology of Maynooth University, Ireland. His expertise lies in the areas of Irish and EU employment and labour law, industrial relations, and social dialogue. He has worked on a number of EU projects on cross-border working terms and conditions, and is a member of several European research networks looking at employment and labour law and policy in the EU.

Silvia Favalli is Assistant Professor in International Law at the Department of International, Legal, Historical and Political Studies of the University of Milan, Italy. She holds a PhD in 'Public Law, Criminal and International Justice' from the Department of Law of the University of Pavia, Italy.

Delia Ferri is Professor of Law at the School of Law and Criminology of Maynooth University (MU), Ireland, and Co-Director of the MU Assisting Living and Learning (ALL) Institute. She is the Principal Investigator of the project 'Protecting the Right to Culture of Persons with Disabilities and Enhancing Cultural Diversity through European Union Law: Exploring New Paths – DANCING', funded by the European Research Council.

Eva S Krolla is Research Assistant at Maynooth University, Ireland and within the project 'Protecting the Right to Culture of Persons with Disabilities and Enhancing Cultural Diversity through European Union Law: Exploring New Paths – DANCING', funded by the European Research Council. She holds a joint Erasmus Mundus Master of Arts in Euroculture from the University of Groningen, The Netherlands, and the University of Udine, Italy.

Charles E O'Sullivan is Assistant Professor at the School of Law and Criminology of Maynooth University, Ireland. His research focuses on the interaction between law and the welfare state, with an emphasis on social inclusion, immigration and disability.

Urška Šadl is Part-time Professor of Law at the European University Institute in Florence, Italy and member of the MOBILE Centre of Excellence at the University of Copenhagen, Denmark.

Gabriel N Toggenburg is Honorary Professor of European Union and Human Rights Law at the University of Graz, Austria and Head of the Human Rights Structures and Mechanisms Sector at the European Union Agency for Fundamental Rights. He holds a PhD from the European University Institute in Florence, Italy and published widely on human rights issues.

Annalisa Volpato is Assistant Professor of European Union Law at the University of Padova, Italy. She is an associate scholar of the Maastricht Centre for European Law, The Netherlands, and member of the Editorial Board of the Review of European Administrative Law and the Maastricht Journal of European and Comparative Law.

Lisa Waddington is the European Disability Forum Professor of European Disability Law at Maastricht University, The Netherlands. Her Chair was established in cooperation with the European Disability Forum. She participates in a number of European networks and projects and is a member of the senior research team and legal research coordinator for the European Disability Expertise network, as well as the Senior Expert on Discrimination on the Ground of Disability in the European Network of Legal Research in Gender Equality and Non-Discrimination. She is also Guest Professor at Hasselt University, Belgium.

Anne Waldschmidt is Professor of Sociology and Politics of Rehabilitation, Disability Studies, and Director of iDiS (International Research Unit Disability Studies) at the University of Cologne, Germany. She is also a founding member of the interdisciplinary Centre for Gender Studies (GeStiK) at the University of Cologne. She was a member of the Academic Network of European Disability Experts and a member of the Scientific Committee of the European Union Agency for Fundamental Rights from 2018 to 2023.

LIST OF FIGURES

LIST OF TABLES

Introduction: Walking Through the Looking Glass

DELIA FERRI AND EVA S KROLLA

1. The Core Aims of the Volume

In the past few years, European Union (EU) law scholars have explored innovative approaches to the study of EU institutions, free movement and, more broadly, the process of European integration.[1] Departing from the traditional, and still dominant, legal doctrinal work, a new wave of academic research has engaged with empirical methods, as well as historical, geographical, sociological, and reflective analyses.[2] Scholars have discussed how knowledge about EU law is produced,[3] illustrating the history and politics of EU law as an academic discipline,[4] and they have investigated the 'lived experience of European integration'.[5] In spite of a critical discourse on interdisciplinarity and the challenges that legal scholarship faces *vis-à-vis* empirical research,[6] several academics have embraced Bailleux's

[1] This new wave has roots in the law-in-context debate dating back to the 1990s and even earlier. See F Snyder, 'New Directions in European Community Law' (1987) 14 *Journal of Law and Society* 167–182; J Shaw, 'European Union Studies in Crisis? Towards a New Dynamic' (1996) 16 *Oxford Journal of Legal Studies* 231–253.

[2] Among many others, A Dyevre, W Wijtvliet and N Lampach, 'The Future of European Legal Scholarship: Empirical Jurisprudence' (2019) 26 *Maastricht Journal of European and Comparative Law* 348–371; PJ Neuvonen, 'A way of critique: What can EU law scholars learn from critical theory?' (2022) 1(1) *European Law Open* 60–88; F de Witte, 'Here be Dragons: Legal geography and EU law' (2022) 1(1) *European Law Open* 113–125; C Kilpatrick and J Scott (eds), *New Legal Approaches to Studying the Court of Justice: Revisiting Law in Context* (Oxford University Press 2020); A Wallerman Ghavanini, 'The EU Court of Justice as a relational actor: an introduction' (2023) 2(2) *European Law Open* 233–243; A Bailleux, 'From the Stage to the High Seas: Concluding Thoughts on the Present and Future of EU Legal Studies' (2022) 18(4) *European Constitutional Law Review* 737–752; A Bailleux and B De Witte (eds), *Lawyering Europe: European Law as a Transnational Social Field* (Hart 2013).

[3] B De Witte, 'Editorial Note: How Much Critical Distance in the Academic Study of European Law?' (2022) 18 *Croatian Yearbook of European Law and Policy*.

[4] M Rasmussen, 'Establishing a Constitutional Practice of European Law: The History of the Legal Service of the European Executive, 1952–65' (2012) 21(3) *Contemporary European History* 375–397; S Kahn, 'Should Europe disturb historians? On the importance of methodology and interdisciplinarity' (2022) 28(4-6) *European Law Journal*.

[5] F de Witte (n 2).

[6] GT Davies, 'Taming Law: The Risks of Making Doctrinal Analysis the Servant of Empirical Research' in M Bartl, P Cebulak and J Lawrence (eds), *Behind the Method: The Politics of European Legal Research* (Edward Elgar 2022).

suggestion that they should 'not turn a blind eye to this 'social' dimension of law', '[w]hile not seeking to replace or mimic social scientists'.[7] Such a perspective encapsulates, as De Witte puts it, 'the possibility to rely on the findings of other disciplines (or, in its more ambitious form, the possibility to engage in interdisciplinary research oneself) in order to offer a better and richer understanding of legal questions'.[8] Muir, in a similar vein, contends that perspectives from other disciplines and interdisciplinary approaches 'are crucial to oxygenate EU legal scholarship' as 'they helpfully complement doctrinal legal work', illuminating a large number of institutional practices that have developed 'in the shadow of the law'.[9]

Recent scholarly endeavours have focused on the role of different institutional and non-institutional actors in EU law,[10] examining what these actors do in a doctrinal fashion, paying attention to constitutional processes, but also reflecting on the 'activities' or 'practices' that are behind the adoption of legal norms, as well as on their implementation, application and interpretation.[11] The analysis of legally relevant practices has become central to harness the benefits of non-doctrinal insights for legal scholars in order to expand our understanding of how EU law is shaped.[12] Thus far, most attention is given to courts, and particularly to the Court of Justice of the European Union (CJEU) and its role within the larger institutional framework of the EU.[13] As illustrated by the introduction to a dedicated special issue of *European Law Open*, the investigation of the CJEU as a 'relational actor' in both its constitutional and its judicial function and the need to go beyond well-rooted case law analysis, is gaining traction.[14] Scholarly contributions on the EU legislature – the Council of the EU (Council) and the European Parliament (EP) – and on the executive – the European Commission

[7] Bailleux (n 2).

[8] B De Witte, 'Legal Methods for the Study of EU Institutional Practice' (2022) 18(4) *European Constitutional Law* Review 637–656.

[9] E Muir, 'How to Introduce the EU Legal Order? Some Thoughts on Framework and Method' in M Claes and E Vos, *Making Sense of European Union Law* (Hart 2022) 136.

[10] R Gadbled and E Muir, 'Actors and Roles in EU Law: Asking 'Who Does What?' in the European Union Legal System' (2022) 18(4) *European Constitutional Law Review* 621–636.

[11] Bailleux and De Witte (n 2).

[12] R Deplano, G Gentile, L Lonardo and T Nowak (eds), *Interdisciplinary Research Methods in EU Law. A Handbook* (Edward Elgar 2024); R van Gestel and H-W Micklitz, 'Why Methods Matter in European Legal Scholarship' (2014) 20(3) *European Law Review* 292–316; JM Smits, 'What is Legal Doctrine? On the Aims and Methods of Legal-Doctrinal Research' (2015) 6 *Maastricht European Private Law Institute Working Paper*.

[13] Among others, T Horsley, *The Court of Justice of the European Union as an Institutional Actor. Judicial Lawmaking and its Limits* (Cambridge University Press 2018); P Craig, 'Institutions, Power, and Institutional Balance' in P Craig and G de Búrca (eds), *The Evolution of EU Law* (Oxford University Press 2021); C Moser and B Rittberger, 'The CJEU and EU (de-)constitutionalization: Unpacking jurisprudential responses' (2022) 20(3) *International Journal of Constitutional Law* 1038–1070; MR Madsen, F Nicola and A Vauchez (eds), *Researching the European Court of Justice. Methodological Shifts and Law's Embeddedness* (Cambridge University Press 2022); E Muir, M Dawson and B De Witte (eds), *Revisiting Judicial Politics in the EU* (Edward Elgar 2024).

[14] Wallerman Ghavanini (n 2).

(Commission) – have also departed from the traditional positivist slant, centring on constitutional processes.[15]

On the basis of such growing EU law literature that leverages on different methodologies, theoretical frameworks and approaches to studying decision-making processes and to critically examining legal sources, this volume adopts an '*actor-oriented* perspective' in pursuing a discrete overarching goal: that of extending our understanding of how EU disability law has actually been shaped. This collection thus takes on Bailleux's exhortation to 'leave the wonderland of law and [walk] through the looking glass'.[16] After an initial part that further articulates methodological and conceptual prolegomena, this volume brings together a series of chapters that interrogate the role of institutional and non-institutional actors in protecting and promoting disability rights within the EU and in moulding current EU disability law.

This volume does not intend to replicate existing academic work on the implementation of the UN Convention on the Rights of Persons with Disabilities (CRPD)[17] in the EU, although many of the chapters do include reflections on the extent to which the CRPD has been implemented.[18] Further, this volume does not focus on the extent to which EU law protects people with disabilities from discrimination, and does not aim to add to the already copious discussion of the shortcomings of Directive 2000/78/EC of 27 November 2000 establishing a general framework for equal treatment in employment and occupation (Employment Equality Directive),[19] and related case law.[20] However, some of the chapters, especially the ones dedicated to the CJEU, do inevitably engage with the Employment Equality Directive and its interpretation by the Luxembourg judges *vis-à-vis* the CRPD.[21]

Ultimately, this collection aims to illustrate the multifaceted contribution of different actors to the shaping of EU disability law as a stand-alone field of EU action. In doing so, it endeavours to critically reflect on the way institutional and non-institutional actors have traced the contours of EU disability law as it stands

[15] Among others, P Leino-Sandberg, C Eckes and A Wallerman Ghavanini (eds), *The Dynamics of Powers in the European Union* (Hart 2024).

[16] Bailleux (n 2).

[17] Annex I UN Convention on the Rights of Persons with Disabilities, 13 December 2006, in force 03 May 2008, UN Doc A/RES/61/106.

[18] Existing work on the implementation of the CRPD in EU law is vast. Among others, D Ferri and A Broderick (eds), *Research Handbook on EU Disability Law* (Edward Elgar 2020); L Waddington, 'The Influence of the UN Convention on the Rights of Persons with Disabilities on EU Anti-Discrimination Law' in U Belavusau and K Henrard (eds), *EU Anti-Discrimination Law beyond Gender* (Hart 2018) 339–361.

[19] Council Directive 2000/78/EC establishing a general framework for equal treatment in employment and occupation [2000] OJ L303/16.

[20] Among others, L Waddington, 'The European Union' in L Waddington and A Lawson (eds), *The UN Convention on the Rights of Persons with Disabilities in Practice: A Comparative Analysis of the Role of Courts* (Oxford University Press 2018) 131–152.

[21] B Cortese, 'The Role of the Court of Justice of the European Union in Protecting Disability Rights' in this volume; CE O'Sullivan, 'National Courts as 'Actors' in the Preliminary Reference Procedure' in this volume.

and it discusses the future role(s) they might take on in advancing the rights of persons with disabilities. The volume uses the term 'disability law' as umbrella term to encompass EU legislative instruments as well as soft law and variegated policy tools, although some of the authors do refer to 'disability law and policy' or to 'disability policies', albeit in a manner that is consistent with the scope of this volume.

2. EU Disability Law as a Stand-alone Field of Academic Enquiry

One of the key premises that underpins each of the contributions collected here is the emergence of disability as a discrete field of EU action and academic enquiry.[22] It is well known that, since the 1970s, and even earlier as Waldschmidt and Krolla highlight in their contribution, the EU has adopted a wide range of legislative and policy measures that address the rights of persons with disabilities. In fact, disability law has been distinctly advanced and elaborated by several institutional and non-institutional actors, informed by their varying mandates. Disability issues have featured in the process of European integration and consolidated in the 'EU disability *acquis*'.

2.1. The EU Disability *Acquis*

Generally, scholars have identified two watershed moments in the emergence of such *acquis*.[23] The first one was the entry into force of the Treaty of Amsterdam, which conferred onto the former European Community the power to combat, *inter alia*, discrimination on the grounds of disability, by virtue of Article 13 EC (now Article 19 of the Treaty on the Functioning of the European Union – TFEU) and supported the adoption of the Employment Equality Directive. The second, and probably most significant, moment was the conclusion by the EU[24] of the CRPD, which triggered a visible shift in the EU's approach to disability.[25] As many authors in this volume recall, the CRPD now forms an 'integral part of the European Union legal order',[26] enjoys a sub-constitutional status within the EU

[22] D Ferri and A Broderick, 'Introduction' in Ferri and Broderick (n 18) (Edward Elgar 2020) 1-10.

[23] L Waddington, *From Rome to Nice in a Wheelchair: The Development of a European Disability Policy* (Europa Law Publishing 2005); Waddington (n 18).

[24] Council Decision 2010/48/EC concerning the conclusion, by the European Community, of the United Nations Convention on the Rights of Persons with Disabilities [2010] OJ L23/35.

[25] D Ferri, 'The Role of Soft Law in Advancing the Rights of Persons with Disabilities in the EU: A 'hybridity' Approach to EU Disability Law' (2023) 28(4-6) *European Law Journal* 134–153.

[26] Joined Cases C-335/11 and C-377/11 *HK Danmark, acting on behalf of Jette Ring v Dansk almennyttigt Boligselskab and HK Danmark, acting on behalf of Lone Skouboe Werge v Dansk Arbejdsgiverforening, acting on behalf of Pro Display A/S* ECLI:EU:C:2013:222, para 30.

legal order, and requires EU secondary law to be interpreted in a manner consistent with it.[27]

After the ratification of the CRPD, the European Disability Strategy 2010–2020 (EDS)[28] was adopted to lay out a comprehensive disability policy framework. The EDS identified legislative and non-legislative measures in eight main areas that traversed the whole spectrum of EU competences: accessibility, participation, equality, employment, education and training, social protection, health, and external action.[29] As planned in the EDS, the EU adopted disability-specific legislation such as the Web Accessibility Directive (WAD),[30] which governs accessibility requirements for websites and mobile applications of public sector bodies, and the European Accessibility Act (EAA),[31] which mandates accessibility standards for a range of products and services. In that regard, the EDS has been a key tool for the advancement of EU disability law. The successor to the EDS, the Strategy for the Rights of Persons with Disabilities 2021–2030 (Strategy 2021–2030),[32] further contributes to the consolidation of EU disability law. It articulates several initiatives to be adopted around four core themes – accessibility; enjoying EU rights; decent quality of life and living independently; and equal access and non-discrimination – that are aimed at ensuring the implementation of the wide-ranging obligations provided for in the CRPD.

From a doctrinal standpoint, EU disability law currently consists of an array of primary and secondary legal sources – including key non-discrimination provisions enshrined in the TFEU, the EU Charter of Fundamental Rights (CFR) and the Employment Equality Directive, the CRPD as 'integral part of EU law',[33] disability-related provisions incorporated in EU legislation as well as disability-specific acts, such as the EAA – and a complex net of soft law, as well as technical standards adopted by standardisation organisations, and variegated policy tools. Further, EU disability law has developed across two axes: the first axis is the judicial development of a capacious protection from discrimination on the grounds of disability through case law; the second is the deployment of an array of legislative and non-legislative measures to protect and promote disability rights. In fact, thus far, scholarly contributions have mostly revolved around these key judicial and legislative developments,[34] with extensive focus

[27] Ibid para 29.

[28] European Commission (Commission), 'European Disability Strategy 2010-2020: A Renewed Commitment to a Barrier-Free Europe' COM(2010) 636 final.

[29] M Lecerf, 'Understanding EU Policies for People with Disabilities' (November 2023) European Parliamentary Research Service PE 698.811 7.

[30] Directive (EU) 2016/2102 of the European Parliament and of the Council on the accessibility of the websites and mobile applications of public sector bodies [2016] OJ L327/1.

[31] Directive (EU) 2019/882 of the European Parliament and of the Council of 17 April 2019 on the accessibility requirements for products and services [2019] OJ L151/70.

[32] Commission, 'Union of Equality Strategy for the Rights of Persons with Disabilities 2021–2030' COM(2021) 101 final.

[33] Joined Cases C-335/11 and C-337/11 *HK Danmark*, para 30.

[34] Among many others, D Ferri, 'The European Accessibility Act and the Shadow of the "Social Market Economy"' (2020) 45 *European Law Review* 660–680; P Watson and A Broderick, 'Disability in

on CJEU case law.[35] While recognising that EU disability law embeds the idea of the 'disablement' faced by persons with disabilities through discriminatory laws, policies and practices,[36] legal scholars have, for the most part, critically addressed the gaps and shortcomings of EU disability law (particularly non-discrimination provisions in the Employment Equality Directive) *vis-à-vis* the CRPD.[37] They have engaged with the field as a unified, yet over time stratified, area of EU action,[38] and, to varying degrees, have contributed to the systematisation of what Kilpatrick and Scott call 'a structured sphere of interaction of legal materials' into a discrete body of EU law.[39] However, with a few exceptions, such as de Búrca's contribution on the way in which EU experimentalist governance has influenced the content of the CRPD itself,[40] legal scholars have paid limited attention to the way in which various actors construct, interpret and ultimately shape EU disability law. In that regard, this volume aims to advance the state of the art and to shine a light on the making of EU disability law by a range of institutional and non-institutional actors interacting in fully constitutionalised processes and through informal participatory governance tools.

2.2. The CRPD as Normative Standard

As noted above, this volume is not about the CRPD *per se*, and, quite deliberately, does not engage with a compliance analysis of EU law *vis-à-vis* the CRPD.

EU non-discrimination law' in Ferri and Broderick (n 18) 121-145; L Waddington, 'Reading a Duty to Provide Accessible Pre-Contractual Information for Consumers with Disabilities into EU Consumer Protection Law' (2022) 45(2) *Journal of Consumer Policy* 307–329; C Conte, *The UN Convention on the Rights of Persons with Disabilities and the European Union. The Impact on Law and Governance* (Hart 2022).

[35] Among others, S Favalli and D Ferri, 'Defining Disability in the European Union Non-Discrimination Legislation: Judicial Activism and Legislative Restraints' (2016) 22 *European Public Law* 541; D Schiek, 'Intersectionality and the Notion of Disability in EU Discrimination Law' (2016) 53 *Common Market Law Review* 35–63; L Waddington, 'Saying all the Right Things and Still Getting it Wrong: The Court of Justice's Definition of Disability and Non-Discrimination Law' (2015) 22 *Maastricht Journal of European and Comparative Law* 576; C O'Brien, 'Union Citizenship and Disability: Restricted Access to Equality Rights and the Attitudinal Model of Disability' in D Kochenov (ed), *Citizenship and Federalism in Europe: The Role of Rights* (Cambridge University Press 2016).

[36] A Lawson, 'Disability Law as an Academic Discipline: Towards Cohesion and Mainstreaming?' (2020) 47(4) *Journal of Law and Society* 558–587; D Ferri, 'The Role of Disability Studies in the Advancement of EU Law Scholarship' in Deplano, Gentile, Lonardo and Nowak (n 12).

[37] A Broderick, 'The United Nations Convention on the Rights of Persons with Disabilities and EU Disability Law: Towards a Converging Vision of Equality?' in T Giegrich (ed), *The European Union as Protector and Promotor of Equality* (Springer 2020) 363–390; L Waddington and A Broderick, 'Combatting disability discrimination and realising equality: A comparison of the UN CRPD and EU equality and non-discrimination law' (European Commission 2018); L Waddington, 'Equal to the Task? Re-Examining EU Equality Law in Light of the United Nations Convention on the Rights of Persons with Disabilities' (2013) 4 *European Yearbook of Disability Law* 169; L Waddington and A Lawson, 'The Unfinished Story of EU Disability Non-Discrimination Law' in A Bogg, C Costello and ACL Davies (eds), *Research Handbook on EU Labour Law* (Edward Elgar 2016).

[38] Ferri (n 25).

[39] C Kilpatrick and J Scott, 'Introduction' in Kilpatrick and Scott (n 2).

[40] G de Búrca, 'The EU in the Negotiation of the UN Disability Convention' (2010) 35(2) *European Law Review*.

However, it is premised on the assumption that this Convention, besides (undeniably) being the major driver for the development of EU disability law, is 'the normative standard to which the EU adheres with regard to the rights of individuals with disabilities'.[41] For this reason, without disentangling the main normative tenets of the CRPD, which have been thoroughly discussed elsewhere,[42] it seems important to set out key facets and the most relevant provisions of this Convention, which are evoked and mentioned at various junctures throughout the volume.

The first notable feature of the CRPD is that it conceives of disability as a social construct,[43] and abandons the outdated medical model of disability. In doing so, the Convention is said to embrace a social-contextual understanding of disability,[44] which centres on the removal of barriers to ensure the equal enjoyment of rights by persons with disabilities. In particular, Article 1 CRPD states that 'disability results from the *interaction* between persons with impairments and attitudinal and environmental barriers that hinder their full and effective participation in society on an equal basis with others'.[45] The distinctive normative cipher of the CRPD is linked to the fact that the CRPD embeds and puts forward the 'human rights model of disability'.[46] As Degener contends, this model underscores the inherent human dignity of persons with disabilities, values impairments as part of human diversity, and 'encompasses both sets of human rights, civil and political as well as economic, social and cultural rights'.[47] The CRPD epitomises the 'human rights model of disability', placing emphasis on the dignity of persons with disabilities and inclusive equality,[48] and making clear that persons with disabilities are holders of the whole panoply of human rights, must live independently and be fully included in society.[49] Admittedly, there is some disagreement among disability scholars on the nature of the human rights model, in particular in its relation to the social model of disability: some consider the human rights model an 'improvement of the social model of disability';[50] and others see the two models as

[41] Ferri and Broderick (n 18); D Ferri, 'The Unorthodox Relationship between the EU Charter of Fundamental Rights, the UN Convention on the Rights of Persons with Disabilities and Secondary Rights in the Court of Justice Case Law on Disability Discrimination' (2020) 16(2) *European Constitutional Law Review* 275–305.

[42] The literature on the CRPD is vast. Among others, V Della Fina, R Cera and G Palmisano (eds), *The United Nations Convention on the Rights of Persons with Disabilities: A Commentary* (Springer 2017).

[43] Committee on the Rights of Persons with Disabilities (CRPD Committee), 'General Comment No. 6 on equality and non-discrimination' (2018) CRPD/C/GC/6.

[44] A Broderick, *The Long and Winding Road to Equality and Inclusion for Persons with Disabilities* (Intersentia 2015) 77.

[45] Emphasis added. See also Preamble para (e) CRPD.

[46] T Degener, 'A New Human Rights Model of Disability' in Della Fina, Cera and Palmisano (n 42) 41.

[47] Ibid.

[48] Ibid; G Quinn and T Degener, 'Human Rights and Disability' (United Nations 2002); CRPD Committee (n 43).

[49] T Degener, 'Disability in a Human Rights Context' (2016) 5(3) *Laws* 35–59.

[50] Most notably T Degener, 'A human rights model of disability' in P Blanck and E Flynn (eds), *Routledge Handbook of Disability Law and Human Rights* (Routledge 2016) 32.

'complementary'.[51] Crucially, however, both iterations consider the human rights model as being able to offer a 'roadmap' for change.[52] Even more, as Lawson and Beckett observe, the prescriptive nature of the human rights model *requires* the progression of disability law and policy 'in line with human rights and principles, as set out in the CRPD'.[53]

The CRPD enshrines the core principles of respect for human dignity, non-discrimination and equality, accessibility, and participation. The principle of non-discrimination has been illustrated as the '*leitmotif*' of the CRPD,[54] in that it applies to both civil and political rights as well as to economic, social and cultural rights. Article 2 CRPD provides a wide-ranging definition of discrimination on the ground of disability, stating that such discrimination comprises the denial of reasonable accommodation, whereby reasonable accommodation is any 'necessary and appropriate modification and adjustments not imposing a disproportionate or undue burden, where needed in a particular case, to ensure to persons with disabilities the enjoyment or exercise on an equal basis with others of all human rights and fundamental freedoms'. As discussed by the UN Committee on the Rights of Persons with Disabilities (CRPD Committee) in General Comment No. 2, accessibility is an essential 'precondition' for the enjoyment of other human rights.[55] Article 9 CRPD requires State Parties to take appropriate measures to ensure that people with disabilities have access to environments, facilities, information and services on an equal basis with others.[56] The principle of participation of people with disabilities is also a core feature of the Convention, mandating the involvement of persons with disabilities in society, and in all spheres of policy-making.[57]

These core principles are subsumed in the concept of inclusive equality, which embraces four intertwined dimensions: a fair *redistributive* dimension, which refers to the need to address socio-economic disadvantages; a *recognition* dimension, which requires the combatting of stigma and the recognition of dignity and intersectionality; a *participative* dimension, which necessitates the recognition of the social nature of people with disabilities as members of society; and an *accommodating* dimension, which entails making space for difference as a matter of human dignity.[58]

[51] A Lawson and AE Beckett, 'The social and human rights models of disability: towards a complementarity thesis' (2021) *The International Journal of Human Rights* 348–379.

[52] Ibid 360, 368; Degener (n 49).

[53] Lawson and Beckett (n 51) 364.

[54] O Mjöll Arnardóttir, 'A Future of Multidimensional Disadvantage Equality' in O Mjöll Arnardóttir and G Quinn (eds), *The UN Convention on the Rights of Persons with Disabilities: European and Scandinavian Perspectives* (Martinus Nijhoff Publishers 2009) 41.

[55] CRPD Committee, 'General Comment No. 2 on accessibility' (2014) CRPD/C/GC/2. See also CRPD Committee (n 43) para 40.

[56] CRPD Committee, 'General Comment No. 2 on accessibility'.

[57] CRPD Committee, 'General Comment No. 7 on the participation of persons with disabilities, including children with disabilities, through their representative organizations, in the implementation and monitoring of the Convention' (2018) CRPD/C/GC/7.

[58] CRPD Committee (n 43) para 11, T Degener and M Uldry, 'Towards inclusive equality: 10 years Committee of the Rights of Persons with Disabilities' (German Federal Ministry of Labour and Social Affairs 2018).

The CRPD protects and promotes the whole spectrum of civil, political, economic, social and cultural rights, but also recognises that the full realisation of these rights depends on governance mechanisms that implement legislation, policies and practices that align with the CRPD. Article 33 CRPD sets forth the obligations to: designate one or more focal points to implement the CRPD (Article 33(1) CRPD); give due consideration to the establishment of a mechanism to coordinate the implementation process (Article 33(1) CRPD); and put in place a structure to protect, promote and monitor the implementation of the Convention (Article 33(2) CRPD). In addition, Article 33(3) CRPD requires State Parties to involve civil society, in particular organisations of persons with disabilities, in monitoring processes. The latter provision tallies with Article 4(3) CRPD, which requires in a general fashion close consultation with, and active involvement of, persons with disabilities, through their representative organisations, in the development and implementation of legislation and policies and in all decision-making processes that concern disability related issues.

Overall, in the EU, the CRPD can be said to have displayed its potential of a 'catalyst for change',[59] having triggered an array of developments as well as advancements in the way that institutional and non-institutional actors have engaged with one another and have dealt with disability rights.

3. Methodological Approaches

3.1. An Overarching 'Law-in-Context' Perspective

This volume on the whole is underpinned by a 'law-in-context' perspective, which embraces Snyder's approach to EU law as 'an intricate web of politics, economics and law' and requires an interdisciplinary, contextual or critical approach.[60] It recognises, as Armstrong posits, that the ever-changing nature of EU governance requires lawyers to give accounts of complex relationships between EU law and politics,[61] and acknowledges the existence of blurred boundaries between 'law and economics, law and politics, law and culture'.[62] It embraces the view that the 'law-in-context' approach allows the use of 'theoretical input to tackle concrete legal questions', which 'far from being methodologically peripheral, is actually key to producing meaningful research on European integration'.[63] It further embraces the

[59] L Arbour, 'Statement by Louise Arbour UN High Commissioner for Human Rights on the Ad Hoc Committee's Adoption of the Convention on the Rights of Persons with Disabilities' (New York, 5 December 2006).

[60] Snyder (n 1).

[61] K Armstrong, 'Legal Integration: Theorizing the Legal Element of Integration' (1998) 36(2) *Journal of Common Market Studies* 155–174.

[62] P Selznick, 'Law in Context Revisited' (2003) 30(2) *Journal of Law and Society* 177–186.

[63] K Caunes, 'Some triple Q reflections: On journal rankings, methodology and scholarship with impact' (2022) 28(4-6) *European Law Journal* 110–123.

current dynamism that characterises the study of EU law, and aims to bring layers of concreteness to the discrete study of EU disability law. However, this volume does not prescribe a specific methodological approach, nor the use of empirical methods. It does not deny the importance, usefulness and value of traditional legal research which, as noted by Davies, 'seeks to analyse the law, as found in legislation or judgments or other sources of law' and often 'expose[s] the implicit values, assumptions, normative claims, and concepts in the law, to show what it expresses, which ideas it nurtures, and which it suppresses'.[64]

The chapters collected here adopt a range of methodological approaches and perspectives. Some chapters are based on qualitative research, such as that authored by Coveney. Others, such as the one authored by Krolla, adopt a socio-legal approach that blends empirical findings and legal/doctrinal research. Other chapters, such as that written by Ferri, engage with a systematic document analysis. Further contributions, such as O'Sullivan's chapter, blend to varying degrees doctrinal and non-doctrinal perspectives. Other authors align with the traditional stream of doctrinal research, which, as noted earlier, is still well rooted and retains significant validity.[65] All of the chapters engage with what role the actor under examination has played – and will arguably play in the future – in shaping, implementing or adjudicating EU disability law. Each of the contributing authors has in fact made deliberate choices on the methodology(-ies) and approaches that best serve to capture and examine the practices and significance of an actor.[66] These choices are briefly explained and contextualised by each contributor in their respective chapters.

3.2. Actorness and Actors

As Volpato thoroughly discusses in her chapter, the investigation of 'who', i.e. the relevant actors, and what they 'do' can reveal important information about their actual 'activities' or 'practices' and how these inform EU disability law, shape its meaning, define its contours, and drive its implementation.

Actorness as a theoretical concept originates in European Studies in relation to the EU's ability to act at international level. However, as Čmakalová and Rolenc point out, the EU's 'actorness' is informed by the internal dimension of its constituent actors and their inherent legitimacy.[67] The term 'actor' has been used by an

[64] Davies (n 6).

[65] Muir (n 9) 136.

[66] Madsen, Nicola and Vauchez (n 13).

[67] For a concise overview of various concepts of 'actorness', K Čmakalová and JM Rolenc, 'Actorness and Legitimacy of the European Union' (2012) 4(2) *Cooperation and Conflict* 260–270; E Drieskens, 'Golden or gilded jubilee? A research agenda for actorness' (2017) 24(10) *Journal of European Public Policy* 1534–1546; M Rhinard and G Sjöstedt, 'The EU as a Global Actor: A new conceptualisation four decades after 'actorness'' (The Swedish Institute of International Affairs 2019).

array of political science scholars. Bressanelli *et al.* in the introduction to a special issue of the *Journal of European Public Policy* entitled 'EU Actors under pressure: politicisation and depoliticisation as strategic responses'[68] distinguish supranational actors, such as the CJEU, the European Central Bank and the Commission, from intergovernmental actors, such as the Council. Meijer *et al.* use the term 'actor' in a general fashion and highlight that '[d]ecisions in the European Union are the consequence of the negotiations between various (oftentimes collective) actors on the European and the national level with conflicting preferences over multiple issues'.[69] When looking at actors, the volume adopts a broad definition, to encompass EU institutions and bodies as well as non-institutional players – such as civil society organisations, social partners and academics – that actually participate in various capacities in EU governance mechanisms and co-produce to differing degrees EU disability law. Part II of the volume discusses a selected number of key institutional actors: the Commission, the EP and the Council (as legislature), the CJEU, national courts (in the role of European courts), as well as the EU Agency for Fundamental Rights (FRA) and the European Ombudsman. The volume acknowledges that other institutions and bodies have contributed to the building of EU disability law – this is the case, for example, of the European Economic and Social Committee which has released several notable opinions on disability legislation and on specific proposals of the Commission. However, it deliberately focuses on a range of actors whose contribution has been more ostensible in actually shaping current EU disability law. Part III looks at the European Disability Forum (EDF) and other disability organisations, social partners and academics. This part of the volume recognises the important role played by civil society, broadly conceived of, in advancing the protection and promotion of disability rights.[70] It also includes a chapter on the CRPD Committee. While this is not an EU actor *strictu sensu*, by reviewing the EU action within the treaty reporting procedure, the CRPD Committee has contributed to orient EU disability law and highlights strengths and weaknesses. It has been noted that the Member States are generally important actors 'owing to the decisive role that they play' in EU law generally.[71] However, this volume purposedly does not engage with them *per se*, but does consider their weight within the legislative process. Further, national courts are considered as specific EU law actors in O'Sullivan's chapter. EU citizens have also been considered as an important actor.[72]

[68] E Bressanelli, C Koop and C Reh, 'EU Actors under pressure: politicisation and depoliticisation as strategic responses' (2020) 27(3) *Journal of European Public Policy* 329–341.

[69] MJ Meijers, CJ Schneider and A Zhelyazkova, 'Dimensions of input responsiveness in the EU: actors, publics, venues' (2019) 26(11) *Journal of European Public Policy* 1724–1736.

[70] L Vanhala, 'Anti-discrimination policy actors and their use of litigation strategies: the influence of identity politics' (2009) 16(5) *Journal of European Public Policy* 738–754; A Waldschmidt, 'Disability Policy of the European Union: The Supranational Level' (2009) 3 *Alter European Journal of Disability Research* 8, 11; C O'Mahony and S Quinlivan, 'The EU Disability Strategy and the Future of EU Disability Policy' in Ferri and Broderick (n 18) 12-28.

[71] Muir (n 9) 137.

[72] Ibid.

Which roles different actors can and do assume has been elaborated both in social sciences and in International Relations (IR) research since the 1960s.[73] While (organisational) role theories were initially focused on the individual to conceptualise and analyse enacted roles, theories in IR applied them to the behaviour of states.[74] Role theories in the IR realm concur that the role(s) actors take on are relational in nature and must be recognised by society.[75] Considering this array of theories, this volume does conceive roles as legal positions that carry expectations as per their purpose.[76] The volume takes into account that the examination of an actor's roles must be carried out by scrutinising the criteria of role expectation, role conceptions, role enactment and identity formation.[77]

As yet, literature that explores which roles actors *within* the EU have assumed, or ought to assume, have primarily been pursued through the prism of European integration theories. In this context, EU institutions are traditionally thought about along the intergovernmental versus supranational axis. On the intergovernmental side, liberal intergovernmentalism has perhaps been the most prominent theory. Developed by Moravcsik, liberal intergovernmentalism sees Member States, and thus the Council, as the drivers of European integration, acting however in that direction to advance national socio-economic interests.[78] On the other hand, supranationalists argue that it is the EU's supranational institutions, most notably the Commission and the CJEU, that urge European integration on. Hodson *et al.* refer to neofunctionalism, neo-neofunctionalism, and supranationalism, as theories that 'see EU institutions as engines of European integration and as key ingredients in political spillover'.[79]

In the last decade, an array of 'new' theories has sprung up on both sides of the debate.[80] Bickerton *et al.* have presented 'new intergovernmentalism', emphasising the dominance of deliberation and consensus-seeking in intergovernmental institutions, as well as the tendency to create '*de novo* bodies' to delegate powers

[73] D Katz and RL Kahn, *The Social Psychology of Organisations* (Wiley 1966); D Katz and RL Kahn, *The Social Psychology of Organisations* (Wiley 1978); BJ Biddle, 'Recent Developments in Role Theory' (1986) 12 *Annual Review of Sociology* 67–92; M Wickham and M Parker, 'Reconceptualising organisational role theory for contemporary organisational contexts' (2007) 22(5) *Journal of Managerial Psychology* 440–464.

[74] S Harnisch, 'Role theory. Operationalization of key concepts' in S Harnisch, C Frank and HW Maull (eds), *Role Theory in International Relations* (Routledge 2011) 7.

[75] Ibid; C Thies, 'Role Theory and Foreign Policy' in RA Denemark (ed), *The International Studies Encyclopedia* (Wiley-Blackwell 2010).

[76] Harnisch (n 74) 8.

[77] Ibid 8-9.

[78] A Moravcsik, 'Negotiating the Single European Act: national interests and conventional statecraft in the European Community' (1991) 45(1) *International Organization* 19–56; A Moravcsik, 'Preferences and Power in the European Community: A Liberal Intergovernmentalist Approach' (1993) 31(4) *Journal of Common Market Studies* 473–524; A Moravcsik, *The Choice for Europe* (Cornell University Press 1998).

[79] D Hodson, U Puetter and S Saurugger, 'Why EU institutions matter: five dimensions of EU institutional politics' in D Hodson, U Puetter, S Saurugger and J Peterson (eds), *The Institutions of the EU* (Oxford University Press 2021) 9.

[80] V Schmidt, 'Rethinking EU Governance: From 'Old' to 'New' Approaches to Who Steers Integration' (2018) 56(7) *Journal of Common Market Studies* 1544–1561.

to rather than to the Commission.[81] According to Schmidt, 'new supranationalists' then view the EU's supranational institutions as 'driving integration through their greater role in policy design and enforcement',[82] while 'new parliamentarians' focus on what they see as an increasing role of the EP.[83] While these theories build on the differences between the traditional intergovernmentalist and supranationalist theories, Schmidt points out that the 'new' approaches all adopt a common framework of analysis of European integration in that they all 'emphasize the importance of sentient actors' ideas and discursive interactions following a constructivist or discursive institutionalist logic, in which actors' ideational powers are constructed through discourse and deliberation'.[84] Schmidt coins a term for this newest form of institutionalism: discursive institutionalism.[85] In essence, this approach 'views EU institutions through the lens of ideas and discourse'.[86] Referencing Schmidt, Hodson *et al.* note that this approach 'takes a dynamic view of institutions, in which ideas and discourse serve as catalysts for change rather than a means of reinforcing the status quo'.[87]

The chapters included in Part II engage with the role of the actor under examination and take into account expectations related to the actor's actions, but do not directly discuss the process of European integration. Rather, they are underpinned by the understanding that exploring who, and how, drives integration dynamics in relation to disability supports an understanding of European governance. Some chapters, such as Bartlett's, also showcase how intergovernmentalist and supranationalist trends manifest themselves in the shaping of EU disability law. When looking at the role of institutional actors, the chapters engage with their constitutional competences and mandates (and their boundaries) as laid down in the Treaties. To varying degrees, chapters on non-institutional actors, i.e. actors outside the formal architecture of the EU legal order, probe the extent to which such actors can be influential outside constitutional processes in EU disability law.

4. Structure of the Volume

Further to this introduction, the volume includes thirteen chapters and is divided into three parts. As noted above, the opening chapters in Part I provide a critical

[81] CJ Bickerton, D Hodson and U Puetter, 'The new intergovernmentalism: European integration in the Post-Maastricht Era' (2015) 53(4) *Journal of Common Market Studies* 703–722.

[82] Schmidt (n 80) 1545; Schmidt refers to MW Bauer and S Becker, 'The Unexpected Winner of the Crisis: The European Commission's Strengthened Role in Economic Governance' (2014) 36(3) *Journal of European Integration* 213–229 and RA Epstein and M Rhodes, 'The Political Dynamics Behind Europe's New Banking Union' (2016) 39(3) *West European Politics* 415–437.

[83] Schmidt (n 80) 1545.

[84] Ibid.

[85] Already in V Schmidt, 'Discursive Institutionalism: the explanatory power of ideas and discourse' (2008) 11 *The Annual Review of Political Science* 303–326.

[86] Hodson, Puetter and Saurugger (n 79) 12.

[87] Ibid.

elaboration of methodological challenges in EU legal scholarship and provide an important bedrock to the study of actors and roles in the context of EU disability law. Part II focuses on institutional actors of the EU legal order and discusses whether, how and to what extent they have contributed to the protection and promotion of disability rights in the EU. Part III considers selected non-institutional actors' impact on EU disability law, similarly addressing whether, how and to what extent they have contributed to the protection and promotion of disability rights in the EU. The volume is concluded by an epilogue that reflects on the concrete relevance of actors and actorness in the development of EU disability law.

Volpato opens Part I of the volume and traces the relevant trajectories and drivers of the complex, multi-actor and multi-level nature of the EU legal order that have contributed to the development of EU disability law. In her analysis she highlights the roles of different actors in EU governance and the collaborative links established between them to critically reflect on their individual contributions to EU disability law. Šadl deepens the discussion by proposing a novel and comprehensive framework for analysing the role of legal actors, in particular Member States' governments, national courts submitting preliminary references and Advocates General as well as relevant factors, such as existing law and politics and their influence over EU law-making. The chapter addresses the key question of which, how much and when these actors and factors impact EU law-making by conceptualising a model of influence that accounts for the direct and explicit as well as the indirect and implicit influence that legal actors can exert. To conclude the opening part and set the scene for Part II, Waldschmidt and Krolla examine the different phases in which EU institutions and other actors have shaped EU disability policy and connects them to general developments and structural changes of the EU and its predecessors since the late 1950s. The chapter functions as a contextual anchor for the contributions included in Part II and Part III.

Part II of the volume focuses on institutional actors of the EU architecture to illuminate and interrogate which role the institutions play, their respective mandates and competences and crucially in which ways they have shaped the development of EU disability law. Besides investigating recent developments and case studies, the chapters in Part II consider which future role the given actor may play in EU disability law and endeavour to draw from experiences in adjacent policy areas, such as non-discrimination law, labour law and internal market law. Krolla posits that the Commission is the principal institutional driving force behind major developments in EU disability law. The author makes use of a socio-legal approach that combines doctrinal research with a set of empirical data from qualitative interviews in the analysis. The roles that the Commission assumes in setting the agenda, initiating and implementing legislation as well as the uses of various consultation processes are teased out. Bartlett critically examines the role of the EU co-legislators – the Council and the EP – by using three case studies that illustrate how they are capable of advancing disability rights and how, due to conflicting interests, they are similarly able to inhibit such advancement. He identifies four common issues that hamper EU social legislation and the development of EU disability law, and points to legal strategies for disability advocates that have proven successful in facilitating the unblocking of legislation with the co-legislators. Turning to the judiciary, the following two chapters, authored by Cortese and O'Sullivan respectively, investigate the CJEU and national courts as EU courts and their roles in protecting disability rights but also in progressively shaping EU disability law. Cortese examines the role of the CJEU in supporting disability rights, but he points to the limits of the Luxembourg case law. O'Sullivan discusses key issues for the preliminary reference procedure on the basis of Article 267 TFEU to be effective in elaborating EU disability law. The chapter highlights that sufficient EU law 'fluency', the willingness to engage with the procedure and the capability of referred cases and questions to expand existing case law, are crucial in this regard. The subsequent chapter, authored by Ferri, considers the European Ombudsman. It identifies, maps and analyses complaints and inquiries related to disability issues, and on foot of that analysis the chapter concludes that the European Ombudsman *de facto* contributes to the advancement of EU disability law. Toggenburg explains the FRA's role and mandate as independent centre of expertise for fundamental rights and examines the Agency's work on the rights of persons with disabilities, as well as its role in the EU monitoring framework under Article 33(2) CRPD.

Turning to actors that sit outside the EU constitutional architecture, Part III of this volume considers various stakeholders. Coveney first investigates how EDF as civil society actor has influenced EU disability policy. The author shows how EDF engages with various EU institutions and individual policymakers through civil society forums, consultations throughout the legislative process and lobbying activities as well as targeted campaigns to shape disability policy. To this end, she discusses three selected campaigns run by EDF and the extent to which stated goals (as well as unintended outcomes) were achieved. Doherty, changing the viewpoint, examines the role(s) that social partners have assumed in the advancement of disability rights. The author critically reflects on the apparent diminution of social partner legitimacy in EU law- and policy-making orders, and on their limited role in promoting disability rights. Using an autoethnographic approach, Waddington outlines and reflects on the role of experts and academics in shaping EU disability law over the past 30 years. Finally, as an actor outside the European geopolitical sphere, the CRPD Committee assumes three distinct yet interrelated roles: as a monitoring body, as a quasi-judicial body and as an expert body. Favalli argues that – despite the fact that the EU has yet to ratify the Optional Protocol of the CRPD that enables the role of a quasi-judicial body for the CRPD Committee *vis-à-vis* parties to the Convention – the CRPD Committee has taken on a leading role in nudging the EU towards a more effective implementation of the CRPD and thus contributes to inform EU disability law and policy.

The volume concludes with an epilogue written by De Witte, that draws on and brings together the analyses of the different institutional and non-institutional actors in the EU disability law arena, and situates these within the larger domain of EU law.

Notably, this volume was conceived of and written within the remit of the project 'Protecting the Right to Culture of Persons with Disabilities and Enhancing Cultural Diversity through European Union Law: Exploring New Paths – DANCING', funded by the European Research Council (Grant Agreement No. 864182) and hosted at Maynooth University, Ireland. While presenting some of the interim findings of this project in dedicated chapters, this volume aims to situate those findings within broader debates in EU law and to realise one of the ambitions of DANCING, that of contributing to the emerging field of EU disability law. Most of the chapters in this volume were finalised at the beginning of June 2024. Thus, the volume covers legal developments that occurred up until 31 May 2024.

PART I

Prolegomena and Methodological Challenges

1

The Voices and the Choir: The Importance of a Contextual Analysis of EU Actors' Roles

ANNALISA VOLPATO

1. Introduction

The development of EU disability law, which has experienced an unequivocable rise in the last decades, has taken place in a normative framework inherently characterised by a complex and multi-layered nature.[1] The implementation of the UN Convention on the Rights of Persons with Disabilities (CRPD) in particular, spans across different levels of governance[2] and involves different relevant actors, including national authorities, the European Commission (Commission), the European Parliament (EP), the European Ombudsman, the EU Agency of Fundamental Rights (FRA) and the European Disability Forum (EDF).[3] Far from being an exception to the rule, the plurality of governance levels and governing actors that we find in EU disability law is an expression of the peculiar manner in which the European legal order, and especially the European administration, has developed in the bulk of the policy fields the EU is active in today.

The actors involved in the implementation of EU disability law are inevitably affected by this evolution which, together with judicial interpretation, impact on their structure and the limits to their powers. To fully grasp their role and action in this policy field, it is therefore important to collocate them in this broader context and to analyse the concrete manner whereby the various actors interact across the different governance levels. Without the ambition of providing a comprehensive picture of the evolution of EU law governance, this chapter aims to retrace the

[1] D Ferri and A Broderick, 'Conclusion to the Research Handbook on EU Disability Law' in D Ferri and A Broderick (eds), *Research Handbook on EU Disability Law* (Edward Elgar 2020) 450.

[2] The term 'governance' refers to the 'rules, processes and behaviour that affect the way in which powers are exercised', as defined in European Commission (Commission), 'White paper on European Governance' COM(2001) 428 final 5.

[3] A Hoefmans, 'The EU Framework for monitoring the CRPD' in Ferri and Broderick (n 1) 76.

main trajectories and the drivers of the evolution in the implementation of EU law to underline the trends that have mostly affected the way in which EU disability law is implemented (section 2). This analysis aims to unveil the peculiarities of the EU legal system that the contributions included in Part II of this edited volume will focus on from distinct perspectives. It further aims to discuss the importance of devoting renewed scholarly attention on institutional and non-institutional actors to better understand the field of EU disability law. It will therefore then put forward some methodological observations on legal analysis of EU law and on the specific approach adopted in this book (section 3), before drawing some conclusions (section 4).

2. From a Duet to a Choir: The Plurality of Actors in EU Law Governance

In the 60 years of European integration, the European legal system has seen an evolution towards a multiplicity of actors which displays reciprocal ties between them. Among the stratified and complex dynamics which have shaped the EU as it is today, for the purpose of this chapter three significant drivers can be identified: (1) the progressive sharing of the exercise of legislative and executive powers among a plurality of actors, in particular with the establishment of comitology; (2) the agencification of EU administration; and (3) the involvement of private actors in EU rule- and policy-making. Such an evolution has entailed the emergence also of collaborative links among these actors, crystallised in peculiar procedures and practices.[4]

2.1. The Early Instances of Plurality and Collaboration

In the original Treaty of Rome, the decision-making power at the European level followed a procedure often summarised with the phrase 'the Commission proposed, and the Council disposed'.[5] While the rule-making power was considered as being the critical instrument for European integration and was solidly put in the hands of these two institutions, less attention was paid in the text to the dimension of the implementation of the rules thus adopted.[6] Still, two distinctive modes for carrying out the implementing tasks necessary for the concretisation of EU policies could already be recognised: the indirect execution at national

[4] On the collaborative nature of EU law, see also B Cortese, *L'ordinamento dell'Unione europea, tra autocostituzione, collaborazione e autonomia* (Giappichelli 2018).

[5] As incisively put by P Craig, 'Case C-133/06, European Parliament v. Council (Delegation of legislative power), judgment of the Grand Chamber of 6 May 2008, [2008] ECR I-3189' (2009) 46 *Common Market Law Review* 1274.

[6] M Chiti, *Diritto amministrativo europeo* (Giuffrè Editore 2011) 287.

level and the direct execution at European level. Indirect execution was generally the rule. According to a model of executive federalism (Vollzugsföderalismus),[7] national administrations took the primary responsibility of operationalising the common rules through the existing administrative bodies at the national level ('les puissantes machineries des Etats', in the words of Monnet) in compliance with the principle of loyal cooperation.[8] Conversely, the European institutions were equipped with a rather thin administrative organisation[9] since implementation could only be carried out directly by the Commission or, in certain cases, by the Council as an exception. In particular, the Commission had 'its own power of decision' in the cases provided for in the Treaties (such as in competition law),[10] but the Treaty of Rome offered also a (flimsy) basis to the Council for conferring to the Commission further implementing powers.[11]

It has been noted that, already in this early phase, this binary distinction of implementation modes did not imply a strict separation of the respective administrations. On the contrary, collaborative links and procedural cooperation started soon to emerge.[12] In indirect execution, the then EC legislator could establish specific patterns of implementation that would involve European institutions and, in spite of the principle of national procedural autonomy, would set the requirements for the administrative procedures that should apply at the national level.[13] Hence, this 'EC-driven indirect administration' generally promoted functional interdependence between the national and the European level, rather than their functional separation.[14]

However, it is in the following decades that the complexity of the EU institutional landscape started to emerge, both for the legislative and the executive powers. As regards the legislative power, the introduction of the co-decision procedure in the Treaty of Maastricht put the EP on equal footing with the Council in a number of policy areas, and made the former institution an important player for rule-making.[15] This role, consolidated in the Treaty of Lisbon, also implied the

[7] K Lenaerts, 'Constitutionalism and the Many Faces of Federalism' (1990) 38 *American Journal of Comparative Law* 230; R Schütze, 'From Rome to Lisbon: 'Executive Federalism' in the (New) European Union' (2010) 47 *Common Market Law Review* 1385.

[8] Article 5 Treaty establishing the European Economic Community (Treaty of Rome).

[9] Article 5(2) Treaty establishing the European Coal and Steel Community (ECSC Treaty), expressly establishing 'un appareil administratif réduit'.

[10] See Articles 155 and 89 Treaty establishing the European Community (EC Treaty) [2002] OJ C325/33.

[11] Article 155 EC Treaty.

[12] H Hofmann, 'European Administration: Nature and Developments of a Legal and Political Space' in C Harlow, P Leino and G Della Cananea (eds), *Research Handbook on EU Administrative Law* (Edward Elgar 2017) 33; C Harlow and R Rawlings, *Process and Procedures in EU Administration* (Hart 2004) 323.

[13] Chiti (n 6) 127.

[14] Ibid.

[15] N Lupo and A Manzella, *Il Parlamento europeo* (Luiss University Press 2019); P Craig, 'Institutions, Power and Institutional Balance' in P Craig and G de Búrca (eds), *The Evolution of EU Law* (Oxford University Press 2011) 46–90.

development of formal[16] and informal[17] procedures to discipline the sharing of the legislative power among these two institutions and to enable compromise in the adoption of legislative acts. Moreover, it gradually became clearer that other actors may have a voice in the process, even without having the formal powers to do so. For instance, the decisive action of the European Council in shaping major legislative developments of EU law,[18] especially in times of crisis,[19] showed unequivocally that in EU rule-making the actors that actually play a role often go beyond those two formally empowered.[20]

As regards the executive power, the possibility of conferring powers to the Commission through an act of the Council paved the way for an extensive delegation of implementing powers to the Commission.[21] Although little in the text of the Treaties could anticipate it, this delegation was in fact accompanied by the establishment of a system of hybrid committees, composed of representatives of the Member States and chaired by the Commission, which began to consistently assist the latter in the exercise of its implementing powers. First developed for the management of the Common Agricultural Policy in the 1960s,[22] this system (named comitology system after the French term for committee) not only allowed the Council to maintain a control over the Commission's exercise of conferred powers, through a power of veto on the draft implementing acts. It also provided the Commission with the technical and scientific expertise it needed to adopt detailed rules in complex policy fields.[23] The involvement of national representatives, moreover, had the positive effect of facilitating the interactions with the

[16] Article 294 Treaty on the Functioning of the European Union (TFEU).

[17] The reference here is to the practice of the trilogues. D Curtin and P Leino, 'In Search of Transparency for EU Law-making: Trilogues on the Cusp of Dawn' (2017) 54 *Common Market Law Review* 1673; J Greenwood and C Roederer-Rynning, 'In the Shadow of Public Opinion: The European Parliament, Civil Society Organisations, and the Politicisation of Trilogues' (2019) 7 *Politics and Governance* 316; M Hillebrandt and P Leino-Sandberg, 'Administrative and Judicial Oversight of Trilogues' (2021) 28(1) *Journal of European Public Policy* 53.

[18] B de Witte, 'Legal Methods for the Study of EU Institutional Practice' (2022) 18 *European Constitutional Law Review* 643–644.

[19] In particular, during the Covid-19 crisis, European Council, 'Conclusions of the meeting of 10 and 11 December 2020' EUCO 22/20.

[20] On the factors and non-institutional actors that influence the passage of EU disability law, O Bartlett, 'The EU Legislative Institutions and Disability Rights: Uncovering the Factors that Block Progress and Offering Insights for Future Advocacy' in this volume.

[21] For a more extensive analysis of delegation of powers in the EU, A Volpato, *Delegation of Powers in the EU Legal System* (Routledge 2022).

[22] For an analysis of the origin and the evolution of the comitology system (after Lisbon, neo-comitology), D Bianchi, *De Comitatibus. L'origine et le rôle de la comitologie dans la politique agricole commune* (L'Harmattan 2012); CF Bergström, *Comitology. Delegation of Powers in the European Union and the Comitology System* (Oxford University Press 2005).

[23] E Vos, 'The Rise of Committees' (1997) 3(3) *European Law Journal* 210; C Joerges and J Neyer, 'From Intergovernmental Bargaining to Deliberative Political Processes: The Constitutionalisation of Comitology' (1997) 3(3) *European Law Journal* 273–299; M Everson and C Joerges, 'Re-Conceptualising Europeanisation as a Public Law of Collisions: Comitology, Agencies and an Interactive Public Adjudication' in H Hofmann and A Türk (eds), *EU Administrative Governance* (Edward Elgar 2006) 512–540.

administrators who were afterwards in charge of the application of the rules at the national level.[24]

As a result of these spillovers of the system, comitology progressively spread across virtually all fields of EU policy, despite the fact that the EP[25] and scholars expressed sharp criticism on the system for its lack of both transparency and democratic credentials.[26] Its existence and procedures are now codified in primary law[27] and in Regulation 182/2011,[28] which establishes specific rules and procedures for the 357 currently existing committees.

However, comitology committees do not represent the only expert groups the Commission can employ. Other, less formalised, *ad hoc* committees or expert groups also began to emerge with the view of providing assistance in the preparation of legislative proposals or of delegated acts,[29] or in the implementation of EU policies. EU disability policy was fertile ground for both kinds of committees. For instance, in the implementation of the Web Accessibility Directive (WAD), the Commission is assisted by the WAD Committee (C49600),[30] a typical comitology committee that votes on the draft implementing acts according to Regulation 182/2011.[31] In parallel, for the elaboration of policy initiatives, the Commission has often sought the support of other expertise-based, specific groups, such as the Academic Network of European Disability experts (ANED), which later has become the European Disability Expertise network (EDE). Although lacking formal powers, this group has still significantly affected the development of EU disability law.[32]

2.2. New Executive Voices: The Agencification of EU Administration

With the expansion of EU competences and the growing complexity of EU rulemaking, a demand for efficiency and expertise grew, increasingly calling on the EU

[24] P Craig, *EU Administrative Law* (Oxford University Press 2012) 113; G Della Cananea, 'Cooperazione e integrazione nel sistema amministrativo delle Comunità europee: la questione della "comitologia"' (1990) 3 *Rivista trimestrale di diritto pubblico* 655–702.

[25] European Parliament Resolution on Committees for the Adaptation of Directives on Technical and Scientific Progress [1984] OJ C172/6.

[26] GJ Brandsma, D Curtin and A Meijer, 'How Transparent Are EU "Comitology" Committees in Practice?' (2008) 14(6) *European Law Journal* 819–838.

[27] Article 291(2) TFEU.

[28] Regulation (EU) No. 182/2011 of the European Parliament and of the Council of 16 February 2011 laying down the rules and general principles concerning mechanisms for control by Member States of the Commission's exercise of implementing powers [2011] OJ L55/13.

[29] Interinstitutional Agreement between the European Parliament, the Council of the European Union and the European Commission on Better Law-Making [2016] OJ L123/1.

[30] Information on the WAD Committee (C49600) can be retrieved from the Comitology Register at <https://ec.europa.eu/transparency/comitology-register/screen/committees/C49600/consult?lang=en>.

[31] Article 11 Directive (EU) 2016/2102 of the European Parliament and of the Council of 26 October 2016 on the accessibility of the websites and mobile applications of public sector bodies (Web Accessibility Directive – WAD) [2016] OJ L327/1.

[32] The impact of EDE, and of academics in general, on EU disability law is discussed by L Waddington, 'The Role of Academics in Shaping EU Disability Law: Some Personal Reflections' in this volume.

administration to regulate fields of significant technical and scientific complexity.[33] The delegation of powers to the existing institutional bodies became thus insufficient and, in some respects, unsuitable, since the excessive empowerment of the Commission allegedly risked upsetting the existing balance and dynamics.[34] The solution adopted at the EU level resulted in the creation of independent bodies, set up by the institutions through secondary legislation, that operate at arm's length from the political actors. Being highly specialised, these non-majoritarian bodies appeared to be well-equipped to deal with complex technical and scientific issues,[35] while at the same time able to maintain a structural independence from political pressures and to confer credibility and output legitimacy on them.[36]

In the last decades, agencification has progressively grown, both in quantitative and qualitative terms.[37] The number of decentralised agencies has risen to more than 30 bodies, which are very diverse and vary significantly in their functions, structures and powers conferred.[38] In this latter regard, while few agencies have genuine decision-making powers,[39] most EU agencies provide scientific advice and/or technical support to EU institutions without adopting formal decisions. This is the case, for instance, of the FRA, which collects and analyses law and data, and then issues publications and reports on fundamental rights, including the rights of persons with disabilities.[40] Scholars have recognised that, albeit non-decision-making, in certain cases these agencies have *de facto* a considerable influence on the decision-making activities of other institutions, being so authoritative that, for instance, the Commission never departs from their opinion.[41]

Although the establishment and the empowerment of EU agencies undeniably represents a formidable development of EU administration, until the Treaty of Lisbon they were not mentioned in primary law, which still does not provide an

[33] G Majone, *Regulating Europe* (Routledge 1996); M Everson, 'Independent Agencies: Hierarchy Beaters?' (1995) 1(2) *European Law Journal* 180.

[34] R Dehousse, 'The Politics of Delegation in the European Union' (2016) 4 *Les Cahiers européens de Sciences Po*.

[35] M Busuioc, *European Agencies: Law and Practices of Accountability* (Oxford University Press 2013) 25.

[36] C Tovo, *Le agenzie decentrate dell'Unione europea* (Editoriale Scientifica 2016) 395.

[37] The literature on EU agencies is abundant. M Everson, C Monda and E Vos, *European Agencies in between Institutions and Member States* (Wolters Kluwer 2014); M Chamon, *EU Agencies. Legal and Political Limits to the Transformation of the EU Administration* (Oxford University Press 2016); E Chiti, *Le agenzie europee. Unità e decentramento nelle amministrazioni comunitarie* (Cedam 2002); J Alberti, *Le agenzie dell'Unione europea* (Giuffrè 2018).

[38] For a recent overview of this phenomenon, E Vos, 'EU Agencies, Common Approach and Parliamentary Scrutiny' European Parliamentary Research Service available at <https://www.europarl.europa.eu/thinktank/en/document/EPRS_STU(2018)627131#:~:text=This%20study%20provides%20an%20overview%20of%20the%20different,Commission%20and%20Member%20States%2C%20stakeholder%20involvement%20and%20transparency>.

[39] For a classification of agencies according to their powers, S Griller and A Orator, 'Everything under Control? The 'Way Forward' for European Agencies in the Footsteps of the Meroni Doctrine' (2010) *European Law Review* 13–15.

[40] On the role of the FRA in EU disability law, GN Toggenburg, 'The Role of the Fundamental Rights Agency in Advancing Disability Rights within the EU' in this volume.

[41] Chamon (n 37) 31.

express legal basis nor clear constitutional boundaries for the delegation of powers to EU agencies,[42] historically raising relevant concerns on the legitimacy of these bodies.[43]

Moreover, EU agencies have been described as 'interesting hybrids'[44] and 'in-betweeners'[45] amidst the EU institutions and the Member States. The peculiar organisational structure (which generally envisages the presence of Member States' representatives on their management boards) and the tasks performed by EU agencies (especially when they act as *primus inter pares* in a network of national specialised agencies) grant strong cooperation with the national administrations.[46] In this sense, the agencification of EU administration shows the signs of an evolution in the implementation model of EU policies, which went beyond the strict dichotomy between direct and indirect administration through the creation of hybrid bodies.[47] At the same time, EU agencies are an expression and are part of the composite EU administration that is characterised by intense cooperation between the different executive levels.[48]

2.3. Voices from the Public: The Involvement of Private Actors in EU Governance

One final driver in the evolution of EU governance landscape can be recognised in the involvement of private actors in EU rule- and policy-making. This involvement was particularly promoted by the European institutions in the last decades, especially since the Interinstitutional Agreement on Better Law-Making[49] and

[42] See the insertion of EU agencies in Articles 263, 265, 267 and 277 TFEU. The 'constitutionalisation' of EU agencies remains, however, 'unfinished' to an important extent, E Vos, 'European Agencies and the Composite EU Executive' in Everson, Monda and Vos (n 37) 43; M Everson and E Vos, 'Unfinished Constitutionalisation: The Politicised Agency Administration and Its Consequences' (Paper presented at the TARN Conference, Florence, 10-11 November 2016) 14.

[43] D Geradin, 'The Development of European Regulatory Agencies: Lessons from the American Experience' in D Geradin, R Munoz and N Petit (eds), *Regulation through agencies in the EU: a new paradigm of European governance* (Edward Elgar 2005) 231; E Vos, 'Reforming the European Commission: What Role to Play for EU Agencies?' (2000) 37(5) *Common Market Law Review* 1113–1134.

[44] M Everson, 'Agencies: The Dark Hour of the Executive?' in H Hofmann and A Türk (eds), *Legal Challenges in EU Administrative Law. Towards an Integrated Administration* (Edward Elgar 2009) 131.

[45] M Everson, C Monda and E Vos, 'European Agencies in between Institutions and Member States' in Everson, Monda and Vos (n 37) 3-8; D Curtin, *Executive Power of the European Union. Law, Practices and the Living Constitution* (Oxford University Press 2009) 174.

[46] E Chiti, 'An Important Part of the EU Institutional Machinery: Features, Problems and Perspectives of European Agencies' (2009) 46 *Common Market Law Review* 1398.

[47] Tovo (n 37) 9.

[48] This is particularly true for the so-called 'network agencies', M Zinzani, *Market integration through 'network governance': the role of European agencies and networks of regulators* (Intersentia 2012) 41–42.

[49] Para 16 Interinstitutional Agreement on Better Law-making [2003] OJ C321/1. 'The three Institutions recall the Community's obligation to legislate only where it is necessary, in accordance with the Protocol on the application of the principles of subsidiarity and proportionality. They recognise the need to use, in suitable cases or where the Treaty does not specifically require the use of a legal instrument, alternative regulation mechanisms'.

more recently in the Better Regulation Package.[50] With a view to reducing the normative gap between EU institutions and citizens, and dealing with the increasing complexity of its system, the EU institutions have explored new modes of governance, seeking to better connect individual citizens and representative associations to the EU policy making. This has taken place within a broader critical reflection on the governance of the Union[51] and on the quality of its law-making.[52] Accordingly, the increased involvement of citizens, and more generally of individuals, is sought not only through the traditional democratic representation in the EP or by the involvement of national democratic institutions in EU decision-making; emphasis is also placed on a new dimension of *direct participation* in policy and law-making.[53] Individual citizens, experts, and representative associations are therefore called to make a substantial contribution in shaping and managing EU policies, providing input that has the potential to make the rules that are enacted closer to their needs.[54] This has been particularly important for the development of EU disability law.

Initially mentioned in the Maastricht Treaty in relation to social policy,[55] the participation of stakeholders and civil society in policy- and rule-making has taken different forms. On the one hand, the involvement of civil society has been inserted in the existing procedures for law-making, creating specific phases or tools for the consultation and participation of stakeholders in the making of new rules.[56] Such forms of participation, epitomised by targeted and public consultations organised by the Commission before the adoption of legislative proposals,[57] required that procedural rights and channels were introduced in legislation to make room for the voice of stakeholders in rule-making procedures, especially in environmental matters.[58] This dialogue has sometimes taken the shape of

[50] Commission, 'Better regulation for better results – An EU agenda' COM(2015) 215 final.

[51] Commission (n 2).

[52] Interinstitutional Agreement on Better Law-making [2003] OJ C321/1; Interinstitutional Agreement between the European Parliament, the Council of the European Union and the European Commission on Better Law-Making [2016] OJ L123/1.

[53] Commission, 'Towards a reinforced culture of consultation and dialogue – General principles and minimum standards for consultation of interested parties by the Commission' COM(2002) 704 final 5.

[54] A Alemanno, 'Unpacking the principle of openness in EU law: transparency, participation and democracy' (2014) 39(1) *European Law Review* 72–90; J Mendes, 'Participation and participation rights in EU law and governance' in Hofmann and Türk (n 44) 257, 259; J Mendes, *Participation in EU Rule-Making: A Rights-Based Approach* (Oxford University Press 2011).

[55] C Barnard, 'The Social Partners and the Governance Agenda' (2002) *European Law Journal* 80–101.

[56] Commission, 'Better regulation: Joining forces to make better laws' COM(2021) 219 final 4.

[57] In particular through Commission, 'Have Your Say Portal', introduced in 2017, available at <https://ec.europa.eu/info/law/better-regulation/have-your-say_en>.

[58] L Squintani and G Perlaviciute, 'Access to Public Participation: Unveiling the Mismatch between what Law Prescribes and what the Public Wants' in M Peters and M Eliantonio (eds), *Research Handbook on EU Environmental Law* (Edward Elgar 2020) 139. With the exception of the environmental field, the approach of the Court of Justice to the recognition of specific participation rights in decision-making is rather restrictive. Case C-104/97 *Atlanta AG and others v Commission of the European Communities and Council of the European Union* ECLI:EU:C:1999:498; Case T-13/99 *Pfizer Animal Health v Council* ECLI:EU:T:2002:209; Mendes, *Participation in EU Rule-Making* (n 54) 142-267.

specific stakeholder groups or civil society fora, such as the Disability Platform, which brings together 14 civil society organisations (as active members) and the European institutions.[59] The existence of these formalised channels goes in parallel with uninstitutionalised lobbying activities, which aim at influencing institutional actors' choices in decision-making in a more informal fashion, and which determine a substantive phenomenon that has nonetheless been the object of political and legal analysis.[60]

On the other hand, in certain fields, private actors have taken also an active role by directly generating the rules applicable to a certain market sector, acting (more or less) autonomously in drafting the content of the rules.[61] This second kind of participation in rule-making most commonly takes the forms of co-regulation and self-regulation of private parties, which arguably represent the most innovative and interesting phenomena from an institutional perspective.[62] Firstly, co-regulation, i.e. the mechanism whereby a legislative act 'entrusts the attainment of the objectives defined by the legislative authority to parties which are recognised in the field',[63] entailed outsourcing the adoption of technical rules to standardisation organisations (private bodies mostly composed by representatives of industry) that determine, in detail, how health and safety requirements established by EU legislation are to be met.[64] Although already used since the 1980s,[65] this regulatory technique has recently gained increasing scholarly attention due to some recent legislative[66] and judicial developments[67] that have fostered a strong debate on the

[59] The role and influence of Disability Platform is also examined in C Coveney, 'The Role of the European Disability Forum and Disability Organisations in Shaping EU Disability Policy' in this volume.

[60] E Korkea-aho, 'No Longer Marginal? Finding a Place for Lobbyists and Lobbying in EU Law Research' (2022) 18 *European Constitutional Law Review* 682–705.

[61] For a recent overview, A Beckers, 'EU Law's Dark Private Legal Space: Researching Private Regulators and the Importance of Legal Doctrine' (2022) 18 *European Constitutional Law Review* 657–681.

[62] H Hofmann, G Rowe and A Türk, *Administrative Law and Policy of the European Union* (Oxford University Press 2011) 582–621.

[63] Para 18 Interinstitutional Agreement on Better Law-making [2003] OJ C321/1.

[64] For an example of the use of harmonised standards in EU disability law, Article 15 Directive (EU) 2019/882 of the European Parliament and of the Council of 17 April 2019 on the accessibility requirements for products and services [2019] OJ L151/70.

[65] Commission of the European Communities, 'Completing the Internal Market. White Paper from the Commission to the European Council (Milan, 28-29 June 1985)' COM(85) 310 final; Council Resolution of 7 May 1985 on a new approach to technical harmonization and standards [1985] OJ C136/1; Council Resolution of 21 December 1989 on a global approach to conformity assessment [1990] OJ C10/1.

[66] Regulation (EU) No 1025/2012 of the European Parliament and of the Council of 25 October 2012 on European standardisation [2012] OJ L316/12.

[67] Case C-588/21 P, *Public.Resource.Org and Right to Know v Commission and Others* ECLI:EU:C:2024:201; Case C-171/11 *Fra.bo. v DVGW* ECLI:EU:C:2012:453; Case T 474/15 *Global Garden Products Italy SpA v Commission* ECLI:EU:T:2017:36; and especially Case C-631/14 *James Elliott Construction Limited v Irish Asphalt Limited* ECLI:EU:C:2016:821, commented in A Volpato, 'The Harmonised Standards before the ECJ: James Elliott Construction' (2017) 54(2) *Common Market Law Review* 591–604; C Colombo and M Eliantonio, 'Harmonized Technical Standards as Part of EU

legal status of standards and on the use of these industry-driven organisations for the pursuit of public interests.[68] Secondly, forms of self-regulation, i.e. 'the possibility for economic operators, the social partners, non-governmental organisations or associations to adopt amongst themselves and for themselves common guidelines at European level',[69] has been used as a soft law instrument in certain policy fields, such as corporate social responsibility[70] or digital markets,[71] to steer market dynamics and behaviour.

At the European level the participation of private actors in rule-making has therefore become an important regulatory mechanism in socially relevant sectors, such as consumer protection, product safety, environmental policy, social corporate responsibility, and financial markets. Civil society has played an important role in advancing the protection and promotion of EU disability rights.[72] This has contributed not only to enhance the democratic legitimacy and acceptance of EU legislation in the eyes of European citizens, but also to enrich the EU landscape with non-institutional actors, whose relevance cannot be underestimated by EU lawyers anymore.[73]

3. Singling Out the Voices of EU Actors: Some Methodological Reflections

Sketching out some of the main drivers and trajectories in the evolution of EU governance has shown how the EU institutional framework is strongly characterised by a plurality of actors – institutional and non-institutional, public and private – which, for certain purposes and to different extents, necessarily cooperate in the definition and implementation of EU policies. The substantive law of a certain policy field, such as EU disability law, is therefore almost inevitably the

Law: Juridification with a Number of Unresolved Legitimacy Concerns?, Case C-613/14 *James Elliot Construction Limited v Irish Asphalt Limited*, EU:C:2016:821' (2017) *Maastricht Journal of European and Comparative Law* 323–340.

[68] H Schepel, 'The New Approach to the New Approach: The Juridification of Harmonised Standards in EU Law' (2013) *Maastricht Journal of European and Comparative Law* 521–533; R Van Gestel and H-W Micklitz, 'European Integration through Standardisation: How Judicial Review is Breaking Down the Club House of Private Standardisation Bodies' (2013) *Common Market Law Review* 145–181; C Daelmans, 'The Legitimacy and Quality of European Standards: The Legitimation of Delegation of Powers and Standard-Setting Procedures' in C Joerges, K-H Ladeur and E Vos (eds), *Integrating Scientific Expertise into Regulatory Decision-Making. National Experiences and European Innovations* (Nomos 1997).

[69] Para 22 Interinstitutional Agreement on Better Law-making [2003] OJ C321/1.

[70] A-L Sibony and A Alemanno, *Nudge and the Law: A European Perspective* (Hart 2015); M Kerr, R Janda and C Pitts, *Corporate social responsibility: a legal analysis* (LexisNexis 2009).

[71] Commission, 'Principles for Better Self- and Co-Regulation and Establishment of a Community of Practice' on the website dedicated to the Digital Single Market available at <https://digital-strategy.ec.europa.eu/en/news/principles-better-self-and-co-regulation-and-establishment-community-practice>.

[72] D Ferri and ES Krolla, 'Introduction: Walking Through the Looking Glass' in this volume.

[73] In the same vein Beckers (n 61).

result of a collaborative, multi-level and multi-actor endeavour in which the action of a single player is often dependent on 'the complex set of interdependencies and interconnections Europeans are embedded into'.[74] In such a choral context, one may therefore question (1) what is the actual meaning and value of a study that aims at singling out the different voices of EU actors, and (2) which methodological approach may suit this enquiry best.

3.1. The 'Who?' Question in EU Law

Focusing on specific actors and their role in a certain policy field is certainly not an unprecedented approach in doctrinal legal analysis. As highlighted by Gadbled and Muir in a recent special issue on actors and roles in EU law, 'asking – and answering – the question "who does what?" in the EU legal system is the core business of EU institutional and constitutional scholars'.[75] Defining the distinctive traits and the competences of a specific actor contributes to shaping the 'intellectual grammar', which is essential for the understanding and systematising of the factual reality within the categories and concepts of the legal order.[76] Traditionally, in EU law, such categories and concepts are determined on the basis of the rich (and to a significant extent, common)[77] history of legal scholarship in the Member States[78] – which provided, for instance, the consolidated distinction of public authorities according to the function they perform (judicial, executive, or legislative),[79] which has been used previously in this chapter to describe the evolution of EU governance – or on the basis of the text of the Treaties itself, which lists institutions and procedures. Accordingly, scholarly attention has typically focused on retracing the State-based concepts in the peculiar features of the EU legal system,[80] or on analysing the seven Treaty-mentioned institutions,[81] with a particular interest on the role of the CJEU.[82]

However, as we have seen in the previous section, nowadays few of the entities that concur to define a policy can be formally classified as EU institutions: committees and agencies, for instance, are an integral part of the EU administrative

[74] To use the wording of L Azoulai, 'Infrastructural Europe: EU Law and Human Life in Times of the Covid-19 Pandemic' (2020) 66 *Revista de Derecho Comunitario Europeeo* 356.

[75] R Gadbled and E Muir, 'Actors and Roles in EU Law: Asking "Who Does What?" in the European Union Legal System' (2022) *European Constitutional Law Review* 621.

[76] Ibid 622.

[77] U Vincenti, *I fondamenti del diritto occidentale* (Laterza 2013).

[78] On the role of common legal traditions also in the case law of the CJEU, Joined Cases C-46/87 and C-227/88 *Hoechst AG v Commission of the European Communities* ECLI:EU:C:1989:337.

[79] This example is taken from Gadbled and Muir (n 75) 630.

[80] D Ritleng, 'L'identification de la fonction exécutive dans l'Union' in J Dutheil de La Rochère (ed), *L'exécution du droit de l'Union, entre mécanismes communautaires et droits nationaux* (Bruylant 2009); K Lenaerts, 'Some Reflections on the Separation of Powers in the European Community' (1991) 28 *Common Market Law Review* 11–35.

[81] In the sense of Article 13 Treaty on European Union (TEU).

[82] Korkea-aho (n 60) 688.

machinery but do not have the status of an institution and, until recently, were not even mentioned in primary law. Some, such as standardisation organisations, lobbying groups or academics, do not even pertain to the public law realm nor can they be easily labelled collectively as entities or bodies. Yet, their ability to influence the legal framework that affects natural and legal persons is, by now, beyond doubt.[83] Including these as objects for a legal analysis has arguably become unavoidable as it allows the interpreter not only to identify more comprehensively the sources of (binding and non-binding) rules of conduct in a given field, but also to have a more complete picture of the interests, dynamics and factors at play in such a field. In fact, it is the inherent diversity of EU law actors that suggest such an analysis: as we have seen, their origins – as much as the rationale, the context and the legal bases for their creation – significantly differ not only from State entities, whose concepts are well known by legal scholars, but also from each other. This, in turn, affects the competences they exercise, the collaborative ties they establish, and the limits that apply to them. For instance, it makes a legally significant difference if their empowerment finds its legal basis in primary or secondary law (or outside the law), if their role is foreseen in the Treaties or if it is the result of a delegation of powers from EU institutions, since the operation of the principles of institutional balance and legality constrain more strictly the latter according to the case law of the CJEU.[84] Only the analysis of the specific nature and limits applicable to each relevant actor at stake can thus unveil how it can inform EU law, shape its meaning, define its contours, and drive its implementation. On the contrary, take the example of harmonised standards: the lack of a clear understanding of their legal status in literature has probably justified ambiguous oscillations in the case law,[85] with negative repercussions on the principles of transparency and the rule of law in the EU, which the CJEU appears to have only recently addressed.[86]

At the same time, this represents a (more or less conscious) choice on the scope and limits of the analysis, which has theoretical and methodological implications even though they often (maybe too often)[87] remain implicit. In this sense, the increasing relevance of non-institutional actors challenges the traditional EU legal scholarship in a similar manner than the one already experienced in the international relations field with the advent of the European integration process. Faced with the inadequacy of the pre-existing categories of international relations or international law (such as legal personality or statehood) to capture the presence and influence of the EU in the global sphere, the focus of researchers shifted from

[83] On the relevance of private actors in rule-making, Beckers (n 61).

[84] Case C-270/12 *Short Selling* ECLI:EU:C:2014:18, paras 45-47. For further analysis, Volpato (n 21).

[85] On the public access to the text of standards, for instance, compare Case T-185/19 *Public.Resource.Org* ECLI:EU:T:2021:445, and Case C-160/20 *Stichting Rookpreventie Jeugd* ECLI:EU:C:2022:101.

[86] Case C-588/21 P, *Public.Resource.Org*.

[87] Gadbled and Muir (n 75) 622; A Bailleux, 'From the Stage to the High Seas: Concluding Thoughts on the Present and Future of EU Legal Studies' (2022) *European Constitutional Law Review* 737–752.

formal categories to the elaboration of the concept of 'actorness',[88] which gradually became a stand-alone notion with different connotations according to the theory adopted.[89] Analogously, the terminological choice – operated for instance in this book – of directing the scholarly attention to 'actors' (rather than just to institutions) carries the intention of taking advantage of the versatility of this term, which has already determined its success in that field, to encompass in the analysis any entity or group that has the capacity to behave actively and deliberatively in relation to others,[90] irrespective of their form.

Like in the academic debate on EU international relations, the discussion on the 'actorness' of the different players is inevitably intertwined with the issue of their legitimacy and effectiveness.[91] Delving into the *distinguo* between the different EU actors and reasoning on their specific legitimacy vectors[92] or assets[93] in comparison to the others, provides the ground for a normative assessment on the acceptability and effectiveness of the exercise of asymmetrical powers by a certain actor in the policy field. Clearly, depending on whether the benchmarks of this assessment are provided by the law itself, following a doctrinal research approach, or drawing from political, economic, societal considerations, in a more interdisciplinary fashion,[94] there may be different perspectives and results to such an evaluation. Still, singling out the different voices and their characteristics appears as a necessary step for those studies which, implicitly or explicitly, combine a descriptive approach to an evaluative one.

3.2. The 'What?' Question in EU Law

While focusing on institutional and non-institutional actors is to be considered not only as a legitimate methodological approach in EU legal studies, but also

[88] E Drieskens, 'Golden or Gilded Jubilee? A Research Agenda for Actorness' (2017) 24(10) *Journal of European Public Policy* 1536. On a similar shift in transnational law and international law, Korkea-aho (n 60) 690.

[89] H Larsen, 'Discourse Analysis in the Study of European Foreign Policy' in B Torna and T Christiansen (eds), *Rethinking European Union Foreign Policy* (Manchester University Press 2004) 62–80. On the different elements defining actorness, compare C Bretherton and J Vogler, 'A global actor past its peak?' (2013) 27(3) *International Relations* 375–390; G Sjöstedt, *The External Role of the European Community* (Saxon House 1977); J Jupille and JA Caporaso, 'States, agency and rules: the European Union in global environmental politics' in C Rhodes (ed), *The European Union in the World Community* (Lynne Rienner 1998) 213–229.

[90] Paraphrasing the definition of actorness by Sjöstedt (n 89).

[91] K Čmakalová and JM Rolenc, 'Actorness and legitimacy of the European Union' (2012) 47(2) *Cooperation and Conflict* 260–270.

[92] Ibid 265.

[93] I Venzke and J Mendes, 'The idea of relative authority in European and international Law' (2018) 16(1) *International Journal of Constitutional Law* 75–100; J Mendes and I Venzke (eds), *Allocating authority: who should do what in European and international law?* (Hart 2018).

[94] B De Witte, 'Legal Methods for the Study of EU Institutional Practice' (2022) 18 *European Constitutional Law Review* 639–640.

often as a compelling necessity if the purpose of the study is to 'make sense of [the EU's] ever-emerging, evolving dimensions'[95] in a given field, the second limb of the 'who does what?' question touches more closely upon methodological choices of the authors. In fact, this 'what' conceals a broader question on what is relevant to legal analysis[96] and, taken to the extreme, what is law as an academic discipline.[97]

In this regard, it is important to highlight that methodological debates have increasingly interested EU scholars in the last decade.[98] The reasons for this piquing of interest have been traced back to endogenous or exogenous factors, including the way that research funding schemes are designed[99] and the multiple crises that the EU as a polity is experiencing.[100] Irrespective of whether this is a sign that 'something is wrong' with the discipline[101] or of the supposed 'maturity' of contemporary EU legal studies,[102] this trend has partially compensated for the traditional lack of interest and self-reflection on methodology of legal scholarship. A vocabulary of legal methodology has therefore flourished, together with the popularity of quantitative and qualitative methods,[103] critical legal studies,[104] new legal realism,[105] and interdisciplinary methodologies.[106]

In particular, legal scholarship tends to divide between (1) a purely *doctrinal* approach, which limits itself to systematise the state of the law or answer particular legal problems within the parameters provided by the law itself; (2) *socio-legal* approaches, which look at the law in action, conceiving it as a social practice; and (3) *normative* legal research, which 'investigates the underlying normative principles and values of the law and thus how the law ought to be interpreted from an external perspective'.[107] Examples of all of these approaches can be found in this book.[108] Within the doctrinal methodology, a further distinction is drawn

[95] J Hunt and J Shaw, 'Fairy Tale of Luxembourg? Reflections on Law and Legal Scholarship in European Integration' in D Phinnemore and A Warleigh-Lack (eds), *Reflections on European Integration: 50 Years of the Treaty of Rome* (Palgrave Macmillan 2009) 96.

[96] Gadbled and Muir (n 75) 636, paraphrasing Bailleux (n 87).

[97] Bailleux (n 87) 738.

[98] R Deplano, G Gentile, L Lonardo and T Nowak (eds), *Interdisciplinary Research Methods in EU Law* (Edward Elgar 2024); K Riesenhuber, *European Legal Methodology* (Intersentia 2021); V Réveillère (ed), 'Debate on Controversies over Methods in EU Law' (*Verfassungsblog*, 18–23 March 2024) available at <https://verfassungsblog.de/category/focus/controversies-over-methods-in-eu-law/>.

[99] R Van Gestel and H Micklitz, 'Why Methods Matter in European Legal Scholarship' (2014) 20(3) *European Law Journal* 292.

[100] V Réveillère, 'Controversies over Methods in EU Law' (*Verfassungsblog*, 18 March 2024) available at <https://verfassungsblog.de/controversies-over-methods-in-eu-law/>.

[101] J Komárek, 'Becoming a (Critical) EU Law Scholar Today' (*Verfassungsblog*, 18 March 2024) available at <https://verfassungsblog.de/becoming-a-critical-eu-law-scholar-today/>.

[102] Gadbled and Muir (n 75) 624.

[103] E Korkea-aho and P Leino, 'Interviewing lawyers: a critical self-reflection on expert interviews as a method of EU legal research' (2019) *European Journal of Legal Studies* 17–47.

[104] Komárek (n 101).

[105] V Nourse and G Shaffer, 'Varieties of New Legal Realism. Can a New World Order Prompt a New Legal Theory?' (2009) 95 *Cornell Law Review* 61.

[106] For a more exhaustive list, R Van Gestel, H-W Micklitz and M Poiares Maduro, 'Methodology in the New Legal World' (2012) *EUI Working Paper LAW* 2012/13 1-2.

[107] Beckers (n 61) 663.

[108] Ferri and Krolla (n 72).

between a *positivist* legal tradition that focuses on the letter of the law, and a more open methodological take which allows using the findings of other disciplines to get 'a better and richer understanding of legal questions'.[109] Introduced in the 1980s and 1990s, this *law-in-context* approach aims at making sense of the law 'by placing legal institutions, rules, dispute settlement processes, and legal professionals in their social, economic, political and cultural contexts'.[110]

According to its promises, the law-in-context approach appears to be the best suited for extending our understanding of how a EU policy field, such as EU disability law, has actually been shaped since it allows not only the combination of the reading of the relevant legal sources with the observation of the actual 'activities' of its actors, but also for many of the practices through which EU law concretely unfolds to be unveiled. This has proved particularly useful for understanding the peculiar evolution of EU governance. As remarked also by De Witte, many institutional innovations happened 'in the shadow of the law' and only later (and often partially) were formalised in positive law.[111] Likewise, as we have seen, the actual role that important actors play, such as the European Council and non-decision-making agencies, would largely remain uncovered should a positivist legal approach be preferred. The very reasons for the establishment of such agencies, which clearly emerged from an historical and political analysis of the context in which they were created,[112] would elude a purely doctrinal research approach. Finally, considering that many of the collaborative ties established among institutional and non-institutional actors are not (or not yet) crystallised in formal procedures, a contextual approach is particularly suitable for providing a more comprehensive account of the collaborative character of the legal system, thus enriching the understanding of the reciprocal relations between actors.

4. Concluding Remarks

With the view of contextualising the peculiarities of EU disability law within the broader evolution of the EU legal system, this chapter has traced what – in a limited and personal perspective – are the most relevant drivers and trajectories of development in EU decision-making, especially with regard to EU policy governance and law implementation. In particular, significant changes in the institutional balance have been recognised in the progressive multiplication of institutional

[109] De Witte (n 94) 654; F Snyder, 'Editorial' (1995) 1 *European Law Journal* 1.

[110] F Snyder, 'Establishing Law in Context: An Insider's Perspective' (*Verfassungsblog*, 20 March 2024) available at <https://verfassungsblog.de/establishing-law-in-context/>; AJ Menéndez, 'The Triumph of EU Law in Context?' (*Verfassungsblog*, 22 March 2024) available at <https://verfassungsblog.de/the-triumph-of-eu-law-in-context/>.

[111] De Witte (n 94) 654.

[112] Such as the one of M Egeberg and J Trondal, 'Agencification of the European administration' (2016) 1 TARN Working Paper 1-17; J Trondal, 'EU Committee Governance and the Multilevel Community Administration' in Hofmann and Türk (n 23) 391-416.

actors involved in decision-making, in the mushrooming of EU agencies, and in the participation of private actors in EU rule-making. The current state of affairs is, in fact, the result of an evolution that has constantly and incrementally shaped the distribution of the power in the EU according to subsequent 'phases'[113] or 'tides'[114] of change, often in the shadow (or in anticipation) of formal changes in EU primary law.

This evolution has involved both the vertical and horizontal axes of power distribution. On the vertical level, the neat distinction between indirect and direct administration – referring respectively to the national and European implementation of EU legislation – is progressively being eroded by the creation of hybrid or in-between bodies and procedures.[115] On the horizontal level, a proliferation of institutional and non-institutional bodies has populated the European administrative space.[116] In this context, one of the trajectories for enhancing the democratic legitimacy and acceptance of EU legislation has been identified in an increased involvement of civil society in rule-making at the European level.[117] As a consequence, more and more decisions are taken in by a wide variety of actors in a wide variety of forums, bodies, and groups.[118]

The plurality of actors that concur in the implementation of EU disability law, therefore, is part and parcel of this broader evolution of EU governance towards a choral execution of EU policies, in which the roles and contributions of the different levels and the different actors becomes increasingly juxtaposed and, to a certain extent, blurred.[119] Yet, each actor is strongly characterised by a different voice which – due to the differences in the legal basis, competences and limits to their powers – maintains a distinct timbre and volume in this process. Singling out the different voices therefore represents an essential endeavour for a comprehensive understanding of whether, how, in what way and to what extent different actors have contributed to shape EU disability law. The methodological choice of encompassing in this analysis both institutional and non-institutional, public and private actors, and of complementing the positivist interpretation of the law with the contextual aspects that affect their activities, appears to be the most suitable approach to this end. Still, it is important to recognise it as what it is: one choice among an increasing variety of methods for making sense of the complex, multi-actor and multi-layered legal system that is the EU.

[113] E Chiti and J Mendes, 'The Evolution of EU Administrative Law' in P Craig and G de Búrca (eds), *The Evolution of EU Law* (Oxford University Press 2021) 339–372; C Harlow, 'Three Phases of EU Administrative Law' in Craig and de Búrca (n 15) 433; Hofmann (n 12) 23.

[114] Curtin (n 45) 8.

[115] S Cassese, 'European Administrative Proceedings' (2004) 68 *Law and Contemporary Problems* 21–36; G Della Cananea, 'The European Union's Mixed Administrative Proceedings' (2004) 68 *Law and Contemporary Problems* 197–218.

[116] Hofmann (n 12) 21.

[117] KA Armstrong, 'Rediscovering Civil Society: The European Union and the White Paper Governance' (2002) *European Law Journal* 102–132.

[118] Curtin (n 45) 1.

[119] H Hofmann, 'Legislation, Delegation and Implementation under the Treaty of Lisbon: Typology Meets Reality' (2009) 15(4) *European Law Journal* 498.

2

Studying the Role of Legal Actors in EU Law: An Outline

URŠKA ŠADL

1. Introduction

The European Union's (EU) legal system persistently transforms and adapts to the changing European reality. Historically envisaged as an economic community committed to securing peace through cooperation in narrowly defined sectors for the common good of the peoples,[1] the EU is seeking to reimagine itself as a democratised and politically ambitious supranational organisation with common values and way of life, expanding the array of its commitments to environmental protection, the promotion of scientific and technological progress, social justice, equality between women and men, and the combating of social exclusion and discrimination – including against people with disabilities.[2] The multiplication of European goals, priorities and policies, the expansion of competences, and geographical enlargements have increased the number and the diversity of actors that directly and/or indirectly participate in the policy-decision and law-making processes at the EU level.

[1] The Rome Treaty established a common market with the view of progressively approximating the economic policies of Member States, a harmonious development of economic activities, a continuous and balanced expansion, an increased stability, an accelerated raising of the standard of living and closer relations between its Member States. Article 2 Treaty of Rome (Treaty establishing the European Economic Community).

[2] In Article 10 of the Treaty on the Functioning of the EU (TFEU), the EU commits to combat discrimination based on sex, racial or ethnic origin, religion or belief, disability, age or sexual orientation in defining and implementing its policies and activities. Article 19(1) TFEU gives the Council of the EU (Council), acting unanimously in accordance with a special legislative procedure and after obtaining the consent of the European Parliament, the power to take appropriate action to combat discrimination based on sex, racial or ethnic origin, religion or belief, disability, age or sexual orientation within the powers conferred upon the Union. Article 19(2) TFEU authorises the European Parliament and the Council to adopt incentive measures in support of the action taken by the Member States contributing to the achievement of these objectives, acting in accordance with the ordinary legislative procedure. The Article expressly excludes any harmonisation of the laws and regulations of the Member States.

The present volume is a timely initiative to collect, organise and deepen the knowledge about institutional and non-institutional actors' roles in the shaping of EU disability law.[3] The approach of interrogating the roles of already well-examined as well as so-far practically unknown participants in the protection and promotion of disability rights, addressing and redressing the disadvantages of persons with disabilities, is important and will offer novel insights into the labour of legal actors and the structures in which they shape the law.[4] This is indispensable for the understanding of the law's legal authority and its power to enforce the established social order legitimately.[5]

Methodologically, this volume nudges all authors to transcend the conception of law as a closed, complete, and autonomous normative system,[6] abiding by its internal logic and developing according to its own dynamics.[7] This forces the 'social universe in which law is produced and in which it exercises its power'[8] upon legal scholars, who might not yet be fully comfortable with the concepts, theory, terminology and methodological tools to fully exploit the acquired methodological freedom. For instance, while the idea of a social role is a popular and long-debated idea in the social sciences, with different strands of role theory and an off-the-shelf methodology, legal scholars that have ventured into socio-legal and empirical investigations of the role of legal actors have spent less time on key concepts, methods, or theory.[9] Borrowing selectively from social science methodologies, this volume makes observable social practices, characteristic behaviours and identities that participants assume in their interactions within groups and *vis-à-vis* institutions or structures, accessible to legal scholars. As chapters such as the one authored by Krolla[10] or the one written by Coveney demonstrate,[11]

[3] D Ferri and ES Krolla, 'Introduction: Walking Through the Looking Glass' in this volume.

[4] Ibid.

[5] P Bourdieu, 'The Force of Law: Toward a Sociology of the Juridical Field' (1986) 38 *Hastings Law Journal* 805.

[6] A Volpato, 'The Voices and the Choir: The Importance of a Contextual Analysis of EU Actors' Roles' in this volume.

[7] Bourdieu (n 5).

[8] Ibid.

[9] Most literature that *theorises* rather than *mentions* legal actors stems from legal sociology. However, see H Schepel and R Wesseling, 'The Legal Community: Judges, Lawyers, Officials and Clerks in the Writing of Europe' (1997) 3(2) *European Law Journal* 165–188; E Stein, 'Lawyers, Judges, and the Making of a Transnational Constitution' (1981) 75(1) *American Journal of International Law* 1–27; JVH Holtermann and M Rask Madsen, 'European New Legal Realism and International Law: How to Make International Law Intelligible' (2015) 28(2) *Leiden Journal of International Law* 211–230; A Vauchez, 'The Transnational Politics of Judicialization. Van Gend en Loos and the Making of EU Polity' (2010) 16(1) *European Law Journal* 1–28. For contributions that use a historical approach, see M Rasmussen, 'The Origins of a Legal Revolution – The Early History of the European Court of Justice' (2008) 14 *Journal of European Integration History* 77–98; V Fritz, 'Activism on and off the Bench: Pierre Pescatore and the Law of Integration' (2020) 57(2) *Common Market Law Review* 475–502.

[10] ES Krolla, 'The Role of the European Commission in Shaping EU Disability Law: A Driver with the Brakes Put On?' in this volume.

[11] C Coveney, 'The Role of the European Disability Forum and Disability Organisations in Shaping EU Disability Policy' in this volume.

empirical research can update or reinvigorate outdated concepts,[12] bringing the legal world closer to the social reality.[13]

To situate the volume in the wider debate, this chapter interprets the role broadly, focusing on judicial actors as a methodological avenue to a deeper understanding of the origins, functioning, maintenance, and authority of EU law. In that regard, it distinguishes between the *influence* that key participants in judicial proceedings wield in defining or constructing the meaning of the law, a *role* that the participants can *play* in the framing of the dispute and in different stages of the judicial proceedings where legal meaning is being minted, and the *effect* of the political context on the Court of Justice of the EU's (CJEU or 'the Court') law-making, including the adopted interpretations, legal concepts, reinterpretation of precedents, and case outcomes. Key participants are typically institutional legal actors, such as Member State governments, national courts submitting preliminary references, and the Advocates General (AG) as the members of the CJEU who assist it with impartial opinions. However, the chapter also discusses the strength of the relationship between a broader political atmosphere on case outcomes and the Court's willingness to engage in law-making as a stand-in for a political process – that is, the Court's autonomous role in the law-making process. The latter, particularly, has been the subject of lively academic debates in legal scholarship and political science.[14] The chapter also highlights the following elements of research: the considerations made when building a framework for the analysis of EU law – which operationalises the insights of the existing literature and theory –, the conceptualisation of legal influence, and the systematic analysis of case law. The framework supports the study of any area of EU law, or any policy. The method of legal hand coding, discussed below, is widely applicable and is used in many different settings to assess the strength of the relationships between legal actors and legally relevant outcomes.

The chapter is structured as follows. Section 2 describes the premises of the analysis, including the conceptual, theoretical, and methodological questions. Section 3 presents two studies that explore the role of the national courts and the CJEU in different stages of the procedure, including the influence on different elements of the law – adopted interpretations, methods of interpretation, the framing of the disputes by embedding them in the existing case law, and case outcomes. Section 4 concludes the chapter.

2. Conceptualising and Operationalising the 'Role' of Legal Actors

A good understanding of legal practice, doctrine, and political context is an indispensable first step to identify sufficiently stable, deep, consequential, and

[12] L Waddington, 'The Role of Academics in Shaping EU Disability Law: Some Personal Reflections' in this volume.

[13] L Azoulai, 'Editorial' (2024) *Common Market Law Review* (forthcoming).

[14] See n 9.

far-reaching connections, relationships and parameters that shape a legal field. The second step involves the construction of an analytical framework to operationalise and analyse these connections. In EU law, the framework is often based on two insights. First, scholars argue that courts engage with legal actors to minimise political conflict and to maintain legal authority.[15] In this sense, the CJEU's alliance with the Commission, its initial *amour* with the scholars, its fruitful collaboration with the national courts, and its quiet approval of the political actors are legion.[16] Second, the CJEU strategically yields to the political will when facing a credible threat of legislative override.[17]

The most evident conceptual challenge is in defining the role or influence of the CJEU and in delimiting it from agreement with the legal actors or other related notions. The methodological challenge is how to process legal texts comprehensively, combining legal detail with an overall analysis of legal trends and shifts in legal meaning, linking legal arguments to legal actors. The practical challenge is access to documents, which is often restricted.

Influence can be directly observed in citations to the previous cases and other sources or indirectly transpires from the CJEU's reasoning, interpretation, and the choice of legal sources (precedents) in the case at hand, as well as in subsequent related cases. Explicit influence can be observed and assessed through direct citations using citation network analysis.[18] Implicit influence can be teased out by combing through legal texts systematically.

Legal hand coding is an alternative to legal analysis and expert coding of text. Researchers read the text of the judgment. This included the facts, the legal framework, and the preliminary questions/claims in direct actions, the reasoning of the Court, and the final ruling and adopted interpretation. They then record the values for each legal characteristic (variable), which approximates the main argument, outcome, and other relevant information that can untangle the role of legal actors on legal texts and legal meaning. Some variables require a more detailed reading and expert knowledge of general EU law as well as the specific policy area, such as the free movement of goods, and legal theoretical knowledge about the Court's methodology and methods of interpretation. In contrast to legal analysis in which the reading of formally binding or non-binding legal sources aims to present a legal problem, provide a correct (or possible) legal solution(s), give a normative critique, or issue a legislative proposal, legal coding is cruder. Its

[15] M Rask Madsen, '"Legal Diplomacy" – Law, Politics and the Genesis of Postwar European Human Rights' in S-L Hoffmann (ed), *Human Rights in the Twentieth Century* (Cambridge University Press 2010).

[16] D Sindbjerg Martinsen, *An Ever More Powerful Court?: The Political Constraints of Legal Integration in the European Union* (Oxford University Press 2015).

[17] O Larsson and D Naurin, 'Judicial Independence and Political Uncertainty: How the Risk of Override Affects the Court of Justice of the EU' (2016) 70(2) *International Organization* 377–408.

[18] W Alschner and D Charlotin, 'The Growing Complexity of the International Court of Justice's Self-Citation Network' (2018) 29 *European Journal of International Law* 83.

perspective is not normative, chronological and linear. Fragmenting a judgment along selected legally relevant characteristics (procedural, conceptual, historic, legal argumentative) threatens to decontextualise such characteristics and to lose important nuance and legal critical understanding. A judgment appears like a set of highlighted categories, not like a legal source. However, systematic reading of selected characteristics offsets the bias inherent in legal doctrinal work in which case selection criteria can remain implicit because the legal community accepts the material's relevance in supporting the interpreter's (author's) conclusions and critique.

Moreover, systematic recording of smaller constitutive parts can offer greater insight than a holistic study. Fragmentation, curiously, contributes to a fuller and more informative input about a subject or a phenomenon.[19] Finally, legal hand coding supports one-off data collections and individual research projects conducted by a single scholar or a small research team tailored to specific research questions, theories of European integration, or a particular model of judicial behaviour. It is also well suited for multi-user projects and for unspecified research questions.

3. Application: Two Studies of Legal Actors' Role

Different phases of the law-making process can be summarised as follows: the national courts initiate and thus frame the dispute, the AG effectively concludes the oral phase of the proceedings, potentially reframing the dispute, and the political actors influence the proceedings and the substance. This section focuses first on national courts and unpacks the role of national referring courts as legal actors that can influence the CJEU by framing the legal issues in the preliminary reference procedure. The analysis complements O'Sullivan's case study, which highlights the power of national courts to force the CJEU into dealing with disability related issues by submitting the *right* questions,[20] discussing the overall willingness of national courts to suggest answers to preliminary questions, and the procedural tools of the Court, such as the reformulation of the preliminary questions, to eschew potentially controversial answers in high profile or politically charged disputes. The second subsection looks at the external constraints for the CJEU to shape the law. It examines the role of political divisions and overall support for European integration, formalised in the Court's choice to rule in a large formation, and the readiness to develop the law by issuing audacious – law-making – rulings *in lieu* of political actors.

[19] D Kahneman *et al.*, 'A Survey Method for Characterizing Daily Life Experience: The Day Reconstruction Method' (2004) 306 *Science* 1776.

[20] CE O'Sullivan, 'National Courts as 'Actors' in the Preliminary Reference Procedure' in this volume.

3.1. The Role of National Courts

This section focuses on the ambition of national courts as potentially influential and powerful allies of the CJEU, to contribute to legal developments, encapsulated in the possibility to explain their view about the interpretation of legal rules, and to suggest answers to preliminary questions, which they submit to the Court in the preliminary reference procedure.[21] The CJEU can theoretically counteract this ambition by reformulating the preliminary questions, thereby eschewing potentially controversial answers in politically contentious disputes – an aspect that makes the study interesting from the interdisciplinary perspective. Compared with O'Sullivan's chapter that discusses the preliminary reference procedure as an important source of EU disability law, this section draws on an earlier study, which explored the relationship between the CJEU and the national courts in broader terms.[22]

Article 267 TFEU states that all national courts can address a preliminary question to the CJEU in cases of doubt about the interpretation or validity of EU law with the courts of last instance having an obligation to refer. The Court must deliver an answer, but it can in practice rephrase or otherwise depart from the question. Reformulation of preliminary questions has become an emblematic part of the preliminary ruling procedure. The Court paraphrases the question using different terms: it joins several questions in one reformulated question and provides a single answer or interpretation;[23] it reverses the order of the questions;[24] it answers some questions and decides that others have become obsolete in the light of previous answers.[25] Modifications can alter preliminary questions substantively,[26] at times leading to a binding interpretation of a provision of EU law, which the referring court did not raise.[27]

[21] Ibid.

[22] U Šadl and A Wallerman, '"The Referring Court Asks, in Essence": Is Reformulation of Preliminary Questions by the Court of Justice a Decision Writing Fixture or a Decision-Making Approach?' (2019) 25 *European Law Journal* 416.

[23] Case C-512/13 *C.G. Sopora v Staatssecretaris van Financiën* ECLI:EU:C:2015:108, para 20: 'Thus, by its questions, which it is appropriate to examine together, the referring court asks essentially'. Here, the Court joins three questions into one.

[24] Case C-219/15 *Schmitt v TÜV Rheinland LGA Products GmbH* ECLI:EU:C:2017:128, para 38: 'By its second and third questions, which it is appropriate to answer first and together'.

[25] Case C-67/14 *Jobcenter Berlin Neukölln v Nazifa Alimanovic and Others* ECLI:EU:C:2015:597, para 47.

[26] Case C-346/05 *Monique Chateignier v Office national de l'emploi (ONEM)* ECLI:EU:C:2006:711, especially paras 19 and 24.

[27] A Rosas, 'The European Court of Justice in Context: Forms and Patterns of Judicial Dialogue' (2007) 1(2) *European Journal of Legal Studies* 121–136; D Sarmiento, 'Half a Case at a Time: Dealing with Judicial Minimalism at the European Court of Justice' in M Claes *et al.* (eds), *Constitutional Conversations in Europe: Actors, Topics and Procedures* (Intersentia 2012). Note the exception in MP Broberg and N Fenger, *Preliminary References to the European Court of Justice* (Oxford University Press 2014).

Legal literature has primarily focused on the principles and doctrines minted in the procedure – from this perspective, the centrality of national courts to integration and legal development can hardly be overstated.[28] Political science scholars focused on the reasons for judicial cooperation,[29] seeking to explain why national courts *would* embrace the guidance of the CJEU and participate in the process of integration.[30] The co-authored study of reformulation, described below, focused on the circumstances under which the CJEU reformulates the preliminary questions, and explores the nature of judicial cooperation, the role of national courts, and the effect of procedural tools on legal substance.

Legal literature[31] suggests that the Court reformulates the preliminary questions mainly to correct deficient drafting, thereby assisting the referring court by pinpointing, clarifying and simplifying the legal issues.[32] Judicial behaviour or judicial politics literature would, however, suggest that the Court uses reformulation strategically, mainly to extend the reach of EU law and its own jurisdiction, in line with the broader integrationist agenda claim.[33] If the Court's main ambition was to simplify and clarify the questions, reformulation would be more common in complex cases with many preliminary questions. If the Court's ambition was to

[28] On the so-called dialogue with the high profile courts – but focused on the reception of direct effect and supremacy, see G de Búrca and J Weiler, *The European Court of Justice* (Oxford University Press 2001).

[29] A Stone Sweet, *The Judicial Construction of Europe* (Oxford University Press 2004); A-M Burtley and W Mattli, 'Europe Before the Court: A Political Theory of Legal Integration' (1993) 47 *International Organizations* 41; A-M Slaughter, A Stone Sweet and J Weiler, *The European Court and National Courts – Doctrine and Jurisprudence: Legal Change in Its Social Context* (Hart 1998); KA Armstrong, 'Legal Integration: Theorizing the Legal Dimension of European Integration' (1998) 36(2) *Journal of Common Market Studies* 155.

[30] Ranging from trust and workload to empowerment, see A Dyevre, 'Domestic Judicial Defiance in the European Union: A Systemic Threat to the Authority of EU Law?' (2016) 35 *Yearbook of European Law* 106; M Glavina, 'Dismissed Preliminary References: Chilling or Learning Effect?' (ACTORE workshop, Antwerp, 2017); A Dyevre, A Atanasova and M Glavina, 'Who Asks Most? Institutional Incentives and Referral Dynamics in the European Union Legal Order' (12 October 2017 SSRN Electronic Journal) (2020) 27(6) *Journal of European Public Policy* 912–930; JA Mayoral, 'In the CJEU Judges Trust: A New Approach in the Judicial Construction of Europe' (2016) 55 *Journal of Common Market Studies* 551; JA Mayoral, U Jaremba and T Nowak, 'Creating EU Law Judges: The Role of Generational Differences, Legal Education and Judicial Career Paths in National Judges' Assessment Regarding EU Law Knowledge' (2014) 21 *Journal of European Public Policy* 1120.

[31] Broberg and Fenger (n 27); K Lenaerts *et al.*, *EU Procedural Law* (Oxford University Press 2014); R Barents, *Remedies and Procedures before the EU Courts* (Kluwer Law International 2016); DWK Anderson and M Demetriou, *References to the European Court* (Sweet & Maxwell 2002).

[32] Broberg and Fenger (n 27); Lenaerts *et al.* (n 31) 235.

[33] KJ Alter, *Establishing the Supremacy of European Law: The Making of an International Rule of Law in Europe* (Oxford University Press 2001); CJ Carrubba and L Murrah, 'Legal Integration and Use of the Preliminary Ruling Process in the European Union' (2005) 59 *International Organization* 399; A Stone Sweet and T Brunell, 'The European Court and the National Courts: A Statistical Analysis of Preliminary References, 1961-95' (1997) 5 *Journal of European Public Policy*; W Mattli and A-M Slaughter, 'Revisiting the European Court of Justice' (1998) 52 *International Organization* 177; G Garrett, 'The Politics of Legal Integration in the European Union' (1995) 49 *International Organization* 171; K Alter, 'Explaining National Court Acceptance of European Court

assist the national court, the latter's framing of the dispute and the question would be decisive, and reformulation limited to the margins (stylistic). If the Court's main ambition were to expand the reach of its jurisdiction, reformulation would expand the scope of the questions (substantive).

The study examined these assumptions and tested these hypotheses derived from legal and political science literature, combining unexplored legal sources, namely the Orders for Reference (OfR) drafted by national judges[34] with over-explored legal materials, that is, the corresponding judgments of the Court. We read and annotated 106 OfR and 94 corresponding judgments in which the phrase 'procedural autonomy' or 'judicial protection' appears in the title or in the text of the judgment.[35]

Three considerations underpin the selection of cases dealing at least partially with procedural matters. The first consideration is expertise and relevance. Procedures and remedies are central to the working of the national courts – both in their daily judicial activity and as a matter of constitutional principle. Hence, national courts have a good understanding of the procedures, and all changes affect them directly. They will be willing and able to clarify the relevant national law[36] and express their legal preference.[37] The second consideration relates to the principle of national procedural autonomy. Cases which challenge the limits of jurisdiction and allow for calculated choices on both sides offer the best platform for examining whether reformulation is a tool of the Court for providing useful answers within the limits of its jurisdiction. The EU and the Member

Jurisprudence: A Critical Evaluation of Theories of Legal Integration' in Slaughter, Stone Sweet and Weiler (n 29); H Rasmussen, *On Law and Policy in the European Court of Justice: A Comparative Study in Judicial Policymaking* (Nijhoff 1986).

[34] Data on file with the author. A Wallerman Ghavanini, 'Sowing Wheat and Reaping Thorns: The Referring Court's (Lack of) Influence on the EU Court of Justice' (ECPR Conference, 26 August 2020); A Wallerman, 'Can Two Walk Together, except They Be Agreed?: Preliminary References and (the Erosion of) National Procedural Autonomy' (2019) 44 *European Law Review* 159; A Wallerman, 'Towards an EU Law Doctrine on the Exercise of Discretion in National Courts? The Member States' Self-Imposed Limits on National Procedural Autonomy' (2016) 53(2) *Common Market Law Review* 339–360.

[35] The analysis is based on a sample of 106 Order for References (OfRs) and 94 judgments, delivered by the Court between 1 January 2008 and 1 April 2017. The selection is supplemented by judgments falling into the same period, listed in the chapter on national procedures and remedies in P Craig and G de Búrca, *EU Law: Text, Cases, and Materials* (Oxford University Press 2015). After reading the selected documents, we excluded those that did not raise any questions concerning remedies and judicial protection, as well as judgments related to the OfRs that were not available due to confidentiality issues. We obtained the OfRs from the Swedish Ministry of Justice in August 2017. The difference in numbers is due to the Court's practice of sometimes joining identical or similar preliminary references issuing from one or several referring courts to render a single judgment in two or more Joined Cases (Article 54 Rules of Procedure of the Court of Justice [2012] OJ L265/1). Each incoming OfR is registered with its own case number (eg C-NN/YYYY), but several cases can share the same Celex number (6YYYYCJNNNN), which denotes the judgment rather than the case.

[36] JHH Weiler, 'A Quiet Revolution. The European Court of Justice and Its Interlocutors' (1994) 26 *Comparative Political Studies* 510, 532.

[37] Either defending (shielding) the national procedural rules and arrangements or not.

States share competence concerning procedures and remedies.[38] Theoretically, this creates a level playing field, which should encourage meaningful conversation and occasional confrontation. Previous research suggests that referring courts articulate the preferred case outcome with more confidence in areas of shared competence.[39] The third consideration is the potential immediate influence of the referring courts on the interpretation of EU law. The referring courts can frame questions that invoke doubts about the interpretation and validity of EU law as substantive *or* procedural. Again, literature suggests that the framing affects the Court's response.[40]

The first analytical step groups different characteristics of the OfR and the judgments of the Court into three categories. These categories relate to the complexity of the case before the national court and the resulting OfR, the national court's outlook on EU law, and the Court's tendency to expand its legal reach. The second analytical step examines which factors increase the scope of reformulation. To determine the scope of reformulation, the study introduces a conceptual framework that distinguishes between stylistic (less significant in scope) and substantive (more significant in scope) reformulation.

The findings indicate that the complexity of the case and its OfR are not decisive. Moreover, the frequency and the scope of reformulation do not coincide with the expansion of the EU's competence. By contrast, and most relevant to the discussion of the role of legal actors in the shaping of EU law, the national court's outlook on EU law seems pivotal.

Substantive reformulation is also more frequent when the referring court indicates that the reasons for referral are procedural and substantive (meaning a combination of both) or does not specify any reasons for referral. Furthermore, the scope of reformulation is independent from the referring court's provisional answers:[41] namely, whether the court enters a concrete discussion on possible answers or expresses a preference for a particular outcome. However, the likelihood of substantive reformulation sharply increases in cases in which the Court's answers conflict with the expressed preference of the referring court.

Reformulation highlights the Court's authority to set the rules of the game and the limited role of the national courts beyond the initial submission of the

[38] W van Gerven, 'Of Rights, Remedies, and Procedures' (2000) 37 *Common Market Law Review* 501; P Haapaniemi, 'Procedural Autonomy: A Misnomer?' in L Ervo, M Gräns and A Jokela (eds), *Europeanization of Procedural Law and the New Challenges to Fair Trial* (Europa Law 2009) 117; M Bobek, 'Why There is No Principle of "Procedural Autonomy" of the Member States' in H-W Micklitz and B De Witte (eds), *The European Court of Justice and the Autonomy of the Member States* (Intersentia 2011).

[39] SA Nyikos, 'Strategic Interaction among Courts within the Preliminary Reference Process – Stage 1: National Court Preemptive Opinions' (2006) 45(4) *European Journal of Political Research* 527, 540.

[40] Wallerman, 'Can Two Walk Together, Except They Be Agreed?' (n 34) section 4.4.

[41] On the term and its definition, R van Gestel and J de Poorter, 'Putting Evidence-Based Law Making to the Test: Judicial Review of Legislative Rationality' (2016) 4 *The Theory and Practice of Legislation* 155.

questions. Three sets of findings validate this conclusion. First, the analysis suggests that a specific kind of engagement of the referring court with EU law is consequential. On the one hand, the Court sanctions ambiguity: reformulating the questions substantively when the referring court states only formal reasons for the referral or fails to distinguish the procedural from the substantive aspects of the dispute in the main proceedings. On the other hand, the Court sanctions tenacity: reformulating the questions substantively when the referring court presents a forceful argument and argues toward one interpretation. However, the CJEU is more likely to edit the preliminary questions lightly when the referring court extracts the relevant questions of EU law from the dispute in the main proceedings, presents the national context in which they arise, explains doubts about the correct interpretation of EU law, and makes an educated but not too forceful deduction.

Overall, the findings indicate that reformulation increases with the risk of interpretative confrontations between the courts of a given Member State or between judicial and political institutions. While this may allow the CJEU to avoid political conflict of limited legal value, it also foregoes potentially meaningful legal interpretative conversations with the referring courts and their limited role in the shaping of EU law. The national courts are not active co-creators but rather passive recipients of the Court's interpretations.[42]

The findings highlight the role of national courts in the preliminary reference procedure and given its centrality to the reshaping of the European legal order into a *sui generis* legal order, in the European integration process. They add some important nuance to the literature, which typically treats the preliminary reference procedure as an instrument for judicial cooperation or conversation[43] that is central to the uniformity, development and enforcement of EU law.[44] Contributing to the debates concerning judicial style and its effect on the substance of EU law, such findings also highlight the importance of a more comprehensive examination

[42] SA Brekke *et al.*, 'That's an Order! How the Quest for Efficiency is Transforming Judicial Cooperation in Europe' (2023) 61 *Journal of Common Market Studies* 58; U Šadl *et al.*, 'Law and Orders: The Orders of the European Court of Justice as a Window in the Judicial Process and Institutional Transformations' (2022) 1 *European Law Open* 549.

[43] Claes *et al.* (n 27); M Claes and M de Visser, 'Are You Networked Yet? On Dialogues in European Judicial Networks' (2012) 8 *Utrecht Law Review*.

[44] GF Mancini, 'The Making of a Constitution for Europe' (1989) 26 *Common Market Law Review* 595, 606; R Dehousse, *The European Court of Justice: The Politics of Judicial Integration* (St Martin's Press 1998) 138; ML Volcansek, *Judicial Politics in Europe: An Impact Analysis* (P Lang 1986) 265; T Tridimas, 'Constitutional Review of Member State Action: The Virtues and Vices of an Incomplete Jurisdiction' (2011) 9 *International Journal of Constitutional Law* 737; T Tridimas, 'Knocking on Heaven's Door: Fragmentation, Efficiency and Defiance in the Preliminary Reference Procedure' (2003) 40 *Common Market Law Review* 9; T Tridimas, 'Dialogue with National Courts' in A Arnull and D Chalmers (eds), *The Oxford Handbook of European Union Law* (Oxford University Press 2015); Lenaerts *et al.* (n 31). For research placing the emphasis on the role of national courts as the main allies of the Court, KJ Alter, *The European Court's Political Power: Selected Essays* (Oxford University Press 2009); JHH Weiler, 'The Transformation of Europe' (1991) 100 *The Yale Law Journal* 2403; FG Jacobs and A Durand, *References to the European Court: Practice and Procedure* (Butterworths 1975).

of judicial practices based on novel empirical materials and alternative analytical focus areas.

The study did not explore developments in the preparatory stages of the preliminary reference procedure, or the autonomous role of the Registry as the unseen legal actor in the exchange of communications with the referring courts, and the effect of the preparatory stages of the preliminary reference procedure on the case outcomes. These stages would include the decisions related to the use of the accelerated procedure, reformulations or withdrawals of the preliminary questions when prompted by the Registry, or the use of reasoned orders to answer preliminary questions. Similarly, the independent role of the AG in proposing either stylistic or substantive reformulation would merit attention, not least because the AG (unlike the Court) might explain what circumstances prompted them to reformulate the preliminary questions.

3.2. The Effect of Political Divisions on the Court's Lawmaking

The second sub-section adds two aspects to the study of legal actors' role. First, it zooms into the effect of legal actors on judicial proceedings, that is, on procedural decisions, which indirectly shape the law. Second, and relatedly, it separates the Court's procedural response to Member State governments' participation in the proceedings from the Court's response to broader political divisions and support for integration. Member State governments are influential political actors that can intervene in the proceedings, representing national interests.

The above-mentioned aspects are discussed in the study, which inquired whether the Court authoritatively settles or cautiously avoids salient legal matters in times of political division.[45] The question is inspired by the theory of integration, according to which the Court acted as the motor of integration, willing and able to step in as a substitute legislator in times of political and legislative impasse, fashioning doctrines and principles that effectively constructed the internal market.[46] Again, two competing accounts present the puzzle: the integration through law and the separation of powers, aka the legislative override theory. The former[47] agrees that the Court was left to pursue and achieve political ends in the absence of an authoritative and united legislator. This narrative also underlines the role of law as a sword and shield,[48] acting as a political tool through technical

[45] U Šadl and S Hermansen, 'The European Court of Justice, an Able and Unwilling Lawmaker: Evidence from 920 Free Movement of Persons Judgments' in M Dawson, E Muir and B De Witte (eds), *Revisiting Judicial Politics in the European Union* (Edward Elgar 2024).

[46] A Arnull, *The European Union and its Court of Justice* (Oxford University Press 2006); Stein (n 9); Weiler (n 44).

[47] Stein (n 9).

[48] Burtley and Mattli (n 29).

language of judge-made doctrines and principles (direct effect, supremacy, pre-emption).[49] The latter focuses on its relationship with the Member States forming the Council of the EU (Council). Originally developed with reference to the United States Congress and the Supreme Court, it suggests that judges enforce their policy agenda when the legislators are unable to overrule their pronouncements and vice versa.[50]

In the EU context, the scholarship supports *and* refutes the theory, highlighting the impotence of the legislator to curb the CJEU's power[51] and demonstrating its effectiveness.[52] The Court addresses politically powerful governments,[53] aligning outcomes with the 'majoritarian' policy view.[54] The precise working of the mechanisms that govern judicial action remains poorly understood and legal scholars question the relevance of the theory altogether.[55]

The existing studies moreover analysed the presence of powerful political actors in the courtroom or in the procedure, exhibiting a direct threat of potential legislative override. The third line of the argument, however, was more sensitive to the effect of a broader political atmosphere on the rulings.[56] Still, the studies did not answer the question of whether or not political division affected the Court's willingness to step into legislative shoes nor the question of whether the Court responded to political divisions and support for integration in the Member States procedurally and substantively.

[49] Stein (n 9); Weiler (n 36); Alter (n 33); T Pavone, *The Ghostwriters: Lawyers and the Politics behind the Judicial Construction of Europe* (Cambridge University Press 2022).

[50] WN Eskridge Jr., 'Overriding Supreme Court Statutory Interpretation Decisions' (1991) 101 *The Yale Law Journal* 331–455.

[51] RD Kelemen, *Eurolegalism: The Transformation of Law and Regulation in the European Union* (Harvard University Press 2011); A Stone Sweet, *Governing with Judges: Constitutional Politics in Europe* (Oxford University Press 2000). The legal opinion seems to side with the scholarship emphasising the difficulty of legislative override, GT Davies, 'Legislative Control of the European Court of Justice' (2014) 51 *Common Market Law Review* 1579–1607.

[52] Sindbjerg Martinsen (n 16).

[53] G Garrett, 'International cooperation and institutional choice: the European Community's internal market' (1992) 46(2) *International Organization* 533–560; G Garrett, RD Kelemen and H Schulz, 'The European Court of Justice, National Governments, and Legal Integration in the European Union' (1998) 52 *International Organization* 149–176.

[54] CJ Carrubba, M Gabel and C Hankla, 'Judicial Behavior under Political Constraints: Evidence from the European Court of Justice' (2008) 102 *American Political Science Review* 435–452; Larsson and Naurin (n 17); J Dederke and D Naurin, 'Friends of the Court? Why EU governments file observations before the Court of Justice' (2018) 57 *European Journal of Political Research* 867–882; CJ Carrubba, M Gabel and C Hankla, 'Understanding the Role of the European Court of Justice in European Integration' (2012) 106 *American Political Science Review* 214–223. The claim is reminiscent of Maduro's majoritarian activism claim, LM Poiares Pessoa Maduro, *We the Court: The European Court of Justice and the European Economic Constitution* (Hart 1998) 61–102.

[55] Davies (n 51).

[56] KJ Alter, LR Helfer and M Rask Madsen, 'How Context Shapes the Authority of International Courts' in KJ Alter, LR Helfer and M Rask Madsen (eds), *International Court Authority* (Oxford University Press 2018).

The study addressed the question with a comprehensive inquiry into the free movement of persons case law, using statistical modelling to evaluate the strength of the relationships. We collected and hand coded all 920 preliminary references related to the free movement of persons issued from 1963 to 2020. Free movement of persons cases are politically controversial, even when legally straightforward,[57] meaning that the so-called easy cases[58] required hard decisions. It is thus also likely to expect that the Court would be especially sensitive to political support for integration and political divisions.

The analysis shows that the Court responds to political division (1) procedurally, by increasing chamber size and (2) substantively, by moderating its decisions and evading authoritative solutions.

Considering the relevance of the sitting formation, it is useful to recall that the number of sitting judges has symbolic importance for the Court and its audiences beyond the parties to the case. Article 16 of the Statute specifies that the Court hears cases in chambers of three or five judges, as well as in the Grand Chamber of 15 judges, including the President, the Vice-President, and at least three Presidents of the chambers of five judges. When it considers that a case before it is of exceptional importance, the Court may decide, after hearing the AG, to refer the case to the full Court composed of all (27) judges. The Court must convene the Grand Chamber at the request of a Member State or an institution of the Union that is party to the proceedings. It should also sit in the Grand Chamber in legally more complex cases.[59]

The Statute of the Court and the Rules of Procedure regulate the procedural steps, detailed in the internal procedural guidelines. When the case reaches the Registry, the Member States receive the invitation to submit observations. The President of the Court appoints a reporting judge who delivers a preliminary report. The Court decides on the chamber size in the plenary meeting after the reporting judge presents their preliminary opinion and the Member States announce their participation.[60]

The sitting formation reveals the Court's understanding of the legal complexity of the case (legal significance), the gravity of the circumstances and exceptional importance. The assessment of legal complexity is not objective, and it is reasonable to expect that the Court interprets the procedural rules on chamber size with political context in mind and is sensitive to the number of filed observations.

[57] An example is the *L.N.* case on student maintenance grants, or the *Metock* judgment. Case C-46/12 *L. N.* ECLI:EU:C:2013:97; Case C-127/08 *Metock and Others* ECLI:EU:C:2008:449; C Jacqueson, 'Metock as a shock? The struggle between rights and sovereignty' in H Koch *et al.* (eds), *Europe: The New Realism: Essays in Honour of Hjalte Rasmussen* (DJØF 2010) 277–296.

[58] Case C-46/12 *L.N.* (Second Chamber).

[59] Article 60 Rules of Procedure of the Court of Justice [2012] OJ L265/1.

[60] In principle, the Member States can refrain from submitting the observations but decide to participate at a hearing (if the Court holds a hearing in the case). Such instances are exceptional.

Chamber size thus also reveals the Court's perceived need to publicly communicate and display its institutional authority, i.e. in potentially conflicted environments.[61] Large formations signal to the parties and the audiences that their legal arguments, considerations, and voices are heard in the courtroom, and that their views are duly considered in the deliberation chamber. They also anonymise judges, contributing to the sense of institutional independence. Finally, even if the Grand Chamber does not contribute to the perception of institutional legitimacy,[62] it is among the most visible – as opposed to the quality of reasoning –[63] signal.[64]

The analysis considers the interest of the governments in the case (case salience) and the political preferences of the Member States (political division, political support). The governments' pro-European scores use information from cabinet parties' electoral manifestos to approximate political division and political support.[65] Political support refers to the support in the Council (following the qualified majority rule).[66] Political division[67] reflects the differences in the support for the EU among the ruling parties across Europe.[68] The divisions are latent or unobserved, expressing the general attitudes of governments towards the European integration project, and not their support for an audacious judgment in a case that would be expressed in their observations.

Case salience is the share of Member State governments that submit observations in the preliminary reference proceedings.[69] Governments have limited resources, and their decision to intervene reveals their priorities. The median case

[61] The Court can simultaneously strengthen its legal authority, for instance by greater reliance on previous case law. For the argument that citations can be mandated by the case or strategic, O Larsson *et al.*, 'Speaking Law to Power: The Strategic Use of Precedent of the Court of Justice of the European Union' (2017) 50 *Comparative Political Studies* 879–907.

[62] Different approach by A Follesdal, 'Survey Article: The Legitimacy of International Courts' (2020) 28 *Journal of Political Philosophy* 476–499.

[63] S Caserta and P Cebulak, 'Resilience Techniques of International Courts in Times of Resistance to International Law' (2021) 70 *International & Comparative Law Quarterly* 737–768; M Madsen, P Cebulak and M Wiebusch, 'Backlash against international courts: explaining the forms and patterns of resistance to international courts' (2018) 14 *International Journal of Law in Context* 197–220.

[64] The membership and the internal organisation of the Court have changed over the 60-year period of study. The Court usually deliberates in chambers of three or five judges. Until the early 1990s it typically deliberated as the full court (seven judges until 1973, nine judges until 1981 and so forth). The analysis accounts for this fact, considering the sitting formation in all cases decided in a given period (that is, not only in the analysed sample dealing with free movement of persons), and the departures from the typical sitting formation in a case.

[65] A Volkens *et al.*, 'The Manifesto Data Collection. Manifesto Project (MRG/CMP/MARPOR)' (2017). These scores range between −2 (Eurosceptic) and 2 (pro-European).

[66] The scores range from 0.04 (low support) to 0.49 (high support).

[67] MJ Gabel and JD Huber, 'Putting parties in their place: Inferring party left-right ideological positions from party manifestos data' (2000) 44(1) *American Journal of Political Science* 94–103.

[68] The scores range from 0.08 (low division) to 0.77 (high division). Measured as the spread (the standard deviation) in governments' policy preferences regarding European integration at the time of the decision.

[69] The selection of preliminary references (omitting direct actions) is justified by the need to contrast comparable cases and ensure that the difference in formal rules applicable to Member State observations in direct actions and preliminary references does not bias the measure of salience.

contains only two observations, typically also from the Member State in which the preliminary reference originates. By contrast, the 10% most salient cases attracted observations from more than 25% of the Member States.[70]

Even if the measure of case salience does not distinguish between legal and political salience, legal considerations have political undertones owing to the *erga omnes* effect of the Court's pronouncements. The decision to allocate scarce resources signals that a Member State wants to express its view before the Court in this form, either to achieve a state friendly outcome or to shape legal developments in specific policy areas.[71] Rarely, a Member State might plead at the hearing without submitting prior written observations.

The sample of 920 preliminary references of the Court, filed between 1963 and 2020 includes all judgments that the Court labelled as free movement of persons or European citizenship. All texts are available from the EUR-Lex portal and the Court's website.

The research assistants (PhD students with expertise in the free movement of persons and citizenship) read and annotated the judgments according to pre-existing guidelines. They considered whether (1) the judgment makes an important or relevant contribution to EU law in the doctrinal sense (doctrinal outcome can be either strong or moderate); (2) the Court ascribes direct effect to a provision of EU law; or (3) the judgment affects the scope of EU competence given the state of the legislation. The Court's judgment can potentially expand or reduce the competence of the EU to regulate a policy area, expanding or reducing the limits of the Treaty. Alternatively, it does not need to alter the competence allocation. The annotation of doctrinal contribution and effects on competence is additionally difficult given that the literature at times disagrees about both.[72]

It is possible to conceptualise at least three forms of authoritative intervention.[73] First, a ruling that *de facto* allocates more competence to the EU than would seem to follow from the literal interpretation (the wording) of the interpreted Treaty provisions; second, a judgment that develops or entrenches judge-made concepts

[70] Given that the EU's membership has increased from the original six to the current 27 states during the period of study, we calculate salience as the proportion of governments that could potentially submit their views.

[71] On the reasons of the Member States to engage in the proceedings, M-PF Granger, 'When governments go to Luxembourg…: the influence of governments on the European Court of Justice' (2004) 29 *European Law Review* 3–31; M Favale, M Kretschmer and PLC Torremans, 'Who is steering the jurisprudence of the European Court of Justice? The influence of Member State submissions on copyright law' (2020) 83 *Modern Law Review* 831–860.

[72] P Craig, 'The ECJ and ultra vires action: A conceptual analysis' (2011) 48 *Common Market Law Review* 395–437.

[73] In inter-institutional disputes, which are not part of the analysis, a pro-integration attitude of the Court would mean more competence to the Commission/Parliament at the expense of the Council (eg power to negotiate international agreements). In disputes related to EU cooperation as opposed to intergovernmental cooperation, the Union can have less (when the task is taken from the Commission and placed on the Council – eg conclusion of international agreements) or more competence (eg when the Union's competence accompanies intergovernmental cooperation).

and doctrines; and third, a judgment that expands the application of EU law by ascribing its provisions direct effect. A judgment can also combine all three or two forms of audacity. For the purposes of the analysis, such authoritative interventions in the political process are conceptualised as audacious judgments.

In the case law touching on disability rights, the judgment in *Assistenzprofis*[74] is audacious because it authoritatively settles the balance between the right of a candidate applying for a position as a personal assistant to a person with disabilities to effective protection against discrimination on grounds of age and the disabled person's right to effective protection against discrimination on the basis of their disability in favour of the latter. This interpretation of Article 2(5) of Council Directive 2000/78/EC of 27 November 2000 establishing a general framework for equal treatment in employment and occupation[75] means that the autonomy and self-determination of a person with a disability can justify discrimination based on age (that is, the rights of others to equal treatment).

Compared to leading cases or landmark cases, audacious judgments are not always known and discussed as such. The concepts overlap, but audaciousness comprises only the legal quality at the time of the decision.[76] One could argue that landmark rulings are a doctrinal construction that selected cases acquire over time and with regular use. Labelling all authoritative interventions as leading cases or ascribing such status to them would be imprecise.

Figures 2.1 and 2.2 are based on the statistical analysis and show the Court's procedural and substantive response to political division.[77] Figure 2.1 shows that the Court increases chamber size when political division increases, relying more on large chambers in free movement of persons cases compared with other cases decided in the same year.[78] Chamber size, however, does not automatically translate into audacious judgments. Figure 2.2 illustrates the inversely proportionate relationship between audacious judgments and political divisions from 1963 to 2020. As divisions grow (solid line), the share of audacious judgments drops (dotted line). Even if the information is unreliable for the early years – there are only a handful of judgments from the 1960s and six Member States –, the direction of the relationship is clear.

[74] Case C-518/22 *J.M.P. v AP Assistenzprofis GmbH* ECLI:EU:C:2023:956.

[75] Council Directive 2000/78/EC of 27 November 2000 establishing a general framework for equal treatment in employment and occupation [2000] OJ L303/16.

[76] For the conception of leading cases, U Šadl and Y Panagis, 'What is a leading case in EU law? An empirical analysis' (2015) 40 *European Law Review* 15–34.

[77] S Hermansen and U Šadl, 'Judicious judging: The effects of political division on decision making in the European Court of Justice' (APSA Annual Meeting & Exhibition, Montreal, September 2022).

[78] The analysis thus compares the chamber size in preliminary reference cases included in the analysis, with all preliminary references issued in the same period in other policy areas (eg free movement of goods, agriculture, or areas of freedom, security, and justice). The share of large chamber cases (adjusted for institutional changes over time) is higher in audacious judgments (28%) than in non-audacious judgments (9%). Ibid.

Figure 2.1 CJEU's reliance on large chamber. The Court's reliance on large chamber becomes disproportionately higher compared to other court cases decided in the same period when political division between Member State governments increases.

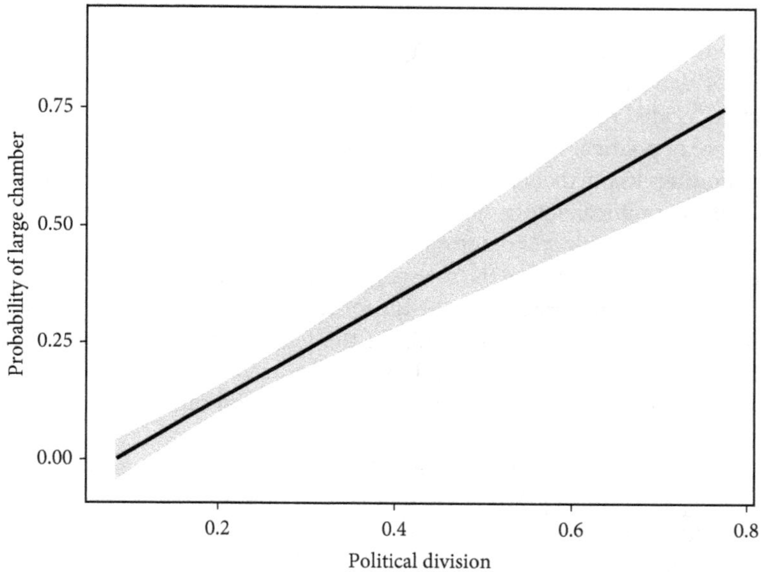

Figure 2.2 CJEU's propensity to issue 'audacious' judgments. The Member State preferences (solid line) and the Court's propensity to issue audacious judgments (dotted line) varied substantively over time. Greater division meant fewer audacious judgments.

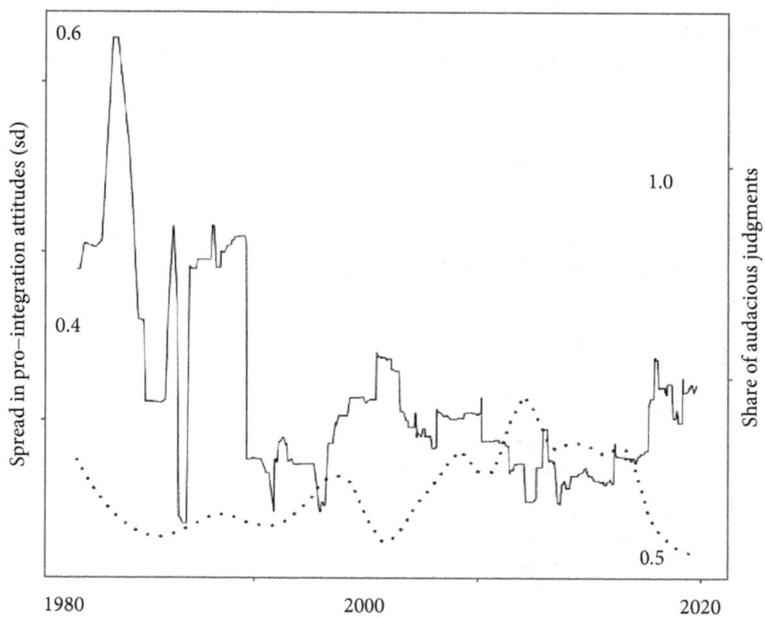

The analysis of the case law shows, among other, that the Court issued more audacious judgments in times of relative pro-European accord, such as in the late-1970s and mid-1990s. The measure of political division, however, as used in this analysis, also includes political ignorance – in which political parties do not explicitly engage with European integration matters in their manifestos. Thus, if the Court decided *Walrave and Koch*,[79] *Cristini*,[80] *Rutili*[81] and *Bonsignore*[82] under political neglect, it decided *Kraus*,[83] *Coonan*,[84] *Schumacker*,[85] *Bosman*[86] and *Dafeki*[87] in the atmosphere of political tolerance and greater sympathy for free movement.

The findings imply that the Court only unwillingly settles divisive legal matters instead of the political actors. On the one hand, case salience triggers the Court to increase chamber size, and authoritatively settle the issue. On the other hand, political division surrounding the case triggers the same procedural response but a legally cautious or moderate solution. The former theoretically increases the legitimacy of the judicial process, legitimising the final product. The latter arguably detaches the Court from the political process by preserving the legal *status quo*. The interaction between procedural and substantive response of the Court is not straightforward.

These findings add nuance to the CJEU's role and political *savoir faire*, also known as legal diplomacy. Studies demonstrated that the Court, fearing political pushback, has sought to align case outcomes with the preferences of the Member States that submitted observations in the case.[88] The findings support a related argument, showing that the Court's sensitivity to the preferences of policymakers has been greater and more nuanced than the separation of powers literature has acknowledged. Even when the Member States do not engage in the procedure with their observations, the Court is unwilling to enforce its own agenda with audacious judgments, avoiding authoritative legal solutions that would break political stalemate or counteract legislative paralysis caused by political disagreement.

4. Concluding Remarks

The chapter contributed to the volume's quest for a more nuanced, comprehensive, and deeper understanding of the legal actors that make up EU disability law by

[79] Case C-36/74 *Walrave and Koch v Association Union Cycliste Internationale and Others* ECLI:EU:C:1974:140.

[80] Case C-32/75 *Cristini v S.N.C.F.* ECLI:EU:C:1975:120.

[81] Case C-36/75 *Rutili v Ministre de l'intérieur* ECLI:EU:C:1975:137.

[82] Case C-67/74 *Bonsignore v Oberstadtdirektor der Stadt Köln* ECLI:EU:C:1975:34.

[83] Case C-19/92 *Kraus v Land Baden-Württemberg* ECLI:EU:C:1993:125.

[84] Joined Cases C-259/91, C-331/91 and C-332/91 *Allué and Others v Università degli studi di Venezia and Others* ECLI:EU:C:1993:333.

[85] Case C-279/93 *Finanzamt Köln-Altstadt v Schumacker* ECLI:EU:C:1995:31.

[86] Case C-415/93 *Union royale belge des sociétés de football association and Others v Bosman and Others* ECLI:EU:C:1995:463.

[87] Case C-336/94 *Dafeki v Landesversicherungsanstalt Württemberg* ECLI:EU:C:1997:579.

[88] Larsson and Naurin (n 17).

unpacking the empirical research process, inquiring into (1) the ambition and the power of referring national courts to delimit their role in the preliminary reference procedure and judicial cooperation, and (2) the effect of the political divisions within the Member States on the Court's willingness and ability to make EU law *in lieu* of the European legislator, hence its role in the process of European market integration.

The purpose of these studies was to show that empirical methods – dissecting legal texts by hand coding and then using the information for qualitative or quantitative analysis – can enrich the knowledge of the law and law-making as a process of meaning-making or meaning construction in which legal actors represent competing voices of varying magnitude. Studying these voices systematically offers a deeper insight into the functioning of the legal system and its power dynamics that mirror the law's power to shape and sustain the social order, authoritatively defining individual rights, duties, and EU competence.

The chapter sketched selected methodological, conceptual and practical considerations in studies that explored the role of legal actors in law-making in EU law. Further analysis can use the presented concepts, methods and research design to explore the interaction between the law, politics and society in individual disputes or in legislative processes, uncovering which narratives emerge as victorious in the process. In this volume, Bartlett's chapter illustrates the obstacles to societal change in disability rights by unpacking the law-politics-civil society interplay of the proposed but never adopted Horizontal Equality Directive.[89] While the disability rights movement enjoyed support in the European Parliament, it encountered insurmountable obstacles in the Council, divided between progressive and more conservative Member States. In this scenario, Bartlett argues, litigation is unlikely to make up for the lack of legislative action.[90] O'Sullivan's chapter unpacks the uneven contribution of national courts to the making of EU disability law, using Irish courts as a case study.[91] The chapter demonstrates how smaller and neglected Member States individually and fittingly solve complex relationships between EU law and the UN Convention on the Rights of Persons with Disabilities on their own, and that the contribution of national courts depends on their composition, a factor in need of further research.

These case studies can balance large-n studies by teasing out the genealogy of legal change, legal ideas and ideologies that compete in the struggle to define EU law, retelling the history of a legal field, offering a deeper understanding of legal concepts.[92]

[89] O Bartlett, 'The EU Legislative Institutions and Disability Rights: Uncovering the Factors that Block Progress and Offering Insights for Future Advocacy' in this volume.

[90] Ibid.

[91] O'Sullivan (n 20).

[92] I thank Fernanda Nicola and Antoine Vauchez for highlighting this (Seminar on Methodological Controversies in EU Law, Aix Marseilles, 2 May 2024).

3

The Surge of EU Disability Policy: Historical Developments, Current Issues and the Role of Different Actors

ANNE WALDSCHMIDT AND EVA S KROLLA

1. Introduction

Disability policy in the European Union (EU) is a complex subject of investigation. This is because it emerges simultaneously at different, intersecting levels, from local or subnational governments to national governments, to the EU level and to international organisations, such as the United Nations (UN). Perhaps most notably, after the adoption of the UN Convention on the Rights of Persons with Disabilities (CRPD) by the UN General Assembly in December 2006,[1] an 'internationalisation' of disability issues has occurred, which, in turn, triggered a renewed attention to disability rights globally. However, the recent focus on the CRPD often disregards that, since the mid-20th century, an array of different actors has significantly influenced and shaped disability policy in Europe.

This chapter focuses on the EU level and expounds on the expansion of EU disability policy. While the overall volume tends to use 'law' as overarching term, this chapter uses 'policy' as an umbrella term, to encompass EU legislative instruments – as well as soft law – and the array of measures adopted to promote disability rights, consistent with the political science lens that it adopts. This chapter aims to complement and support legal and socio-legal chapters elsewhere in this volume, proffering an overview of past and current developments. Sitting at the intersection of political science and law it contextualises the analyses of institutional and non-institutional actors provided by other authors in this edited volume. In that vein, it critically reviews the objectives that underpin EU disability

[1] On the CRPD, among others, see T Degener and E Diehl (eds), *Handbuch Behindertenrechtskonvention. Teilhabe als Menschenrecht – Inklusion als gesellschaftliche Aufgabe* (Bundeszentrale für politische Bildung 2015).

policy, and, differently from earlier scholarly works,[2] points to the institutional and non-institutional actors that influence the shaping of this field.[3] In this respect, the chapter gauges relevant 'political dynamics', and contrasts the development of disability policy *vis-à-vis* EU social policy within the remit of the European integration process.

This process has unfolded through a steady enlargement of the Member States, which was particularly driven forward in the mid-2000s with the entry of Eastern European countries. Founded by only six nation-states, the EU consisted of a total of 28 Member States until recently. Since 2020, as a result of the British referendum against EU membership in 2016 (Brexit), the EU has 27 Member States; although preparations are being made for new countries to join.[4] The Treaty of Lisbon, in force since 2009, has impacted on the interplay of the EU institutions, elevating the significance of supranationalism and strengthening the position of the European Parliament (EP). However, while qualifying as a constitutional system[5] and embedding the separation of powers of classic nation-states, the EU is not a state.

For the purpose of this analysis, and in line with the volume, the following seven institutional actors are considered as being significant for the shaping of EU disability policy. Through intergovernmental cooperation in the European Council (the heads of state and government), the main political direction of the EU is steered. The Council of the EU (Council) in its various ministerial configurations by policy specialisation has (together with the EP) a primary legislative function.[6] In addition to these intergovernmental institutions, the European Commission (Commission) has a special position due to its supranational influence and its ability to shape policies, which it uses confidently by submitting proposals for EU legislative acts, such as regulations and directives.[7] It is subdivided into Directorates-General (DGs), which function as departments for the individual policy areas. The Directorate-General for Employment, Social Affairs and Inclusion (DG EMPL) includes a unit responsible for disability policy. Another important institution of the EU is the EP as the elected representative of the EU

[2] L Waddington, *From Rome to Nice in a Wheelchair. The Development of European Disability Policy* (Europa Law Publishing 2005); C O'Mahony and S Quinlivan, 'The EU Disability Strategy and the Future of EU Disability Policy' in D Ferri and A Broderick (eds), *Research Handbook on EU Disability Law* (Edward Elgar 2020) 12–28; D Ferri, 'The Role of Soft Law in Advancing the Rights of Persons with Disabilities in the EU: A 'Hybridity' Approach to EU Disability Law' (2023) 28(4–6) *European Law Journal* 134–153.

[3] See recently also MC Nisco, 'Disability in EU's institutional discourse: An analysis of terminology' (2024) 30(1) *Terminology. International Journal of Theoretical and Applied Issues in Specialized Communication* 107–133.

[4] European Commission (Commission), '2023 Communication on EU Enlargement Policy' COM(2023) 690 final.

[5] G Martinico, *The Tangled Complexity of the EU Constitutional Process. The Frustrating Knot of Europe* (Routledge 2023).

[6] O Bartlett, 'The EU Legislative Institutions and Disability Rights: Uncovering the Factors that Block Progress and Offering Insights for Future Advocacy' in this volume.

[7] ES Krolla, 'The Role of the European Commission in Shaping EU Disability Law: A Driver with the Brakes Put On?' in this volume.

population, which has been given a greater say through several amendments of the Treaties. However, the EP's legislative powers are not comparable to those of national parliaments. As laid down in Article 294 of the Treaty on the Functioning of the European Union (TFEU), the EP co-legislates with the Council through the so-called ordinary legislative procedure. The Court of Justice of the European Union (CJEU) represents the main judicial institution of the EU.

Furthermore, there are additional institutions, bodies and a large number of agencies which influence or support to varying degrees EU policy-making.[8] Particularly relevant for EU disability policy are the European Union Agency for Fundamental Rights (FRA),[9] which has been involved in monitoring the implementation of the CRPD in the EU since 2013, and the European Ombudsman[10] who has prompted the EU institutions to adhere to current international standards on the rights of persons with disabilities.

In addition, non-institutional actors (i.e., actors outside the formal architecture of the EU legal order) are considered to varying degrees. These include civil society organisations, in particular the European Disability Forum (EDF).[11] The impact of the UN Committee on the Rights of Persons with Disabilities (CRPD Committee) and its role in shaping the development of EU disability policy as an external, non-institutional actor in the EU is discussed elsewhere in this volume.[12]

In order to analyse disability policy at the EU level, it is important to realise that policy-making on issues relevant to persons with disabilities is not confined to the framework of traditional social policy, but encompasses almost all areas of life, be it education, employment, living in the community, sexuality and having a family or access to culture and leisure, technologies and civil society engagement. The following broad definition of disability policy therefore also applies at the EU level; it refers 'to the totality of policy measures, with intended or unintended consequences, for the welfare, living conditions, autonomy, participation and dignity of persons with disabilities [...]'.[13] In this chapter, we see 'disability policy as covering broad areas of policy and sectors of society that may or may not have "disability" or similar terms in their names [...]'.[14] Even though this definition is helpful as a heuristic tool, it proves difficult to implement in practice, which

[8] In the context of EU disability policy, the European Economic and Social Committee, the Committee of the Regions and the European Central Bank are noteworthy; however, their analysis goes beyond the scope of this chapter and volume.

[9] GN Toggenburg, 'The Role of the Fundamental Rights Agency in Advancing Disability Rights within the EU' in this volume.

[10] D Ferri, 'The Role of the European Ombudsman in Protecting Disability Rights' in this volume.

[11] D Ferri and ES Krolla, 'Introduction: Walking Through the Looking Glass' in this volume; C Coveney, 'The Role of the European Disability Forum and Disability Organisations in Shaping EU Disability Policy' in this volume.

[12] S Favalli, 'The Role of the Committee on the Rights of Persons with Disabilities in Nudging the EU towards Compliance with the Convention on the Rights of Persons with Disabilities' in this volume.

[13] R Halvorsen *et al.*, 'Diversity and dynamics of disability policy in Europe. An analytical framework' in R Halvorsen *et al.* (eds), *The Changing Disability Policy System. Active Citizenship and Disability in Europe Volume* 1 (Routledge 2017) 13.

[14] Ibid.

is why, in this chapter, we mostly refer to policy documents in which disability and/or persons with disabilities are explicitly mentioned.

In the remainder of the chapter, the development of the EU's disability policy from the late 1950s to the beginning of the 21st century is assessed. The chapter then moves on to deal with current issues in EU disability policy. First, we look at the provisions relevant to persons with disabilities in the EU Treaties; second, we focus on disability-specific policy measures; and third, we discuss collective actors in EU disability policy. The concluding remarks provide a summary and identify thematic areas that are investigated further in this volume, but that require future research as well.

2. Disability Policy of the EU: Historical Development

The history of EU disability policy has taken place against the backdrop of the eventful, and somewhat 'conflicted', ongoing process of European integration. As disability policy was initially a sub-area of social policy, its development into an independent policy field goes hand in hand with the history of EU social policy, at least until the end of the 20th century. Building on other contributions[15] and previous work,[16] the subsequent discussion is intended to trace the history of EU disability policy over the past six decades. Overall, we propose that the emergence of this particular policy field at the EU level can be divided into four periods. We further differentiate between eight phases, two of which are identified per period. We first describe the general social policy activities of the EU and its predecessors, as they provide the larger context, before focusing on explicit disability policy measures.

2.1. The First Period of EU Disability Policy: 1958–1979

The first phase of the first period covers the early years of the EU's predecessor, the then European Economic Community (EEC). The years from 1958 to 1973 were

[15] P Becker, 'Sozialpolitik' in W Weidenfeld and W Wessels (eds), *Europa von A bis Z* (Nomos 2006) 334–337; W Däubler, 'Die Europäische Union als Wirtschafts- und Sozialgemeinschaft' in W Weidenfeld (ed), *Die Europäische Union. Politisches System und Politikbereiche* (Bundeszentrale für politische Bildung 2006) 273–288; O'Mahony and Quinlivan (n 2).

[16] The historical presentation in section 2 is an updated account of earlier versions based on A Waldschmidt, 'Disability Policy of the European Union: The supranational level' (2009) 3(1) *ALTER: European Journal of Disability Research* 8–23 and A Waldschmidt and K Lingnau, 'Abschlussbericht zum Forschungsprojekt Soziale Teilhabe in Europa: Eine Studie zu den Ordnungsprinzipien europäischer Sozial- und Gleichstellungspolitik am Beispiel der Politiken für behinderte Menschen auf supranationaler und nationaler Ebene' Bewilligungsnummer W-06-2-012, Berichtszeitraum 01.04.2007–31.03.2009, gefördert von der RheinEnergieStiftung Jugend/Beruf, Wissenschaft, Köln, unveröffentlicht (Universität zu Köln 2009).

characterised by the absence of any real social policy initiatives. The only exceptions were two regulations that concerned the discrimination against migrant workers.[17] In light of the economic boom and full employment at the time, there was an apparent lack of socio-political problems that would have required action at the EEC level.[18] Remarkably, in 1965, the European Social Fund was confronted with the problem of having to find new fields of activity as a result of dwindling unemployment rates.[19] Yet, during the same phase no Community initiatives were specifically aimed at persons with disabilities. In fact, the beginning of a EEC disability policy can only be set at a later date, namely in the years from 1974 to 1979.

This second phase was ushered in by the Paris Summit of Heads of State and Government in 1972, at which the enlargement of the EEC was decided.[20] As a consequence of this decision, the Council of Ministers of Labour and Social Affairs adopted the first Social Action Programme[21] at the EEC level in 1974. Its main objectives were the fight against unemployment, the improvement of working and living conditions and the democratisation of enterprises. On the basis of this programme, directives were issued that still inform the core of EU labour law to this day, such as the Equal Pay Directive,[22] the Equal Treatment Directive[23] and the Directive on the Implementation of the Principle of Equal Treatment for Men and Women in the field of social security.[24] Even though the programme's promises were not ultimately fulfilled, Däubler argues that from an employee point of view, the phase from 1974 to 1979 can be seen as the 'golden age' of former Community social policy.[25]

In the same phase, only one major activity within disability policy is worth mentioning. In 1974, within the framework of the first Social Action Programme, the Council also adopted the first Community Action Programme for the vocational

[17] Council Regulation No 38/54/EEC of 25 March 1964 on freedom of movement for workers within the Community [1964] OJ L62/965; Council Regulation No 1612/68/EEC of the Council of 15 October 1968 on freedom of movement for workers within the Community [1968] OJ L257/2.

[18] Däubler (n 15) 274.

[19] O Blanchard, 'European Unemployment: The Evolution of Facts and Ideas' (November 2005) NBER Working Paper 11750.

[20] European Communities, 'Statement from the Paris Summit (19 to 21 October 1972)' available at <https://www.cvce.eu/en/search?q=Statement+from+the+Paris+Summit+%2819+to+21+October+1972%29>.

[21] Council Resolution of 21 January 1974 concerning a social action programme [1974] OJ C13/1.

[22] Council Directive 75/117/EEC of 10 February 1975 on the approximation of the laws of the Member States relating to the application of the principle of equal pay for men and women [1975] OJ L45/19.

[23] Council Directive 76/207/EEC of 9 February 1976 on the implementation of the principle of equal treatment for men and women as regards access to employment, vocational training and promotion, and working conditions [1976] OJ L39/40.

[24] Council Directive 79/7/EEC of 19 December 1978 on the progressive implementation of the principle of equal treatment for men and women in matters of social security [1979] OJ L6/24.

[25] Däubler (n 15).

rehabilitation of handicapped persons.[26] This programme aimed at improving labour market participation and was part of the EEC's efforts to strengthen the common market; the relatively high unemployment rates among workers with disabilities as a result of the 1973 oil crisis and the subsequent economic recession were to be combated and gainful employment increased. Simultaneously, it laid the foundation for EU disability policy.

2.2. The Second Period of EU Disability Policy: 1980–1996

The next period can also be divided into two phases. The first phase is from the end of the 1970s until 1985 and saw no progress in social policy. All of the Commission's proposals (e.g. on minimum protection for temporary employment, fixed-term employment and part-time work) failed due to the British veto. The then Conservative government of the United Kingdom (UK) under Margaret Thatcher pursued a course of strictly liberal economic deregulation. For this reason, social policy initiatives of the Commission had no prospect of a favourable vote in the Council, especially as the EEC Treaty in force did not yet permit majority decisions.

Disability policy in this phase can also be described as largely stagnant. Only the 'International Year of Disabled Persons' of the UN in 1981 proved to be a source of impetus, albeit a weak one. It stimulated a Council Resolution on the social integration of persons with disabilities[27] and a corresponding Commission Communication;[28] these two documents were, however, not published until December 1981.

In the second phase, the EEC began to coalesce as a more significant social policy actor. In the so-called Single European Act of 1986, the concept of the internal market was defined for the first time and two social policy provisions were included. The competences of the Council were extended to enable it to take majority decisions in the field of the working environment and the Commission was mandated to promote dialogue between trade unions and employers. The emerging internal market also prompted trade unions to call for EEC-wide social rights. In response, the Community Charter of the Fundamental Social Rights of Workers (CFSRW)[29] was adopted in December 1989 by eleven of the then twelve

[26] Council Resolution of 27 June 1974 establishing the initial Community action programme for the vocational rehabilitation of handicapped persons [1974] OJ C80/30.

[27] Council Resolution of the Representatives of the Governments of the Member States of the European Communities, Meeting within the Council of 21 December 1981 on the social integration of handicapped people [1981] OJ C347/1.

[28] Commission of the European Communities, 'The Social Integration of Disabled People – A Framework for the Development of Community Action' COM(81) 633 final.

[29] Commission of the European Communities, 'Community Charter of the Fundamental Social Rights of Workers' (Office for Official Publications of the European Communities 1990).

Member States – the UK did not sign this Charter until 1997, following Tony Blair's election as Prime Minister. Although primarily a political declaration, without any legally binding effects, it provided the basis for legitimising further initiatives. Amongst other measures,[30] the Framework Directive on Occupational Safety and Health[31] was released in 1989. Building on the CFSRW, the 1991 Maastricht Summit concluded a legally binding agreement on social policy – the Social Policy Protocol – though again without the UK. During this time the European Social Funds were also reformed.[32]

Simultaneously, increased activities can be observed in the area of disability policy in the late 1980s and early 1990s. Several initiatives dealt with the employment of persons with disabilities in the Community and pursued the goal of greater labour market integration. Of particular note in this context is the HELIOS I programme,[33] which focused on vocational education and rehabilitation and was issued as second Community Action Programme for the benefit of persons with disabilities. In addition, the Council adopted a Resolution on inclusive education in 1990.[34]

During the second phase, the Maastricht Treaty entered into force in November 1993.[35] As the founding Treaty of the EU it represented a major step towards greater integration of the formerly disparate communities and areas of cooperation at the Community level. Further, the Economic and Monetary Union was decided upon, as a result of which the Euro was introduced as common currency across 11 out of the then 15 Member States in 1999. The Maastricht Treaty also brought about some important (albeit not radical) changes in social policy. The above-mentioned Social Policy Protocol of 1991 was annexed to the Treaty. Directives were to be issued by the Member States (except the UK) unanimously or by a qualified majority in almost all areas of labour and social law. At the same time, the principle of subsidiarity was emphasised, which requires that the EU only intervenes when neither the Member States nor social partners are able to produce adequate solutions.

[30] See, eg, Council Directive 91/308/EEC of 10 June 1991 on prevention of the use of the financial system for the purpose of money laundering [1991] OJ L166/77; Council Directive 93/104/EC of 23 November 1993 concerning certain aspects of the organization of working time [1993] OJ L307/18.

[31] Council Directive 89/391/EEC of 12 June 1989 on the introduction of measures to encourage improvements in the safety and health of workers at work [1989] OJ L183/1.

[32] For an overview see EP, 'European Social Fund Plus' available at <https://www.europarl.europa.eu/factsheets/en/sheet/53/european-social-fund-plus>; Commission, 'Growth, Competitiveness, Employment. The Challenges and Ways forward into the 21st Century White Paper' (Office for Official Publications of the European Communities 1994).

[33] Council Decision 88/231/EEC of 18 April 1988 establishing a second Community action programme for disabled people (Helios) [1988] OJ L104/38. HELIOS is the acronym for 'Handicapped People in the European Community Living Independently in an Open Society'.

[34] Resolution of the Council and the Ministers of Education Meeting within the Council of 31 May 1990 concerning integration of children and young people with disabilities into ordinary systems of education [1990] OJ C162/2.

[35] Waddington (n 2); D Ferri and A Broderick, 'Introduction' in Ferri and Broderick (n 2) 1-10.

The spirit of optimism that prevailed in European politics at that time was also evident in disability policy. On the one hand, the HELIOS II programme[36] continued the promotion of vocational and social integration. On the other, the Commission Communication of 30 July 1996 on equality of opportunity for people with disabilities[37] and a corresponding Resolution of the Council[38] brought about a clear turning point in EU disability policy. From that moment onwards, the focus was no longer on vocational rehabilitation alone; equality of persons with disabilities also became a key issue.

2.3. The Third Period of EU Disability Policy: 1997–2009

The first phase of the third period, which spans from approximately 1997 to 1999, was characterised by both the consolidation of the social policy agenda and the establishment of the right to non-discrimination. The Treaty of Amsterdam, adopted in 1997 and in force since 1999, integrated the Social Policy Protocol of the Maastricht Treaty as Title X.[39] Social policy objectives of the EU were also expanded to include a reference to the CFSRW and the European Social Charter[40] of the Council of Europe.[41] With the overall aim of achieving equal treatment in the labour market, the EU was now empowered with the competence to adopt non-discrimination legislation, *inter alia*, on the ground of disability by virtue of former Article 13 EC, now Article 19 TFEU. Additionally, in this phase, several soft law initiatives were issued. For example, the Council adopted a Recommendation on a parking card for people with disabilities in 1998[42] and a Resolution on equal employment opportunities for people with disabilities in 1999.[43] On the one hand, this was to ensure mobility in terms of transport, on the other, labour market policy initiatives were continued.

Marking the second phase, the years from 2000 to 2009 were a particularly eventful time for the EU. One important milestone was the Treaty of Nice, which

[36] Council Decision of 25 February 1993 establishing a third Community action programme to assist disabled people (Helios II 1993 to 1996) [1993] OJ L56/30.

[37] Commission, 'Communication of the Commission of 30 July 1996 on equality of opportunity for people with disabilities: A New European Community Disability Strategy' COM(96) 406 final.

[38] Resolution of the Council and of the Representatives of the Governments of the Member States meeting within the Council of 20 December 1996 on equality of opportunity for people with disabilities [1996] OJ C12.

[39] Articles 136–145 Treaty establishing the European Community (TEC), now Articles 151–161 Treaty on the Functioning of the European Union (TFEU).

[40] Council of Europe, European Social Charter, adopted 18 October 1961, in force since 26 February 1965, ETS No 035; European Social Charter (revised), adopted 3 May 1996, in force since 1 July 1999, ETS No 163; G Palmisano, 'The European Social Charter and Disability' in Ferri and Broderick (n 2) 431-447.

[41] Article 136 TEC, now Article 151 TFEU.

[42] Council Recommendation 98/376/EC of 4 June 1998 on a parking card for people with disabilities [1998] OJ L167/25.

[43] Council Resolution of 17 June 1999 on equal employment opportunities for people with disabilities [1999] OJ C186/3.

was signed in 2001 and came into force in 2003. Prior to this, in 2000, the Charter of Fundamental Rights of the European Union (CFR)[44] was adopted as a non-binding declaration by the EP, the Council and the Commission. At the same time, the European Council in Nice adopted the European Social Agenda,[45] with which the EU presented its social policy work programme until 2005. The aim was to implement the so-called Lisbon Strategy[46] – a programme to make the EU the most competitive and dynamic knowledge-based economic area in the world within ten years – and to add a social policy dimension. In the European Social Agenda, the EU compiled current and future challenges and formulated aims for a common social policy. Ambitious objectives, such as the creation of more and better jobs, the modernisation of social protection systems, equality between men and women and the fight against poverty and discrimination were pursued. By virtue of the Open Method of Coordination (OMC), first introduced in 1993 and extended in 2000, coordination and monitoring processes of employment policy and later further policy fields were established at the EU level.[47] The Member States were encouraged to regularly report on their labour market, education, health, and social policies, to receive recommendations and to learn from one another.

On the one hand, efforts were made to better coordinate common social and equality policies. On the other, the attempt to give the EU a constitutional treaty failed in 2007 due to national referenda in France and the Netherlands. The end of the decade was characterised by the Treaty of Lisbon, which was adopted in 2007 and has been in force since 2009.[48] It established the legally binding nature of the CFR, making it an integral part of the EU's political system. Moreover, the EU acquired legal personality[49] and gained a more decisive role in the international arena, engaging with international organisations, such as the UN.[50]

These years can be considered critical in relation to disability policy because of increased activities in the field of non-discrimination. In 2000, both the Employment Equality Directive[51] and the Community Action Programme to

[44] Charter of Fundamental Rights of the European Union [2000] OJ C364/01.

[45] European Parliament (EP), 'European Council – Nice 7-10 December 2000 Conclusions of the Presidency Annex I – European Social Agenda' available at <https://www.europarl.europa.eu/summits/nice2_en.htm>.

[46] Council of the EU (Council), 'Lisbon European Council (23–24 March 2000) – Presidency Conclusions' available at <https://www.europarl.europa.eu/summits/lis1_en.htm>.

[47] DM Trubek and LG Trubek, 'Hard and Soft Law in the Construction of Social Europe: the Role of the Open Method of Co-ordination' (2005) 11(3) *European Law Journal* 343–364; S Devetzi and H-W Platzer (eds), *Offene Methode der Koordinierung und Europäisches Sozialmodell. Interdisziplinäre Perspektiven* (ibidem Verlag 2009); K Armstrong, 'The Open Method of Coordination – Obstinate or Obsolete?' (2016) 45 *University of Cambridge Faculty of Law Research Paper*.

[48] O Leiße (ed), *Die Europäische Union nach dem Vertrag von Lissabon. Europäische Politik im 21. Jahrhundert* (VS Verlag für Sozialwissenschaften 2010).

[49] Article 47 Treaty on European Union (TEU).

[50] Article 21 TEU.

[51] Council Directive 2000/78/EC of 27 November 2000 establishing a general framework for equal treatment in employment and occupation (Employment Equality Directive) [2000] OJ L303/16.

combat discrimination,[52] which ran from 2001 to 2006, were adopted. Both signified important milestones for disability policy too.[53] Moreover, in other policy areas measures were adopted that specifically addressed the situation of persons with disabilities. Accessibility to the internet-based knowledge and information society[54] and to cultural institutions, equal opportunities for pupils and students with disabilities in education[55] as well as the promotion of employment and social inclusion were important issues.[56] In addition, the European Year of People with Disabilities in 2003[57] provided impetus for further development. As a result of the Year, a series of biennial Disability Policy Action Plans[58] were implemented at the EU level between 2003 and 2010. Advances were also made in electronic communications networks and services,[59] transport[60] as well as public procurement[61] legislation with the adoption of several regulations and directives that established common standards and requirements, which included disability-related provisions.[62] Moreover, in 2007 the Commission recommended that the Council sign the CRPD.[63]

[52] Council Decision 2000/750/EC of 27 November 2000 establishing a Community action programme to combat discrimination (2001 to 2006) [2000] OJ L303/23.

[53] Waddington (n 2); Ferri and Broderick (n 35).

[54] Commission, 'eEurope 2002: Impact and Priorities A communication to the Spring European Council in Stockholm, 23-24 March 2001' COM(2001) 140 final.

[55] Council Resolution of 5 May 2003 on equal opportunities for pupils and students with disabilities in education and training [2003] OJ C134/6.

[56] Commission, 'Joint Report on Social Inclusion' (Office for Official Publications of the European Communities 2002).

[57] Council Decision 2001/903/EC of 3 December 2001 on the European Year of People with Disabilities 2003 [2001] OJ L335/15.

[58] Commission, 'Equal opportunities for people with disabilities: A European Action Plan' COM(2003) 650 final.

[59] Directive 2002/22/EC of the European Parliament and of the Council of 7 March 2002 on universal service and users' rights relating to electronic communications networks and services (Universal Service Directive) [2002] OJ L108/51.

[60] Regulation (EC) No 1899/2006 of the European Parliament and of the Council of 12 December 2006 amending Council Regulation (EEC) No 3922/91 on the harmonisation of technical requirements and administrative procedures in the field of civil aviation [2006] OJ L377/1; Regulation (EC) No 1107/2006 of the European Parliament and of the Council of 5 July 2006 concerning the rights of disabled persons and persons with reduced mobility when travelling by air [2006] OJ L204/1; 2006/87/EC Directive of the European Parliament and of the Council of 12 December 2006 laying down technical requirements for inland waterway vessels [2006] OJ L389/1; Regulation (EC) No 1370/2007 of the European Parliament and of the Council of 23 October 2007 on public passenger transport services by rail and by road [2007] OJ L315/1; Regulation (EC) No 1371/2007 of the European Parliament and of the Council of 23 October 2007 on rail passengers' rights and obligations [2007] OJ L315/14.

[61] Directive 2004/17/EC of the European Parliament and of the Council of 31 March 2004 coordinating the procurement procedures of entities operating in the water, energy, transport and postal services sectors [2004] OJ L134/1; Directive 2004/18/EC of the European Parliament and of the Council of 31 March 2004 on the coordination of procedures for the award of public works contracts, public supply contracts and public service contracts [2004] OJ L134/114.

[62] D Ferri and N Šubic, 'The European Union. Federal Trends in Disability Rights' in D Ferri, F Palermo and G Martinico (eds), *Federalism and the Rights of Persons with Disabilities. The Implementation of the CRPD in Federal Systems and Its Implications* (Hart 2023) 30.

[63] Council Decision 2010/48/EC of 26 November 2009 concerning the conclusion, by the European Community, of the UN CRPD [2010] OJ L23/35; EP, 'EU Implementation of the UN Convention on

In summary, during this third period, EU disability policy began to take on a contoured and more complex shape.

2.4. The Fourth Period of EU Disability Policy: 2010–2024

The fourth and final period that we identify in the development of EU disability policy proved to be particularly crisis-ridden. Against the backdrop of the global financial crisis of 2007 to 2008, the ensuing European debt crisis and the resulting economic recession, social policy once again took centre stage in the EU. At the Social Summit in Gothenburg in 2017, EU Member States adopted the so-called European Pillar of Social Rights (EPSR).[64] The EPSR encompasses twenty fundamental principles in the areas of equal opportunities, labour and employment as well as in social inclusion, but does not commit the countries to any concrete measures and is thus a non-binding declaration of intent for social rights in the EU. Social policy issues continue to be decided at national level; however, social policy has simultaneously been increasingly Europeanised,[65] mainly indirectly through the aforementioned OMC.

The first phase from 2010 to 2019 also saw significant events in EU disability policy. Important steps were taken with regard to the CRPD, which the EU ratified as a 'regional integration organisation'[66] in 2010.[67] This resulted in the Convention becoming legally binding at the EU level.[68] As a party to the CRPD, the EU undertook to report regularly to the UN on its implementation and submitted its first report on the CRPD in 2014;[69] one year later, the first formal review was conducted before the CRPD Committee, which published its observations and recommendations in October 2015.

The European Disability Strategy 2010–2020 (EDS)[70] was adopted in 2010, almost simultaneously with the ratification of the CRPD, and included

the Rights of Persons with Disabilities (CRPD) European Implementation Assessment' (European Parliamentary Research Service 2016) 6-7.

[64] Interinstitutional Proclamation on the European Pillar of Social Rights [2017] OJ C428/10.

[65] C de la Porte, 'Round Table. From Lisbon to Porto: taking stock of developments in EU social policy: Opening up the Pandora's Box of EU Social Rights' (2021) 27(4) *Transfer: European Review of Labour and Research* 513–519. For a critical account see E Muir, 'Drawing Positive Lessons from the Presence of 'The Social' Outside of EU Social Policy Stricto Sensu' (2018) 14(1) *European Constitutional Law Review* 75–95. Most recently see also the trio programme of the Spanish, Belgian and Hungarian presidencies of the Council, 'Taking forward the Strategic Agenda 18-month Programme of the Council (1 July 2023–31 December 2024)' 10597/23 which aims to enhance the 'social dimension of Europe' and establishes some continuity across the rotating presidencies.

[66] Article 44 UN Convention on the Rights of Persons with Disabilities (CRPD).

[67] Council Decision 2010/48/EC of 26 November 2009 concerning the conclusion, by the European Community, of the UN CRPD [2010] OJ L23/35.

[68] M Chamon, 'Negotiation, Ratification and Implementation of the CRPD and its Status in the EU Legal Order' in Ferri and Broderick (n 2) 52-70.

[69] Committee on the Rights of Persons with Disabilities (CRPD Committee), 'Initial Report of States Parties due in 2012 European Union' (5 June 2014) CRPD/C/EU/1.

[70] Commission, 'European Disability Strategy 2010–2020: A Renewed Commitment to a Barrier-Free Europe' COM(2010) 636 final.

a comprehensive programme with eight priorities.[71] Accessibility also became an important issue in this phase.[72] First, the Web Accessibility Directive (WAD)[73] was adopted in 2016 to harmonise accessibility standards of public sector bodies' websites and mobile applications across the Union. It was followed by the so-called Marrakesh Package,[74] which was enacted to implement the Marrakesh Treaty to Facilitate Access to Published Works for Persons Who are Blind, Visually Impaired or Otherwise Print Disabled adopted by the World Intellectual Property Organisation.[75] The latter legislative package regulates exceptions to copyright obligations to facilitate the access to printed works for persons who are blind, visually impaired or otherwise print disabled, thus with a more limited personal scope than the CRPD and other EU acts and not universally relevant for persons with disabilities. Access to audiovisual content was fostered through the revision of the Audiovisual Media Services Directive (AVMSD) recast in 2018[76] as well as the European Accessibility Act (EAA)[77] which was passed in 2019 and aims to harmonise accessibility requirements across certain services and products in the internal market placing a range of obligations on manufactures, importers, distributors and service providers both in the public and private sectors.[78]

In the division proposed, the final phase commenced in 2020. While it is still too early to take proper stock, it is important to highlight that EU disability policy has advanced amid an array of crises: the Covid-19 pandemic, the Russian war against

[71] O'Mahony and Quinlivan (n 2); DL Hosking, 'Staying the Course: The European Disability Strategy 2010–2020' (2013) 4 *European Yearbook of Disability Law* 73–98.

[72] D Ferri, 'The Role of the European Union in Ensuring Accessibility of Cultural Goods and Services: All About that … Internal Market?' (2023) 48(3) *European Law Review* 257–280.

[73] Directive (EU) 2016/2102 of the European Parliament and of the Council of 26 October 2016 on the accessibility of the websites and mobile applications of public sector bodies [2016] OJ L327/1.

[74] Regulation (EU) 2017/1563 of the European Parliament and of the Council of 13 September 2017 on the cross-border exchange between the Union and third countries of accessible format copies of certain works and other subject matter protected by copyright and related rights for the benefit of persons who are blind, visually impaired or otherwise print-disabled [2017] OJ L242/1; Directive (EU) 2017/1564 of the European Parliament and of the Council of 13 September 2017 on certain permitted uses of certain works and other subject matter protected by copyright and related rights for the benefit of persons who are blind, visually impaired or otherwise print-disabled and amending Directive 2001/29/EC on the harmonisation of certain aspects of copyright and related rights in the information society [2017] OJ L242/6.

[75] World Intellectual Property Organisation, 'Marrakesh Treaty to Facilitate Access to Published Works for Persons Who Are Blind, Visually Impaired, or Otherwise Print Disabled' available at <https://www.wipo.int/wipolex/en/text/301019>; Council Decision (EU) 2018/254 of 15 February 2018 on the conclusion on behalf of the European Union of the Marrakesh Treaty to Facilitate Access to Published Works for Persons who are Blind, Visually Impaired, or otherwise Print Disabled [2018] OJ L48/1.

[76] Directive (EU) 2018/1808 of the European Parliament and of the Council of 14 November 2018 amending Directive 2010/13/EU on the coordination of certain provisions laid down by law, regulation or administrative action in Member States concerning the provision of audiovisual media services (Audiovisual Media Services Directive) in view of changing market realities [2018] OJ L303/69.

[77] Directive (EU) 2019/882 of the European Parliament and of the Council of 17 April 2019 on the accessibility requirements for products and services (EAA) [2019] OJ L151/70.

[78] Ferri (n 72) 266.

Ukraine since 2022, and, at the time of writing, the crisis in the Gaza strip. The main policy initiative under the banner 'Union of Equality' was the new Strategy for the Rights of Persons with Disabilities 2021–2030 (Strategy 2021–2023).[79] Further, in September 2023 the Commission released its proposal for a European Disability Card and a revised European Parking Card,[80] which was subsequently negotiated and adopted by the Council and EP in record time.[81] Last but not least, the CRPD remains a high priority on the EU's disability policy agenda. The next review by the CRPD Committee is scheduled for March 2025 during the 32nd session of the body.[82] To this end, civil society organisations have submitted their alternative reports[83] and the EU has provided answers to the List of Issues, which constitute its combined second and third state report under the simplified reporting procedure.[84] This review process might in fact be the starting point of a new period (or phase) of EU disability policy. Additionally, the new legislative term, following the European elections in June 2024, that saw a right-wing surge in the EP, might affect EU's future approach to disability.

This brief historical review clearly shows a dynamic development of EU disability policy with remarkable progress. It also shows setbacks and phases of stagnation. In the preceding analysis, we have also highlighted parallel and encroaching developments of disability policy and social policy. In the area of

[79] Commission, 'Union of Equality: Strategy for the Rights of Persons with Disabilities 2021–2030' COM(2021) 101 final.

[80] Commission, 'Proposal for a Directive of the European Parliament and of the Council establishing the European Disability Card and the European Parking Card for persons with disabilities' COM(2023) 512 final. The proposal was substantiated on 31 October 2023 by a proposal extending the provisions to third country nationals legally residing in a Member State, see Commission, 'Proposal for a Directive of the European Parliament and of the Council extending Directive [XXXX] to third country nationals legally residing in a Member State' COM(2023) 698 final; Bartlett (n 6).

[81] Council, 'Council and Parliament pave the way for a European disability card and a European parking card for persons with disabilities' (Press Release, 8 February 2024) available at <https://www.consilium.europa.eu/en/press/press-releases/2024/02/08/council-and-parliament-pave-the-way-for-a-european-disability-card-and-a-european-parking-card-for-persons-with-disabilities/>. The compromise text was adopted by the EP in its April session following the approval by Coreper I on 16 February 2024. Council, 'Council and Parliament pave the way for a European disability card and a European parking card for persons with disabilities' (Press Release, 8 February 2024, updated 16 February 2024) available at <https://www.consilium.europa.eu/en/press/press-releases/2024/02/08/council-and-parliament-pave-the-way-for-a-european-disability-card-and-a-european-parking-card-for-persons-with-disabilities/>; EP, 'Parliament adopts EU-wide Disability and Parking Cards' (Press Release, 24 April 2024) available at <https://www.europarl.europa.eu/news/en/press-room/20240419IPR20572/parliament-adopts-eu-wide-disability-and-parking-cards>.

[82] CRPD Committee, 'When will my country be considered by the Committee?' (Updated 7 October 2024) available at <https://view.officeapps.live.com/op/view.aspx?src=https%3A%2F%2Fwww.ohchr.org%2Fsites%2Fdefault%2Ffiles%2Fdocuments%2Fhrbodies%2Fcrpd%2FTentative_forecasts_Country_reviews.docx&wdOrigin=BROWSELINK>.

[83] CRPD Committee, 'European Union' available at <https://tbinternet.ohchr.org/_layouts/15/treatybodyexternal/TBSearch.aspx?Lang=en&TreatyID=4&CountryID=218>.

[84] CRPD Committee, 'Combined second and third reports submitted by the European Union under article 35 of the Convention, pursuant to the optional reporting procedure, due in 2021' (4 May 2023) CRPD/C/EU/2-3.

general social policy measures, the EU continues to have a relatively weak profile, even if this policy field has taken on stronger contours over time. With the inclusion of the prohibition of discrimination in EU primary law, the EU has created a new field of action from which persons with disabilities benefit. The scope of EU disability policy has increased considerably since the end of the 1990s. However, the EU's specific constellation of competences – weak powers in the field of social rights and strong powers in equality policy – is reflected in disability policy as well.

Table 3.1 Overview of EU Social and Disability Policy 1958–2024

	EU Enlargements	EU Social Policy	EU Disability Policy
1958–1973	*1958*: EEC-6 *1972*: EEC-9	(1) Low level of social policy coordination	(1) No activities relevant to disability policy
1974–1979		(2) *1974*: First Social Action Programme is installed	(2) First Community Action Programme for the vocational rehabilitation of disabled people is installed
1980–1985	*1981*: EEC-10 *1985*: EEC-12	(3) British veto causes social policy stagnation	(3) Stagnation in disability policies
1986–1996	*1995*: EU-15	(4) The European Community is formed as a social policy actor; Maastricht Treaty establishes the EU and creates new rules of the game; Open Method of Coordination is introduced	(4) Increased measures for labour market integration are introduced; the programmes HELIOS I (1988–1991) and HELIOS II (1993–1996) focus on vocational and social integration
1997–1999		(5) Consolidation of the social policy agenda; anchoring the right to non-discrimination (Amsterdam Treaty)	(5) Reorientation in European disability policy: from vocational rehabilitation to non-discrimination and equal opportunities (6) *1998*: EU parking card is introduced

(continued)

Table 3.1 ***(Continued)***

	EU Enlargements	EU Social Policy	EU Disability Policy
2000–2009	*2004*: EU-25 *2007*: EU-27	(6) *2000–2003*: EU Charter of Fundamental Rights (CFR) and European Social Agenda are adopted in Nice; Open Method of Coordination is extended (7) *2007–2009*: Constitutional Treaty fails; Euro crisis begins; Lisbon Treaty reforms the institutional structure of the EU; CFR becomes legally binding	(7) *2000–2003*: New impetus through non-discrimination policy: Employment Equality Directive; 'European Year of People with Disabilities' (8) *2002–2007*: Sectoral legislation with disability-related provisions are released (9) *2003–2010*: Disability policy action plans are implemented (10) *2007–2008*: EU Commission recommends signing the UN Convention on the Rights of Persons with Disabilities (CRPD) and presents proposal for new Horizontal Equality Directive
2010–2019	*2013*: EU-28	(8) Financial crisis; Economic recession; European debt crisis (9) *2015*: European refugee crisis (10) *2016–2019*: Brexit and exit negotiations with the UK (11) *2017*: European Pillar of Social Rights is declared	(11) *2010–2015*: EU ratifies CRPD in 2010; first report in 2014; first review by CRPD Committee in 2015 (12) *2010*: 'European Disability Strategy 2010–2020: A Renewed Commitment to a Barrier-Free Europe' is adopted (13) *2019*: European Accessibility Act is passed

(continued)

Table 3.1 ***(Continued)***

	EU Enlargements	EU Social Policy	EU Disability Policy
2020–2024	*2020*: EU-27	(12) *2020–2023*: Covid-19 pandemic (13) *2021*: The European Pillar of Social Rights Action Plan is introduced (14) *2022–2024*: EU supports Ukraine in the fight against Russia's war	(14) *2021*: 'Union of Equality: Strategy for the Rights of Persons with Disabilities 2021–2030' is adopted; first meeting of Disability Platform (15) *2023*: European Commission proposes Directive establishing European Disability Card and revised European Parking Card (16) *2024*: Co-legislators adopt EU-wide Disability and Parking Cards

3. Disability Policy in the EU: Current Issues

Over the last six decades, disability policy has increasingly been established as an independent policy field of the EU, although certain issues remain unaddressed. After having adopted a diachronic perspective, we therefore now focus on current issues. The following discussion is roughly guided by three basic political science dimensions:[85] the level of 'polity' which includes, *inter alia*, the institutional set-up, structures and fundamental values, norms and principles; the dimension of 'policy', which comprises the political measures and programmes that are applied to solve specific societal problems; and the dimension of 'politics', which is used to describe the representation of interests of various collective actors.

3.1. 'Disability' in the Polity of the EU

The current polity of the EU is framed by the Treaty on European Union (TEU) and the TFEU, as well as the earlier-mentioned Charter of Fundamental Rights (CFR). Disability is addressed in Article 19(1) TFEU which provides that Council and EP

[85] T Meyer, *Was ist Politik?* (VS Verlag für Sozialwissenschaften 2010); MG Schmidt, F Wolf and S Wurster (eds), *Studienbuch Politikwissenschaft* (Springer VS 2013).

may take appropriate action to combat discrimination based on, *inter alia*, disability. The same wording was first used in the Treaty of Amsterdam; in this respect, non-discrimination policy is characterised by continuity rather than innovation. In the CFR disability appears in two provisions: Article 21, which deals with the right to non-discrimination, lists disability among other prohibited grounds of discrimination; Article 26 is entitled 'Integration of persons with disabilities' and is thus explicitly dedicated to this group of persons.[86]

It is noteworthy that in the CFR both Articles are included in the so-called 'Title III: Equality'. At least Article 26 would also have fitted into 'Title IV: Solidarity', which contains the provisions traditionally assigned to social policy, such as 'social security and social assistance'[87] or 'health care'.[88] This categorisation shows that within the framework of the EU, the living situation of persons with disabilities is progressively viewed from the perspective of equality.

3.2. 'Disability' in Current Policies of the EU

As far as current EU disability policies are concerned, they are, as noted above, no longer solely about the goal of occupational participation, but also about equality and non-discrimination. Yet, the EU retains only limited competences in some central areas, such as social security,[89] which is why social policy at the EU level is characterised by policy reporting tools such as the OMC. In addition, symbolic measures such as the European Day of Persons with Disabilities,[90] or the 'Access City Award',[91] which has been awarded within an annual conference since 2010, have been introduced. Furthermore, the EU's ratification of the CRPD established its implementation as a policy in its own right, which deserves its own consideration.[92] In this chapter, however, we only selectively look at the

[86] In the original '[t]he Union recognises and respects the right of persons with disabilities to benefit from measures designed to ensure their independence, social and occupational integration and participation in the life of the community'.

[87] Article 34 Charter of Fundamental Rights (CFR).

[88] Article 35 CFR.

[89] AP van der Mei, 'Freedom of movement for persons with disabilities and coordination of social security within the EU' in Ferri and Broderick (n 2).

[90] Commission, 'European Day of Persons with Disabilities 2023' available at <https://ec.europa.eu/social/main.jsp?catId=88&furtherEvents=yes&eventsId=2129&langId=en>. The EU celebrates this Day at the end of November and the beginning of December in alignment with the International Day of Persons with Disabilities on 3 December.

[91] Commission, 'Access City Award' available at <https://ec.europa.eu/social/main.jsp?catId=1141#:~:text=The%20Access%20City%20Award%20is%20an%20EU%20initiative,authorities%20to%20promote%20and%20share%20their%20best%20practices>. Note that symbolic measures are hosted by DG EMPL.

[92] L Waddington, 'The European Union and the United Nations Convention on the Rights of Persons with Disabilities: A Story of Exclusive and Shared Competences' (2011) 18(4) *Maastricht Journal of European and Comparative Law* 431–453; S Quinlivan, 'The United Nations Convention on the Rights of Persons with Disabilities: an introduction' (2012) 13 *ERA Forum* 71–85; W Schär and W Angermann,

EU's Disability Strategies as well as non-discrimination and accessibility as cornerstones of current EU disability policy.

3.2.1. Disability Strategies as Instruments in EU Disability Policy

Following the European Year of People with Disabilities and the three Disability Policy Action Plans, the Commission adopted the first European Disability Strategy 2010–2020 (EDS) in 2010.[93] Provided with a ten-year term, this comprehensive programme was based on the CRPD and aimed to contribute to its implementation. It included measures in eight areas: 'Accessibility'; 'Participation'; 'Equality'; 'Employment'; 'Education and training'; 'Social security'; 'Health' and 'Foreign policy'.[94]

In February 2017 an interim report on the progress on the implementation of the broadly designed EDS was published emphasising, amongst others, the adoption of a directive on cross-border healthcare in 2011[95] and the Web Accessibility Act in 2016.[96] Additionally, the pilot project on the European Disability Card[97] ran between 2016 and 2018. This trialled the facilitation of access to special conditions and particularly in the areas of culture, leisure, sport and transport. Moreover, the ErasmusPlus programme that allows for more mobility for students with disabilities, as well as the efforts towards the European Accessibility Act, were mentioned.[98]

The second and current disability-related Strategy 2021–2030 is, as mentioned above, under the heading 'Union of Equality' and structured somewhat differently from the previous one. It is divided in four broad headings: 'Accessibility'; 'Enjoying EU Rights'; 'Decent Quality of Life and Living Independently'; and 'Equal Access and Non-Discrimination'. Further, it is characterised by so-called 'flagship initiatives' as policy goals.[99] Other sections of the Strategy 2021–2030 pertain to awareness-raising and to the implementation of policy objectives and CRPD obligations internally as well as externally.

'Die Europäische Union als Vertragspartei der UN-Behindertenrechtskonvention' in T Degener and E Diehl (eds), *Handbuch Behindertenrechtskonvention. Teilhabe als Menschenrecht – Inklusion als gesellschaftliche Aufgabe* (Bundeszentrale für politische Bildung 2015) 352–364.

[93] Commission (n 70).

[94] O'Mahony and Quinlivan (n 2); L Waddington and A Broderick, 'The Post-2020 European Disability Strategy' Policy Department for Citizen's Rights and Constitutional Affairs (European Parliament 2020).

[95] Directive 2011/24/EU of the European Parliament and of the Council of 9 March 2011 on the application of patients' rights in cross-border healthcare [2011] OJ L88/45.

[96] Directive (EU) 2016/2102 of the European Parliament and of the Council of 26 October 2016 on the accessibility of the websites and mobile applications of public sector bodies [2016] OJ L327/1.

[97] D Ferri, 'Analysis of the European Disability Card. The Proposed Directive: Shortcomings, Strengths and Opportunities' Committee on Employment and Social Affairs, Policy Department for Economic, Scientific and Quality of Life Policies (European Parliament 2023) 22.

[98] Commission, 'Progress Report on the implementation of the European Disability Strategy (2010–2020)' SWD(2017) 29 final 5-6, 11-12.

[99] Commission (n 79).

Notably, the Strategy 2021–2030 sets out a timeline for the review of several pieces of accessibility legislation and the introduction of a resource centre on accessibility,[100] called AccessibleEU, which was set up by the Commission in 2022.[101] Continuation can further be detected insofar as the European Disability Card and European Parking Card have been given priority with a designated flagship initiative.[102] As indicated earlier, the Commission released relevant proposals that the Council and EP subsequently negotiated and adopted in April 2024. Similarly, following an implementation report on the Employment Equality Directive,[103] and in line with the Strategy 2021–2030 objectives, the Commission proposed directives to strengthen the role of equality bodies.[104] Remarkably, the Commission explicitly[105] calls on the Member States, and in doing so on the Council, to facilitate the adoption of the proposed Horizontal Equality Directive of 2008[106] in this strategy. While this notion exemplifies a soft natured approach to nudging the Council towards horizontal equality, it shows that the Commission has not let go of the objective and indeed states its aim in an official strategy; whether it will bear fruit, however, remains to be seen.

Lastly, it is important to highlight the setting up of the Disability Platform, which is another flagship initiative included in the Strategy 2021–2030.[107] This Platform, which is discussed in the subsequent section, represents a further development of the participatory mechanisms available to persons with disabilities and their input on EU disability policy. It replaces the former High Level Group on Disability (HLGD), comprising national CRPD focal points as well as organisations of persons with disabilities, and functions as an expert group.[108]

3.2.2. Non-Discrimination as Cornerstone of EU Disability Policy

Since 1999 the EU has developed the policy field of equality and non-discrimination through several directives. The Employment Equality Directive of 2000[109] is

[100] Ibid 5.

[101] Commission, 'AccessibleEU' available at <https://accessible-eu-centre.ec.europa.eu/index_en>.

[102] Commission (n 79) 6.

[103] Commission, 'Report from the Commission to the European Parliament and the Council on the application of Council Directive 2000/43/EC implementing the principle of equal treatment between persons irrespective of racial or ethnic origin ('the Racial Equality Directive') and of Council Directive 2000/78/EC establishing a general framework for equal treatment in employment and occupation ('the Employment Equality Directive')' COM(2021) 139 final.

[104] Commission (n 79) 11.

[105] Ibid 14.

[106] Commission, 'Proposal for a Council Directive on implementing the principle of equal treatment between persons irrespective of religion or belief, disability, age or sexual orientation' COM(2008) 426 final.

[107] Commission (n 79) 5, 24.

[108] Ibid 24; Commission, 'Commission Decision of 27.10.2021 setting up the group of experts "Disability Platform"' COM(2021) 7591 final; Commission, 'Disability Platform' available at <https://ec.europa.eu/transparency/expert-groups-register/screen/expert-groups/consult?lang=en&groupId=3820&fromMembers=true&memberType=4&memberId=97587>.

[109] Employment Equality Directive (n 51).

currently the only non-discrimination legislation that includes disability as a prohibited ground of discrimination; it also introduced the principle of reasonable accommodation[110] in the context of employment and training.[111]

Clearly, equality policy aimed at persons with disabilities was originally closely linked to employment policy; in this respect, one can speak of a 'piggyback' strategy: The tried and tested method, namely the goal of integrating persons with disabilities into the general labour market, served as a vehicle for a reorientation in the sense of horizontal equality policy that took into account the multidimensionality of discrimination. As a result, the EU's non-discrimination policy triggered a corresponding alignment at the Member State level, as the latter were obliged to transpose the directives or would have to pay heavy fines in case of non-compliance. For instance, the General Equal Treatment Act[112] in Germany would likely not exist without the EU equal treatment directives;[113] with this law, an infringement procedure, which the Commission had already initiated, was just averted.

In this respect, tangible results have been achieved in this policy field, even if further development has stagnated for some time. Indications of what the EU's future non-discrimination policy could look like exist following the abovementioned proposed Horizontal Equality Directive of the Commission. It provides for an extension of the scope of prohibition of discrimination, *inter alia* on the ground of disability, beyond the labour market to the areas of social security, health services, social benefits, education as well as access to goods and services.[114] In this regard, there are gaps in the current protection against discrimination, as only the Racial and Gender Equality Directives[115] cover these areas.

Some advancements have been made regarding the functioning of equality bodies across the Union with proposals put forward by Commissioner for Equality, Helena Dalli. In December 2022, two proposals for new directives on the standards for equality bodies in the fields of equal treatment in employment and occupation were published[116] and subsequently negotiated by the Council and EP.

[110] A Broderick and D Ferri, 'Disability Discrimination in European Union Law' in A Broderick and D Ferri, *International and European Disability Law and Policy. Text, Cases and Materials* (Cambridge University Press 2019).

[111] Article 5 Employment Equality Directive.

[112] Allgemeines Gleichbehandlungsgesetz vom 14 August 2006, BGBL I 1897, zuletzt geändert durch Artikel 8 des Gesetzes vom 3 April 2013, BGBL I S 610.

[113] F Welti, 'Germany. Is Cooperative Federalism Generating Multi-Level Barriers or Facilitating Multi-Level Inclusion?' in Ferri, Palermo and Martinico (n 62).

[114] Commission (n 106).

[115] Council Directive 2000/43/EC of 29 June 2000 implementing the principle of equal treatment between persons irrespective of racial or ethnic origin [2000] OJ L180/22; Directive 2002/73/EC of the European Parliament and of the Council of 23 September 2002 amending Council Directive 76/207/EEC on the implementation of the principle of equal treatment for men and women as regards access to employment, vocational training and promotion, and working conditions [2002] OJ L269/15.

[116] Commission, 'Proposal for a Council Directive on standards for equality bodies in the field of equal treatment between persons irrespective of their racial or ethnic origin, equal treatment in the field of employment and occupation between persons irrespective of their religion or belief, disability,

Following their adoption and entry into force in May 2024, these directives strengthen the independence of these bodies, and support their representative action before national courts.[117] Notably, equality bodies in the Member States, as collective actors, contribute to varying degrees to the promotion and protection of disability rights; thus their strengthening will likely support the advancement of disability policy both at Member State and EU level.

3.2.3. Accessibility as Cornerstone of EU Disability Policy

While an array of sectoral accessibility legislation has been released in the last two decades, the European Accessibility Act (EAA) serves as example and case study here, as it is the latest adopted. In 2015, the Commission presented a proposal for a directive on accessibility requirements for products and services that the Council spoke in favour of in 2017. However, the title gave rise to misunderstandings; it was by no means an all-encompassing directive that would realise accessibility in all areas of life. The Commission promised many advantages for users with disabilities, but at the same time emphasised that the economy would benefit from cost reductions, the facilitation of cross-border trade and increased marketing opportunities with regard to accessibility.[118] In the end, however, market goals and a digitalised future were given highest priority.

The agreement reached between the EP and Council in 2018 is entirely along these lines with critics pointing out that the adopted directive 'leaves out the real world environment where persons with disabilities live', such as housing, everyday objects or public spaces.[119]

Ultimately, the material scope of the EAA covers common accessibility requirements for key products and services, such as phones, computers, payment

age or sexual orientation, equal treatment between women and men in matters of social security and in the access to and supply of goods and services, and deleting Article 13 of Directive 2000/43/EC and Article 12 of Directive 2004/113/EC' COM(2022) 689 final; Commission, 'Proposal for a Directive of the European Parliament and of the Council on standards for equality bodies in the field of equal treatment and equal opportunities between women and men in matters of employment and occupation, and deleting Article 20 of Directive 2006/54/EC and Article 11 of Directive 2010/41/EU' COM(2022) 688 final.

[117] Council, 'Equality bodies: Council agrees on final text to strengthen their role across the EU' (Press Release, 20 February 2024) available at <https://www.consilium.europa.eu/en/press/press-releases/2024/02/20/equality-bodies-council-agrees-on-final-text-to-strengthen-their-role-across-the-eu/#:~:text=This%20directive%20will%20significantly%20strengthen%20the%20role%20of,an%20important%20step%20towards%20a%20Union%20of%20Equality>; Council Directive (EU) 2024/1499 of 7 May 2024 on standards for equality bodies in the field of equal treatment between persons irrespective of their racial or ethnic origin, equal treatment in matters of employment and occupation between persons irrespective of their religion or belief, disability, age or sexual orientation, equal treatment between women and men in matters of social security and in the access to and supply of goods and services, and amending Directives 2000/43/EC and 2004/113/EC [2024] OJ L2024/1499.

[118] Commission, 'Employment, Social Affairs & Inclusion: Policies and Activities: European Accessibility Act' available at <https://ec.europa.eu/social/main.jsp?catId=1202&langId=en&>.

[119] EDF, 'Immediate Release: Disappointing Compromise on EU Accessibility Act' (8 November 2018) <https://www.accessibletourism.org/resources/06_11_2018_press_release_accessibility_act_final01.pdf>.

terminals or self-service terminals, banking services, electronic communications – including the 112 emergency number –, access to audio-visual media services, e-books, e-commerce and some elements of transport services[120] as a minimum harmonising instrument.[121] Those products and services that fall within the remit of the directive must adhere to EU harmonised standards and the Commission retains the power to adopt implementing acts where no such standards exist yet.[122] Thus, they might progressively be enhanced through Commission action. As alluded to before, next to accessibility obligations throughout the production and market chain, the EAA integrates monitoring and implementing mechanisms that are supported by an enforcement mechanism.[123] The latter sets the EAA apart and aims to reinforce the accessibility requirements. Yet, the limited material scope together with several exceptions to the application of the scope of the EAA are illustrative of the piecemeal accessibility legislation currently in place at the EU level.[124]

While this overview of some key EU disability policies has shown that progress continues to be connected to internal market objectives and employment policies, recent developments point to a stronger emphasis on equality and non-discrimination. This is also reflected and enhanced by the Strategy 2021–2030, which has yielded some notable achievements so far including the AccessibleEU centre, the European Disability Card, the strengthening of equality bodies, the continuous review of accessibility legislation and, last but not least, the Disability Platform.

3.3. 'Disability' in the Politics of the EU

How do disability policies actually come about? Who conceives them, in which contexts, and how are decisions made? These questions touch on the last dimension of our analysis in this chapter and address the overarching rationale of this volume, namely furthering our understanding of how EU disability law and policy is shaped by various institutional and non-institutional actors. While Part II of this volume is entirely dedicated to institutional actors, this section, discusses the interaction of institutional and non-institutional actors, with a focus on participatory mechanisms that facilitate policy input by persons with disabilities.

The following section thus deals with politics in the narrower sense, i.e. the representation of interests and the participation of civil society in political decision-making processes.[125] Even at this level, we can only consider a part of the

[120] Commission (n 118).
[121] S Charitakis, 'Accessibility of Goods and Services' in Ferri and Broderick (n 2) 233.
[122] Article 4(9) EAA; Ibid 234.
[123] Articles 19–22 EAA.
[124] Ferri (n 72) 271.
[125] See H-W Platzer, 'Interessenverbände und europäischer Lobbyismus' in W Weidenfeld (ed), *Die Europäische Union. Politisches System und Politikbereiche* (Bundeszentrale für politische

complex power structure of the EU. It therefore makes sense to first examine the role of institutional actors in the EU political system in enabling political participation for and by persons with disabilities. Next, we provide an overview of some of the non-institutional actors that are active in disability policy.

3.3.1. The Interaction between Institutional and Non-Institutional Actors in EU Disability Policy

Besides individual participation in EP elections, there are a number of formal and informal access points to the EU institutions that interest groups can use as actors of collective political participation. In particular, the EP and the Commission are considered relatively open to lobbying from outside interests.[126]

Since 2011, and on the basis of an interinstitutional agreement that was revised and extended to cover the Council in 2021,[127] access to the EP is subject to approval of registrants in the Transparency Register by the EP. Interest groups and individuals, who register voluntarily and are approved, are given access to the buildings and sessions of the EP, including being speaker at committee events, intergroup or delegation meetings. It should be borne in mind that participatory observation can certainly be helpful, but that direct contact with members of the EP (MEPs) and their staff in informal ways is probably more effective in terms of influence. As far as contacts between the EP and civil society in disability policy are concerned, the 'Disability Intergroup'[128] is a key venue. Founded in 1980 it is one of the oldest parliamentary working groups of informal nature, and regularly brings together MEPs from all parties and organisations representing persons with disabilities.

There are also a number of civil society contacts within the Commission, in particular in DG EMPL's unit D.3.[129] This unit set up the Academic Network on European Disability Policy experts (ANED) under the funding programme PROGRESS and since 2008 experts have produced regular reports on the status

Bildung 2008) 187–205. This section is further based on A Sturm *et al.*, 'Exercising Influence at the European Level: Political Opportunity Structures of Disability Rights Advocacy and the Impact of the UN CRPD' in Halvorsen *et al.* (n 13) 159-176. Ferri and Krolla (n 11).

[126] P Bernhagen, A Dür and D Marshall, 'Information or context: what accounts for positional proximity between the European Commission and lobbyists?' in J Beyers, C Braun and H Klüver (eds), *Legislative Lobbying in Context. The Policy and Polity Determinants of Interest Group Politics in the European Union* (Routledge 2016) 124–138; E Korkea-aho, 'No Longer Marginal? Finding a Place for Lobbyists and Lobbying in EU Law Research' (2022) 18(4) *European Constitutional Law Review* 682–705.

[127] Interinstitutional Agreement of 20 May 2021 between the European Parliament, the Council of the European Union and the European Commission on a mandatory transparency register [2021] OJ L207/1.

[128] EP, 'Intergroup on Disability [IG9-11]' available at <https://www.europarl.europa.eu/meps/en/intergroup/details/6298/Intergroup%20on%20Disability>.

[129] This unit also heads the 'Inter-Service Group on Disability', a working group of the Commission on disability issues, in which EU officials from all DGs coordinate political measures with the aim of 'disability mainstreaming' at EU level.

of various policies at the national level. This initiative was replaced in 2020 with the European Disability Expertise (EDE) network,[130] which is funded under the Rights, Equality and Citizenship Programme. In the context of ANED's annual conferences and other thematically focused events, personal exchanges between responsible EU staff, academic experts and disability rights organisations have been fostered.

Expert groups of the Commission, which have both formal and informal character, with invitations to membership stemming from the Commission's unit in charge, also provide opportunities for advocacy. Of particular importance was the already named High Level Group on Disability (HLGD);[131] this was an informal and indefinite expert group that usually met twice a year. Its task was set out in a Council resolution of 1996 with the aim of facilitating cooperation which was formulated as 'promot[ing] – in collaboration with the Member States and with non-governmental organisations of and for persons with disabilities – the exchange of useful information and experience especially concerning innovative practices and good practice'.[132] The Disability Platform, introduced by the Strategy 2021–2030, replaced the HLGD.[133] The tasks of the new body are to support the implementation of the Strategy 2021–2030; to facilitate cooperation between the Commission and Member States for the implementation of the CRPD; to assist in the preparation of policy and legislative proposals; and to establish and foster the implementation of EU legislation, programmes and policies as well as to exchange experiences and good practices.[134] Meetings are held regularly and sub-groups have been created to address specific policy initiatives, such as for the European Disability Card.[135]

3.3.2. The Role of Civil Society and Organisations of Persons with Disabilities as Non-Institutional Actors in EU Disability Policy

When examining the question of who the collective actors are that represent persons with disabilities *vis-à-vis* the EU institutions, one finds that there is a lack of empirical data and only a rough picture can be drawn. For example, the list of

[130] Human European Consultancy, 'European Disability Expertise' available at <https://www.human-consultancy.com/projects/european-disability-expertise-ede>; Commission, 'European Disability Expertise' available at <https://ec.europa.eu/social/main.jsp?catId=1532&langId=en>; L Waddington, 'The Role of Academics in Shaping EU Disability Law: Some Personal Reflections' in this volume.

[131] See further Sturm *et al.* (n 125) 163.

[132] Resolution of the Council and of the Representatives of the Governments of the Member States Meeting within the Council of 20 December 1996 on Equal Opportunities for Persons with Disabilities [1997] OJ C12/1-2, Part III, Article 2.

[133] Krolla (n 7).

[134] Article 2 Commission Decision of 27.10.2021 setting up the group of experts "Disability Platform" COM(2021) 7591 final.

[135] Article 8 Commission Decision of 27.10.2021 setting up the group of experts "Disability Platform" COM(2021) 7591 final.

organisations included in a previous study[136] on the practice of European advocacy in disability policy from 2017, comprises both impairment-specific, rather medically-oriented[137] as well as cross-disability associations.[138] Most of them are umbrella organisations made up of associations that operate at national level. European branches have been founded by traditional disability associations,[139] parents' associations[140] as well as organisations of the disability rights movement.[141] There are European self-advocacy organisations with long histories[142] and others formed more recently.[143]

Moreover, there are new formations,[144] among which the European Disability Forum (EDF) stands out. Created in 1996 on the initiative of the Commission as part of the HELIOS II programme, EDF has evolved over the past two decades into an influential organisation that represents the interests of persons with disabilities.[145] EDF fulfils this role in several ways. As a formally structured association, whose membership is divided into four categories – 'full', 'ordinary', 'observer', 'associate' – it comprises the national councils for persons with disabilities of 29[146] European countries and 25 disability rights organisations as 'full' members.[147] With this structure, EDF rather resembles a network-like 'advocacy coalition' than a simple umbrella organisation. For this reason, EDF can be considered a 'hybrid' organisation.[148]

Yet, EDF is also a member of other coalitions that exist at the European level in disability-related policy fields. Here again, the strong influence of EDF can be observed. While some of the organisations with full EDF membership are also represented in various networks, EDF is the only collective actor in EU disability policy that is also represented in the three important coalitions 'European Social Platform', 'European Patients Forum' and 'European Coalition of Community Living'. Previously, EDF was a member of the HLGD of the Commission as a non-governmental organisation and has now joined the Disability Platform.[149] Moreover, EDF is responsible for the secretariat of the 'Disability Intergroup' of the EP.

[136] Sturm *et al.* (n 125).

[137] eg, European Alliance of Muscular Dystrophy Association or International Federation of Spina Bifida and Hydrocephalus.

[138] eg, European Action of Persons with Disabilities/Action Européenne des Personnes Handicapées.

[139] eg, Rehabilitation International.

[140] eg, Inclusion Europe.

[141] eg, Disabled People's International Europe or European Network on Independent Living.

[142] eg, European Blind Union.

[143] eg, European Network of [ex-]Users and Survivors of Psychiatry.

[144] eg, European Association of Service Providers for Persons with Disabilities.

[145] Sturm *et al.* (n 125); J Malleier, *Lobbying für Behinderte: Interessenvermittlung am Beispiel des Europäischen Behindertenforums in der Europäischen Union* (Peter Lang Internationaler Verlag der Wissenschaften 2011).

[146] Besides the 27 EU Member States, Iceland and Norway are represented.

[147] 12 organisations are 'ordinary' members; national disability councils of four EU candidate countries have 'observer' status and 42 organisations are 'associated' with EDF.

[148] Sturm *et al.* (n 125) 168.

[149] Commission (n 108).

The fact that EDF is considered to be a central European network actor in disability policy can also be inferred from its role in the CRPD monitoring at the EU level.[150] With the exception of EDF, no other (self-)advocacy organisation or coalition is involved in the monitoring. In this context, EDF has, at times, assumed management tasks. While the Commission was responsible for secretariat tasks, the Forum led the so-called 'monitoring framework' from 2013 to 2015.[151] Subsequently, the already mentioned FRA took over the secretariat, and leadership now alternates. This example shows particularly clearly that the networking structures of disability policy advocacy at the EU level are not only highly complex, but also neo-corporatist. Which impacts this has on the concrete goals, practices and strategies of disability policy actors more generally has hardly been investigated. However, the chapter by Coveney in this volume looks at precisely that: the concrete goals (and their knock-on effects) as well as the practices and strategies employed by EDF as the most prominent collective actor in disability policy at the EU level and from a disability advocacy perspective.[152]

4. Concluding Remarks

On the whole, this chapter aimed to trace the development of disability policy as a distinct field of EU action from the early stages of the 1950s to today. By considering the changing institutional architecture of the EU and its predecessors as well as the available competences to address disability rights at the EU level, this chapter has highlighted the ambivalent relationship between social policy and equality policy of the EU. Measured against its own aspirations, this stock taking remains sobering. It is striking that the EU still hardly advances in the field of social policy and is confined to concentrating on policy areas that relate to the four fundamental freedoms, namely the mobility of persons, services, goods, and capital in the context of the internal market. Against the background of the EU's focus on the internal market and its organisation, it would be worthwhile to examine the extent to which disability policy at EU level is also primarily market-liberal rather than social policy-oriented.

Yet, since the late 1990s, a remarkable contouring of EU disability policy has taken place. The current state of this policy area in relation to the levels of 'polity' and 'policy' is characterised by a focus on the issues of non-discrimination and accessibility. At the level of 'politics', the EU institutions offer a range of opportunities for the participation of persons with disabilities in particular through the

[150] Sturm *et al.* (n 125) 168-172.

[151] The so-called EU monitoring framework for the CRPD is made up of the EP, the European Ombudsman, the FRA and EDF. Until 2015, the Commission was also a member; it withdrew as a result of the recommendations of the CRPD Committee. CRPD Committee, 'Concluding observations on the initial report of the European Union' (2 October 2015) CRPD/C/EU/CO/1 para 77.

[152] Coveney (n 11).

Disability Platform and more informal contacts with Commission and EP staff. However, the arena of civil society advocacy likens that of a 'closed shop', since EDF has assumed a comprehensive and prominent role as the central representative of disability issues in the EU legal order that often subsumes the input from other actors in this sphere.

In terms of institutional actors, the Commission and the EP have been prominent in advancing disability policies while the Council has often held a more reluctant position. Thus, policies and soft law rather than binding legislation have dominated EU disability law and policy. However, the latest developments include increasing disability-specific legislation and the mainstreaming of disability rights across sectors. As Toggenburg shows in his chapter, the FRA as an institutional, but formally independent body within the EU legal order[153] monitors and strengthens disability policy and CRPD compliance.

This chapter has thus hinted at the main drivers and principal dynamics of EU disability law and policy, and many of the issues highlighted are further elaborated by other contributions in this volume. Future research may however supplement and further elucidate our understanding of the role of institutional and non-institutional actors active in EU disability law and policy. In particular, the role of organisations of persons with disabilities apart from EDF, their advocacy practices and impact on EU disability law and policy have not yet been comprehensively explored; these may also be examined in terms of democratic legitimacy and principal function within the formal EU legal order. In light of the strengthening of equality bodies, the dynamics and interactions between organisations of persons with disabilities and equality bodies should be observed, especially in terms of mainstreaming disability rights in the work and advocacy of equality bodies. Evaluating and assessing the Strategy 2021–2030 will be a continuous research task that includes comparative insights with its predecessor and will inform research on potential successive strategies. Similarly, research into current policies for and with persons with disabilities outside the realm of labour market participation, non-discrimination, equality and accessibility are also important research topics in addition to the regular study of the progressive implementation of the CRPD in the EU. Future research may also focus on case studies to further detect effects of Europeanisation trends in this policy field.

[153] Article 16 Council Regulation (EC) No 168/2007 of 15 February 2007 establishing a European Union Agency for Fundamental Rights [2007] OJ L53/1; Toggenburg (n 9).

PART II

The Role of Institutional Actors in Shaping EU Disability Law

4

The Role of the European Commission in Shaping EU Disability Law: A Driver with the Brakes Put On?

EVA S KROLLA*

1. Introduction

The European Commission (Commission) is a much debated institution within the European Union (EU) legal order.[1] On the one hand, as a result of the changing nature of the institutional balance in the EU, many commentators point to the Commission's relative decline *vis-à-vis* the European Council and the European Parliament (EP) since the Maastricht Treaty.[2] The strengthening of the European Council is perceived as emphasising the intergovernmental dimension of the EU and is deemed to be detrimental to the Commission's agenda-setting and leadership roles.[3] On the other hand, the rise of the

* This chapter has been written within the remit of the project 'Protecting the Right to Culture of Persons with Disabilities and Enhancing Cultural Diversity through European Union Law: Exploring New Paths – DANCING'. This project has received funding from the European Research Council (ERC) under the European Union's Horizon 2020 Research and Innovation Programme (Grant Agreement No 864182). Sincere thanks to the participants in our study for their contributions. Furthermore, I would like to thank Delia Ferri for her generous patience, guidance and critical review of previous drafts that greatly supported the development of this chapter.

[1] Among others, N Nugent and M Rhinard, *The European Commission* (Bloomsbury Academic 2015).

[2] H Kassim *et al.*, *The European Commission of The Twenty-First Century* (Oxford University Press 2013); A Wille, *The Normalization of the European Commission* (Oxford University Press 2013); MW Bauer, J Ege and S Becker, 'The European Commission and the Disintegration of Europe – Taking Stock and Looking Ahead' in J Ege, MW Bauer and S Becker (eds), *The European Commission in Turbulent Times. Assessing Organizational Change and Policy Impact* (Nomos 2018) 9–31.

[3] Article 15 Treaty on European Union (TEU); CJ Bickerton, D Hodson and U Puetter (eds), *The New Intergovernmentalism. States and Supranational Actors in the Post-Maastricht Era* (Oxford University Press 2015); L Van Middelaar, *Alarums and Excursions: Improving Politics on the European Stage* (Agenda Publishing Limited 2019).

EP as co-legislator[4] and its increased influence on the appointment of the Commission[5] have changed the institutional balance and power between the Commission, EP and Council of the EU (Council). In spite of the perceived more constrained role of the Commission in EU policy-making, this chapter argues that the EU executive has in fact played an instrumental role in advancing the EU's disability agenda.

Building on the copious scholarship that examines how the Commission has responded to bureaucratic and civil service tasks,[6] how it uses its right of initiative and its effectiveness in proposing law and policy,[7] this chapter discusses the role of the Commission as collegiate body that takes joint stances, following the lead of the responsible Commissioner(s) and Directorate(s)-General (DG), in shaping EU disability law. It considers the period following the ratification of the UN Convention on the Rights of Persons with Disabilities (CRPD) in 2010,[8] and covers three legislative terms, with three different Commission formations.

Employing a socio-legal and mixed method approach, this chapter is based on a blend of legal doctrinal research and on a set of ten qualitative interviews with staff at the Commission, the EP and other bodies whose work either centres on or concerns the rights of persons with disabilities. While small, this set of interviews comprises key informants that provide rich and comprehensive data to support the legal analysis. Participants were identified and recruited through purposeful sampling, with consideration for their respective expertise, and were drawn from different DGs and interlocutors who play a significant role in the initiating, drafting and negotiation of EU legislation with an influence on the Commission's work.[9] The semi-structured interviews were conducted between December 2023 and March 2024 and form part of a larger interdisciplinary research project.[10] Prior to interviews, participants were provided with information on the overall

[4] S Hix and B Høyland, 'Empowerment of the European Parliament' (2013) 16 *Annual Review of Political Science* 171–189.

[5] Article 17 TEU; N Nugent, 'The European Parliament' in N Nugent, *The Government and Politics of the European Union* (Palgrave Macmillan 2017) 206–209; M Egeberg, 'The European Commission' in M Cini and N Pérez-Solórzano Borragán (eds), *European Union Politics* (Oxford University Press 2022) 146.

[6] Wille (n 2) 188; N Nugent, 'The European Commission' in Nugent (n 5) 129; J Blom-Hansen and R Senninger, 'The Commission in EU Policy Preparation' (2021) 59(3) *Journal of Common Market Studies* 627.

[7] G Tsebelis and G Garrett, 'Legislative Politics in the European Union' (2000) 1(1) *Euphorion* 9–36; S Becker *et al.*, 'The Commission: Boxed in and constrained, but still an engine of integration' (2016) 39(5) *West European Politics* 1011–1031; Egeberg (n 5) 144; N Yordanova and A Zhelyazkova, 'Legislative Control Over Executive Law-Making: Delegation of Quasi-Legislative Powers to the European Commission' (2020) 58(2) *Journal of Common Market Studies* 345–364.

[8] Council Decision of 26 November 2009 concerning the conclusion, by the European Community, of the United Nations Convention on the Rights of Persons with Disabilities [2010] OJ L23/35.

[9] LA Palinkas *et al.*, 'Purposeful Sampling for Qualitative Data Collection and Analysis in Mixed Method Implementation Research' (2015) 42(5) *Administration and Policy in Mental Health and Mental Health Services Research* 533–544.

[10] The project entitled 'Protecting the Right to Culture of Persons with Disabilities and Enhancing Cultural Diversity through European Union Law: Exploring New Paths – DANCING' funded by the European Research Council. Data was collected by Prof. Delia Ferri, Dr. Ann Leahy and Eva S. Krolla. For the purpose of the present chapter, data was analysed by Eva S. Krolla.

research, specific information on privacy, anonymisation and data storage and gave informed, written consent to participate. The relevant ethical approval was obtained from the Maynooth University Ethics Committee. The interviews were informed by an interview guide that was responsive to individual participants, to allow for the presentation of information that was most relevant from the interviewee's point of view. This was functional to the overall data collection as it more closely observed when, where and how disability rights concerns feature in the initial stages of EU law- and policy-making. Interviews were conducted online and transcribed verbatim before being analysed by using a reflexive approach to thematic analysis following Braun and Clarke.[11] To preserve anonymity, participants are indicated with a general identifier EU_PM (policymaker), accompanied by the interview number when using extracts from the interviews conducted.

The chapter is structured as follows: section 2 considers the legal bases and mandates of the Commission in establishing which principal roles it can assume. Section 3 discusses the Commission as agenda-setter, while section 4 examines it as legislative initiator on the basis of Article 17(2) of the Treaty on European Union (TEU). Section 5 investigates the delegated powers of the Commission regarding EU disability law. Section 6 explores how the Commission supports implementation at Member State level, before section 7 looks at the consultation processes the Commission utilises to inform its work. Finally, section 8 provides some concluding remarks.

2. The European Commission

The role and manifold functions of the Commission are set out in Article 17 TEU. Generally considered to be the executive in the EU legal order,[12] its principal mission is to act in the 'general interest'[13] of the Union; and its members are to be 'persons whose independence is beyond doubt'.[14] Further, no instructions shall be taken from any government or other entity underpinning its (theoretically) non-partisan character.[15] The Commission is thus endowed with a host of oversight, coordinating and implementing tasks.[16]

[11] V Clarke and V Braun, 'Thematic Analysis' (2017) 12(3) *The Journal of Positive Psychology* 297–298; V Braun, *Thematic Analysis: A Practical Guide to Understanding and Doing* (Sage 2021).

[12] S Hix, *The Political System of the European Union* (Palgrave Macmillan 2005).

[13] Article 17(1) TEU.

[14] Article 17(3) TEU.

[15] For a discussion of political influence on and in the Commission, M Hartlapp, 'Politicization of the European Commission: When, How, and with What Impact?' in MW Bauer and J Trondal (eds), *The Palgrave Handbook of the European Administrative System* (Palgrave Macmillan 2015) 145–160; H Kassim *et al.*, 'Managing the House: the Presidency, Agenda Control and Policy Activism in the European Commission' (2017) 24(5) *Journal of European Public Policy* 653–674; C Koop, C Reh and E Bressanelli, 'Agenda-setting under pressure: Does domestic politics influence the European Commission?' (2021) 61(1) *European Journal of Political Research* 46–66.

[16] Article 17(1) TEU.

Among the Commission's tasks is, however, also the near monopoly on legislative initiative,[17] which enables it to put forward legislative proposals to the co-legislators in almost all fields of EU action.[18] Besides proposing legislation, the Commission is moreover responsible for annual and multiannual programming 'with a view to achieving interinstitutional agreement'.[19] The programming activities are framed by the political guidelines of an incoming Commission president that outline the priorities for the ensuing term. To concretise these priorities and objectives, the Commission develops annual work programmes that detail its planned actions including legislative and non-legislative measures. These are further explicated in strategic and management plans per DG and support the accountability of Commission activity, which is reported on annually.[20] The interinstitutional dimension of programming was strengthened in 2016 when the Commission, Council and EP agreed on their first 'Joint Declaration' of policy priorities under the Interinstitutional Agreement on Better Law Making,[21] which have since been adopted annually. A set of multiannual 'Joint Conclusions' for 2020-2024 complements this process,[22] which allows the Commission an opportunity to influence broader policy priorities at the EU level – but also facilitates influence of the co-legislators on the Commission's activities.

The Commission also has important responsibilities regarding the implementation of EU law. Upon delegation, the Commission can adopt executive rules,[23] i.e. implementing or delegated acts pursuant to Articles 290 and 291 of the Treaty on the Functioning of the European Union (TFEU). Moreover, on the basis of Articles 258 and 260 TFEU the Commission may initiate infringement procedures against non-compliant Member States.[24]

The Commission also executes the budget, manages programmes and represents the EU externally.[25] However, these latter tasks, or roles, are not the focus of the present chapter. Instead, this contribution concentrates on the Commission in its agenda-setting, legislative initiating and executive roles of implementing and monitoring EU disability law.

[17] Legislation can also be proposed by a quarter of Member States pursuant to Article 76 Treaty on the Functioning of the European Union (TFEU); The Council and EP can prompt the Commission to put forward a legislative proposal pursuant to Articles 225 and 241 TFEU. B Oztas and A Kreppel, 'Power Or Luck? The Limitations of the European Commission's Agenda Setting Power and Autonomous Policy Influence' (2022) 60(2) *Journal of Common Market Studies* 408, 411.

[18] Common Foreign and Security Policy is exempted from this prerogative and in further instances as laid down in the Treaties. Article 17(1) TEU.

[19] Article 17(1) TEU.

[20] P-J Loewenthal, 'Article 17 TEU' in M Kellerbauer, M Klamert and J Tomkin (eds), *The EU Treaties and the Charter of Fundamental Rights* (Oxford University Press 2019) 162–163.

[21] Interinstitutional Agreement between the European Parliament, the Council of the European Union and the European Commission on Better Law-Making (Better Law Making Agreement) [2016] OJ L123/1; Joint Declaration on the EU's Legislative Priorities for 2017 [2016] OJ C484/02.

[22] Joint Conclusions of the European Parliament, the Council of the European Union and the European Commission on Policy Objectives and Priorities for 2020-2024 [2021] OJ C451 I/02.

[23] Blom-Hansen and Senninger (n 6) 627.

[24] Article 260(2) TFEU.

[25] Article 17(1) TEU.

3. The Commission as Disability Agenda-Setter

The Commission engages in the agenda-setting of EU law and policy in various ways. By devising soft law tools, such as dedicated strategies, it significantly contributes to elevating a policy issue and supports coordinated EU action. Further, by working towards including certain policy issues in interinstitutional agreements, such as Joint Declarations and Joint Conclusions and larger policy frameworks, the Commission can highlight the importance of a given matter and nudge the co-legislators towards more tangible actions. These documents also serve to mainstream policy issues, especially where EU competence is limited. Although these documents are not legally binding, they do create relevant legal and practical effects, including expectations in EU citizens to which the Commission is held answerable.[26]

Regarding EU disability law, the Commission has been the driving force behind an increasingly coherent and pan-European approach to disability, especially after the ratification of the CRPD by the EU, which has strengthened the EU's mandate to act on disability rights protection.

3.1. Disability Strategies

Disability is decidedly a cross-cutting issue, and in support of the implementation of the CRPD, the Commission has devised two strategies, each with a ten-year term since 2010.[27] While building on action plans that were devised before the CRPD, these strategies are far more comprehensive and outline specific measures to fulfil obligations under the CRPD – importantly, at both EU and national level. Yet, it must be kept in mind that while the Commission can prescribe actions for itself, it can only suggest and encourage actions or measures to be taken by other EU institutions and by the Member States.

The former European Disability Strategy 2010-2020 (EDS),[28] comprised eight areas of action to be addressed at EU level and to support Member State measures. The Commission's role was not only to develop the strategy but also to enact many of the objectives set out in it. Besides working with Member States to eliminate existing barriers, the Commission intended to make use of legislative instruments

[26] D Ferri, 'The Role of Soft Law in Advancing the Rights of Persons with Disabilities in the EU: A 'Hybridity' Approach to EU Disability Law' (2023) 28 *European Law Journal* 134–153; F Snyder, 'The Effectiveness of European Community Law: Institutions, Processes, Tools and Techniques' (1993) 56(1) *The Modern Law Review* 19–54; OA Stefan *et al.*, 'EU Soft Law in the EU Legal Order: A Literature Review' (2019) King's College London Law School Research Paper Series available at <https://papers.ssrn.com/sol3/papers.cfm?abstract_id=3346629>.

[27] For a concise discussion of EU disability strategies preceding the EDS, C O'Mahony and S Quinlivan, 'The EU Disability Strategy and the Future of EU Disability Policy' in D Ferri and A Broderick (eds), *Research Handbook on EU Disability Law* (Edward Elgar 2020) 12–28.

[28] European Commission (Commission), 'European Disability Strategy 2010-2020: A Renewed Commitment to a Barrier-Free Europe' COM(2010) 636 final.

and soft law measures to address policy aims in each of the identified areas, such as accessibility or equality.[29] Moreover, the Commission was assigned a central role in implementing the EDS through awareness raising, funding, statistics and data collection for monitoring purposes as well as reporting duties.[30]

The current Union of Equality: Strategy for the Rights of Persons with Disabilities 2021-2030 (Strategy 2021-2030)[31] builds on the EDS. Yet, it differs from its predecessor in some respects. The Strategy 2021-2030 is divided into four broader categories of action, each detailing specific tasks the Commission will undertake.[32] These are complemented by six flagship initiatives spearheaded by the Commission. While the Strategy 2021-2030 acknowledges the nature and limits of shared and supporting competences, it emphasises the need to coordinate at national and EU level alike.[33] The Commission aims to lead by example regarding the implementation of the CRPD and to advance EU disability law intra-institutionally.[34] To this end, the establishment of 'disability coordinators' under the Strategy 2021-2030 appears to be a positive development in mainstreaming disability into the work of the DGs.[35] 'Disability coordinators' are designated per DG and are responsible for ensuring that disability is duly considered in the DG's work, especially in legislative proposals. Additionally, 'disability coordinators' work across the DGs to facilitate exchange on relevant developments and to foster the transversal protection of disability rights. One participant commented on this as follows:

> … we have the inter-service group and here we have participants from all the DGs and they nominated a person that takes care and is responsible, is our contact point for disability in the DGs, yes. [EU_PM3]

A consolidating effect of disability mainstreaming *within* the Commission can thus be observed that now compounds the work of the designated – at least under the current Von Der Leyen Cabinet – Disability Unit in DG Employment, Social Affairs and Inclusion (EMPL).[36] Moreover, the Commission encourages

[29] Ibid 5-6.

[30] Ibid 9-10.

[31] Commission, 'Union of Equality: Strategy for the Rights of Persons with Disabilities 2021-2030' COM(2021) 101 final.

[32] An overview of measures taken/completed under the Strategy 2021-2030 is available at Commission, 'Monitoring Framework' available at <https://ec.europa.eu/social/main.jsp?catId=1552&langId=en>.

[33] Commission (n 31) 2.

[34] Ibid.

[35] Ibid 23.

[36] Commission, 'DG EMPL – EMPL.D3 Disability and Inclusion' available at <https://commission.europa.eu/document/download/d150d9fe-adf5-4d95-88c6-987ce95e0066_en?filename=EC_DG-EMPL_Organigramme_15-Jan-2024.pdf>. This trend has further been substantiated by the establishment of a Task Force on Equality, created to support the work of the Commissioner for Equality consisting of 'Equality Coordinators' from all DGs and the External Action Service. Commission, 'The Task Force on Equality of the European Commission' available at <https://commission.europa.eu/strategy-and-policy/policies/justice-and-fundamental-rights/union-equality/task-force-equality-european-commission_en>.

other EU institutions, bodies and agencies to assign 'disability coordinators' as well as the Member States to mainstream disability.[37] This effort relies on voluntary compliance by the respective institutions and the Member States, with the Commission having no power to enforce in this instance.

Targeted disability strategies devised by the Commission lay out detailed actions and measures to be taken. In doing so, they play a central, anchoring role in EU disability law. Here, in its role as agenda-setter, the Commission has the ability to drive disability rights forward by ambitiously developing and leading their implementation – including by increasingly adopting internal measures to lead by example.

3.2. Policy Priorities and Other Policy Frameworks

Besides disability strategies, the Commission has advanced the inclusion of disability concerns in interinstitutional documents and overarching policy frameworks contributing to the embedding of disability rights in EU action.

Considering that Joint Declarations and Joint Conclusions encompass numerous policy objectives and are less elaborate and overt – and possibly less incisive –, specific reference to and prioritisation of disability is generally scarce and evasive of detail. Only the Joint Conclusions of 2017 include an explicit commitment to disability-specific legislation, namely the European Accessibility Act (EAA)[38] – which was proposed by the Commission in 2015[39] and ultimately adopted in 2019 – and further legislation under the Digital Singel Market efforts.[40] However, disability appears to be subsumed under commitments to fundamental rights protection and non-discrimination, moving away from primarily employment-oriented measures towards broader efforts to advance disability rights in line with CRPD obligations and in compliance with the 'human rights model' of disability by the Commission.

Disability is further mainstreamed through other policy frameworks. The protection of disability rights features in policy documents, such as the Europe 2020 Strategy[41] and the European Platform against Poverty.[42] Both documents pursued socio-economic policy goals 'to turn the EU into a smart, sustainable and

[37] Commission (n 31) 22-23.

[38] Directive (EU) 2019/882 of the European Parliament and of the Council of 17 April 2019 on the accessibility requirements for products and services [2019] OJ L151/70.

[39] Commission, 'Proposal for a Directive of the European Parliament and of the Council on the approximation of the laws, regulations and administrative provisions of the Member States as regards the accessibility requirements for products and services' COM(2015) 278 final.

[40] Points 2 and 5 Joint Declaration on the EU's legislative priorities for 2017 [2016] OJ C484/7.

[41] Commission, 'Europe 2020 A Strategy for Smart, Sustainable and Inclusive Growth' COM(2010) 2020 final 19.

[42] Commission, 'The European Platform against Poverty and Social Exclusion: A European Framework for Social and Territorial Cohesion' COM(2010) 758 final 17-18.

inclusive economy delivering high levels of employment, productivity and social cohesion'.[43] Released as part of the European Year for Combating Poverty and Social Exclusion in 2010,[44] the Commission included measures that addressed persons with disabilities under this banner, albeit in seemingly rather vague terms.

Similarly, the Strategy 2021-2030 links to broader EU policy documents – such as to the European Pillar of Social Rights (Pillar),[45] which serves as a general compass,[46] and to the Pillar's Action Plan.[47] Principle 17 of the Pillar concerns persons with disabilities specifically – albeit with an emphasis on labour market participation, it also encompasses rights to participate in society and life in dignity –[48] and the Commission has released several soft law tools to support its realisation, including the Disability Employment Package[49] and the proposals for a European Disability Card (EDC) and a European Parking Card.[50] The latter constitutes one of the flagship initiatives of the Strategy 2021-2030 and was adopted by the co-legislators in October 2024. The Strategy 2021-2030 is complementary to the 'sister' strategies under the 'Union of Equality' banner of the current Commission and supports policy frameworks that concern the digital and green transitions.[51] Taken together, the Commission aims to use these policies to achieve the UN Sustainable Development Goals and to bolster its external role in protecting human rights internationally.[52] There is evidence in these strategies and action plans of mainstreaming disability, and cross-references to the Strategy 2021-2030 in other documents do support such mainstreaming.

On the whole, disability rights have become a feature in both interinstitutional agreements on policy priorities – albeit to a limited extent – and increasingly in horizontal policy frameworks, such as in the Pillar. Some documents also make specific reference to the Strategy 2021-2030.[53] In this respect, the Strategy

[43] Commission (n 41) 10.

[44] Decision No 1098/2008/EC of the European Parliament and of the Council of 22 October 2008 on the European Year for Combating Poverty and Social Exclusion (2010) [2008] OJ L298/20.

[45] Interinstitutional Proclamation on the European Pillar of Social Rights [2017] OJ C428/09.

[46] Commission (n 31) 1.

[47] Ibid 3; Commission, 'The European Pillar of Social Rights Action Plan' (Publications Office of the European Union 2021) 26.

[48] Principle 17 Inclusion of People with Disabilities Interinstitutional Proclamation on the European Pillar of Social Rights [2017] OJ C428/10.

[49] Commission, 'Disability Employment Package' available at <https://employment-social-affairs.ec.europa.eu/policies-and-activities/social-protection-social-inclusion/persons-disabilities/union-equality-strategy-rights-persons-disabilities-2021-2030/disability-employment-package-improve-labour-market-outcomes-persons-disabilities_en>.

[50] Commission, 'European Disability Card and European Parking Card for persons with disabilities' available at <https://ec.europa.eu/social/main.jsp?catId=1139>.

[51] Commission (n 31) 3.

[52] Ibid.

[53] Commission, '2021 Rule of Law Report The rule of law situation in the European Union' COM(2021) 700 final 2; Commission, 'A more inclusive and protective Europe: extending the list of EU crimes to hate speech and hate crime' COM(2021) 777 final 5; Commission, 'EU strategic framework on health and safety at work 2021-2027 Occupational safety and health in a changing world of work' COM(2021) 323 final 13; Commission, 'Better regulation: Joining forces to make better laws' COM(2021) 219 final 5.

2021-2030 seems to become a tool for positive change across the span of EU action complementing the more concrete flagship initiatives.

4. The Commission as Driver of Disability Legislation

Besides setting the agenda, the Commission distinctly shapes EU disability law by proposing legislation. In the last two decades, the Commission has put forward an array of legislative proposals that either directly or indirectly affect the rights of persons with disabilities. The proposal for a Horizontal Equality Directive[54] on the basis of Article 19 TFEU (formerly Article 13 EC) – which provides for the adoption of secondary legislation combating discrimination, *inter alia*, on the ground of disability following the special legislative procedure requiring unanimity – is probably the most notable example, yet the least successful. As one participant commented:

> I mean, we don't give up, of course … And I see it regularly once per year. … So, the problem is unanimity …. Otherwise it would have been adopted for a long while, … I mean we have to, we have to deal … with what we have … But no, I mean, nobody [is] giving up, and we regularly get questions and we and whenever we get the question, we also mention it and say listen, look this is on the table it's, I mean, it's certainly not us … who are the culprits of not having it adopted now. [EU_PM2]

It predates the conclusion of the CRPD, but clearly embeds, with regard to disability, the approach of the Convention in many respects. To this end, it is illustrative of the ambition of the Commission. However, it also shows that such ambition remains unfulfilled if the co-legislators do not embrace the spirit of a proposal. With regard to legislation based on Article 19 TFEU the requirement of unanimity is certainly a major hurdle.[55] Modelled on the Racial Equality Directive[56] in its material scope, the Commission intended to extend the protection against discrimination to groups under Article 19 TFEU that are not yet protected outside the field of employment,[57] i.e. to persons irrespective of their

[54] Commission, 'Proposal for a Council Directive on implementing the principle of equal treatment between persons irrespective of religion or belief, disability, age or sexual orientation' COM(2008) 426 final.

[55] L Waddington, 'Future prospects for EU equality law: lessons to be learnt from the proposed Equal Treatment Directive' (2011) 36(2) *European Law Review* 163–184.

[56] Council Directive 2000/43/EC of 29 June 2000 implementing the principle of equal treatment between persons irrespective of racial or ethnic origin (Racial Equality Directive) [2000] OJ L180/22.

[57] Council Directive 2000/78/EC of 27 November 2000 establishing a general framework for equal treatment in employment and occupation (Employment Equality Directive) [2000] OJ L303/16 has a broad personal scope that protects persons irrespective of their religion or belief, disability, age or sexual orientation against discrimination in employment and occupation, and thus has a narrow material scope.

religion or belief, disability, age or sexual orientation. Impasse in Council appears to be due to disagreement about EU competence to legislate, the multi-ground nature of the proposal and, with regard to disability, the specifics of provisions and obligations relating to reasonable accommodation, amongst others.[58] As the Commission holds no legislative decision-making powers it is reliant on the Council and EP in terms of adoption of a given piece of legislation. As one interviewee pointed out:

> … I mean, once you have made your proposal, you can only try to get it sailed through without too much harm. But you never muster what the legislators do with it. And there's only so much you can influence in the end. [EU_PM2]

This also alludes to the limitation in ultimately defining the scope and substance of a law. The Commission can propose but the fate and final shape of a legislative act remains in the hands of the co-legislators. During the negotiation phases, the Commission can nevertheless assume a functional role in facilitating compromise between the EP and Council during 'trilogue' meetings. Due to its generally perceived neutrality and privilege of being privy to almost all formal and informal meetings between the co-legislators during the legislative phase, it has inside knowledge of preferences and red tape and is thus well-positioned to broker a common stance.[59] It is important to note that regarding legislation proposed on Article 19 TFEU, however, the EP only has a right to consent rather than to fully act as co-legislator. Thus, the Council has the most influence over the scope and substance but also over resolving impasses.

The Commission is hence constrained in mediation. Still, one option would be to utilise *passarelle* clauses under Article 48 TEU, which 'could do away with the unanimity there, so it would not even need a Treaty change'[60] to move from unanimity to qualified majority voting in Council facilitating the adoption of legislation – especially where principal and majority support exists.[61] Indeed, the Commission did propose to consider using *passarelle* clauses in the context of EU non-discrimination legislation, including to address the stalling of the 2008 proposal in 2019.[62] Yet again, it is not for the Commission to decide

[58] M Bell, 'Advancing EU Anti-Discrimination Law: the European Commission's 2008 Proposal for a New Directive' (2009) 3 *The Equal Rights Review* 11; Waddington (n 55) 164-166, 168; O Bartlett, 'The EU Legislative Institutions and Disability Rights: Uncovering the Factors that Block Progress and Offering Insights for Future Advocacy' in this volume; Council of the European Union (Council), 'Proposal for a Council Directive on implementing the principle of equal treatment between persons irrespective of religion or belief, disability, age or sexual orientation – Progress Report' (2023) 9043/23 2, 4.

[59] Nugent and Rhinard (n 1) 313, 316.

[60] EU_PM1.

[61] Council (n 58) 2; Council, 'Proposal for a Council Directive on implementing the principle of equal treatment between persons irrespective of religion or belief, disability, age or sexual orientation' (2024) 8616/1/24 REV 1 2.

[62] Commission, 'More efficient decision-making in social policy: Identification of areas for an enhanced move to qualified majority voting' COM(2019) 186 final 9-10; Bartlett (n 58).

but merely to initiate. Using *passarelle* clauses, which has not happened yet,[63] depends on the decision by the European Council, the consent by the EP and on the absence of dissent by the national parliaments.[64]

More subtly, the Commission can renew attention to proposed legislation by repeatedly including it in policy documents, such as in the Strategy 2021-2030, or in its work programmes,[65] thereby giving prominence to an issue and building public expectations. In this way, the Commission can pressure the Council and EP into some kind of action. Regarding the proposed Horizontal Equality Directive, the unrelenting commitment to more comprehensive non-discrimination legislation has been visible in the Commission's policy action and the call for adoption of the proposed directive has been reiterated many times,[66] including by the Commissioner for Equality.[67] Several participants in our study commented on this aspect, with one stating:

> … the Commission doesn't want to give it up because it is important and an important file, and no one wants to see the file taken off the agenda, but it is not on the Commission to actually proceed with the file. [EU_PM9]

However, the unsuccessful trajectory of the Horizontal Equality Directive proposal appears to be a 'lesson learnt' with disability legislation being proposed primarily within the remit of market integration. It is notable that the most successful proposals are based on Article 114 TFEU. This does not require unanimity in the Council and the functioning of the internal market is a cross-cutting competence that allows the Commission to propose rather capacious legislation. The Web Accessibility Directive (WAD),[68] EAA and the so-called Marrakesh Directive[69] were all proposed and ultimately adopted on the basis of Article 114 TFEU. The latter Directive 2017/1564 on certain permitted uses of certain works and other subject matter protected by copyright and related rights for the benefit of persons

[63] European Parliamentary Research Service, 'Passerelle clauses in the EU Treaties Opportunities for more flexible supranational decision-making' (2020) PE 659.420 1.

[64] Article 48(7) TEU.

[65] Commission (n 31) 14; 'A New Start for Europe: My Agenda for Jobs, Growth, Fairness and Democratic Change Political Guidelines for the next European Commission' (Strasbourg, 15 July 2014) Jean-Claude Juncker Candidate for President of the European Commission point 7; Commission, 'Commission Work Programme 2020 A Union that strives for more' COM(2020) 37 final Annex III Priority pending proposals No 116.

[66] Commission (n 31) 14; Commission, 'Countering racism and xenophobia in the EU: fostering a society where pluralism, tolerance and non-discrimination prevail' SWD(2019) 110 final 2-3; Commission (n 47).

[67] European Parliament, 'Commitments made at the hearing of Helena Dalli Commissioner-designate Equality' Policy Department for Citizens' Rights and Constitutional Affairs (2019) PE 621.919 2.

[68] Directive (EU) 2016/2102 of the European Parliament and of the Council of 26 October 2016 on the accessibility of the websites and mobile applications of public sector bodies [2016] OJ L327/1.

[69] Directive (EU) 2017/1564 of the European Parliament and of the Council of 13 September 2017 on certain permitted uses of certain works and other subject matter protected by copyright and related rights for the benefit of persons who are blind, visually impaired or otherwise print-disabled and amending Directive 2001/29/EC on the harmonisation of certain aspects of copyright and related rights in the information society [2017] OJ L242/6.

who are blind, visually impaired or otherwise print-disabled was complemented by Regulation 2017/1563 on the cross-border exchange between the Union and third countries of accessible format copies of certain works and other subject matter protected by copyright and related rights for the benefit of persons who are blind, visually impaired or otherwise print-disabled[70] on the basis of Article 207 TFEU. Although, as one interviewee stated, '[disability accessibility] it's scattered around […] and- equality [is] not always mentioned',[71] internal market legislation has bolstered the EU disability *aquis* beyond employment.

The latest proposals on the EDC further intend to facilitate the enjoyment of equal treatment and freedom of movement rights for persons with disabilities. To this end, the EDC proposal[72] is based on Article 21(2) TFEU as residual clause on freedom of movement as well as on Articles 53(1) and 62 TFEU on service provisions. Furthermore, as this proposal also regulates the new European parking card for persons with disabilities, Article 91 TFEU is utilised.

Moreover, the Commission has contributed to the inclusion of important disability provisions in sectoral legislation ranging from transport[73] and procurement[74] to the recast European Electronic Communications Code (EECC)[75] and Audio-visual Media Service Directive (AVMSD),[76] and most recently to the Directive on combating violence against women and domestic violence,[77] which complement this body of EU law.[78] While the EECC is based on Article 114 TFEU,

[70] Regulation (EU) 2017/1563 of the European Parliament and of the Council of 13 September 2017 on the cross-border exchange between the Union and third countries of accessible format copies of certain works and other subject matter protected by copyright and related rights for the benefit of persons who are blind, visually impaired or otherwise print-disabled [2017] OJ L242/1.

[71] EU_PM9.

[72] Commission, 'Proposal for a Directive of the European Parliament and of the Council establishing the European Disability Card and the European Parking Card for persons with disabilities' COM(2023) 512 final.

[73] Regulation (EC) No 1107/2006 concerning the rights of disabled persons and persons with reduced mobility when travelling by air [2006] OJ L150/70; Regulation (EU) No 1177/2010 concerning the rights of passengers when travelling by sea and inland waterway and amending Regulation (EC) No 2006/2004 [2010] OJ L334/1; Regulation (EU) No 181/2011 concerning the rights of passengers in bus and coach transport and amending Regulation (EC) No 2006/2004 [2011] OJ L55/1; Regulation (EU) 2021/782 on rail passengers' rights and obligations (recast) [2021] OJ L172/1.

[74] Directive 2014/25/EU of the European Parliament and of the Council of 26 February 2014 on procurement by entities operating in the water, energy, transport and postal services sectors and repealing Directive 2004/17/EC [2014] OJ L94/243; Directive 2014/24/EU of the European Parliament and of the Council of 26 February 2014 on public procurement and repealing Directive 2004/18/EC [2014] OJ L94/65.

[75] Directive (EU) 2018/1972 of the European Parliament and of the Council of 11 December 2018 establishing the European Electronic Communications Code (Recast) (EECC) [2018] OJ L321/36.

[76] Directive (EU) 2018/1808 of the European Parliament and of the Council of 14 November 2018 amending Directive 2010/13/EU on the coordination of certain provisions laid down by law, regulation or administrative action in Member States concerning the provision of audiovisual media services (Audiovisual Media Services Directive) in view of changing market realities [2018] OJ L303/69.

[77] Directive (EU) 2024/1385 of the European Parliament and of the Council of 14 May 2024 on Combating Violence against Women and Domestic Violence [2024] OJ L1385/1.

[78] For a comprehensive overview of disability relevant provisions, see Commission, 'Annotated review of European Union law and policy with reference to disability' (Publications Office of the European Union 2024).

other relevant legislation utilise a plethora of Treaty bases that, *inter alia*, support the protection and promotion of disability rights in EU law.

An exception to this trend is the proposal for the standards of Equality Bodies, including equal treatment in the field of employment and occupation between persons irrespective of their religion or belief, disability, age or sexual orientation,[79] which is based on Article 19(1) TFEU. While requiring unanimity in Council, the proposal appears functional to advancing existing EU non-discrimination legislation. Equality Bodies are critical in assisting and defending victims of discrimination on various grounds and their establishment has been required, for instance, by the Racial Equality Directive.[80] Considering that much of legal enforcement in this area is complaint-based,[81] such bodies are an important instrument for protected groups and were thus included in the Horizontal Equality Directive proposal.[82] Albeit a piecemeal approach, the proposal for standards of Equality Bodies for groups covered, *inter alia*, by the Employment Equality Directive, might best be understood as a pragmatic attempt by the Commission to fill the gaps in non-discrimination legislation in the absence of agreement on horizontal non-discrimination legislation. On the chances of legislation being passed by unanimity, one participant commented as follows:

> … we expect that there will be an agreement soon on the Article 19 [TFEU] proposal [on Equality Bodies] as well, which would be the one applying also to disability. And there you see that it is, if it happens, you … should never take things for granted, but if it happens, it would show that it is still possible to have secondary law under unanimity even nowadays, so not everything is lost for the 2008 proposal. [EU_PM2]

Indeed, the Council adopted, *inter alia*, the proposal on the basis of Article 19 TFEU in May 2024.[83]

[79] Commission, 'Proposal for a Council Directive on standards for equality bodies in the field of equal treatment between persons irrespective of their racial or ethnic origin, equal treatment in the field of employment and occupation between persons irrespective of their religion or belief, disability, age or sexual orientation, equal treatment between women and men in matters of social security and in the access to and supply of goods and services, and deleting Article 13 of Directive 2000/43/EC and Article 12 of Directive 2004/113/EC' COM(2022) 689 final. The Commission released a parallel proposal for equality bodies in the field of equal treatment and equal opportunities between men and women on the basis of Article 157(3) TFEU.

[80] Article 13 Racial Equality Directive.

[81] Bell (n 58) 15.

[82] Article 12 Commission (n 54).

[83] Council, 'Strengthening the role of equality bodies across the EU: Council adopts two directives' (Press Release, 7 May 2024) available at <https://www.consilium.europa.eu/en/press/press-releases/2024/05/07/strengthening-the-role-of-equality-bodies-across-the-eu-council-adopts-two-directives/>; Council Directive (EU) 2024/1499 of 7 May 2024 on standards for equality bodies in the field of equal treatment between persons irrespective of their racial or ethnic origin, equal treatment in matters of employment and occupation between persons irrespective of their religion or belief, disability, age or sexual orientation, equal treatment between women and men in matters of social security and in the access to and supply of goods and services, and amending Directives 2000/43/EC and 2004/113/EC [2024] OJ L1499/1.

The still pending proposal for a Horizontal Equality Directive appears as a stark reminder of the liminal space the Commission enjoys when attempting to advance EU (disability) law – especially comprehensive non-discrimination legislation. Yet, the Commission has undoubtedly played an instrumental role in advancing disability-specific legislation as well as mainstreaming disability provisions. While the adoption of sectoral laws is incremental – and fragmented at times –[84] making for seemingly rather small steps than big leaps in EU disability law, there is a compounding effect that should not be neglected. The latest proposals indicate the impact of dedicated disability strategies as a roadmap that fosters the Commission's efforts in initiating ambitious legislation to facilitate the full enjoyment of rights of EU citizens with disabilities. The swift adoption of the proposals on the EDC and Equality Bodies and the supportive stance of recent Council presidencies might signify some momentum for the advancement of EU disability law following the Commission's lead.

5. The Commission's Delegated Power

Another avenue for the Commission to substantiate the growing EU disability *aquis* is through executive rule making by way of delegated and implementing acts. As with the majority of legislative proposals, the Commission has the right of initiative for executive rules.[85] Delegated acts function as supplement or amendment to a legislative act with technical specifications of general application and in accordance with Article 290 TFEU.[86] Implementing acts, pursuant to Article 291 TFEU, specify measures to facilitate uniform conditions for implementation of a given law across the Union.[87]

The Commission duly engages with these mechanisms and in doing so has, for instance, substantiated the EECC with a delegated regulation that specifically details and fleshes out the provisions on the 112 emergency number with a view of ensuring effective access to emergency communication for persons

[84] D Ferri, 'The Role of the European Union in Ensuring Accessibility of Cultural Goods and Services: All About that … Internal Market?' (2023) 48(3) *European Law Review* 257–280.

[85] Blom and Senninger (n 6) 638. Note that changes in tertiary law-making since the Lisbon Treaty have impacted on the institutional balance, provoking questions of democratic legitimacy, when such powers are conferred to the Commission, and political sensitivities attached, yet they go beyond the scope of the present chapter. For critical accounts, Nugent and Rhinard (n 1) 322-326; Yordanova and Zhelyazkova (n 7); J Mendes, 'The Making Of Delegated and Implementing Acts Legitimacy Beyond Institutional Balance' in CF Bergström and D Ritleng (eds), *Rulemaking by the European Commission* (Oxford University Press 2016) 233–254; G Bellenghi and E Vos, 'Rethinking the Constitutional Architecture of EU Executive Rulemaking: Treaty Change and Enhanced Democracy' (2024) *European Journal of Risk Regulation* 1–19.

[86] Nugent and Rhinard (n 1) 323.

[87] Nugent and Rhinard (n 1) 324.

with disabilities across the Union.[88] Moreover, on the basis of Article 4(9) EAA it released an implementing decision on a standardisation request to the European standardisation organisations (ESOs).[89] The Commission thereby requests a new harmonised standard for the accessibility requirements of products and services covered under Article 2(1) and (2) EAA be developed by the ESOs to ensure the high level of accessibility prescribed by Article 4 EAA.[90] The resulting Mandate 587 for revising the EN 301 549 standard is currently under execution.[91] Importantly, the implementing decision links the revision of the harmonised standard to the WAD and even covers aspects of the EECC with respect to emergency communication[92] streamlining the applicable standards.

Standardisation serves as an important policy tool and the Commission has made use of this instrument to support disability accessibility across policy areas and legislation for a long time.[93] These recent efforts show continuity and commitment to interoperability – an objective pursued with internal market interests at heart – yet one that undoubtably benefits persons with disabilities in terms of more reliable accessibility of products and services across the Union.

Where the Commission has been authorised to issue non-legislative acts – it should be noted here that no such powers have been conferred in the AVMSD or in the Marrakesh Directive – it executes them comparatively quickly since their release is set with a given time frame.[94]

However, the Commission does not enact executive rules on its own. The growing mechanism of 'comitology' whereby representatives of the Member States form expert committees to assist the Commission in drawing up delegated and implementing acts was ultimately enshrined in Article 291(2) and (3) TFEU and is regulated through Regulation (EU) No 182/2011.[95] It grants the Member States

[88] Commission Delegated Regulation (EU) 2023/444 of 16 December 2022 Supplementing Directive (EU) 2018/1972 of the European Parliament and of the Council with measures to ensure effective access to emergency services through emergency communications to the single European emergency number '112' [2023] OJ L65/1.

[89] Commission, 'Commission Implementing Decision of 14.9.2022 on a standardisation request to the European standardisation organisations as regards the accessibility requirements of products and services in support of Directive (EU) 2019/882 of the European Parliament and of the Council' COM(2022) 6456 final.

[90] Ibid Recitals 1 and 2.

[91] Commission, 'eNorm Platform – C(2022)6456 – Standardisation Request M/587' available at <https://ec.europa.eu/growth/tools-databases/enorm/mandate/587_en>.

[92] Recitals 4, 8 and 9, Article 1(2) Commission (n 89); Commission, 'Accessibility of ICT Products and Services (RP2023)' available at <https://interoperable-europe.ec.europa.eu/collection/rolling-plan-ict-standardisation/accessibility-ict-products-and-services-rp2023>.

[93] D Hosking, 'Disability and Standardization' in Ferri and Broderick (n 27) 243-262.

[94] Parts V, VII Point 42 and Annex Better Law Making Agreement.

[95] Regulation (EU) No 182/2011 of the European Parliament and of the Council of 16 February 2011 laying down the rules and general principles concerning mechanisms for control by Member States of the Commission's exercise of implementing powers [2011] OJ L55/13.

veto rights on draft acts thus strengthening their influence on eventual executive rules *vis-à-vis* the Commission.[96]

6. The Commission and National Implementation

6.1. Supporting National Implementation

The national implementation of EU disability law is supported by tailored initiatives of the Commission. To facilitate implementation of EU disability law in law and in practice, the Commission uses several tools including guidelines that clarify implementation and reporting duties.[97]

Moreover, as one of the flagship initiatives under the Strategy 2021-2030, the Commission established the AccessibleEU centre[98] in 2022 to pool expertise and experience and thereby advise on how to best comply with and implement EU disability accessibility legislation and policy. It specifically supports the implementation of EU disability law and compliance with EU accessibility legislation and standards.[99] Through both the collection of country reports by national experts and the provision of additional guidelines across sectors,[100] this centre supplements the Commission's efforts of implementing and monitoring EU disability law. Forming the starting point of a more stringent disability accessibility monitoring, this flagship initiative also acts as a venue for bringing together national authorities to engage with and discuss EU disability legislation, particularly in its practical application. The Commission thereby contributes to the tightening of network structures between Member States and civil society that strengthens the consolidation and mainstreaming of disability accessibility throughout the Union and across sectors.

[96] A Volpato, 'The Voices and the Choir: The Importance of a Contextual Analysis of EU Actors' Roles' in this volume; D Curtin, H Hofmann and J Mendes, 'Constitutionalising EU Executive Rule-Making Procedures: A Research Agenda' (2013) 19(1) *European Law Journal* 1–21; Mendes (n 85).

[97] Communication from the Commission Guidelines on the practical application of the essential functionality criterion of the definition of a 'video-sharing platform service' under the Audiovisual Media Services Directive [2020] OJ C223/3; Communication from the Commission Guidelines pursuant to Article 13(7) of the Audiovisual Media Services Directive on the calculation of the share of European works in on-demand catalogues and on the definition of low audience and low turnover [2020] OJ C223/10; Communication from the Commission Guidelines pursuant to Article 33a(3) of the Audiovisual Media Services Directive on the scope of Member States' reports concerning measures for the promotion and development of media literacy skills [2023] OJ C66/3.

[98] Commission (n 31) 5; Commission, 'AccessibleEU' available at <https://accessible-eu-centre.ec.europa.eu/index_en>.

[99] Commission, 'Accessibility Monitoring' available at <https://accessible-eu-centre.ec.europa.eu/accessibility-monitoring-0_en>.

[100] Commission, 'Guidelines and Support Materials' available at <https://accessible-eu-centre.ec.europa.eu/guidelines-and-support-materials_en>.

6.2. Reporting on National Implementation

The monitoring of EU disability law implementation at Member State level is complemented by regular application reporting by the Commission.[101] This can take different forms, from application reports to reviews and evaluations, and is regulated through provisions in a given law, typically explicating the date for the release of such reports and frequency of reporting, where applicable. However, as provisions and foreseen reporting vary across legislation, there is no consistent and immediately comparable reporting available for legislation discussed above. Instead, the Commission has published a multitude of policy documents that report on or review and evaluate the implementation of relevant laws to date. While these processes are mandatory, the Commission gave further symbolic weight to them by explicitly committing to its legal obligations in the Strategy 2021-2030.[102]

Reports on the Employment Equality Directive[103] and the AVMSD[104] serve an interesting example. Here, the Commission variously builds on information provided by the Member States, Eurobarometer survey data, surveys conducted by the Fundamental Rights Agency of the EU, studies[105] or settled Court of Justice of the EU (CJEU) case law[106] to inform its analysis of application. However, the Commission is faced with several challenges in drawing up these reports: first, it is reliant on the Member States to transpose and implement a given EU law. As long as not all Member States implement the law in question fully, application reports cannot be developed for lack of relevant information. Second, once all Member States have transposed a law, the analysis of adopted legislation and/ or measures and their effectiveness is often inhibited by the fact that late transposition, incomplete transposition or non-compliance create discrepancies in the lengths of time such measures have had relevant practical effect. This makes comprehensive comparative analysis difficult and often renders it indicative

[101] The Better Law Making Agreement in section VII and VIII further regulates reporting by the Commission to the co-legislators and performance checks to evaluate whether legislation would benefit from amendments or new proposals. The latter have contributed to the Commission's proposals for the recast AVMSD and EECC.

[102] Commission (n 31) 4-5.

[103] Commission, 'Report from the Commission to the European Parliament and the Council on the application of Council Directive 2000/43/EC implementing the principle of equal treatment between persons irrespective of racial or ethnic origin ('the Racial Equality Directive') and of Council Directive 2000/78/EC establishing a general framework for equal treatment in employment and occupation ('the Employment Equality Directive')' COM(2021) 139 final.

[104] Commission, 'Commission Staff Working Document Reporting on the application of Directive 2010/13/EU "Audiovisual Media Services Directive" as amended by Directive (EU) 2018/1808, for the period 2019-2022' COM(2024) 4 final.

[105] Commission (n 103) 2-3.

[106] Commission (n 104) 3.

rather than conclusive. Regarding the AVMSD, one participant described this difficulty as follows:

> … [we had a general problem] on the directive that of course was reflected also on accessibility, that is one of the measures. … [D]ue to this late transposition and of course also our assessment of the real implementation of the directive now because you have of course the transposition that is a check if Member States have transposed the rules. And then *something more*, that as you were saying, just to see how the rules have been implemented and how they work. So we have, for us it is mandatory to provide every three years a report on the application of the directive. But of course one of the things that we said in the report is exactly this, due to the late transposition we are not able to have really a complete picture on how practically the directive was implemented in Member States.[107] [EU_PM4]

Inherently, legislation must be in place for a while to reveal how it works in practice and affects persons with disabilities before useful conclusions can be drawn to inform the state of play, amendments or further legislative proposals. This complication will remain until the recent EU disability law efforts have settled and consolidated in law and in practice, exacerbating the variation in analysis conducted by the Commission for the time being.

6.3. Monitoring National Implementation

Nonetheless, the Commission has another important monitoring power, namely that of initiating infringement procedures against non-compliant Member States on the basis of Articles 258 and 260 TFEU. As one interviewee put it, 'this is one of the powerful tools' in the hands of the Commission.[108]

Where Member States fail to notify or to report measures taken to transpose, or fail to fully implement or comply with EU legislation, the Commission can, on the basis of Article 258 TFEU, open infringement procedures by sending letters of formal notice to request required information from Member States, followed by reasoned opinions. When Member States fail to comply with a reasoned opinion – a formal request to comply with EU law that explicates why the Commission believes a Member State is breaching EU law and requires the Member State to communicate measures taken to remedy the situation – within a specified time frame, the Commission can take action before the CJEU against the Member State(s) in question. In cases in which the CJEU finds a given Member State as infringing EU rules, Member States must comply with the judgment as laid down in Article 260(1) TFEU. Failure to do so allows the Commission to take action against the Member State again and, in case the CJEU finds the Member State non-compliant with its judgment, to propose financial sanctions in the form of lump

[107] Emphasis added.
[108] EU_PM7.

sums and/or daily payments that the CJEU ultimately determines in its ruling.[109] This gives the Commission both monitoring powers and influence over the penalty of a Member State in the event of an infringement.

Scholars have noted that, in the context of EU disability law, this procedure has proven functional.[110] For instance, the infringement procedure against Germany in the early 2000s for failure to transpose the equal treatment directives ultimately led to the adoption of the General Equal Treatment Act (*Allgemeines Gleichbehandlunsgesetz*) in 2006. This law, *inter alia*, explicitly prohibits discrimination on the ground of disability[111] and besides other legislation, transposes the Employment Equality Directive. Similarly, an infringement procedure was pursued against Italy for failing to comprehensively protect persons with disabilities against discrimination in the workplace under Article 5 Employment Equality Directive;[112] following the CJEU's judgment, Italy amended legislation to rectify the shortcomings in transposing the Directive.

Considering more recent disability-specific legislation, the Commission has pursued infringement procedures regarding almost all relevant legislation, such as the WAD, the Marrakesh Directive and the EAA. The majority of infringement procedures address failures in communication on transposition or timely transposition and resolve without any action taken before the CJEU. Non-communication and delayed transposition are, as discussed above, serious shortcomings, that hamper the effectiveness of existing EU disability law and contribute to its unevenness across the Union.

Some infringement procedures however reveal more severe failings in the implementation of disability relevant provisions. For instance, in the proper implementation of the EECC and AVMSD. While most Member States received formal notices and reasoned opinions for failure of timely transposition of these laws, five Member States were specifically pursued for failures in effectively implementing rules on the 112 emergency number for users with disabilities in accordance with Directive 2002/22/EC, now the EECC.[113]

Moreover, pursuant to Article 260(3) TFEU, Czechia, Ireland, Romania, Slovakia and Spain were referred to the CJEU for failure to transpose the AVMSD in due course.[114] While four cases were subsequently resolved, the infringement

[109] Article 260(2) and (3) TFEU.

[110] A Waldschmidt, 'Behindertenpolitik (In) der Europäischen Union. Geschichte und Aktueller Stand' in T Degener and M Von Miguel (eds), *Aufbrüche und Barrieren. Behindertenpolitik und Behindertenrecht in Deutschland und Europa seit den 1970er Jahren* (Transcript Verlag 2019) 95; F Welti, 'Germany. Is Cooperative Federalism Generating Multi-Level Barriers or Facilitating Multi-Level Inclusion?' in D Ferri, F Palermo and G Martinico (eds), *Federalism and the Rights of Persons with Disabilities. The Implementation of the CRPD in Federal Systems and Its Implications* (Hart 2023) 43–63.

[111] Article 1 Allgemeines Gleichbehandlungsgesetz vom 14 August 2006, BGBL I S 1897, das zuletzt durch Artikel 15 des Gesetzes vom 22 Dezember 2023 BGBL 2023 I Nr 414 geändert worden ist.

[112] Case C-312/11 *Commission v Italy* ECLI:EU:C:2012:149.

[113] Commission, 'July Infringement Package: Key Decisions' (Press Release, 25 July 2019) available at <https://ec.europa.eu/commission/presscorner/detail/en/INF_19_4251> point 3.

[114] Infringement Procedures INFR(2020)0510 Czechia; INFR(2020)0555 Romania; INFR(2020)0563 Slovakia; INFR(2020)0521 Spain.

procedure against Ireland triggered modified financial sanctions in September 2023 and remains active at the time of writing.[115] Amongst others, Ireland has been found to have failed to transpose the insertion of Chapter IXa, entitled 'Provisions applicable to video-sharing platform services'.[116] This includes Article 28b AVMSD under which Member States shall ensure appropriate measures to protect, *inter alia*, 'the general public from programmes, user-generated videos and audiovisual commercial communications containing incitement to violence or hatred directed against a group of persons or a member of a group based on any of the grounds referred to in Article 21 of the Charter'[117] are taken by video-sharing platform providers under their jurisdiction. As persons with disabilities are a protected group under Article 21 of the Charter of Fundamental Rights, this is most concerning. It leaves persons with disabilities potentially disproportionately vulnerable to violence or hatred on certain platforms and moreover reveals the lack of relevant non-discrimination provisions in that Member State.

Yet, the Commission's pursuit of non-compliant Member States will necessarily remain restricted to those sectors where relevant legislation exists. Infringement proceedings thus cannot, in any way, fill the gaps in protection against discrimination. As one interviewee stated:

> I think you would need the 2008 proposal and we see it if we look at the racial discrimination, which is basically apart from women and men now, but from the other grounds, it is the only one where we have a non-employment protection. There you can do many more things like you've certainly seen, in April, we decided to take Slovakia to the Court over segregation of Roma kids in schools. Which is possible on the basis of the Racial Equality Directive, because it goes beyond employment and because there we had the courage as an EU to adopt a more comprehensive framework. [EU_PM2]

This renders the Commission's power to pursue non-compliant Member States functional but not as effective as desirable from a citizen perspective. While financial sanctions can incentivise Member States to transpose legislation, they do not necessarily translate into the speedy adoption of required national measures nor into tangible positive change for persons with disabilities. Yet, the Commission is currently not empowered to enforce compliance by any other means, highlighting that the effectiveness of EU disability legislation continues to lie in the hands of the Member States.

7. Consulting Stakeholders and Experts

The Commission plays a seminal role in ensuring interaction with non-institutional actors. In this respect, the Commission has probably been the leading

[115] Infringement Procedure INFR(2020)0531 Ireland.
[116] Case C-679/22 *Commission v Ireland* ECLI:EU:C:2024:178.
[117] Article 28b(b) AVMSD.

institution in setting up structured dialogue with disability stakeholders, and in particular with organisations of persons with disabilities. This includes organisations active at the national level as well as pan-European organisations. The European Disability Forum is the most prominent umbrella organisation at EU level[118] comprising 112 member organisations that are active at national and EU level and across different types of disabilities, and is a long-standing collaborator of the Commission. However, other civil society actors, such as the European Social Network or the European Network of Equality Bodies are relevant stakeholders that the Commission engages with in the disability realm. Well-established practices of working with expert groups that input on the Commission's legislative preparatory work and expert analyses provided by researchers and academics are similarly noteworthy in this regard.

The consultation of stakeholders throughout the policy cycle is embedded and detailed in the toolbox that accompanies the Better Law Making agreement.[119] It outlines how and when stakeholders, in particular EU citizens, individually or collectively, are to be involved in the preparation and evaluation of legislation and policy. This applies to disability law and is reinforced under Article 4(3) CRPD, which obliges State Parties to 'closely consult with and actively involve persons with disabilities' in the development and implementation of legislation implementing the CRPD.

As such, the Commission has to observe these obligations but also has ample reason to use these consultation processes as a resource, benefitting from expert advice, professional insights and lived experiences to tailor and draft solid disability law. In fact, the Commission has steadily developed into a venue for disability dialogue between civil society, experts and Member States, both through formal and informal channels.

Generally, EU citizens can input on legislative proposals and impact assessments through the 'Have your say' tools on the Commission's website during 'Calls for Evidence' and 'Public Consultations'. These are increasingly made accessible through different available formats to facilitate the broadest possible engagement, including that of persons with disabilities. However, these processes remain opaque in that it is unclear whether and to what extent the collected information ultimately features in official Commission documents.

Concerning the Strategy 2021-2030, however, it appears that the Commission made a dedicated effort to engage with civil society and stakeholders to develop a satisfying outcome that took on board lived experiences and expert advice. One interviewee recalled the process as follows:

> … in the discussions of, that the European Commission organised, DG Employment organised, regarding how, when the disability strategy was being planned. That was a

[118] A Waldschmidt and ES Krolla, 'The Surge of EU Disability Policy: Historical Developments, Current Issues and the Role of Different Actors' in this volume; C Coveney, 'The Role of the European Disability Forum and Disability Organisations in Shaping EU Disability Policy' in this volume.

[119] Commission, 'Better regulation toolbox – Chapter 7 Stakeholder Consultation' (2023) available at <https://commission.europa.eu/law/law-making-process/planning-and-proposing-law/better-regulation/better-regulation-guidelines-and-toolbox/better-regulation-toolbox_en>.

> fascinating process because I don't think that it's, DG Employment does a really good job, I think, in including right-holders organisation and stakeholders organisation in the discussions of their strategies; which I'm not sure that it happens in the same level .... [EU_PM9]

Adding that:

> ... I was able, once the disability strategy was published, to really see and connect the input that had been given to what it was written in the Strategy. Evidently not everything can be included, but there [was a] very clear link .... [EU_PM9]

Further, expert advice is garnered through the European Disability Expertise (EDE) network.[120] This network succeeded the Academic Network of European Disability (ANED) experts that had provided independent scientific research on disability data and disability policy and law. The networks were formally established on the basis of respective public tenders and comprise academics across the EU. Although both of these networks assist(ed) the Commission with independent analyses, it should be noted that the Commission has (had) influence over the thematic foci, thereby impacting on the direction of the research conducted and the advice received. This point is further elaborated elsewhere in this volume.[121]

Informal interactions, such as through long collaboration and nurtured contacts between Commission staff and experts or civil society representatives, as well as active lobbying, impact on the Commission's work on disability. Their influence varies and multiple factors play a role. However, it appears that especially lobbying efforts by disability advocates are most effective when addressing the co-legislators rather than the Commission.[122]

7.1. A Two-Pronged Approach to Disability Dialogue

Under the Strategy 2021-2030, the Commission has intensified its formal and permanent consultation with disability stakeholders. Besides the AccessibleEU centre, the co-called Disability Platform was established as an expert group in 2021.[123] It replaces the previous High Level Group on Disability. The Disability Platform comprises national focal points under the CRPD and Member States' representatives, 14 civil society organisations as full members,[124] Equinet – the

[120] Commission, 'European Disability Expertise' available at <https://employment-social-affairs.ec.europa.eu/policies-and-activities/social-protection-social-inclusion/persons-disabilities/european-disability-expertise_en>.

[121] L Waddington, 'The Role of Academics in Shaping EU Disability Law: Some Personal Reflections' in this volume.

[122] Coveney (n 118).

[123] Commission Decision of 27.10.2021 setting up the group of experts "Disability Platform" COM(2021) 7591 final.

[124] Commission, 'Equality: All members of the new Disability Platform now known' (Press Release, 13 December 2021) available at <https://ec.europa.eu/social/main.jsp?langId=en&catId=89&newsId=

European Network of Equality Bodies (Equinet) and other umbrella bodies as observers, as well as Commission staff. It is tasked with supporting and advising on the implementation of the CRPD, the Strategy 2021-2030, existing EU disability law as well as legislative preparation. Next to general Disability Platform meetings, sub-groups can and have been formed to provide relevant input on specific policy issues, such as on the EDC or independent living.[125] Its functionality appears twofold: as venue for the Commission to engage with civil society as well as with the Member States outside the trilogue format, and as a forum for mutual learning. As one interviewee commented:

> Yeah it is useful, it is in principal continuation, more structured continuation of the [previous] High Level Group on Disability and there are Member States and civil society. So it is necessary for mutual learning and discussions. And here as well we are exchanging examples of good practices and Member States can interact with civil society, so yeah it is useful. [EU_PM3]

This is also reflected in the working practices and programming of the Disability Platform:

> I think that they are doing a great job in trying to include somehow – [...] for instance, in getting input from the [civil society organisations] and stakeholders regarding the work plan for the Platform for next year. [EU_PM9]

In this respect, the Commission also seems to contribute to enhancing and facilitating the exchange between Member States/national authorities and civil society, similar to the efforts under the AccessibleEU flagship. In fact, it appears that the two-pronged approach of establishing the Disability Platform and AccessibleEU centre strengthens the Commission's role as a facilitator of disability rights in law and in practice. Both convene on the initiative of the Commission and offer the Member States and civil society actors opportunities to discuss and exchange views on EU and national disability law in politically more neutral venues, which reduces complicating factors. Whereas the AccessibleEU centre is a more practice-oriented endeavour that focuses primarily on implementation and mutual learning in best practices, it feeds into the monitoring and reviewing tasks of the Commission. In turn, the Disability Platform offers a forum to reflect on best practices on the basis of lived experiences and to discuss existing legislation as well as remaining gaps and future objectives. While the Commission assumes a rather subtle role in the AccessibleEU centre, it holds more decisive powers in the Disability Platform. Ultimately, it can use this venue to garner insights and preferences from the Member States as well as civil society

10124&furtherNews=yes>; Commission, 'Register of Expert Groups. Disability Platform (E03820) – Members' available at <https://ec.europa.eu/transparency/expert-groups-register/screen/expert-groups/consult?lang=en&groupId=3820&fromMembers=true&memberType=4&memberId=97587>.

[125] Article 8 Commission Decision of 27.10.2021 setting up the group of experts "Disability Platform" COM(2021) 7591 final; Commission, 'Disability Platform (E03820) – Subgroups' available at <https://ec.europa.eu/transparency/expert-groups-register/screen/expert-groups/consult?lang=en&groupId=3820&fromMembers=true&memberType=4&memberId=97587>.

stakeholders but can determine which and to what extent it incorporates information into its forthcoming proposals on EU disability law and policy.

8. Concluding Remarks

This chapter examined the extent to which the Commission has shaped EU disability law. It aimed at illuminating our understanding of this institutional actor by utilising both desk-based and qualitative research. Main roles have been identified as agenda-setter, legislative initiator and a set of executive roles that pertain to the implementation and monitoring of EU disability law. The set up with 'disability coordinators' across DGs, complementing the inter-service group on disability, and a designated Commissioner for Equality supported by the Task Force on Equality, have consolidated a renewed and stronger focus on disability.

Despite general questions around its leadership and agenda-setting roles, it appears that the Commission is a strong driver behind recent developments in EU disability law. Dedicated strategies and the increasing mainstreaming of disability into larger policy frameworks and interinstitutional agreements has been key in placing disability front and centre in EU disability policy. Albeit in small steps, the increasing integration of disability into larger frameworks seemingly contributes to the advancement of disability rights protection outside the realm of employment. The establishment of 'disability coordinators' within the Commission, under the Strategy 2021-2030, contributes to a mainstreaming within the institution that is increasingly reflected in its work and legislative proposals. As agenda-setter, the Commission further aims to lead by example and thus far has used the Strategy 2021-2030 as a clear roadmap for its flagship initiatives and legislative proposals alike.

When it comes to legislative initiative, while the Commission has demonstrated its ambition to advance disability rights through an array of legislation, successful adoption is outside its remit.[126] A continued commitment to comprehensive non-discrimination legislation protecting, *inter alia*, persons with disabilities can be detected in the Commission's unrelenting emphasis on the need to adopt the Horizontal Equality Directive proposal. Recent successes in strengthening Equality Bodies and adopting the EDC might even indicate a useful momentum. Although the co-legislators can easily put the brakes on the Commission's ambitions, it might be able to capitalise on this momentum to further advance EU disability law.

The Commission can also support the implementation of EU disability law at the national level. It has done so through soft governance mechanisms, such

[126] Bartlett (n 58).

as the Disability Platform and the AccessibleEU centre. In very different ways these mechanisms facilitate an interface for Member States and civil society to engage, exchange and reflect on best practice in law and its application. While this is a subtle way of fostering implementation and mainstreaming across the Union, there are indicators that these venues have proven to be useful for a more uniform application of EU disability law. It has further done so through its important power of initiating infringement proceedings against non-compliant Member States.

The new Commission, following the European elections in June 2024, might further support the protection and promotion of disability rights in the EU legal order. EU disability law might thus continue to be embedded and mainstreamed into EU action across the board, especially if the organisational set-up of the Commission featuring a Commissioner for Equality and the Task Force on Equality, were to continue. These dynamics and potential further innovations in this respect should therefore be closely observed.

5

The EU Legislative Institutions and Disability Rights: Uncovering the Factors that Block Progress and Offering Insights for Future Advocacy

OLLIE BARTLETT

1. Introduction

The European Disability Strategy 2010–2020 (EDS),[1] adopted in 2010, laid out a comprehensive disability policy framework that identified several legislative measures. Its successor, the European Union's (EU) Strategy for the Rights of Persons with Disabilities 2021-2030 (Strategy 2021–2030)[2] also outlines an ambitious agenda for change that will not be achievable without the adoption of EU legislation. The institutions that comprise the EU legislature – the Council of the European Union (Council) and the European Parliament (EP) – have thus played and will continue to play an important role in advancing the protection of disability rights for the 101 million European citizens over the age of 16 who have some form of disability.[3] However, adopting progressive EU disability legislation is no easy task. The legislative process can be long, is sometimes unhelpful for social rights initiatives, and is always vulnerable to influence.

This chapter evaluates the ability of the EU legislature to adopt progressive disability legislation. Using case studies, it demonstrates that the EU legislature

[1] European Commission (Commission), 'European Disability Strategy 2010-2020: A Renewed Commitment to a Barrier-Free Europe' COM(2010) 636 final.

[2] Commission, 'Union of Equality: Strategy for the Rights of Persons with Disabilities 2021-2030' COM(2021) 101 final.

[3] See Eurostat, 'Level of disability (activity limitation) by sex, age and income quintile' available at <https://ec.europa.eu/eurostat/databrowser/view/hlth_silc_12/default/table?lang=en>.

does have the capacity to strongly protect disability rights, but only under the right political conditions. In this respect, disability policy within the EU is very similar to other contested social policy issues, in particular public health policy, which is similarly characterised by difficult resource allocation decisions and a highly polarised set of stakeholders.[4] Far from being a source of frustration, this should give disability advocates the opportunity to learn from comparable social policy issues in which coalitions of progressives have beaten the odds to build the consensus required for the adoption of legislation that offers meaningful protection to European citizens.

The chapter employs a mixed methodological approach. Initially it employs doctrinal and textual analysis to identify the legal and political mandate for progressive disability policies. It then employs mainstream policy analysis, particularly focussing on advocacy coalitions within the legislative process,[5] to extract from the case studies the factors that block or promote progressive disability rights legislation.

After this introduction, the second section outlines the legal competence and the political mandate that the EU has for legislating on disability issues. The third section presents case studies of three pieces of EU disability legislation at different stages of the legislative process – the Directive establishing the European Disability Card and European Parking Card,[6] the European Accessibility Act (EAA),[7] and the Horizontal Equality Directive.[8] It examines the negotiation of these pieces of legislation to identify the key factors that might block the progress of EU disability legislation. The fourth section compares the disability case studies to others elsewhere in the social policy field to demonstrate that these blocking factors are not unique to disability policy, but rather are common to most areas of social policy. The fifth section then discusses how advocacy strategies that have been developed through other social policy sagas might be adopted by disability advocates to potentially help the progress of current or future EU disability legislation. The sixth section offers some concluding remarks.

[4] See A Waldschmidt and ES Krolla, 'The Surge of EU Disability Policy: Historical Developments, Current Issues and the Role of Different Actors' in this volume.

[5] For an overview of mainstream policy analysis, and the advocacy coalition approach, see J Browne *et al.*, 'A guide to policy analysis as a research method' (2019) 34 *Health Promotion International* 1032–1044.

[6] Commission, 'Proposal for a Directive of the European Parliament and of the Council establishing the European Disability Card and the European Parking Card for persons with disabilities' COM(2023) 512 final.

[7] Directive (EU) 2019/882 of the European Parliament and of the Council of 17 April 2019 on the accessibility requirements for products and services [2019] OJ L151/70.

[8] Commission, 'Proposal for a Council Directive on implementing the principle of equal treatment between persons irrespective of religion or belief, disability, age or sexual orientation' COM(2008) 426 final.

2. The Competence and Mandate to Adopt EU Disability Legislation

The EU has recently adopted certain important pieces of disability legislation as envisaged in the EDS. Of the case studies examined in this chapter, the EAA, which was indicated among the key initiatives in the EDS, is now law, and the Directive establishing the European Disability and Parking Cards, which features as one of the flagship initiatives in the Strategy 2021-2030, shortly will be; both aim to make it easier for persons with disabilities to use essential technology and services. The Employment Equality Directive[9] ensures that reasonable accommodation is provided to persons with disabilities in the course of their employment or training. The Patient's Rights Directive[10] allows persons with disabilities to seek medical treatment connected to their disability in another Member State. The EU has also had some success at mainstreaming disability issues into other policy areas. For example, the Audiovisual Media Services Directive contains provisions to promote the accessibility of audiovisual media content for persons with disabilities,[11] and the Work-Life Balance Directive contains provisions that ensure adaptations to parental leave arrangements are made for parents with a disability or with children who have a disability.[12]

The Strategy 2021-2030 identifies the adoption of the long-delayed Horizontal Equality Directive as a clear legislative target. However, the Strategy 2021-2030 also commits the EU institutions to identifying gaps in existing legislation. The proactive protection of disability rights through the adoption of legislation has a clear legal basis in the EU Treaties. Article 19 of the Treaty on the Functioning of the European Union (TFEU) provides the power to adopt non-discrimination legislation through the special legislative procedure, which Article 10 TFEU more broadly mandates the EU to mainstream action against disability discrimination into other policy areas. The power to adopt harmonising legislation for the removal of internal market barriers, provided by Article 114 TFEU, can also be used to achieve social policy objectives as long as there is a simultaneous genuine

[9] Directive 2000/78/EC of 27 November 2000 establishing a general framework for equal treatment in employment and occupation [2000] OJ L303/16.

[10] Directive 2011/24/EU of the European Union and of the Council of 9 March 2011 on the application of patients' rights in cross-border healthcare [2011] OJ L88/45.

[11] Article 7(1) Directive (EU) 2018/1808 of the European Parliament and of the Council of 14 November 2018 amending Directive 2010/13/EU on the coordination of certain provisions laid down by law, regulation or administrative action in Member States concerning the provision of audiovisual media services (Audiovisual Media Services Directive) in view of changing market realities [2018] OJ L303/69.

[12] Article 5(8) Directive (EU) 2019/1158 of the European Parliament and of the Council of 20 June 2019 on work-life balance for parents and carers and repealing Council Directive 2010/18/EU [2019] OJ L188/79.

effort to improve internal market functioning.[13] Moreover, there is a strong political and legal mandate for the adoption of EU disability legislation.

The political mandate for legislative action to protect disability rights is not only encapsulated in the Strategy 2021-2030, but also in Article 17 of the European Pillar of Social Rights.[14] Both institutions of the EU legislature have put on record their support for greater action on disability rights protection. The EP in particular has been clear on the need for a revised EU disability strategy that expanded disability rights protection, and on the actions required at Member State and EU level to secure equal rights for persons with disabilities.[15] The Council has also advocated for greater disability protections in the labour market[16] and for greater access to sport for persons with disabilities.[17] Impetus also comes from the United Nations (UN) level – the Committee on the Rights of Persons with Disabilities (CRPD Committee) issued a range of recommendations for improved EU implementation of the CRPD following the EU's first implementation report in 2014,[18] while the UN Special Rapporteur has also encouraged the EU to continue its work on disability rights protection,[19] and there is consistent commentary from civil society advocates[20]

[13] Case C-380/03 *Germany v Parliament and Council* ECLI:EU:C:2006:772.

[14] The text of the 'Pillar', as well as the Commission's Action Plan for its implementation are available at <https://ec.europa.eu/social/main.jsp?catId=1226&langId=en>.

[15] European Parliament (EP), 'European Parliament resolution of 18 June 2020 on the European Disability Strategy post-2020' 2019/2975(RSP).

[16] Council, 'Council Conclusions on inclusive labour markets: Improving the employment of people in a vulnerable position in the labour market' (2019) 14646/19.

[17] Conclusions of the Council of the European Union and the Representatives of the Member States meeting within the Council on Access to sport for persons with disabilities [2019] OJ C192/18.

[18] For a summary of the implementation report, Committee recommendations, and the EU's work in addressing these recommendations, see J Smits, 'The implementation of the 2015 Concluding Observations of the CRPD Committee by the EU' (European Parliament 2021).

[19] See United Nations, 'UN expert hails EU commitment to disability rights' (Press Release, 31 March 2022) available at <https://www.ohchr.org/en/press-releases/2022/03/un-expert-hails-eu-commitment-disability-rights>. See also S Favalli, 'The Role of the Committee on the Rights of Persons with Disabilities in Nudging the EU towards Compliance with the Convention on the Rights of Persons with Disabilities' in this volume.

[20] The European Disability Forum (EDF) is one of the most prominent civil society organisations campaigning on disability rights, and regularly releases public commentary and statements on the necessity of including disability rights protection in EU legislation. See eg their open letter on the removal of the CRPD from the Corporate Sustainability Due Diligence Directive. EDF, 'Open letter: EU policy makers pass up opportunity to ensure companies respect the rights of persons with disabilities and other marginalised groups' (20 January 2024) available at <https://www.edf-feph.org/publications/open-letter-eu-policy-makers-pass-up-opportunity-to-ensure-companies-respect-the-rights-of-persons-with-disabilities-and-other-marginalised-groups/>. Coalitions of civil society actors also regularly call for particular legislative actions that would improve the protection of disability rights – see eg the joint open letter calling for greater disability protections in the AI Act ('Ensure fundamental rights protections in the Council position on the AI Act' (17 October 2022) available at <https://edri.org/wp-content/uploads/2022/10/CZ-Minister-Digitalisation-letter-AI-act.pdf>) and the joint statement calling for the adoption of the Horizontal Equality Directive ('Joint NGO Statement on the 10th Anniversary of the Horizontal Directive Ten years on and nothing to show for it' (July 2018) available at <https://www.age-platform.eu/draft-eu-horizontal-non-discrimination-directive-ten-years-on-and-sadly-nothing-to-show-for-it/>).

and academia[21] on the legislative actions required for strong disability rights protection.

There is also a clear legal mandate for advancing disability rights protection through EU legislation. In 2007 the EU took the unique step of becoming the first regional organisation to sign an international human rights treaty, when it signed the UN Convention on the Rights of Persons with Disabilities (CRPD).[22] Much subsequent commentary has focused on how the EU should adopt legislation to discharge its obligations under the CRPD.[23] Indeed, it has been argued that the EU should be bold and proactive in adopting legislation on the basis of its accession to the CRPD in areas in which it holds exclusive legislative competence.[24] While the CRPD provides direct legal justification for progressive EU disability legislation, the equivocation of the Court of Justice of the European Union (CJEU) and the divergent legislative practices of EU Member States provide a certain indirect legal justification. Although the CJEU has actively developed jurisprudence on issues of disability rights protection, it has declined to make certain advances and has left key questions unanswered and in need of resolution,[25] especially on the question of defining disability.[26] Some commentators have also noted a possible stagnation of the CJEU's progressive approach to the interpretation of EU disability legislation. This invites the EU legislator to pick up where the CJEU appears to have left off. Meanwhile, the Member States have adopted divergent implementations of EU disability legislations in areas such as employment,[27] access to culture,[28] the accessibility of

[21] See, eg, R Whittle, 'Disability Rights after Amsterdam: the way forward' (2000) 1 *European Human Rights Law Review* 33–48; M Anišić Campbell, 'Disability Rights and the EU Labour Market: An Analysis of Legislation and Policy' (2020) 6(1) *Croatian Yearbook of European Law and Policy* 231–264; M Bell, 'People with intellectual disabilities and labour market inclusion: What role for EU labour law?' (2020) 11(1) *European Labour Law Journal* 3–25.

[22] Council Decision of 26 November 2009 concerning the conclusion, by the European Community, of the United Nations Convention on the Rights of Persons with Disabilities [2010] OJ L23/35.

[23] M Chamon, 'Negotiation, ratification and implementation of the CRPD and its status in the EU legal order' in D Ferri and A Broderick (eds), *Research Handbook on EU Disability Law* (Edward Elgar 2020); A Hoefmans, 'The EU Disability Framework under Construction: New Perspectives through Fundamental Rights Policy and EU Accession to the CRPD' (2012) 3 *European Yearbook of Disability Law* 35; L Waddington, 'Equal to the Task? Re-Examining EU Equality Law in Light of the United Nations Convention on the Rights of Persons with Disabilities' (2013) 4 *European Yearbook of Disability Law* 169; T Degener, 'The Impact of the UN Convention on the Rights of Persons with Disabilities on EU Anti-Discrimination Law' in T Giegerich (ed), *The European Union as Protector and Promoter of Equality* (Springer 2020).

[24] L Waddington, 'The European Union and the United Nations Convention on the Rights of Persons with Disabilities: A Story of Exclusive and Shared Competences' (2011) 18(4) *Maastricht Journal of European and Comparative Law* 431.

[25] S Favalli and D Ferri, 'Defining Disability in the European Union Non-discrimination Legislation: Judicial Activism and Legislative Restraints' (2016) 22(3) *European Public Law* 541.

[26] L Waddington, 'Saying all the right things and still getting it wrong: The Court of Justice's definition of disability and non-discrimination law' (2015) 22(4) *Maastricht Journal of European and Comparative Law* 576.

[27] A Lejeune, 'Disability Rights and Cross-National Disparities in Europe' (2022) 121(833) *Current History* 90–95.

[28] D Ferri, 'The role of the European Union in ensuring accessibility of cultural goods and services: All about that … internal market?' (2023) 48(3) *European Law Review* 257.

published works,[29] and the accessibility of audiovisual media services.[30] This also invites stronger and deeper harmonisation efforts from the EU to close the discrepancies in disability rights protection that persist across the EU. Indeed, the revision of the Audiovisual Media Services Directive provides a good example of a relatively successful attempt to close divergent implementation of EU disability rights protection through the revision of the legislation that establishes those protections.[31]

In summary, the EU has the necessary competence to adopt legislation that strongly protects disability rights, both legislative institutions have at various points publicly supported the adoption of progressive disability legislation, and there are sound political and legal rationales for the adoption of such legislation. However, the EU legislative institutions have not always found it straightforward to make good on their responsibility to protect the quarter of Europe's population who have a disability. The rest of this chapter examines this difficulty. The following section presents three case studies of EU disability legislation for the purpose of extracting common factors that might block the passage of progressive EU disability legislation.

3. Case Studies of EU Disability Legislation

As the title of this chapter suggests, the EU's record in legislating on disability rights is mixed. There have been some successes that have been hailed as triumphs for advancing the disability rights agenda. There have been some gains that, although will no doubt improve the lives of persons with disabilities, are clearly missed opportunities to adopt more comprehensive protections. There have also been frustrating delays in the adoption of essential protections that persons with disabilities living in modern Europe should expect to enjoy. This section considers an example of each. First, it considers the Directive establishing the European Disability Card and European Parking Card, which was adopted very swiftly and represents a clear win for disability rights advocates. Second, it considers the EAA, which was passed after several years of negotiations, but was far more limited in scope than disability rights advocates called for. Finally, it considers the stalled Horizontal Equality Directive, a piece of legislation proposed by the Commission in 2008, but which has no realistic prospect of being adopted in the near future, despite the increasing exasperation of both politicians and civil society. These

[29] D Ferri and K Donnellan, 'The Implementation of the Marrakesh Directive: A Comparative Analysis across Six EU Member States' (2022) 44(5) *European Intellectual Property Review* 257.

[30] V Tudisco, 'Accessibility of Audiovisual Media Services for Persons with Disabilities in the European Union: Lights and Shadows of the Audiovisual Media Services Directive' (2022) 6 *Sant'Anna Legal Studies Research Paper*.

[31] Ibid.

three case studies are presented with a view to then identifying the factors that might block the passage of progressive disability rights legislation.

3.1. The Directive Establishing the European Disability Card

The adoption of legislation to create a European Disability Card has been lauded by disability advocates as a 'major advance' for the freedoms of people with disabilities in the EU, which met most of the demands they made during the legislative negotiations.[32] The legislation creates a card[33] that serves as recognised proof of disability in all Member States, and which grants special conditions and preferential treatment when accessing public or private services.

There is a strong rationale for introducing the card. The Strategy 2021-2030 notes that people with disabilities may experience difficulties in having their disability status recognised in another Member State. These difficulties are well known,[34] and were reinforced by the results of the Commission's public consultation.[35] To test the benefits that mutual recognition of disability status could offer to persons with disabilities, a pilot European Disability Card was organised in eight Member States. The Commission's proposal[36] for a Directive establishing the European Disability Card in all Member States, published in September 2023, noted the success of the pilot in improving the lives of people with disabilities.[37]

Negotiations on the legislation were rapid. The Council adopted its position on the Commission proposal unusually quickly, pushed forward by the Spanish Presidency.[38] The EP adopted its position even faster, working directly with civil

[32] EDF, 'Agreement on the European Disability Card: major advance for freedom of movement' (8 February 2024) available at <https://www.edf-feph.org/agreement-on-the-european-disability-card-major-advance-for-freedom-of-movement/>.

[33] The legislation also enhances the current European Parking Card, however the focus of this case study will be on the European Disability Card as a new initiative.

[34] F Sanden, 'For a European Disability Card that makes the freedom of movement accessible' (19 January 2023) available at <https://enil.eu/for-a-european-disability-card-that-makes-the-freedom-of-movement-accessible/>.

[35] Commission, 'More than 2,500 persons with disabilities contribute to the European Disability Card initiative' (Press Release, 4 September 2023) available at <https://employment-social-affairs.ec.europa.eu/news/more-2500-persons-disabilities-contribute-european-disability-card-initiative-2023-09-04_en>.

[36] Commission, 'Proposal for a Directive of the European Parliament and of the Council establishing the European Disability Card and the European Parking Card for persons with disabilities' COM (2023) 512 final.

[37] As detailed in Commission, 'Study assessing the implementation of the pilot action on the EU Disability Card and associated benefits – Final report' (Publications Office of the European Union 2021).

[38] EDF, 'European Disability Card: unusually fast agreement on Council of the EU's position' (5 December 2023) available at <https://www.edf-feph.org/european-disability-card-unusually-fast-agreement-on-council-of-the-eus-position/>.

society to adopt amendments that broadened the scope of the Commission's proposal. Although there were notable discrepancies between the positions of the Council and the Parliament – the most salient being whether access to social security and disability support services would be covered by the legislation – these discrepancies were resolved during only two trilogue sessions that lasted less than one month. Political agreement on the legislation was reached in February 2024, less than six months after the publication of the Commission's proposal.

The speed of the negotiations is likely attributable to the absence of a clash of vested interests over any of the key aspects of the legislation, as well as to the broad base of support for the issue of improving service access for persons with disabilities. Virtually every amendment requested by the EP could be agreed to by the Council because they were largely of a technical nature, with few resource allocation implications. The one point of disagreement on access to social security may have been resolved quickly because there were strong legal reasons for the Council not to move from its position. The Commission impact assessment had already dismissed any option that would impact social security arrangements as lacking political feasibility.[39] A common definition of disability and harmonisation of disability assessment procedures, which would have led to social security access being covered by the card, was further dismissed due to a lack of proportionality and legal basis for harmonisation. There was also clear opposition by the Member States, who were not willing to give up their national competence over disability assessment. Moreover, the coordination of social security is already regulated at EU level. Consequently, the one potential blockage was disposed of quickly, and the legislation could move forward.

3.2. The European Accessibility Act

The European Accessibility Act[40] was a long time in the making, and when finally adopted was greeted with mixed feelings by disability advocates, who regretted the limited scope of the legislation but still acknowledged the step forward for disability rights that it represented.[41] The legislation aims to improve the functioning of the internal market for accessible products, and in so doing set out a series

[39] Commission, 'Commission Staff Working Document Executive Summary of the Impact Assessment Report Accompanying the document Proposal for a Directive the European Parliament and of the Council establishing the European Disability Card and the European Parking Card for persons with disabilities' SWD(2023) 290 final.

[40] Directive (EU) 2019/882 of the European Parliament and of the Council of 17 April 2019 on the accessibility requirements for products and services [2019] OJ L151/70.

[41] EDF, 'Our analysis of the European Accessibility Act' (7 June 2019) available at <https://www.edf-feph.org/newsroom-news-our-analysis-european-accessibility-act/>; European Blind Union, 'The European Accessibility Act' (5 February 2020) available at <https://www.euroblind.org/campaigns-and-activities/finished-campaigns-and-activities/european-accessibility-act>.

of accessibility requirements that must be met by products and services, largely in the digital sector. Computers, ATMs, television and telephony equipment, audio-visual media services, banking services and e-books are among the products and services covered.

There was again a strong rationale for this legislation. Persons with disabilities have always faced barriers in the use of many products and services. The increasing importance of digital technologies complicates this, since these technologies offer opportunities to close the accessibility gap while raising accessibility issues themselves.[42] Lack of accessibility to products and services deprives persons with disabilities of important consumer rights,[43] and often can constitute discrimination.[44] Moreover, economic operators face market barriers both where persons with disabilities cannot access their products or services, as well as where there is less demand for accessible products and services in the absence of requirements for them to be easily available to persons with disabilities.[45] Scholars have noted the relative ineffectiveness of general human rights frameworks in securing product and service accessibility and consequently the increased importance of specific legislative intervention.[46] Again, the Commission's Impact Assessment and public consultation confirmed the significant added value to both free trade and rights protection of EU accessibility legislation.[47]

The proposal of the EAA was therefore a significant opportunity to create accessibility protections for persons with disabilities that improved their socio-economic participation across various sectors. Indeed, the Commission's legislative proposal[48] envisaged horizontal action on the basis that 'accessibility is at the heart of the [CRPD]' and that an 'environment where products and services are more accessible allows for more inclusion and participation of citizens in society'.[49] However, the negotiations produced a piece of legislation

[42] F Botelho, 'Accessibility to digital technology: Virtual barriers, real opportunities' (2021) 33(1) *Assistive Technology* 27–34.

[43] A Micovic, 'Consumer Right to Product Accessibility' (2020) 54 *Zbornik Radova* 1433–1452.

[44] M Liisberg, 'Accessibility of services and discrimination: Concentricity, consequence, and the concept of anticipatory reasonable adjustment' (2015) 15(1-2) *International Journal of Discrimination and the Law* 123–144.

[45] Deloitte, 'Study on the socio-economic impact of new measures to improve accessibility of goods and services for people with disabilities – Final Report' (European Commission 2015).

[46] J Miller, 'Strengthening the Rights of Persons with Disabilities in Europe to Access Goods and Services' (2024) 15(2) *European Journal of Legal Studies* 173–213.

[47] Commission, 'Commission Staff Working Document Impact Assessment Accompanying the document Proposal for a Directive of the European Parliament and of the Council on the approximation of the laws, regulations and administrative provisions of the Member States as regards accessibility requirements for products and services' SWD(2015) 264 final.

[48] Commission, 'Proposal for a Directive of the European Parliament and of the Council on the approximation of the laws, regulations and administrative provisions of the Member States as regards the accessibility requirements for products and services' COM(2015) 615 final.

[49] Ibid 2.

that was considerably more restricted in scope, confined largely to the digital sector. Conflict during the negotiations was precipitated by the largely divergent positions adopted by the EP and the Council. The EP eventually advocated a reasonably progressive and broad act[50] despite the initial rapporteur report[51] having rejected the mainstreaming of accessibility into product and services regulation.[52] The Council, by contrast, embraced a limited sectoral approach[53] that prioritised the interests of economic operators. Negotiations were consequently long, requiring seven trilogues, but ultimately reached a position of compromise. It appears that a major factor in the ability of negotiators to reach this position was a belief that there was a balance to be struck between protecting disability rights and protecting businesses. The balance eventually struck may not have pleased everyone, but the institutions nonetheless were committed to the idea – several of the leading negotiators made a point of speaking publicly about it, including the EP's rapporteur[54] and the EEP Group's Shadow Rapporteur.[55]

Despite the EAA and the Directive establishing the European Disability Card both being pieces of legislation that were designed to enhance disability rights protection, the difference in negotiating experience was stark. This difference can possibly be attributed to the extent to which vested interests were implicated by the content of the EAA. The EP's Committee on Petitions produced an analysis in 2016 that noted the concerns raised in the Council's Working Party on Social Questions regarding the allegedly disproportionate burden that the proposed legislation would have on businesses. Business groups across various sectors were vocal about their opposition to the scope of the legislation,[56] and the Member States themselves were hesitant to endorse horizontal action that would have

[50] EP, 'Amendments adopted by the European Parliament on 14 September 2017 on the proposal for a directive of the European Parliament and of the Council on the approximation of the laws, regulations and administrative provisions of the Member States as regards the a directive on the accessibility requirements for products and services' P8_TA(2017)0347.

[51] EP, 'Draft report on the proposal for a directive of the European Parliament and of the Council on the approximation of the laws, regulations and administrative provisions of the Member States as regards the accessibility requirements for products and services' PR\1113653EN.

[52] For criticism from advocates, see Age Platform Europe, 'Age Sends Joint Letter to Members of the European Parliament on EU Accessibility Act' available at <https://www.age-platform.eu/age-sends-joint-letter-to-members-of-the-european-parliament-on-eu-accessibility-act/>.

[53] Council, 'Proposal for a Directive of the European Parliament and of the Council on the approximation of the laws, regulations and administrative provisions of the Member States as regards the accessibility requirements for products and services – General approach' 15586/17.

[54] Parlementaire Monitor, 'European Accessibility Act: Parliament and Council negotiators strike a deal' (8 November 2018) available at <https://www.parlementairemonitor.nl/9353000/1/j9vvij5epmj1ey0/vktapthhubzf?ctx=vi03gkztbfkx&tab=1&start_tab0=430>.

[55] EPP Group, 'The European Accessibility Act: What did Europe and the EPP Group do for me?' (7 May 2019) available at <https://www.eppgroup.eu/newsroom/the-european-accessibility-act>.

[56] EurActive, 'Special Report European Accessibility Act' (5–9 December 2016) available at <https://euractiv.eu/wp-content/uploads/sites/2/special-report/EURACTIV-Special-Report-European-Accessibility-Act-1.pdf>.

heavy financial implications for businesses.[57] Indeed, lobbying from the business sector on the scope of the legislation was intense – lobbyists were hired to convince the EU institutions to weaken the Commission's proposal and clearly had some success: the EP's Internal Market and Consumer Protection Committee (IMCO Committee) produced a report in April 2017 that distinctly reflected business interests.[58] Of course, lobbying from disability advocates was equally intense and with equal effectiveness – some of the protections removed by the IMCO Committee report were reinserted by final amendments placed before the plenary vote of the EP on the proposal.[59] Business groups vowed to fight the more progressive amendments and signalled their intention to lobby the Council to resist a broad scope for the legislation.[60]

The clear polarisation between industry and civil society over the scope of the EAA was a central factor in the length and difficulty of the negotiations. Key sticking points were the extent to which accessibility requirements applied to the built environment, the obligations placed on small businesses, and the variety of services covered. Member States were evidently fearful of the significant investment required in public infrastructure, and most clearly could not countenance a law that caused difficulties for industry, who themselves were unwilling (under the guise of concern that accessibility requirements could stifle innovation that eventually leads to greater accessibility) to trade profits for disability protections. The theme of conflict of interests also characterises the negotiations on the Horizontal Equality Directive – however, where the conflicts could be resolved in the case of the EAA, this has not been possible for the Horizontal Equality Directive.

3.3. The Horizontal Equality Directive

The proposed Horizontal Equality Directive has been the most controversial and frustrating piece of EU legislation in recent years for the disability rights movement. The purpose of the legislation is to extend prohibitions on discrimination on grounds of disability, religious belief, age and sexual orientation to

[57] Council, 'Proposal for a Directive of the European Parliament and of the Council on the approximation of the laws, regulations and administrative provisions of the Member States as regards the accessibility requirements for products and services – Progress Report' 14463/16.

[58] European Union of the Deaf, 'Adoption of a European Parliament committee report on the draft European Accessibility Act' (14 July 2017) available at <https://www.eud.eu/adoption-of-a-european-parliament-committee-report-on-the-draft-european-accessibility-act/>.

[59] Z Radosavljevic, 'Løkkegaard: Amended Accessibility Act should pass in Parliament' (*EurActive*, 12 September 2017) available at <https://www.euractiv.com/section/public-transport-accessibility/interview/lokkegaard-mep-amended-accessibility-act-should-pass-in-parliament/>; C Coveney, 'The Role of the European Disability Forum and Disability Organisations in Shaping EU Disability Policy' in this volume.

[60] Business Europe, 'Plenary vote on European Accessibility Act: several steps in the right direction' (Press Release, 14 September 2017) available at <https://www.businesseurope.eu/publications/plenary-vote-european-accessibility-act-several-steps-right-direction>.

situations outside of employment and training. The proposal[61] for the Directive was published by the Commission in 2008, but negotiations are currently blocked by the Council.[62]

As with the European Disability Card and the EAA, there is a convincing rationale for EU legislation that extends the prohibition of discrimination on grounds including disability outside the workplace. As with those other pieces of disability legislation, this proposal is a progression rather than a revolution, given that it will build on multiple existing equal treatment directives.[63] Indeed, it will not be the first to extend equal treatment rights in a social context, since the Race Equality Directive provides for equal treatment in all areas. As many civil society organisations have pointed out, it is unacceptable that a hierarchy of discrimination grounds exists within EU law, with persons with disabilities in particular still not enjoying basic equality protections in many aspects of daily life. Although this hierarchy is a product of political realities rather than a conscious decision that some types of equality are more worthy than others,[64] weaker protection of the right to equality for people with disabilities is the practical effect of current EU law. The need for the EU to act in this space is evident, in light of the highly uneven levels of protection against disability discrimination across the Member States.[65]

Consequently, the Commission's proposal for a Horizontal Equality Directive that extends the right to equal treatment for persons with disabilities to all areas was warmly welcomed by disability advocates. However, the hope has turned to exasperation, as negotiations between the EP and the Council have been stuck for a number of years,[66] with little realistic prospect of them progressing in the

[61] Commission, 'Proposal for a Council Directive on implementing the principle of equal treatment between persons irrespective of religion or belief, disability, age or sexual orientation' COM(2008) 426 final.

[62] Several Member States have at some point expressed reservations about the proposal, but most worryingly Germany seems to be opposed to the legislation. See Equinet, 'Horizontal Equal Treatment Directive (Fifth Directive) – The state of play' (June 2015) available at <https://equineteurope.org/wp-content/uploads/2015/07/annegaspard-equinet_presentation_state_of_play-berlin_en.pdf>.

[63] Directive 2000/43/EC of 29 June 2000 implementing the principle of equal treatment between persons irrespective of racial or ethnic origin [2000] OJ L180/22; Directive 2000/78/EC of 27 November 2000 establishing a general framework for equal treatment in employment and occupation [2000] OJ L303/16; Directive 2004/113/EC of 13 December 2004 implementing the principle of equal treatment between men and women in the access to and supply of goods and services [2004] OJ L373/37.

[64] E Howard, 'The Case for a Considered Hierarchy of Discrimination Grounds in EU Law' (2006) 13(4) *Maastricht Journal of European and Comparative Law* 445–470.

[65] T Bratan *et al.*, 'Implementation of the UN Convention on the Rights of Persons with Disabilities: A Comparison of Four European Countries with Regards to Assistive Technologies' (2020) 10(4) *Societies* 74–99; Lejeune (n 27).

[66] In the latest progress report, Czechia and Denmark are maintaining parliamentary scrutiny reservations, while all Member States are maintaining general scrutiny reservations. Council, 'Proposal for a Council Directive on implementing the principle of equal treatment between persons irrespective of religion or belief, disability, age or sexual orientation – Progress Report' 13070/22.

near future.[67] In a similar manner to the EAA, the EP recommended extensions to the scope and substance of the Commission proposal.[68] In recent years, the EP have issued statements of support that have grown increasingly insistent and frustrated.[69] However, unlike the process for adopting the EAA, the Horizontal Equality Directive is based on the competence provided by Article 19 TFEU, which calls for use of the special legislative procedure in which the Council is the sole legislator and the EP has only a right of consent. Article 19 TFEU also calls for unanimity in the Council, and since the Council has been unable to agree on the contents of this Directive, the negotiations have stalled. Although several issues have been resolved, the remaining points of contention appear to be, at least according to the Council itself, questions over whether the Directive respects the principles of legal certainty and subsidiarity, concerns over the implementation costs of the Directive, and the need for clarification on the effects of the reasonable accommodation provisions.[70]

There have been multiple attempts to unblock the Council's negotiations. Some Member States proposed use of the enhanced cooperation procedure, but this was rejected, sensibly so because it would have widened already existing differences in disability rights protection between the Member States.[71] The Commission proposed the activation of the *passarelle* clauses in the TFEU to move non-discrimination to a policy that is subject to the ordinary legislative procedure and thus qualified majority voting in the Council,[72] but this has not been taken up. Many revisions have been made to the substance of the proposal in an effort to generate agreement, yet common ground has proven elusive and some revisions have even been counterproductive. For example, one of the latest revisions inserted a provision that allowed Member States to temporarily exempt themselves from the reasonable accommodation requirement. This was widely acknowledged, including by several Member States, to be incompatible with the CRPD, and hence it received mixed support and subsequently was removed.[73]

[67] '[T]here is clearly a need for significant further work before the required unanimity can be reached in the Council'. Council, 'Proposal for a Council Directive on implementing the principle of equal treatment between persons irrespective of religion or belief, disability, age or sexual orientation – Progress Report' 9043/23 5.

[68] EP, 'European Parliament legislative resolution of 2 April 2009 on the proposal for a Council directive on implementing the principle of equal treatment between persons irrespective of religion or belief, disability, age or sexual orientation' P6_TA(2009)0211.

[69] EP, 'Resolution of 21 January 2021 on the EU Strategy for Gender Equality' P9_TA(2021)0025; 'Resolution of 10 November 2022 on racial justice, non-discrimination and anti-racism in the EU' P9_TA(2022)0389; 'Resolution of 19 April 2023 on combatting discrimination in the EU – the long-awaited horizontal anti-discrimination directive' P9_TA(2023)0111.

[70] Steering note prepared by Council Presidency on the policy debate, 13070/22, 26 May 2023; Progress report of 23 May 2023.

[71] Equinet (n 62).

[72] Commission, 'More efficient decision-making in social policy: Identification of areas for an enhanced move to qualified majority voting' COM(2019) 186 final.

[73] Council, 'Proposal for a Council Directive on implementing the principle of equal treatment between persons irrespective of religion or belief, disability, age or sexual orientation – Progress Report' 13070/22.

The factors causing the impasse on the Horizontal Equality Directive within the Council are similar to those that slowed the passage of the EAA, in that there is a lack of political enthusiasm on the part of some Member States[74] to commit themselves and economic operators to the significant financial investment that is required to fully realise the rights of persons with disabilities. As has been pointed out, this economic argument is invalid due to the known gains in productivity and reductions in financial dependence that would result from the fuller participation of persons with disabilities.[75] While the Member States were able to agree a balance between protection of disability rights and protection of business interests in the case of the EAA, the same strategy is not possible in the case of the Horizontal Equality Directive. As civil society organisations have pointed out, equal treatment is not something that can be balanced – people are either protected from discrimination on particular grounds or they are not.[76] The economic consequences of extending equal treatment rights into many new social circumstances may therefore prompt some Member States to reject equal treatment rather than accept the economic consequences. This may also be the case in relation to the impact upon a Member State's legal system. One of the sticking points for the Directive seems to be the articulation and scope of the right to reasonable accommodation for persons with disabilities. Although the exact motivations of the reticent Member States are unknown, some may be unwilling to accept the significant changes to their national legal system that would be prompted by the adoption of an already contested concept[77] in a far broader piece of EU equality law. Indeed, in the absence of a harmonised EU approach to the activation of the reasonable accommodation duty in the employment context,[78] Member States have adopted many very different legal approaches to the issue.[79] A report for the Commission that analysed how Member States have approached the reasonable accommodation duty outside the employment field found immense diversity, with only a partial overlap between existing national duties and the scope of the proposed Horizontal Equality Directive, and some State constitutions expressly adopting a functional understanding of disability in

[74] It is widely known that Germany has long been a strident opponent of the legislation, although the exact reasons remain unclear.

[75] K Hugendubel, 'Germany's equality paradox' (*EUObserver*, 23 July 2015) available at <https://euobserver.com/health-and-society/129747>.

[76] Age Platform Europe, 'Equality for all: NGOs work together to unblock non-discrimination directive' (23 March 2015) available at <https://www.age-platform.eu/equality-for-all-ngos-work-together-to-unblock-non-discrimination-directive/>.

[77] L Waddington, 'When It is Reasonable for Europeans to be Confused: Understanding When a Disability Accommodation is Reasonable from a Comparative Perspective' (2008) 29 *Comparative Labor Law & Policy Journal* 317–340; P Daly and D Whelan, 'Disability in employment equality law: A reappraisal of the reasonable accommodation duty and issues arising in its implementation' (2021) 28(6) *Maastricht Journal of European and Comparative Law* 744–759.

[78] Although there is no legislative harmonisation, the CJEU has engaged in a judicial harmonisation of the meaning of reasonable accommodation and the circumstances in which the duty arises, although there are still gaps in its interpretations. T Gyulavári, 'Recent CJEU case law on 'reasonable accommodation' at work: towards the recognition of a new discrimination form' (2023) 24 *ERA Forum* 361–377.

[79] Daly and Whelan (n 77).

contrast to the social model adopted by the CRPD.[80] Consequently, it is entirely plausible that some Member States are resistant to EU law that would force fundamental reforms to such delicate areas of national law, or even the need for constitutional revision.

4. Common Issues that Delay or Block EU Social Legislation

The comparison between these case studies reveals important factors that determine the ability of the EU legislative institutions to adopt progressive social legislation. Primarily, these factors concern conflict in the legislative process – some relate to the conflict between different policy interests, and to the conflict between policy ideas and legal doctrine. The success of the EU legislator in adopting progressive disability rights legislation is ultimately therefore determined by how well this conflict can be overcome, or at least managed. In many ways this is not surprising – the EU legislative process is often characterised by institutional conflict, given it is designed to balance the needs of EU citizens with the needs of Member States. However, what these case studies reveal is that the substance of progressive disability rights proposals has the potential to exacerbate and sharpen the inherent conflict in the EU legislative process, such that the passage of these proposals becomes more an exercise in finding a compromise between stakeholder interests than in problem-solving what will best improve European society.[81] Given this, the EU legislature plays a key role as a forum for finding compromise – a role that it is sometimes, but not always, able to fulfil.

The key factors explored below are the capture of legislative institutions (4.1.), the polarisation of stakeholder positions (4.2.), the competence gap in EU disability policy (4.3.), and the legal weakness of the EU's disability mainstreaming obligations (4.4.). Factors related to conflicting ideas and doctrines will likely always prevent the adoption of certain progressive legislation, however factors related to conflicting interests are possible to overcome. These factors are explored below in a manner that demonstrates that they are not unique to disability policy.

4.1. Legislative Capture

The case studies most clearly demonstrate that the 'capture'[82] of one of the legislative institutions by corporate interests will slow, if not stop, the progress of

[80] L Waddington *et al.*, 'Disability law and reasonable accommodation beyond employment: A legal analysis of the situation in EU Member States' (European Commission 2016).

[81] P Elgoibar *et al.*, 'Conflict Management' in *Oxford Research Encyclopedia of Psychology* (Oxford University Press 2017).

[82] For a theorisation of capture, see C Devaux, 'Towards a legal theory of capture' (2018) 24 *European Law Journal* 458–473.

progressive social legislation. Legislative capture occurs when the legislative branch is persuaded by vested interests (usually corporations) through lobbying to think in the same way and to adopt their preferred stance on a particular policy issue. Capture of the Parliament[83] and the Council[84] is equally possible for different reasons. The Council might be attractive as a target because it offers a number of indirect access points through legislatures and public bodies in the Member States; lobbyists can lean on sensitive national interests, and only a small number of Council members are required to fundamentally alter the direction of EU policy. Conversely, the EP might also be an attractive target on account of a similarly large number of access points through committees and the large number of MEPs, and the fact that lobbyists can play to the political ambitions or personal beliefs of MEPs. The best capture strategy for special interest groups depends upon the nature of the issue

Capture of the legislature and legislative process can have a profound impact upon the direction of entire social policy fields,[85] depending on whether the interests of powerful stakeholders are sufficiently engaged. The European Disability Card raised no significant resource redistribution issues, while the EAA and the Horizontal Equality Directive raised them to a moderate extent and a severe extent respectively. It is unsurprising that with lower pressure of vested commercial interests in the legislative process,[86] the European Disability Card was rapidly negotiated, while the EAA and the Horizontal Equality Directive, in contexts involving significant pressure from economic operators, have been respectively delayed and halted. It is possible that the Council has been captured on the issues of reasonable accommodation and implementation costs and thus is largely responsible for the stalling of the Horizontal Equality Directive. There are several Council members that wish to press ahead with the Directive, however a minority do not, and in a policy area that employs unanimous voting one member is all that is required to capture the whole Council.

The impact of corporate capture is evident in other areas of EU social policy. The capture of the Council has been evident recently in the last-minute delay to the adoption of the Supply Chain Directive,[87] which several of the large

[83] For an example of EP capture, see H Meier *et al.*, 'The Capture of EU Football Regulation by the Football Governing Bodies' (2023) 61(3) *Journal of Common Market Studies* 692–711.

[84] For examples of how the UK (while a Member State) was a channel for capture of the Council on various policy initiatives, see Corporate Europe Observatory, 'Captured states: when EU governments are a channel for corporate interests' (6 February 2019) available at <https://corporateeurope.org/en/2019/02/captured-states#:~:text=Member%20states%20play%20a%20hugely%20important%20role%20in,can%20do%20about%20it.%20Download%20the%20full%20report.>.

[85] J MacLean, 'Striking at the Root Problem of Canadian Environmental Law: Identifying and Escaping Regulatory Capture' (2016) 29 *Journal of Environmental Law and Practice* 111–128.

[86] As has been pointed out, vested interests are incentivised to intervene in the policymaking process when faced with legislative developments that threaten them. Conversely, where legislative developments are benign to vested interests, there is less reason for them to press against them. T Moe, 'Vested Interests and Political Institutions' (2015) 130(2) *Political Science Quarterly* 277–318.

[87] Commission, 'Proposal for a Directive on Corporate Sustainability Due Diligence and amending Directive (EU) 2019/1937' COM(2022) 71 final.

Member States temporarily refused to back because of concerns surrounding business competitiveness. The lack of support from at least two large Member States meant that the qualified majority threshold was not reached, and the passage of the Directive was held up while last minute wrangling took place.[88] The EP is equally open to influence and capture[89] – this is evident, for example, in the recent votes against the prospect of harmonised rules that the Commission has promised to propose on health warning labels for alcoholic beverages. A number of MEPs have recited alcohol industry arguments regarding warning labels during debates, and the evident lack of support amongst MEPs has generated a significant risk that, in the context of a policy field in which the Commission is already reticent to propose legislation, the Commission's appetite for pursuing this policy will disappear.

4.2. Stakeholder Polarisation

The case studies also demonstrate that polarisation of the positions of stakeholders – usually civil society on one side and industry on the other – on a policy issue will create conditions in which it is far easier for the legislative institutions to allow policy development to stagnate. The public consultation undertaken to inform the adoption of the European Disability Card showed that there was broad stakeholder support for such a card.[90] The consultations conducted by the Commission in advance of proposals for the EAA[91] and the Horizontal Equality Directive[92] demonstrated that stakeholders were far more polarised in their views.

Stakeholder polarisation can also be observed in other social policy areas in which progress on progressive legislation has been slow or non-existent. Alcohol policy again provides a good example. The conflict between the alcohol

[88] The blockage was cleared when Italy's interests in the content of the directive were satisfied, and it switched sides to back it. P Blenkinsop, 'EU backs supply chain audit law after Italy switches sides' (15 March 2024) available at <https://www.reuters.com/sustainability/boards-policy-regulation/eu-envoys-clear-proposed-supply-chain-audit-law-belgian-presidency-says-2024-03-15/>.

[89] M Rasmussen, 'The Battle for Influence: The Politics of Business Lobbying in the European Parliament' (2015) 53(2) *Journal of Common Market Studies* 365–382.

[90] Commission, 'Factual summary report of the online public consultation in support of the European Disability Card and the European Parking Card initiative' Ares(2023)5961542.

[91] For example, on the contentious question of accessibility requirements in the built environment, the public consultation found that businesses considered such requirements difficult and costly while feeling that a greater level of progress had been achieved in increasing accessibility in the built environment, while citizens considered built environment accessibility requirements to be of high importance while feeling that a weaker level of progress had been achieved in this area. See Deloitte, 'Study on the socio-economic impact of new measures to improve accessibility of goods and services for people with disabilities: Public Consultation Analysis' available at <https://ec.europa.eu/social/BlobServlet?docId=14842&langId=en>.

[92] Citizens and NGOs expressed a desire for legislation, but businesses expressed the opposite. Commission, 'Commission Staff Working Document accompanying the Proposal for a Council Directive on equal treatment: Summary of the Impact Assessment' SEC(2008) 2181.

industry and civil society creates a policy space in which the Commission is caught between two incompatible policy positions,[93] and it is unsurprising therefore that the Commission has been slow in making progress on alcohol control policies. A similar polarised policy space can be observed in other controversial social policy areas such as environmental policy,[94] illustrating that this is a common phenomenon where sensitive policy proposals that have a direct impact upon the financial interests of powerful businesses are being debated. In such situations there is a clear disincentive for the EU legislative institutions to spend political capital on reconciling incompatible policy positions, making inaction an attractive and oft-taken solution.

4.3. Competence Gap

The case studies also demonstrate that the EU's legislative competences still do not match the social policy ambitions of the Commission. There is no specific competence for disability legislation, only a requirement to mainstream disability equality concerns into other EU policy activities. The fact that the Council must still take decisions by unanimity with respect to alternative competences that are employed to advance EU social policy acts as a distinct brake on progress. The Equal Treatment Directive clearly illustrates this – the requirement of Article 19 TFEU for unanimity puts non-discrimination legislation at the mercy of national political priorities and corporate interests. The European Disability Card also illustrates the problem of decision-making by unanimity in social policy areas, since access to social security and disability services was excluded from the scope of the card on account of the difficulty of getting Member States to agree on further harmonisation of their social security policies, another area subject to unanimous decision-making in the Council. The need to use alternative competences to advance disability policy in the absence of a specific competence has further knock-on effects for the adoption of disability legislation. The EAA provides a good illustration of how the use of the internal market harmonisation competence to advance a social policy objective can lead to compromises in the substance of the legislation.[95] In the case of the EAA, the need to remove internal market barriers

[93] For example, the Commission recently consulted on whether to extend the scope of labelling requirements in the Food Information to Consumers Regulation to alcoholic beverages through physical labelling or online information provision. All stakeholder groups apart from the alcohol industry were overwhelmingly in favour of physical labels, while the alcohol industry was clearly in favour of online provision or nothing at all. Commission, 'Factual summary report of the online public consultation in support of the revision of the Food Information to Consumers regulation' Ares(2022)3403916.

[94] A Bunea, 'Sharing ties and preferences: Stakeholders' position alignments in the European Commission's open consultations' (2015) 16(2) *European Union Politics* 281–299.

[95] For a broader discussion how the use of non-social policy competences to achieve social policy objectives can both facilitate and hinder the achievement of those objectives, see E Muir, 'Drawing Positive Lessons From the Presence of 'The Social' Outside of EU Social Policy Stricto Sensu' (2018) 14 *European Constitutional Law Review* 75–95.

probably generated a window for arguments on business competitiveness to influence lawmakers away from adopting those standards that would have required the greatest level of investment.[96]

This competence gap is not by any means unique to disability policy. Alcohol and tobacco policy again provide good examples. The Commission for many years attempted to raise the minimum rates of alcohol excise that Member States must collect. The existing legislation[97] was adopted under Article 113 TFEU, the competence to harmonise tax rules, which also requires unanimity in the Council. After proposing revised legislation in 2006, the Commission eventually dropped the proposal in 2015, citing the improbability of agreement in the foreseeable future.[98] Although the EU's tobacco policy is generally thought to be progressive and successful, the original Tobacco Advertising Directive[99] would have gone much further than the Directive that was eventually adopted,[100] since the need to use Article 114 TFEU in the absence of a competence to harmonise Member State laws for the purpose of protecting public health meant that the legislature did not have the power to regulate forms of tobacco advertising which are not cross-border in nature.

4.4. Weak Mainstreaming Obligations

The case studies are also illustrative of the lack of legal force that the policy mainstreaming obligations in Articles 9 and 10 TFEU seem to have. As Muir and colleagues have observed, these provisions have at times influenced the policy-making process, so the problem of why they have not played a more significant role in the achievement of EU social policy objectives seems not to be attributable to any inherent political reticence to use them, but rather to their lack of legal substance.[101] The fact that some successful mainstreaming of disability rights has been achieved in the context of relatively uncontroversial issues that require little

[96] There is not only a need to visibly address internal market barriers when using Article 114 TFEU, but the range of social policy interventions possible under Article 114 TFEU is also necessarily limited. V Delhomme, 'Emancipating Health from the Internal Market: For a Stronger EU (Legislative) Competence in Public Health' (2020) 11 *European Journal of Risk Regulation* 747–756.

[97] Council Directive 92/84/EEC on the approximation of the rates of excise duty on alcohol and alcoholic beverages [1992] OJ L316/29.

[98] Commission, 'Commission Work Programme 2015 – A New Start' COM(2014) 910 final Annex 2 para 24.

[99] Directive 98/43/EC of the European Parliament and of the Council of 6 July 1998 on the approximation of the laws, regulations and administrative provisions of the Member States relating to the advertising and sponsorship of tobacco products [1998] OJ L213/9.

[100] Directive 2003/33/EC of the European Parliament and of the Council of 26 May 2003 on the approximation of the laws, regulations and administrative provisions of the Member States relating to the advertising and sponsorship of tobacco products [2003] OJ L152/16.

[101] E Muir *et al.*, 'The Horizontal Equality Clauses (Arts 8 & 10 TFEU) and their Contribution to the Course of EU Equality Law: Still and Empty Vessel?' (2022) 7(3) *European Papers* 1381–1403.

resource redistribution indeed points to the latter explanation. Conversely, where policies that could have an impact upon disability rights protection necessitate significant redistribution of resources, there seems to be no possibility to compel the institutions to engage in the policymaking process through a disability rights lens. This is evident in the negotiation of the EAA, where the Council simply refused to countenance the prospect of transport and built environment policy contributing to the objective of achieving equal treatment for persons with disabilities, even though disability advocates were clear that this was a major area of public policy in which persons with disabilities still face discrimination.

The weakness of Treaty mainstreaming obligations extends beyond disability policy. The vagueness of the mainstreaming obligation contained in Article 168 TFEU, and the consequent failure to put them into practice, is well known.[102] While the revision of the Audiovisual Media Services Directive was a relatively rare occasion on which disability concerns were successfully mainstreamed, it is also a glaring example of the short-sighted refusal of the opportunity to legislate in a way that better protects health.[103] The EU often struggles to adopt mainstreaming approaches to social policy issues when there is a competing initiative – sometimes there are structural[104] or political[105] factors at play, but in all instances the weakness of the Treaty obligations themselves must be considered a major reason for mainstreaming of social concerns being neglected.

5. Creative Advocacy Strategies to Unblock Legislation

The previous sections illustrated the factors that have slowed the passage of progressive disability legislation, and through a comparison to other social policy areas they further showed that these factors run deeper and broader than just disability policy. Some are clearly entrenched and will be a persistent disruptor to progress in EU social policy in the absence of Treaty reform. Competence issues and structural blocks on implementing mainstreaming approaches fall into this

[102] O Bartlett and A Naumann, 'Reinterpreting the health in all policies obligation in Article 168 TFEU: the first step towards making enforcement a realistic prospect' (2021) 16(1) *Health Economics, Policy and Law* 8–22; R Geyer and S Lightfoot, 'The Strengths and Limits of New Forms of EU Governance: The Cases of Mainstreaming and Impact Assessment in EU Public Health and Sustainable Development Policy' (2010) 32(4) *European Integration* 339–356.

[103] K Lauber and E Brooks, 'A missed opportunity for public health: How impact assessment shaped EU rules on the marketing of unhealthy commodities to children' (2024) 5 *SSM – Qualitative Research in Health* 1–25.

[104] G Allwood, 'Horizontal policy coordination and gender mainstreaming: The case of the European Union's Global Approach to Migration and Mobility' (2015) 48 *Women's Studies International Forum* 9–17.

[105] C Godziewski, 'Evidence and Power in EU Governance of Health Promotion: Discursive Obstacles to a "Health in All Policies" Approach' (2020) 58(5) *Journal of Common Market Studies* 1307–1324.

category. However, political blocks are not impossible to overcome. They are created by the interaction and alignment of vested and national interests, and thus the application of pressure in the right places could realign these interests. Disability rights advocates have been undertaking this work for decades. The adoption of the European Disability Card and the EAA are two of their prominent successes. The Horizontal Equality Directive remains a source of frustration though. When a policy impasse is reached, an effective way of advocating for progress can sometimes involve the use of litigation. Disability rights advocates are no strangers to litigation,[106] however they still have opportunities to explore alternative avenues for litigation. The European Disability Forum (EDF) states that 'EDF has mainly been intervening before the European Court of Human Rights by submitting third party interventions, also called amicus curiae briefs. EDF will also continue looking into opportunities at other regional human rights mechanisms such as the European Court of Justice or the European Social Rights Committee'.[107] This section explores the possibilities for legal strategies through which disability rights advocates could continue to apply pressure on the EU legislative institutions with the objective of securing the conditions in which interests can align towards progressive disability policy. It will draw from the experiences of civil society organisations in other policy areas which have achieved success through such strategies.

One possibility is to take advantage of the right to request documents from the EU institutions to uncover information that will help civil society to apply lobbying pressure to the EU institutions. The Council has rightly been described as a 'black hole'[108] by EDF when it comes to accessing documents. There are some sound reasons for document secrecy within the Council, however some reasons for keeping documents secret may not be so legitimate. ClientEarth has very recently achieved a major success before the General Court in this respect. In *ClientEarth and Päivi Leino-Sandberg v Council*,[109] ClientEarth argued that the Council's refusal to provide access to the opinion of its legal service on proposed revisions to the Aarhus Regulation[110] on access to justice in environmental matters was in breach of their access to documents obligations under Regulation 1049/2001. The Council had defended the partial release of the document on the

[106] See, eg, the recent complaint to the European Committee of Social Rights, European Disability Forum and Inclusion Europe v France, Complaint no 168/2018.

[107] EDF, 'Legal Remedies' available at <https://www.edf-feph.org/legal-remedies/>. See Coveney (n 59) for further discussion on advocacy strategies pursued by EDF.

[108] EDF, 'Did EU know? Council documents and how to find them' (25 November 2019) available at <https://www.edf-feph.org/newsroom-news-did-eu-know-council-documents/>.

[109] Joined Cases T-682/21 and T-683/21 *ClientEarth and Päivi Leino-Sandberg v Council* ECLI:EU:T:2024:165.

[110] Council, 'Opinion of the Legal Service. Commission proposal for a Regulation amending the "Aarhus Regulation" (Regulation (EC) No 1367/2006) – Scope of application of the proposal, and 2021 Advice of the Aarhus Convention Compliance Committee on the proposal' 8721/21 (document partially accessible to the public (6 August 2021)).

basis that the information it contained was linked to negotiations on an international agreement. However, the General Court rejected these and other arguments concerning the sensitivity of the document, and the right of access to documents was declared to be infringed by the Council's disclosure refusal. This is interesting from a disability policy perspective since it is the Council that is holding up the progress of the Horizontal Equality Directive. This is not the only success that ClientEarth has had with access to documents litigation. In *ClientEarth v Commission*[111] the CJEU held on appeal that no general presumption of confidentiality applied to Impact Assessment documents, which the Commission had refused to supply to ClientEarth on the basis that they were part of an ongoing legislative process. Disability rights advocates would have cause to explore the possibility of access to documents litigation before the CJEU to generate greater transparency in the legislative process.[112] The primary objectives would be, for example, to obtain information that would give advocates greater lobbying leverage, or to better understand the discussions and debates occurring within the institutions as to why legislation cannot move forward.

Another possibility is to engage in strategic rights litigation to target possible breaches by the Member States and the EU institutions of the rights of persons with disabilities under the EU Charter of Fundamental Rights (CFR). Disability rights advocates have already had notable successes in a variety of Member States,[113] however the use of litigation to develop a strong link between EU legislation, particularly equality legislation, and the non-discrimination rights in the CFR has been underwhelming and possibly incoherent.[114] This is perhaps one of the reasons why the Council's failure to progress the Horizontal Equality Directive has been politically decried but not challenged for so long. Projects such as LITI-GATE, which aims to 'promote enforcement of the EU Charter of Fundamental Rights with strategic litigation activities to address breaches of the fundamental rights of persons with intellectual and/or psychosocial disabilities' are therefore welcome developments.[115] The purpose of strategic rights litigation

[111] Case C-57/16P *ClientEarth v Commission* ECLI:EU:C:2018:660.

[112] There is evidence of only one ongoing attempt by a disability rights advocate to engage in access to documents litigation. See Case T-640/20 *Order of the General Court in Validity v Commission* delivered 22 November 2022; Case C-51/23P *Application for appeal against the order of the General Court* in Case T-640/20 brought on 1 February 2023.

[113] See the successful litigation undertaken by Validity in EU countries including Hungary and Czechia, available at <http://validity.ngo>. For further analysis of this work, see B Méhes, 'Strategic Litigation in Action: A Practical Experience of Litigating on Behalf of People with Psychosocial Disabilities' in S Okpaku (ed), *Innovations in Global Mental Health* (Springer 2021).

[114] A Ward, 'The Impact of the EU Charter of Fundamental Rights on Anti-Discrimination Law: More a Whimper than a Bang?' (2018) 20 *Cambridge Yearbook of European Legal Studies* 32–60.

[115] See the LITI-GATE project available at <https://forumhr.eu/strategic-litigation-as-a-gateway-to-address-the-rights-of-persons-with-disabilities-in-the-european-union/#:~:text=From%201%20September%202023%20to,Disabilities%20in%20the%20European%20Union>.

is not only to improve the access to justice that persons with disabilities are entitled to under the CRPD but often find themselves denied,[116] but also, specifically in the context of blocked EU disability rights legislation, it has the purpose of increasing pressure on the EU institutions and Member States to adopt such legislation by calling out key gaps in rights protection.

One strategy to avoid is an attempt to challenge the legislature's failure to discharge its Treaty mainstreaming obligations. Although these are obligations of primary law, it is very hard to meet the threshold required to prove that the institutions have breached them. A comparison with health mainstreaming is instructive. Although enacted EU legislation does not always ensure a high level of health protection as Article 168 TFEU demands, there has never been an instance of EU legislation being struck down because it was not protective enough of health.[117] This is because the CJEU gives the EU institutions wide discretion to determine what they consider to be a high level of health protection.[118] The same issues will apply to the disability mainstreaming obligation in Article 10 TFEU, and likely even more acutely since the phrasing 'shall aim' in Article 10 TFEU is weaker than the phrasing 'shall be ensured' in Article 168 TFEU. Although the disability mainstreaming obligation has yet to be interpreted by the CJEU, multiple Advocates General have opined that Article 10 TFEU does not in fact generate enforceable legal obligations for the EU, but merely 'articulates a particular policy aim to which the European Union is committed'.[119] If this is true, then grounding litigation in the argument that the EU should be required to make a greater effort to tackle disability discrimination appears to be a non-starter.

6. Concluding Remarks

This chapter has aimed to illustrate, through cases studies, the contribution of the EU legislature to shaping EU disability policy. To date, this contribution has been mixed and has depended upon how well conflicting interests are resolved through compromise. In many ways, the EU legislative institutions can be seen as a forum or arena for exactly this purpose, and indeed this is how they have been conceptualised in other fields of social policy that raise sensitive questions

[116] E Flynn and A Lawson, 'Disability and Access to Justice in the European Union: Implication of the United Nations Convention on the Rights of Persons with Disabilities' (2013) 4 *European Yearbook of Disability Law* 7–44.

[117] Bartlett and Naumann (n 102).

[118] Case T-177/13 *Test Bio Tech* ECLI:EU:T:2016:736.

[119] Opinion of Advocate General Wahl delivered on 26 September 2013 in Case C-363/12 *Z v A Government department and The Board of management of a community school* EU:C:2013:604, para 112; Opinion of Advocate General Jääskinen delivered on 17 July 2014 in Case C-354/13 *Fag og Arbejde (FOA) v Kommunernes Landsforening (KL)* ECLI:EU:C:2014:2106, para 23.

of resource allocation and interest conflict.[120] In the case of disability policy, the fundamental tension lies in the fact that adequately resourcing the full and equal participation of persons with disabilities in society is a significant financial and legal undertaking, and both states and economic actors are hesitant to make such commitments. What disability advocates see as a matter of fundamental rights, businesses see as a (sometimes existential) matter of competitiveness. The progress of disability rights legislation depends on the ability to find the compromise between these two positions.

The case studies revealed that there were a number of factors that affected the ability of the legislative institutions to act as a functioning forum for overcoming conflict and finding this compromise. It is clear that capture of one or the other legislative institution will preclude compromise as that institution's position will be tied to the usually intractable position of a special interest group. Stakeholder polarisation also clearly makes compromise harder since it erodes the middle ground in which the search for compromise must take place. Competence gaps and weak mainstreaming obligations both offer convenient legal rationales for those holding conservative or non-progressive positions to refuse to move closer to those holding more socially progressive positions.

The greater the economic implications of proposed disability legislation, the more pronounced these factors are, and the more likely that the EU legislature cannot serve effectively as a forum for inevitable conflict resolution. In particular, the Council has been particularly sensitive to the economic implications of disability legislation, has not always been able to facilitate a negotiated compromise between the Member States, and thus has been the main source of blockage to disability rights legislation. The secrecy and reticence that surrounds Council debates on some disability matters, in contrast to the quite open and candid manner in which MEPs have discussed the issues and arguments on such matters, means that without an effective lobbying access point it is very difficult for external stakeholders to contribute targeted arguments that might add to the search for compromise. It is tempting to see the Council as the villain of the disability rights narrative, given the way that the Parliament has proven to be an arena in which progressive sentiment flourished, with the effect of strengthening disability rights legislation. The Council is not consigned to always play this role though – the Spanish Council Presidency's facilitation of the unusually rapid agreement by the Council on the substance of the European Disability Card is evidence that the Council as an institution can be a force for advancing progressive disability legislation. The fact that the Council has also relatively quickly agreed upon the

[120] On the EP as arena in the field of climate change policy, see F Wendler, 'The European Parliament as an Arena and Agent in the Politics of Climate Change: Comparing the External and Internal Dimension' (2019) 7(3) *Politics and Governance* 327–338. On the Council as arena in the field of Covid-19 policy see T Zgaga *et al.*, 'The European Council: Actor and Arena of Dominance?' (ARENA Centre for European Studies 2023).

substance of directives to strengthen the role of equality bodies across the EU[121] is evidence that the Council is not fundamentally opposed to progressive action on disability rights, but rather that it might be prevented from acting as a force for change when issues of resource allocation and business competitiveness become impacted by proposed legislation. Unfortunately, much of the legislative interventions needed to suitably protect the rights of people with disabilities do have this impact, so it can be imagined that the Council will still at times constitute an obstacle to progressive disability legislation.

This chapter also explored potential legal strategies through which disability rights advocates could seek to loosen existing blockages to legislation. Fundamentally, the ability of disability rights advocates to influence the EU's legislative process concerns the balance of power. Vested economic interests hold considerable sway with the Parliament and the Council, while civil society organisations tend not to enjoy comparable influence with the EU's lawmakers. It is for this reason that a civil society strategy for the EU is being advocated[122] – such a strategy would aim to give civil society organisations a clearer presence in the EU Treaties and a more formal route and right of access to the EU policy process. However, the realistic prospect of Treaty and policy reform of this magnitude seems remote. For this reason, creative legal strategies are important for disability rights advocates as a way of tipping the balance of power in legislative negotiations as far as possible.

The balance certainly does need tipping. Disability rights advocates made the point in 2018, the 10th anniversary of the proposal for the Horizontal Equality Directive, that populist politics is on the rise, and that this increases the risk of marginalised groups such as persons with disabilities being scapegoated for social problems.[123] Even if not related to populism, there are worrying instances of disability rights being rolled back in some Member States,[124] let alone the widespread failings across the EU to properly implement the rights enshrined in the CRPD. People with disabilities need the EU institutions to lead by example, and in this respect the leadership of the EP and the Council is crucial. It is welcome that the

[121] Commission, 'Proposal for a Council Directive on standards for equality bodies in matters of social security and in the access to and supply of goods and services' COM(2022) 689 final; Commission, 'Proposal for a Directive of the European Parliament and Council on standards for equality bodies in matters of employment and occupation' COM(2022) 688 final.

[122] European Civic Forum, 'Towards Vibrant European Civic and Democratic Space: The case for a European civil society strategy and preliminary reflections on the gaps, challenges and opportunities to be addressed' (May 2022) available at <https://civic-forum.eu/wp-content/uploads/2022/05/European-civil-society-strategy-report-2022_European-Civic-Forum.pdf>.

[123] 'Joint NGO Statement on the 10th Anniversary of the Horizontal Directive Ten years on and nothing to show for it' (July 2018) available at <https://www.age-platform.eu/draft-eu-horizontal-non-discrimination-directive-ten-years-on-and-sadly-nothing-to-show-for-it/>.

[124] Validity, 'Czech Republic rolls back on inclusive education for children with disabilities' (11 June 2019) available at <https://validity.ngo/2019/06/11/czech-republic-rolls-back-on-inclusive-education-for-children-with-disabilities/>.

disability rights movement has found consistent support from the EP. However, the same cannot be said of the Council. Although the progressive approach to disability rights of several Member States has helped certain legislation to progress, the national interests of other Member States have prevented progress in other areas. Litigation, while potentially helpful in specific cases, is unlikely to be enough to change the way in which economic influences change the thinking of some Member States on disability rights. A more fundamental political shift is required.

6

The Role of the Court of Justice of the European Union in Protecting Disability Rights

BERNARDO CORTESE

1. Introduction: The Challenge of Looking at the Court of Justice Through a 'Relational' Prism

While sitting on a bench, and thinking about how late I was with my chapter on how the Court of Justice of the European Union ('the Court' or CJEU) has shaped disability law in the European Union (EU), I heard a rabbit protesting it was late … I followed it, and entered, with curiosity, its hole, like Alice did.[1] There, I found a kaleidoscopic prism, namely a theory of relationality in the operation of courts of law,[2] and, like Alice, I started falling and falling and falling … While in the loop of thoughts and visions, reality transformed, I saw strange relational animals – this time not Dodos, nor Mock Turtles, but *DDPs*[3] telling their stories, and a relational Queen, the CJEU – giving orders to its soldiers – the national courts … In the end, I found it was all just on paper … A dream or reality? Like Alice, I have to find my way through this enigma. That is why, in this chapter, I examine the CJEU's contribution to the protection of disability rights, by taking into account a number of relational factors.

First, the CJEU does not act in isolation, and relies upon the collaboration of other actors in order to exercise its jurisdiction: first and foremost, the national courts, within the framework of preliminary ruling procedures, as discussed by

[1] L Carroll, *Alice's Adventures in Wonderland* (Macmillan 1865).

[2] U Šadl, 'Studying the Role of Legal Actors in EU Law: An Outline' in this volume; A Wallermann Ghavanini, 'The EU Court of Justice as a relational actor: an introduction' (2023) 2(2) *European Law Open* 233–243.

[3] The CJEU jargon for order for reference, taken from its *langue de travail* (French) *demande de décision préjudicielle*. The chapter refers to official English translation of CJEU decisions, where available. With regard to CJEU decisions only available in languages other than English, the translation is my own.

O'Sullivan in this volume.[4] Further, the parties are trying to tell their story, quite often only to get outplayed by the Commission's observations, or confused by those of the Member States (MS) – quite as much as Alice, the Lory and the Duck interfere with the Mouse's story.

Second, a further, important relational factor concerns the exercise of the CJEU jurisdiction in infringement proceedings, which depends on a discretionary decision by the Commission to open – or not – such infringement procedure, and to define the scope of the contested national measures. An idea as disturbing, sometimes, as that of the moving arches in the Queen's croquet game.

Advocates General (AGs) may also address the CJEU, while looking through all others' observations and arguments, before finally issuing their Opinion, and then leaving the scene like the hookah-smoking Caterpillar. Relational is also the fact that AGs, like the judges, sometimes look beyond the docket's file to read legal journals and newspapers too, but on other occasions, they seem to prefer some reality-detached internal references to previous CJEU decisions, even to those ones dealing with rather different issues, not so far away from the egregious example of the cutting-off exercise applied to the head of the Cheshire Cat.

Further, a relational approach is needed to fully appraise how the Court's decisions interact, how they relate to those of national referring courts, and the extent to which they ensure the coherent development of case law as well as a unitary legal regime. The unavoidable consideration the CJEU must give to the laws and competences of MS, in their relationship with those of the EU, as well as the interaction between different sources of EU law, and between that law and international law also demands a relational approach. Finally, relational is the reality of the law as a complex construct, at times an ambiguous one, emerging from facts, and taking from them part of its signification.

Now, having quite confusedly recalled this kaleidoscopic list of relational factors that can impact on the way in which the CJEU takes its decisions, and on how the principles elaborated therein can be assessed … well … if I were Alice in relationality wonderland, I would now risk drowning in a pool of tears. Why? Because of first impressions, but because of second thoughts, too. The first impression is that, taken as such, these factors seem to be quite trivial for the EU lawyer used to the CJEU procedure. However, first impressions are not always reliable. The handling of CJEU decisions is often done in abstract terms, if not cursorily. So, one might take the CJEU cases linked to disability rights, and, in particular, those that relate to the Employment Equality Directive,[5] as *just* a story of successful endorsement of the relevant norms of the UN Convention on the Rights of Persons with Disabilities (CRPD) and the Charter of Fundamental Rights (CFR), leading to an ever-growing protection of such rights. This 'story'

[4] CE O'Sullivan, 'National Courts as 'Actors' in the Preliminary Reference Procedure' in this volume.

[5] Directive 2000/78/EC of 27 November 2000 establishing a general framework for equal treatment in employment and occupation [2000] OJ L303/16.

is one where you will find the possibility of recognising labour rights such as the right to paid annual leave of sheltered workers,[6] as well as that of expanding the notion of disability to include long-term illness,[7] and then obesity,[8] and temporary inability of uncertain duration.[9] It is a story where, you will find the notion of reasonable accommodation interpreted as including adjustments of the working time,[10] and even the reassignment to another post.[11] A story where you will see the interpretation of the notion of 'genuine and determining occupational requirement' as not justifying the total exclusion of a blind person from participation as juror in criminal proceedings,[12] or an absolute bar to the employment of a prison officer whose auditory acuity does not meet the minimum standards of sound perception prescribed by the relevant national law.[13] Further, on that bright side you will find a positive (i.e. more protective of disability rights) trajectory with regard to the non-discrimination principle as applied to different groups of persons with disabilities,[14] as well as the endorsement of individual choices made by persons with disabilities in need of personal assistance, as justification of a difference in treatment based on the age of the personal assistance workers.[15] Brightest among the bright lights, you will find the qualification of the dismissal of an employee caring for a child with disability as harassment related to disability.[16]

And they lived happily ever after? Well, maybe, maybe not. So, coming to the second thoughts now, let us try to look at the … dark side of the case law – which is quite often to be found in the same judgments. Now, it is precisely through some 'relational prisms' that this dark side becomes visible.

One of these relational prisms is the interaction between national laws (and residual competences), and the definition of some fundamental concepts used by

[6] See the evolution from Case C-344/87 *I. Bettray v Staatssecretaris van Justitie* ECLI:EU:C:1989:226 to Case C-316/13 *Gérard Fenoll v Centre d'aide par le travail "La Jouvene" and Association de parents et d'amis de personnes handicapées mentales (APEI) d'Avignon* ECLI:EU:C:2015:200.

[7] From Case C-13/05 *Sonia Chacón Navas v Eurest Colectividades SA* ECLI:EU:C:2006:456 to Joined Cases C-335/11 and C-377/11 *HK Danmark, acting on behalf of Jette Ring v Dansk almennyttigt Boligselskab and HK Danmark, acting on behalf of Lone Skouboe Werge v Dansk Arbejdsgiverforening, acting on behalf of Pro Display A/S* ECLI:EU:C:2013:222.

[8] Case C-354/13 *FOA acting on behalf of Karsten Kaltoft v KL acting on behalf of the Municipality of Billund* ECLI:EU:C:2014:2463; Case C-270/16 *Carlos Enrique Ruiz Conejero v Ferroser Servicios Auxiliares SA and Ministerio Fiscal* ECLI:EU:C:2018:17.

[9] Case C-395/15 *Mohamed Daouidi v Bootes Plus SL, Fondo de Garantía Salarial, Ministerio Fiscal* ECLI:EU:C:2016:917.

[10] See Joined Cases C-335/11 and C-377/11 *HK Danmark*.

[11] Case C-485/20 *XXXX v HR Rail SA* ECLI:EU:C:2022:85; Case C-631/22 *Ca Na Negreta* ECLI:EU:C:2024:53.

[12] Case C-824/19 *TC, UB v Komisia za zashtita ot diskriminatsia and VA* ECLI:EU:C:2021:862.

[13] Case C-795/19 *XX v Tartu Vangla* ECLI:EU:C:2021:606.

[14] Case C-406/15 *Petya Milkova v Izpalnitelen direktor na Agentsiata za privatizatsia i sledprivatizatsionen control* ECLI:EU:C:2017:198; Case C-16/19 *VL v Szpital Kliniczny im. dra J. Babińskiego Samodzielny Publiczny Zakład Opieki Zdrowotnej w Krakowie* ECLI:EU:C:2021:64.

[15] Case C-518/22 *AP Assistenzprofis* ECLI:EU:C:2023:956.

[16] Case C-303/06 *S Coleman v Attridge Law and Steve Law* ECLI:EU:C:2008:415.

the Employment Equality Directive. If we use such a prism, we might check both the degree of uniformity of the system, and its predictability for the individual. A further useful prism is the role played by the CJEU, on one hand, and the role of referring judges, on the other hand, in the framework of preliminary ruling. Through such a prism, one could also better assess what weight was given, in the CJEU rulings, to CRPD and CFR provisions. Further, in some cases it might be really useful to check how disability-related facts have entered (or sometimes altered) the CJEU case law. Still, as to facts, a change of prism – focusing on real-life facts first – might help to understand if all relevant disability-related factual situations were dealt with by the CJEU, or if there is something out there that still has to be adequately considered. Throughout this relational analysis exercise, two interrelated relational qualities of that case law need to be assessed, namely the degree of legal certainty it produces for individuals, and its effectiveness in ensuring that persons with disabilities enjoy their right to full and effective participation in professional life on an equal basis with other workers. They are strictly interrelated for at least a couple of reasons. As a matter of principle, legal certainty is an essential precondition of access to justice, and this is particularly true in our area.[17] Further, given the actual model of enforcement of EU disability law – which is highly dependent on individual action before a national court leading to a reference for preliminary ruling to the CJEU, to have it then establish the actual content of EU disability law rules and principles –, legal certainty influences effective protection of EU based rights of persons with disabilities, and vice versa effective protection in individual cases produces legal certainty for future cases.

After this introduction, thus, I move on to examine the most relevant CJEU decisions, trying to make use of these relational prisms. In particular, section 2 considers the CJEU's notion of 'worker', while section 3 looks at the notion of 'disability' in the Court's case law. Section 4 moves on to examine the concept and dimensions of reasonable accommodation. Section 5 considers areas in which the CJEU might refine its rulings by looking particularly at cases that are related to non-discrimination between different categories of persons with disabilities and the choice of individuals with disabilities regarding their caregivers. Sections 6 and 7 discuss aspects that thus far have received little attention from the CJEU, namely non-birthing mothers and main carers of children with severe disabilities. The chapter closes by offering some concluding remarks and includes an epilogue reflecting on some personal 'conflicts of interest'.

The methodological starting point of this chapter is the assumption that the first task of a legal scholar is to explain the complex interplay between different layers of legal rules that form a specific legal system (or a legal order). Such a

[17] On the manifold dimension of the question of access to justice in the disability field see E Flynn and A Lawson, 'Disability and Access to Justice in the European Union: Implications of the United Nations Convention on the Rights of Persons with Disabilities' (2013) 5 *European Yearbook of Disability Law* 7–44.

task allows the author to propose solutions to the inevitable ambiguities and *lacunae* within this system, as well as to highlight inconsistencies that characterise the written rules of the same. Coming from a civil law tradition – and having myself worked for some years inside the CJEU as a *référendaire* – I tend not to assume the Court's rulings, as such, as sources of the law but as 'legal doctrines', albeit formulated by an authoritative interpreter of the law. They are ultimately historical facts determined by the choices of historical individuals, letting a possible solution emerge to the abovementioned questions regarding the EU legal order. As such, they are open to criticism. Such criticism is one of the key tasks of legal scholarship, which is one of the few 'counterbalances' to a court of supreme instance, and can focus on the legal soundness of rulings. This involves checking their coherence with the applicable legal principles and rules of the EU legal order, including those that mandate a certain relationship with principles and rules whose origin is external to it, and those that require more generally the law to be certain, reasonable, and capable of actually protecting the fundamental rights of individuals. Criticism of the Court's ruling can, and should, however, also focus on its appropriateness, i.e. on the extent to which these rulings address actual needs of the society. I am convinced, in fact, of the theoretical soundness of an institutional approach to the law, namely one that defines a legal order not just as the (abstract) result of legal rules built around a formal *Grundnorm*, or rule of recognition, but as the outcome (and the basis) of a given society.[18] I consider, therefore, that the application of the law needs to be adjusted to the needs of that society.

I recognise, moreover, as an essential (starting) point to be considered in any methodological approach to EU law is the special nature of the EU legal system, which is a 'new legal order [...] the subjects of which comprise not only member states but also their nationals'.[19] This starting point, conversely, means that the relevant society here – as its law – is a mixed one. It is not just one organising the coexistence of individuals on an EU-wide scale, but it does this while respecting the existence of states inside the same territorial dimension, each one carrying its own legal system (and 'caring' for a given national society). As a consequence, I certainly consider the need to respect the autonomous, uniform features of most EU law rules, but I cannot accept that such autonomy be pushed so far as to become autopoietic.[20] Yet, I cannot rule out of this picture the phenomenon of

[18] S Romano, *L'ordinamento giuridico* (Sansoni 1946); C Schmitt, *Über die drei Arten des rechtswissenschaftlichen Denkens* (Hanseatische Verlaganstalt 1934); C Mortati, *La costituzione in senso materiale* (Giuffrè 1940). For the use of a similar approach in the anglophone cultural sphere, although moving from a normativist standpoint, N MacCormick, 'Beyond the Sovereign State' (1993) *Modern Law Review* 11.

[19] Case C-26/62 *NV Algemene Transport- en Expeditie Onderneming van Gend & Loos v Netherlands Inland Revenue Administration* ECLI:EU:C:1963:1.

[20] I have detailed my understanding of the main features of the EU legal order, in its necessary relationship with national laws and with international law, in some previous works. B Cortese, 'A la recherche d'un parcours d'autoconstitution de l'ordre juridique interindividuel européen: essai d'une lecture pluraliste 50 ans après Van Gend en Loos et Costa' (2015) *Il Diritto dell'Unione europea* 271–315; B Cortese, *L'ordinamento dell'Unione europea* (Giappichelli 2018); B Cortese, 'Carta, CEDU e

an overarching EU constitutionalism *in the making*. One where common values are *emerging* as possible building blocks of a unitary 'political community of principles'[21] connecting individuals in a transnational legal system, the effectiveness of which cannot be simply pushed through *despite* the national legal systems, but needs to be won in a *collaborative* approach with them.[22]

In the end, therefore, I am following a doctrinal legal methodology, but one that is neither inclined to black letter interpretation, nor blind to the need to take into account – at times conflicting – societal evolution. In this respect, the relational prisms indicated above fit perfectly into this approach to legal research.

2. Sheltered Workers versus Normal Workers

After having set some methodological coordinates, in this section I finally start analysing the CJEU case law relevant from an EU disability law perspective. The starting point is the delimitation of the field of 'work', and therefore the notion of 'worker', when it comes to activities carried out by persons with (intellectual) disabilities in the labour market.[23] This is a decisive issue – rightly so because of the peculiar features of the EU legal system referred to at the end of the previous section – that requires a clear delimitation of its scope of application *vis-à-vis* MS legal systems. Roughly speaking, that delimitation revolves around the existence of EU law measures that harmonise various issues in the field of work, while the provision of care or rehabilitation services is essentially left to MS social policies. It is in this fact – the EU being 'present' in the former field, requiring a uniform set of rules and principles to be respected by its MS – that the key to transforming the international guarantees mandated by the CRPD into *EU law* guarantees lies,[24] as well as making those stemming from the CFR applicable to situations that would be otherwise confined to the realm of national laws.

Costituzioni nazionali: un processo di codificazione tra autonomia, autopoiesi e international collaborative law' in A Annoni, S Forlati and F Salerno (eds), *La codificazione nell'ordinamento internazionale e dell'Unione europea / Codification in International and European Union Law, Società Italiana di Diritto Internazionale e di Diritto dell'Unione Europea – XXIII Annual Conference* (Editoriale Scientifica 2019) 457–506.

[21] R Dworkin, *The Laws Empire* (Harvard University Press 1986).

[22] C Kessedjian, *Le droit international collaborative* (Pedone 2016).

[23] M Bell, 'People with intellectual disabilities and labour market inclusion: What role for EU labour law?' (2020) 11(1) *European Labour Law Journal* 3–25.

[24] On the consequences of the EU conclusion of the UN Convention on the Rights of Persons with Disabilities (CRPD) on its status, and the relevant enforcement mechanisms towards Member States, see M Chamon, 'Negotiation, ratification and implementation of the CRPD and its status in the EU legal order' in D Ferri and A Broderick (eds), *Research Handbook on EU Disability Law* (Edward Elgar 2020) 52–70.

The CJEU in *Fenoll* tells us that the term 'worker' used in the Working Time Directive,[25] and in Article 31(2) CFR, 'may include a person admitted to a work rehabilitation centre'.[26] Great, but who decides if it does? And who decides whether it means that that worker cannot be treated differently from others? In the actual case, despite the fact that the CJEU had gone a long way into suggesting to the referring court how it could adjudicate the actual case in favour of Mr. Fenoll, the French *Cour de cassation* finally rejected his appeal.[27] And it could do that, according to the relevant national law conditions, whose role is recognised by the Working Time Directive. Whether that difference in treatment could also be admitted according to the Employment Equality Directive, or by the non-discrimination provisions in the CFR, was not debated before the national court, nor before the CJEU. Could the issue have been dealt with differently? Surely, at the national level, and probably also at the CJEU level. The Court could have, in fact, widened the scope of the relevant EU legal provisions to include the Employment Equality Directive and Articles 21 and 26 CFR.

As a matter of fact, the CJEU feels free to do that when it finds it necessary to give a useful answer to the referring court. It did so even in that case, as it shifted the reference from Article 1 to Article 7 of the Working Time Directive. However, at the very least, the CJEU could have included a safeguard clause that raised the attention of the referring court to such issues. It chose not to do so. So, we landed back at square one, with no legal certainty.

3. Expanding the Notion of Disability

Let us now move to the rulings through which the Court expands the notion of disability, taking into account the evolution marked by the EU accession to the CRPD.

In *Chacón Navas* the CJEU had been asked to assess the compatibility of the dismissal of a person who had been on 'sickness leave' for eight months, and had been dismissed solely on that ground, with the Employment Equality Directive. After having stated, in abstract terms, that the concepts of 'disability' and 'sickness' are different,[28] and after having further explained that, based on an interpretation of the notion of disability in light of the internal systematic of that Directive, disability means a 'limitation' that will probably 'last for [a] long time'[29] the CJEU

[25] Directive 2003/88/EC of 4 November 2003 concerning certain aspects of the organisation of working time [2003] OJ L299/9.

[26] Case C-316/13 *Gérard Fenoll*, para 50.

[27] *Cour de cassation, civ., Chambre sociale*, Jugement of 16 December 2015, No 11-22.376, ECLI:FR:CCASS:2015:SO02243.

[28] Case C-13/05 *Chacón Navas*, para 44.

[29] Ibid para 45.

excluded that workers are protected 'as soon as they develop any type of sickness',[30] and declared that a dismissal based 'solely on account of sickness' could not be equalled to one based on disability,[31] without raising the question of whether the facts of the case should lead to a qualification of disability.

So, contrary to the prevalent description of that judgment,[32] it is not in my view the notion of disability that is definitely 'outdated' here. The CJEU shows rather a restraint in giving any useful answer to the referring judge, in order not to push a decision based on the Employment Equality Directive too far – again. After the *Mangold* case,[33] which risked to spark a clash with the German constitutional court,[34] the Court is clearly exerting some cautiousness. Such a (relational and defensive) restraint is openly demanded by AG Geelhoed, who 'advocate[s] a more restrained interpretation and application of Directive 2000/78 than [that] adopted by the Court in the *Mangold* case'.[35]

As a consequence, when the Court in *HK Danmark (Ring and Skouboe Werge)* reached the conclusion that a 'curable or incurable illness' entailing a long-term limitation 'can be covered by the concept of disability',[36] it was elaborating and refining a definition that was already in the making. Quite importantly, though, it did so by referring to the CRPD, which adds a social-contextual dimension to that notion.[37]

The problem with this evolutionary, rather than revolutionary, approach, lies in a kind of 'sticky' bond between illness and disability, making it quite unavoidable for the Court to find a medical condition at the basis of a disability. That bond is there in *Kaltoft*,[38] and further in *Ruiz Conejero*,[39] where the CJEU considers that obesity might be 'covered by the concept' of disability, in particular if there are 'medical conditions preventing him from carrying out his work or causing discomfort when carrying out his professional activity', or if the obese worker is hindered by 'reduced mobility'. While the Court pays lip service to a social notion of disability, linking impairment and 'various barriers', there is hardly any reference to those barriers. The only ones seem to be implicit, and include merely physical barriers (in the 'reduced mobility' hypothesis), or the 'medical condition' itself.

[30] Ibid para 46.

[31] Ibid para 47.

[32] L Waddington, 'Case C-13/05 *Sonia Chacón Navas v. Eurest Colectividades SA*, judgment of the Grand Chamber of 11 July 2006' (2007) 44 *Common Market Law Review* 487; D Ferri, '*Daouidi v Bootes Plus SL* and the Concept of 'Disability' in EU Anti-Discrimination Law' (2019) 10(1) *European Labour Law Journal* 70.

[33] Case C-144/04 *Werner Mangold v Rüdiger Helm* ECLI:EU:C:2005:709.

[34] Bundesverfassungsgericht (BVerfG), Order of the Second Senate of 6 July 2010 – 2 BvR 2661/06.

[35] Opinion of Advocate General Geelhoed delivered on 16 March 2006 in Case C-13/05 *Sonia Chacón Navas v Eurest Colectividades SA* ECLI:EU:C:2006:184, para 56.

[36] Joined Cases C-335/11 and C-377/11 *HK Danmark*, para 41.

[37] Ibid paras 37-38. On the definition of 'social-contextual' model, to which the CJEU refers in that judgment and in the following case law, see A Broderick, *The Long and Winding Road to Equality and Inclusion for Persons with Disabilities: The United Nations Convention on the Rights of Persons with Disabilities* (Intersentia 2015).

[38] Case C-354/13 *Kaltoft*, para 60.

[39] Case C-270/16 *Ruiz Conejero*, para 30.

What can be inferred from this? Essentially, that the CJEU transforms an open notion,[40] based on the interaction between some form of impairments and social barriers (including 'attitudinal' ones),[41] like the one used in the CRPD, into a closed one, in which either a functional impairment or a long-term illness limits working capacities.

What if my employer sacks me because I did not lose weight despite having been offered a free gym, as in *Kaltoft*? Is that not an impairment – even if it is ascribed to me, and not necessarily an objectively functional one – that together with a social barrier deprives me of a right? What if my employer is superstitious and thinks of me, as a person with albinism,[42] or with epilepsy, or with a scar or a bubo, that I am 'disgraced', and makes me a person carrying a stigma, and actually excludes me from the enjoyment of my rights? Would I need to prove that my albinism, epilepsy or scar or bubo involve a functional impairment? Maybe, or maybe not. So, here again, we have a lot of people landing back at square one, with no legal certainty. However, why is the CJEU using such a shortsighted approach? I guess, because it is 'scared' to step into fields it perceives as not clearly falling into EU competences. We could call it the '*Mangold* reflex': do you want to avoid confrontation in the social rights area? Fly low.

4. Expanding the Meaning of Reasonable Accommodation: From *HK Danmark* to *HR Rail* and *Ca Na Negreta*

I now turn to examine the trajectory of CJEU case law that led to an expansive interpretation of the concept of reasonable accommodation. The starting point of this trajectory is to be found again in *HK Danmark*, where it is said that a reduction in working hours 'may constitute' a reasonable accommodation, if it 'make[s] it possible for the worker to continue employment'.[43] To reach that result, the CJEU refers to Article 2 CRPD as setting the goal relevant in the interpretation of Article 5 of the Employment Equality Directive, namely that of ensuring the enjoyment or exercise of the right to full and effective participation in professional life on an equal basis with other workers.

In its relationship with the referring court, the CJEU follows its quite traditional approach, leaving to that court the task of applying the legal principle to

[40] S Favalli and D Ferri, 'Defining Disability in the European Union Non-discrimination Legislation: Judicial Activism and Legislative Restraints' (2016) 22(3) *European Public Law* 541, 548.

[41] Preamble letter (e) CRPD.

[42] On the possible inclusion of albinism in the concept of disability, linked to the persecution faced by people with albinism in some regions, Committee on the Rights of Persons with Disabilities, *Mr. X v Tanzania*, Communication No 22/2014, Views of 31 August 2017, CRPD/C/18/D/22/2014.

[43] Joined Cases C-335/11 and C-377/11 *HK Danmark*, para 56.

the actual facts of the case. In particular, it leaves to the referring court to ascertain whether or not an accommodation entails a disproportionate burden for the employer.[44] In doing so, however, the CJEU appears to be a bit too timid, as the facts of the case, quite clearly, showed that such a measure did not, in fact, entail a disproportionate burden.[45]

The next two cases that provide an extensive interpretation of the obligation to provide a reasonable accommodation are *HR Rail* and *Ca Na Negreta*, decided in 2022 and 2024 respectively. In these cases, the CJEU includes the reassignment to another job among the measures that 'may' constitute a reasonable accommodation.[46] The reasoning, in both cases, resorts to Articles 21 and 26 CFR to embolden the interpretation of Article 5 of the Employment Equality Directive. In *Ca Na Negreta* the reference to Article 27 CRPD is further added.[47]

4.1. *HR Rail* and *Ca Na Negreta*: Elevating the Facts of the Cases to a Special (Unnecessary) Condition

The way in which the facts of the two cases are used to frame the relevant legal principle seems puzzling. It has something to do with Alice's hookah-smoking Caterpillar, which, after having listened to Alice's inconclusive arguments about who she is and who she was, and after having discussed the best size to be – no matter if you are a young girl or a caterpillar – comes up with the unexpected story about the effects of eating the mushroom he was sitting upon. Quite like in Lewis Carroll's allegory of a world built on misunderstandings and caprices, AG Rantos' Opinion in *HR Rail* picks from the facts of the actual dispute a fortunate and undisputed element, and – apparently building on a similar argument made by the Commission – elevates it to a principle called upon to decide similar future cases, suggesting that 'the possibility of assigning a disabled person to another job is […] aimed at the situation where there is *at least one vacancy* which the worker concerned is able to occupy, so as not to impose a disproportionate burden on the employer', and noting that otherwise the reassignment could 'result in depriving another worker of his or her job or forcing the latter to swap jobs'.[48]

That is quite a topsy-turvy world, where the actual facts that show that reassignment as a reasonable accommodation is not a disproportionate burden in that special case, are elevated to being the *only* possible condition for such a measure not to constitute a disproportionate burden in future cases. This is based on the evident fallacy that, otherwise, someone else will have to be fired or (unwillingly)

[44] Ibid paras 58-61.

[45] Ibid para 62.

[46] Case C-485/20 *HR Rail*, paras 41, 43; Case C-631/22 *Ca Na Negreta*, para 44.

[47] Case C-631/22 *Ca Na Negreta*, para 50.

[48] Opinion of Advocate General Rantos delivered on 11 November 2021 in Case C-485/20 *XXXX v HR Rail SA* ECLI:EU:C:2021:916, para 77.

reassigned: while this might be the case in a small undertaking, a bigger one might well enjoy enough organisational leeway to create an *ad hoc* appropriate vacancy, without having to impact on other workers' situations, and without bearing a disproportionate burden. What is even more disturbing is that the CJEU adopts a restrictive qualification of the obligation to reassign, as if it were an article of faith. The statement that 'in any event, the possibility of assigning a disabled person to another job is only available where there is at least one vacancy that the worker in question is capable of holding' is inserted by the Court both in its *HR Rail* judgment,[49] and in most recent *Ca Na Negreta* ruling.[50]

Ca Na Negreta refers to a similar situation in which the employer had already reassigned the worker, after the latter experienced a partial inability following a workplace accident, but dismissed him without any reason when the worker had his partial inability recognised by the Spanish social security. The vacancy to be filled was there – or had been there –, and the facts of the situation spoke for themselves, showing quite clearly that a reassignment – besides being clearly appropriate for the worker – would not be a disproportionate burden.

4.2. Back to Horizontal Effects of the General Principles?

That being said, if looked at from a relational perspective, and considering the CJEU approach to actual *and* future preliminary ruling cases, *HR Rail* and *Ca Na Negreta* evidence an important difference between the Court's reasoning and the operative part of the judgment. While in the former the Court elaborates its statements with a certain degree of detail and constructs its language as leaving the task of applying the relevant principles in the actual case to the referring national judge, in the latter the language is much more direct.

In the reasoning, in both cases, the CJEU explains how a reassignment 'may' be a reasonable accommodation. In the operative part of the *HR Rail* ruling, though, the Court directly declared that the Employment Equality Directive 'requires' the reassignment of 'a worker, including someone undertaking a traineeship' who 'has been declared incapable of performing the essential functions of the post that he or she occupies', except where this would impose a disproportionate burden. It is quite a striking evolution from *HK Danmark*, where the operative part followed the same prudent language of the reasoning, in stating that a reduction in working hours 'may constitute one of the accommodation measures' foreseen by Article 5 of the Employment Equality Directive.

Further, in *Ca Na Negreta*, the operative part squarely inserts into the Spanish legislation the requirement that, prior to terminating a contract on the basis of a permanent inability to perform the contractual tasks, the employer needs first

[49] Case C-485/20 *HR Rail*, para 48.
[50] Case C-631/22 *Ca Na Negreta*, para 45.

'to make or maintain reasonable accommodation in order to enable that worker to keep his or her job'. The way in which the two judgments operate in relationship with the relevant individuals, and the national laws, are quite remarkable, and differ from one another.

In *HR Rail* the Court derives a direct obligation for the employer from the content of a directive provision, namely Article 5 of the Employment Equality Directive. This seems already a bold move if looked at from a general systematic perspective: as a matter of principle, directives cannot directly impose obligations on individuals.[51] It is true that this rule is not applicable to entities controlled by MS,[52] and *HR Rail* is essentially controlled by the Belgian State. Nonetheless, the Court did not stress this issue in its judgment, leading to the impression that the relevant directive provision does produce horizontal direct effects on individuals. This ambivalence is not new in the present field. At least since *HK Danmark*, the Court has ruled in ways that clearly imply a horizontal direct effect: while the defendant in Ms. Ring's case was again an entity controlled by a public administration, this was not the case for Pro Display, the defendant in Ms. Skouboe Werge's case. Still, in that case, the Danish courts were able to use the principle affirmed by the CJEU when applying Danish non-discrimination law, so as to exclude any issue of horizontal direct effects of the Directive.[53] The issue was there, though, and it would soon thereafter 'explode' as a matter of confrontation between the *Højesteret* and the CJEU in the *Ajos* case, which involved the general non-discrimination provision of the same Directive, meant by the Court to be an embodiment of a horizontally applicable general principle of EU law.[54]

In *Ca Na Negreta*, however, not only is the defendant before the national court a fully private entity, but also the relevant interpretation of Spanish law having led to the contested dismissal directly derives from the Spanish Supreme Court case law. It is therefore quite striking that the CJEU interprets the Directive as opposing to an application of the relevant Spanish law permitting the termination of the employment relationship *if not complemented* by an obligation 'to make or maintain reasonable accommodation'. This is, despite the formulation of the operative part of the judgment trying to mask it, a situation in which the content of a horizontal private relationship is directly derived from a provision of a directive, as the 'non-application' obligation of the referring judge requires in fact *adding* to the

[51] Case 152/84 *M. H. Marshall v Southampton and South-West Hampshire Area Health Authority (Teaching)* ECLI:EU:C:1986:84, para 48; Case C-91/92 *Paola Faccini Dori v Recreb Srl* ECLI:EU:C:1994:292, paras 24-25.

[52] Case 152/84 *Marshall*, para 49; Case C-188/89 *A. Foster and others v British Gas plc* ECLI:EU:C:1990:313, para 20.

[53] Højesteret, Judgment of 23 June 2015, Case 25/2014 *Dansk Arbejdsgiverforening acting for Pro Display A/S under konkurs v HK Danmark acting on behalf of A*. For a thorough discussion of the confrontation between the two courts see U Šadl and S Mair, 'Mutual Disempowerment: Case C-441/14' (2017) 13 *European Constitutional Law Review* 347–368.

[54] Højesteret, Judgment of 6 December 2016, Case 15/2014, *Dansk Industri acting on behalf of Ajos A/S v Estate of A*.

relevant national legal regime a condition for the dismissal that it does not foresee. Moreover, that horizontal effect is linked to an *innovative interpretation* of the relevant Directive provision having first emerged in *HR Rail*, which is now applied to a dispute whose relevant facts date back to 2018.

That is probably why, in *Ca Na Negreta*, the CJEU no longer derives such effects from Article 5 of the Employment Equality Directive only, but links them also to Articles 21 and 26 CFR and Articles 2 and 27 CRPD. The CJEU seems to be driving back to *Mangold*, *Kücükdeveci*[55] and *Dansk Industri*,[56] with the emboldened approach of a fundamental rights court, but without caring too much about explaining what it is doing. Despite the lack of clear reference to that line of case law, the return to that approach is not just a scholarly *ex post* rationalisation, but is 'relationally' confirmed. *Danks Industri* is precisely the CJEU ruling relied upon by the national court in the *Ca Na Negreta* case,[57] the *Tribunal Superior de Justicia* (TSJ) of the Balearic Islands, to justify what it calls a direct effect of the Directive as interpreted by the CJEU. Possibly, the CJEU should have looked at that in a closer dialogue with the referring court as the same TSJ goes on criticising the Spanish Supreme Court for not having changed its interpretation of the relevant provision of the *Estatuto de los Trabajadores*, taking into account the duty to make (or maintain) a reasonable accommodation as mandated by the Employment Equality Directive, *and thus* by relevant Spanish transposition provisions.[58] The ambivalence of the Spanish court's reasoning is justified, here. It 'feels' the direct effect indication that stems from the operative part of the *Ca Na Negreta* judgment, emerging from the 'evolutionary' non-application it imposes on national courts in a case of clear horizontal dimension: that is why it directly refers to *Dansk Industri*. On the other hand, when entering a dialogue with its supreme court, the *Tribunal Supremo*, asking for an inclusion of the new CJEU interpretation in the latter's case law, the TSJ uses, without referring to it, the empowering effect of the CJEU answer to *Kücükdeveci*'s second question,[59] albeit in a slightly different situation. The TSJ is not in a situation where, as the German referring court in *Kücükdeveci*, it should have otherwise needed to wait for a constitutional court's appraisal of

[55] Case C-555/07 *Seda Kücükdeveci v Swedex GmbH & Co. KG* ECLI:EU:C:2010:21.

[56] Case C-441/14 *Dansk Industri (DI), acting on behalf of Ajos A/S v Estate of Karsten Eigil Rasmussen* ECLI:EU:C:2016:278.

[57] Tribunal Superior de Justicia (TSJ) Illes Balears, Judgment 19 March 2024, No 147/2024.

[58] TSJ Illes Balears, No 147/2024, para 12, in which the court qualifies the lack of statutory provision or case law guidance to the effect as 'incomprehensible', and concludes that it cannot oppose to a direct application of Article 5 Directive 2000/78 ('*resulta incomprensible que ni el legislador ni la jurisprudencia hayan atendido al claro mandato de la Directiva 2000/78 [... p]ero ello ni impide la aplicación directa de tal mandato ni exonera a las empresas en caso de incumplimiento*'); and para 13, with reference to the *Ley General de derechos de las personas con discapacidad* BOE No 289 (3 December 2013) BOE-A-2013-12632.

[59] Namely, the one concerning the power of national courts to disapply provisions of national law contrary to the principle of non-discrimination, without any need to wait for a CJEU ruling, despite the clear and 'non-interpretable' provision of a conflicting national legal provision otherwise applicable to horizontal legal relationships.

the relevant national provision, but still has its own supreme court having already confirmed the viability of the national (discriminatory) provision.

As anticipated, in such a framework, it would have been for the CJEU to take a clearer stance on such structural issues that concerned the relationship between the Directive's reasonable accommodation obligation, the non-discrimination clause as a general principle of EU law, the CFR and the CRPD provisions. To do so, however, it should have been guided by a dedicated AG Opinion in the case,[60] and should have addressed the case in a larger formation of judgement, as advisable when it has to deal with a 'difficult' case.[61] Instead, the CJEU chose to … go stealth, with no AG Opinion, and with no assignment to the Grand Chamber, probably relying on the interpretative margin that is in principle left to the national courts in such cases, because of the very existence of a general implementing measure foreseeing the reasonable accommodation as a duty of any employer.

That leads us back to a decade earlier, between 2011 and 2013, when the Commission introduces, and the Court then decides, the only infringement case to date concerning disability law. The issue at stake then was not the lack of a coherent approach 'designed to ensure [the] independence, social and occupational integration and participation in the life of the community'[62] of persons with disability in Italian law – something that Italy probably has –, but rather the lack of a specific legal provision 'introducing a requirement for all employers to make reasonable adjustments, where needed in a particular case, for all persons with disabilities'.[63]

4.3. The Notion of 'Genuine and Determining Occupational Requirement': Some Relational Variations

For different reasons, therefore, the case law on the widening of the reasonable accommodation obligation involves a non-negligible degree of uncertainty. Nonetheless, the fact remains that in both *HR Rail* and *Ca Na Negreta* the CJEU restricts the margin left to the referring judge when applying the legal principle to the actual case. A similar approach is followed in two decisions, adopted by the CJEU in 2021 that deal with the definition of what constitutes a 'genuine and determining occupational requirement' justifying a difference of treatment based on disability for the purpose of Article 4 of the Employment Equality Directive: *Tartu Vangla* and *TC, UB*. In both cases, the CJEU reached a result, in the operative part of its judgment, that excluded the application of that provision on a genuine and determining occupational requirement. Moreover, even in the reasoning, the

[60] As foreseen by Article 20 of the Statute of the CJEU, making it possible for the Court to decide 'without a submission from the Advocate General', but only when 'the case raises no new point of law'.

[61] According to Article 60 Rules of Procedure of the Court of Justice [2012] OJ L265/1.

[62] Article 26 CFR.

[63] Case C-312/11 *Commission v Italy* ECLI:EU:C:2013:446.

CJEU put forward an approach that, while nominally leaving it to the referring judge to apply the relevant principle in the pending dispute, tended to exclude any actual uncertainty. This was made possible by the accurate explanation made by the referring judge of the facts of the case,[64] and where necessary also of the relevant national legislation.[65] On this side, thus, there is a consistent (relational) approach in the two cases.

Curiously enough, however, while in one case the CFR was directly referred to in the reasoning, as was the CRPD, and the relevant norms thereof were also included in the operative part of the judgment (*TC, UB*), in the other there was no role for the CFR, and the Convention was only mentioned in the reasoning (*Tartu Vangla*). Now, if one looks at the content of the orders for reference, and of the AG Opinions in the two cases, there is no explanation for these divergent approaches to the use of the CFR. In *TC, UB*, the national judge's request for a preliminary ruling only refers to the CRPD and to the Employment Equality Directive. AG Saugmandsgaard Øe, in his Opinion, referred to both the CRPD and the CFR, but in the proposed operative part of the judgment he limited the reference to the CRPD. The Second Chamber of the CJEU, however, included both the CFR and the CRPD in the operative part of its judgment, as well as in its reasoning. In *Tartu Vangla*, on the contrary, despite the fact that the AG Opinion discussed both the CFR and the Convention, the same Second Chamber of the CJEU included only a passing reference to the CRPD in its reasoning, and did not mention the CFR, while the operative part of the judgment was confined to a mention of the relevant provisions of the Employment Equality Directive, sticking to the essential content of the order for reference made by the Estonian Supreme Court. One is therefore left with the impression that the CJEU lacks a systematic approach and is not yet ready to play a decisive role as a fundamental rights court, even when it actually chooses a path that leads to a stronger fundamental rights protection.[66]

5. Further Areas of Improvement

5.1. Non-discrimination between Different Categories of Persons with Disabilities

The same kind of undecided attitude, as to the role the CJEU is ready to play when it comes to protecting the fundamental rights of persons with disabilities, which

[64] Case C-795/19 *XX v Tartu Vangla* ECLI:EU:C:2021:606, paras 15, 47, 51; Case C-824/19 *TC, UB*, para 64.

[65] Case C-795/19 *Tartu Vangla*, paras 45-46.

[66] On the CFR in discrimination disputes see *inter alia* A Ward, 'The Impact of the EU Charter of Fundamental Rights on Anti-Discrimination Law: More a Whimper than a Bang?' (2018) 20 *Cambridge Yearbook of European Legal Studies* 42 *et seq.*

was discussed above in section 4, emerges with a closer look at other – all in all positive – developments of its recent case law, that I examine herewith.

One such development regards the difference of treatment among groups of persons with disabilities. There, the quite disappointing ruling adopted in 2017 by the Second Chamber in the *Milkova* case seems to have been overcome by the Grand Chamber judgment adopted in 2021 in the *Szpital Kliniczny* case. This is true, at least, for the choice of the CJEU, in the former case, not to connect a difference in the applicable national legislation – which foresaw a protection against dismissal for private employees with a psychiatric illness, while not providing any such protection for public employees in the same situation – to the provision of Article 2 of the Employment Equality Directive.

In *Milkova*, the CJEU adopted a formalistic qualification of the situation as non-discriminatory, based on the undiscussed acceptance of the referring court's position: the difference in treatment between two groups of workers with disability would not be based on their disability, but on the employment relationship itself.[67]

That formalistic view is abandoned in *Szpital Kliniczny*, where the CJEU came back to a fundamental assumption about non-discrimination it relied upon in previous cases, including disability related ones such as *Coleman*. What is essential, in order to trigger the application of the non-discrimination principle of the Directive, is that the 'disadvantage at issue is experienced as a result of' one of the grounds referred to in its Article 1. As a consequence, there can be a discrimination based on disability when a comparison between two groups of persons with disabilities shows a difference in treatment, despite the use of a different formal criterion of differentiation in the relevant legislation. In *Szpital Kliniczny*, this argument was made by resorting to a number of systematic arguments of interpretation, including a very abstract reference to the link between the Directive and the general principle of non-discrimination 'now enshrined in Article 21 of the Charter'.[68] At the same time, however, the *Szpital Kliniczny* case marks, to a certain extent, a step backwards.

In fact, in this instance the CJEU operated at the very abstract level of principles, without making any real attempt to guide the referring judge in its application of such principles to the actual dispute. This is quite striking, as the case seemed too perfect to be true, if one wants the CJEU to play an active role in fundamental rights adjudication. The criterion that had led to a distinction between the two categories of employees with disabilities at the Cracow hospital, whose equal treatment as to salary was at stake before that city's regional court, was of such a blunt arbitrariness, that not to seize the occasion to declare such a practice not only in violation of the Directive, but also of the relevant CFR and CRPD provisions, seems to be a deliberate choice of inertia, rather than appropriate judicial self-restraint towards the referring national court.

[67] Case C-406/15 *Milkova*, paras 40-44.
[68] Case C-16/19 *Szpital Kliniczny*, para 33.

5.2. Individual Choices of Persons with Disabilities as to their Caregivers

The second area worth looking into is that of the protection granted to the choices that persons with disabilities might express as to the qualities of their caregivers. Here, too, we have a rather significant ruling in terms of the protection of disability rights by the CJEU, namely the one rendered in December 2023 by the Second Chamber in the *AP Assistenzprofis* case. The issue at the core of the dispute, there, was the exclusion of a person working as a professional caregiver from the selection process that a centre for caregiving services had launched to provide assistance to a young person with a disability, a university student, because of the express demand formulated by that person to be assisted by a caregiver preferably of an age close to their own age.

The answer given by the CJEU to the request for a preliminary ruling submitted by the German *Bundesarbeitsgericht* is quite appropriate in its result, as well as in its underpinning legal assumptions. In essence, its operative part, in fact, reads the Employment Equality Directive in the light of Article 26 CFR and Article 19 CRPD, to exclude that it precludes the recruitment of a caregiver being subject to an age requirement, insofar as this is 'necessary for the protection of the rights and freedoms' of a person with a disability in need of caregiving. In the reasoning, it is moreover clearly suggested to the referring court that such a measure:

> is likely to promote respect for that person's right to self-determination in the provision of those personal assistance services, inasmuch as it appears reasonable to expect that a person within the same age range as the disabled person will fit more easily in that person's personal, social and university circle.[69]

What is regrettable, however, is the lack of courage by the CJEU in (not) linking this right of choice directly to Article 26 CFR and Article 19 CRPD, but choosing instead to make it dependent on a choice by the relevant national legislation[70] whose appropriate character is then assessed under EU law parameters.[71]

However, what about persons with disabilities in need of caregiving services in other MSs, where no equivalent provisions to Article 8(1) *Sozialgesetzbuch IX* (German Social Code – SGB) and Article 33 SGB I apply, according to which:

> when deciding on personal assistance services and in the performance of those services intended to promote the disabled person's participation in the community, the legitimate wishes of the persons entitled to receive those services are to be respected, insofar as those wishes are reasonable and by taking account of those persons' personal circumstances, age, sex, family and religious and philosophical needs?[72]

[69] Case C-518/22 *AP Assistenzprofis*, para 65.
[70] Ibid para 54 *et seq.*
[71] Ibid para 57 *et seq.*
[72] Ibid para 55.

For the CJEU, EU disability law merely permits such a national approach, but does not mandate it. This derives from a – relationally questionable – hermeneutic choice. The choice made by the CJEU is to read the situation at stake through the prism of the Employment Equality Directive. Thus, here the focus is not on the right of the person with a disability, but on the limit to the prohibition to treat professional caregivers differently based on age or sex, religious and philosophical stance, as the case might be for other choices made by the person in need of care and considered by the relevant German provision. A strict interpretation of Article 2(5) of that Directive, as an exception to the non-discrimination provisions contained therein, leads the CJEU to require that the choice expressed by the person with a disability in need of care be foreseen by an applicable provision of national law. The CFR and CRPD only play a role at the final stage of the assessment, that of the justification of the exceptional national measure, as to its goals and to its proportionality.[73]

Could the Court have followed a different path that led to a greater level of uniformity within EU disability law? In my view, yes. Once it is clear that this kind of choice, as expressed by the person with a disability in need of receiving care by a professional personal caregiver, refers to a situation that falls within the scope of application of the Employment Equality Directive, because the professional personal caregiver is going to be hired as an employee – either directly by the interested person with a disability, or indirectly, by a public or private organisation, that will then be in charge of formally providing the service to that person – the CFR becomes applicable, and the need arises to interpret the Directive in light of the CFR.[74] Moreover, the Directive, as well as the whole EU legal system, then needs to be interpreted in light of the CRPD, in itself an expression of general principles of EU law and of its MS' common constitutional approaches. If this is true, then nothing opposes an interpretation of Article 26 CFR as *imposing* on MS, while transposing the Employment Equality Directive, the respect of such a choice, as expressed by the relevant individual, and as warranted by Article 19 CRPD. The appropriate perspective would not then be that of permitting an exceptional national regime derogating a general EU principle, and thus to be interpreted restrictively.

Rather, it would be a question of balancing competing rights: that of the worker not to be subject to discrimination on the basis of age, and that of the person with a disability to express choices and to self-determination, independence, social and occupational integration and participation in the life of the community. Such a balancing exercise could not be done by the CJEU alone in the framework of

[73] Ibid paras 61-62.

[74] This distinguishes such a situation from one where Articles 21 and 26 CFR are relied upon to challenge a discretionary choice by the EU (or national) legislator, as the CJEU was asked to do in case C-356/12 *Wolfgang Glatzel v Freistaat Bayern* ECLI:EU:C:2014:350. On the role of Article 26 CFR in the disability law field, in connection with Article 21 CFR, Ward (n 66) 39 *et seq.*; D Ferri, 'Disability in the EU Charter of Fundamental Rights' in Ferri and Broderick (n 24) 37 *et seq.*

a preliminary ruling procedure. However, the CJEU, provided by the national judge with the knowledge of the relevant facts, could play a decisive role in such process.

6. Some Thoughts on What is Left Outside this Picture

Having considered some positive, and some less positive developments of EU disability law, as shaped by the CJEU case law, this section discusses areas that either have been raised, but rejected as non-disability questions, or were never raised before the CJEU. An example of the first sort is the question of maternity leave for non-birthing mothers. An example of the second sort is the situation of main carers of persons (especially children) with severe disabilities, under the reasonable accommodation perspective.

6.1. Non-birthing Mothers

In *Z v. A Government Department*[75] the Grand Chamber of the CJEU delivered a truly disappointing ruling on a case that involved the refusal by an Irish school to pay a leave equivalent to maternity leave or adoptive leave to a worker who had a baby as a non-birthing mother, thanks to a surrogacy arrangement after in vitro fertilisation of her own eggs, because of a rare syndrome that prevented Ms. Z, having no uterus, from carrying any child. The referring judge formulated two separate questions, advancing two separate hypotheses of discrimination: one based on sex, one based on disability. The CJEU excluded both, treating them as fully separate issues. Moreover, the Court addressed the qualification of the relevant facts under the two relevant directives through quite restrictive, formal approaches. As to Directive 2006/54,[76] the CJEU excluded the facts of the case from its scope by first excluding that any difference in treatment is there between a woman in Ms. Z's situation and any male worker,[77] and by then referring to the term 'pregnancy' as only referring to a birthing mother. As to the Employment Equality Directive, the CJEU confirms that the notion of disability, to be interpreted in light of the CRPD, revolves around an impairment and some barriers, whose interaction results in hindering the 'full and effective participation of the person concerned in professional life on an equal basis with other workers'.

[75] Case C-363/12 *Z. v A Government Department and The Board of management of a community school* ECLI:EU:C:2014:159.

[76] Directive 2006/54/EC of 5 July 2006 on the implementation of the principle of equal opportunities and equal treatment of men and women in matters of employment and occupation [2006] OJ L204/23.

[77] Case C-363/12 *Z. v A Government Department*, para 54.

According to the Court, though, while not having a uterus means having a long-term impairment, it does not appear 'from the order for reference' that such a limitation suffered by Ms. Z 'by itself made it impossible for her to carry out her work or constituted a hindrance to the exercise of her professional activity',[78] with the consequence that her condition is not a 'disability' and the Directive does not apply to her case.

All that sounds so artificial. Let us try to tell it from a relational viewpoint: how far was the Court (and its AG, whose Opinion is no less disappointing)[79] looking, to reach its decision? Did it really look at anything outside its file? Did it look through its windows – albeit indirectly, through a request for clarifications directed at the referring judge, as foreseen by Article 101 of its Rules of Procedure? Did it consider its own case law as emerging from the facts of the case, or did it apply previous solutions to novel situations, without considering the differences? Did it really consider the CRPD approach to disability, which – as it correctly states – binds the Union? Did it have a look at the scholarly debates? It seems quite easy to answer no to all such questions. Just a couple of observations about the most puzzling of such failures.

Let us start with the relevant concept of disability. The CJEU does not seem to bother much with the clear concept that, under the CRPD, disability is a social construct. This implies several things. First, that law – in this case, EU law, national law – is part of the social construct that can hinder the enjoyment of human rights on an equal basis with others. So, the fact that Irish law does not foresee that a maternity, nor an adoptive leave to be applied to the case of surrogacy, should have been considered as a social barrier hindering Ms. Z, because of her impairment, to enjoy her right to equality of opportunities as 'to all matters concerning all forms of employment, including conditions […] of employment'.[80]

Let us continue with the idea of intersectionality, not only as a scholarly tool to better understand and address discrimination,[81] but also as a concept clearly endorsed by the CRPD – as confirmed, *inter alia*, by its Preamble[82] and its Article 6.[83] Nothing of the sort is to be found in the *Z* ruling, sticking to the formal distinction between the two concepts – discrimination on the basis of sex, and on

[78] Ibid para 81.

[79] Opinion of Advocate General Wahl delivered on 26 September 2013 in Case C-363/12 *Z. v A Government Department and The Board of management of a community school* ECLI:EU:C:2013:604.

[80] Article 27(1)(a) CRPD. See also Article 3(1)(c) Employment Equality Directive. For the qualification of the Irish statutory regime as the relevant barrier, L Waddington, 'Saying All the Right Things and Still Getting It Wrong: The Court of Justice's Definition of Disability and Non-Discrimination Law' (2015) 4 *Maastricht Journal of European and Comparative Law* 585.

[81] D Schiek, 'Intersectionality and the Notion of Disability in EU Discrimination Law' (2016) 53(1) *Common Market Law Review* 35–63.

[82] Preamble letter (p) CRPD, recalling the 'concern about the difficult conditions faced by persons with disabilities who are subject to multiple or aggravated forms of discrimination'.

[83] Article 6 CRPD, recognising 'that women and girls with disabilities are subject to multiple discrimination', and the Parties to the Convention shall in this regard 'take measures to ensure the full and equal enjoyment by them of all human rights and fundamental freedoms'.

the basis of disability –, and the two directives, and further not taking into account gendered approaches that would have shown how Ms. Z is worse off than her male colleagues, and also worse off than her female colleagues that did not have a similar condition, because of her gender *and* disability.

And, finally, the way in which case law is referred to (or not): why is there a concentration on hindrance (or its absence) about 'having access to, participating in or advancing in employment', rather than considering the economic conditions attached to a quite normal situation for female workers, namely maternity? The contrast with the only infringement case in this area is striking: there, as already recalled, the whole point was about Italy not having a legislative framework that benefited 'all people with disabilities, covering the *various aspects of employment and work*'.[84]

6.2. … and Reasonable Accommodation for the Main Carers of Children with Severe Disability

A last field deserves closer attention, namely that of workers caring for their children with severe disabilities – or other persons with a severe disability of whom they are the main carers. Apparently, this is an area where the CJEU has already spoken – 16 years ago – and has done so with a commending, progressive judgment issued by its Grand Chamber in *Coleman*, protecting the mother of a child with a severe disability against an abusive dismissal clearly linked to her status of a caring person, and qualifying such a situation as a prohibited harassment. Bravo. But then, if one reads it carefully, one finds the devil in the details.

In fact, the Court there clearly distinguishes between the prohibition of direct discrimination provided for by Article 2 of the Employment Equality Directive, which applies to a situation where 'disability […] is the ground for the less favourable treatment',[85] including in particular the situation of harassment,[86] on one side, and the obligation to provide reasonable accommodation, on the other. Reasonable accommodation would apply, so the CJEU, 'only to disabled people',[87] and this is 'because they are specific measures which would be rendered meaningless or could prove to be disproportionate if they were not limited to disabled persons only'.[88]

[84] Case C-312/11 *Commission v Italy*, para 67.
[85] Case C-303/06 *Coleman*, para 50.
[86] Ibid para 58.
[87] Ibid para 39.
[88] Ibid para 42. For an accurate description of the debate about extending or not extending reasonable accommodation to persons associated with disability, including in the very choices of Ms Coleman's legal team, G Quinn and E Flynn, 'Transatlantic Borrowings: The Past and Future of EU Non-Discrimination Law and Policy on the Ground of Disability' (2021) 60(1) *American Journal of Comparative Law* 43 *et seq*.

Now, this reasoning seems outdated, in light of the subsequent conclusion by the Union of the CRPD. In fact, Article 2 CRPD clearly states that 'discrimination on the basis of disability […] includes […] denial of reasonable accommodation'. This wider understanding of the notion of discrimination is now expressly recalled by two of the recent CJEU rulings on reasonable accommodation, in *HR Rail*[89] and *Ca Na Negreta*.[90] Still, both cases involve the lack of reasonable accommodation for workers having a personal situation of impairment, leading to disability. It cannot therefore be excluded that the CJEU, provided with a question concerning the refusal to provide reasonable accommodation to a main carer of a person with a severe disability, maintains its position about the possible disproportionate nature of such measures, if 'not limited to disabled persons only'.

7. Concluding Remarks

In order to assess the extent to which the CJEU has actually shaped EU disability law, two issues need to be highlighted. First, when addressing the protection of rights of persons with disabilities, the CJEU is treading on an unstable terrain, where the scope of EU law interacts with areas of law that MS would claim to be within the remit of their competences (i.e. social policy). That is why the Court's attitude is not sharp enough to avoid considering the consequences of its decisions in that area. Too often, therefore, it recognises a certain leeway to national measures and entrusts the referring judge with the difficult task of checking the proportionality of the relevant national measure. Second, the relevant CJEU case law is developing, as it often does, mostly in the rails set by requests for preliminary rulings proposed by national courts, while the only notable exception – the infringement action brought by the Commission against Italy for not having implemented Article 5 of the Employment Equality Directive with a general and directly applicable provision – follows essentially the same path. The focus is, therefore, on individual enforcement, i.e. on cases brought to national courts first and then via the preliminary ruling procedure to the attention of the CJEU. Is this the best approach to 'shape' EU disability law? I frankly doubt it.

Disability entails weakness in the management of bilateral legal relationships. A worker is always the weak party in the employment relationship, a worker with disability is even weaker in that relationship. If not rebalanced by strong, effective social support, both in the form of social services and in that of a supportive trade unionism, this especially weak position might involve accepting less than optimal working conditions. The very idea of reasonable accommodation through mutually acceptable special terms of employment might be a slippery slope, and lead to disguised discriminations, not at all likely to emerge before courts.

[89] Case C-485/20 *HR Rail*, para 38.

[90] Case C-631/22 *Ca Na Negreta*, para 42.

Let us consider some raw numbers that relate to the situation we last took into consideration, that of working parents caring for a child with a disability. According to Eurostat,[91] in 2023, 6.9 per cent of the EU population between the ages of 16 and 19 had 'some or severe' disability, while 1.4 per cent had 'severe' disability. Further Eurostat data[92] – the last available refer to 2021 –, indicate that 3.4 per cent of children under the age of 16 have 'moderate or severe' disability, while 1 per cent of EU children of that age have 'severe' disability. One can thus infer from the two relevant Eurostat statistic datasets that between 1 and 1.4 per cent of EU minors have 'severe' disability. As the EU population in 2023 was 448.4 million inhabitants, it means that, in the same year, between 4.5 million and 6.3 million couples/single caring parents had to take care of a child with severe disability. Only ONE (absolute number!) reference for a preliminary ruling reached the CJEU since the entry into force of the Employment Equality Directive, concerning the working situation of a person who is a primary caregiver of one of those children, in a case involving an incredibly crude form of villainy. Since 2006, no other case reached the CJEU in this area. This can only mean two things, but only one is true: either we live in the most perfect of worlds, or the system is not working. Unfortunately, I guess the second alternative is true. How do we fix the system? We would need the Commission to assume in this area, too, a 'main actor' role, like the one it played when it came to start developing an EU approach to disabilities in the 1980s, with the idea of contributing to the UN Decade of Disabled Persons.[93] In order for the Commission do this, however, a number of structural (organisational) and operational issues would probably need to be addressed.

As to the organisational issues, let me just mention the need to de-politicise the infringement procedure, through a modification of the Commission's practices and of its Rules.[94]

As to the operational conditions for the Commission to take such a 'main actor' role, it should undertake a comprehensive, reliable and proactive assessment of the MS's policies and practices in the disability area, as a precondition for discussing their benchmarks, and for initiating infringement actions where such benchmarks are not satisfactory. But, in this game we are all at square one, as it appears quite clearly by the essential lack of precise and comparable statistical data: the Eurostat data referred to above are based on self-declaration, and they essentially lack precision and comparability among Member States.[95]

[91] Eurostat, 'Level of disability (activity limitation) by sex, age and income quintile' available at <https://ec.europa.eu/eurostat/databrowser/product/page/HLTH_SILC_12>.

[92] Eurostat, 'Children with limitation in activities due to health problems, by income group, household composition and age' available at <https://ec.europa.eu/eurostat/databrowser/product/page/ILC_HCH13>.

[93] Quinn and Flynn (n 88) 35 *et seq*.

[94] B Cortese, 'The ban on collective expulsions and the betrayal of the Union's legal system at its external borders' (2023) 40(2) *Anales de derecho* 46.

[95] European Court of Auditors, 'Special Report: Supporting people with disabilities' (European Court of Auditors 2023).

Epilogue

Conflict of Interest Note, as a Way of Personal Conclusions

Let me add a very personal note, and highlight, candidly, a conflict of interest that has influenced this chapter's content: living myself with a child with severe disability, I know what I am talking about …

It is about having your child excluded from the European School in Luxembourg because 'she's not autonomous, and we're not bound to take her', and knowing that that international organisation's secluded complaint system is steady about there being no full right to inclusion for children with severe disabilities.

It is then about not having any other meaningful choice, for our family, than to move to a Member State where inclusive education is at least a full right you can oppose to any non-cooperative administrations – and we have found some of them … –, to force them to comply with their duties, or face a certain rout in court.

It is about my wife, the child's mother, not having any other choice than to take a long leave on personal grounds from her work in a EU institution, because of that situation.

It is further – and that is now about the co-carer father position – about having to count on your colleagues' goodwill and kindness when it comes to defining your working hours, so that you can share that care.

It is about a promotion system that foresees no different criteria for parents of a child with severe disability and their colleagues not having to face any comparable issue.

It is about having to bear the essential weight of your child's out-of-school time and needs because of an underfunded social service.

It is about knowing you are a privileged couple of working parents having both managed to keep your posts and succeed in fulfilling both your caring duties and your professional ones, while you see almost all other families in comparable situations forced to make much heavier compromises.

7

National Courts as 'Actors' in the Preliminary Reference Procedure

CHARLES E O'SULLIVAN

1. Introduction

The procedure of making a preliminary reference, as contained within Article 267 Treaty on the Functioning of the European Union (TFEU), has helped to shape the development of European Union (EU) law and, particularly, the protection of fundamental rights in significant ways. This is not only because it ensures that EU law is 'given an autonomous and uniform interpretation throughout the European Union',[1] but also because it acts as a 'means of eliminating difficulties which may be occasioned by the requirement of giving [EU] law its full effect'.[2]

These preliminary references represent a facet of the 'cooperative federalism'[3] that characterises the EU constitutional identity whereby the 'national court, in collaboration with the Court of Justice, fulfils a duty entrusted to them both of ensuring that in the interpretation and application of the Treaties the law is observed'.[4] That is to say, the process is an entirely 'court to court' procedure, where a national 'court or tribunal' has questions it cannot itself answer on the interpretation or validity of EU rules that are central to the legal scenario in the case currently pending before it and it could otherwise not issue a final determination.[5] It 'establishes between the Court of Justice and the national courts direct cooperation as part of which the latter are closely involved in the correct application and uniform interpretation of European Union law and also in the

[1] Case C-281/09 *Commission v Spain* ECLI:EU:C:2011:767, para 42.

[2] Case C-166/77 *Rheinmühlen-Düsseldorf v Einfuhr- und Vorratsstelle für Getreide und Futtermittel* ECLI:EU:C:1974:3, para 2.

[3] R Schütze, *From Dual to Cooperative Federalism: The Changing Structure of European Law* (Oxford University Press 2009).

[4] Case C-244/80 *Pasquale Foglia v Mariella Novello* ECLI:EU:C:1981:302, para 1.

[5] Case C-75/63 *Mrs M.K.H. Hoekstra v Bestuur der Bedrijfsvereniging voor Detailhandel en Ambachten* ECLI:EU:C:1964:19; and Joined Cases C-338/04, C-359/04 and C-360/04 *Placanica and Others* ECLI:EU:C:2007:133.

protection of individual rights conferred by that legal order'.[6] Elsewhere, this has also been expressed as a means of contributing towards a 'complete system of legal remedies and procedures'[7] and 'ensuring that in all circumstances this law is the same in all states of the [EU]'.[8]

The collaboration ensures that the remit of both the national court system and the Court of Justice of the European Union (CJEU) are respected – the latter only provides the answers to the questions provided to it, and the national court will apply those to the case once the proceedings recommence, with the national law being dealt with by national courts, and the monopoly on the interpretation of EU law being retained by the CJEU.[9]

The contribution made to the development of EU law by the preliminary reference procedure is vast and has led to fundamental shifts within its status and effect. Indeed, EU law would likely not have become 'a new legal order of international law for the benefit of which the State have limited their sovereign rights, albeit within limited fields',[10] at least at the point in time that it did, without the ability of the CJEU to use this body of cases being sent to them as the raw material for the development of key principles. This also extends to the notion of primacy,[11] and even the principles of equivalence[12] and effectiveness.[13]

However, as much – but not all[14] – of the academic commentary has emphasised,[15] and as Cortese examines elsewhere in this volume,[16] the focus within this procedure has centred on the CJEU and how it uses Article 267 TFEU to

[6] Opinion 1/09 *Opinion Pursuant to Article 300(6) EC* ECLI:EU:C:2011:123, para 84.

[7] Case C-50/00 *P Unión de Pequeños Agricultores v Council of the European Union* ECLI:EU:C:2002:462, para 40.

[8] Case C-166/73 *Rheinmühlen-Düsseldorf*, para 2.

[9] TC Hartley, *The Foundations of European Community Law* (Clarendon Press 2002) 270–271; Case C-54/96 *Dorsch Consult Ingenieurgesellschaft mbH v Bundesbaugesellschaft Berlin mbH* ECLI:EU:C:1997:413.

[10] Case C-26/62 *NV Algemene Transport- en Expeditie Onderneming van Gend & Loos v Netherlands Inland Revenue Administration* ECLI:EU:C:1963:1.

[11] Case C-6/64 *Flaminio Costa v E.N.E.L.* ECLI:EU:C:1964:66.

[12] Case C-33/76 *Rewe-Zentralfinanz eG and Rewe-Zentral AG v Landwirtschaftskammer für das Saarland* ECLI:EU:C:1976:188.

[13] Case C-14/83 *Sabine von Colson and Elisabeth Kamann v Land Nordrhein-Westfalen* ECLI:EU:C:1984:153.

[14] K Alter, 'The European Court's Political Power' (1996) 19 *West European Politics* 458, 466-467 takes a provocative view of the way in which lower national courts can use Article 267 TFEU to innovate and bolster their own remit.

[15] A Wallerman Ghavanini, 'The Court of Justice as a Relation Actor: An Introduction' (2023) 2(Special Issue 2) *European Law Open* 233–243; C Kilpatrick and J Scott, *New Legal Approaches to Studying the Court of Justice: Revisiting Law in Context* (Oxford University Press 2020); U Šadl and A Wallerman, '"The Referring Court asks, in Essence": is reformulation of preliminary questions by the Court of Justice a decision writing fixture or a decision-making approach?' (2019) 25(4) *European Law Journal* 416–433.

[16] B Cortese, 'The Role of the Court of Justice of the European Union in Protecting Disability Rights' in this volume.

drive forward European integration and maintain the integrity of the EU project and its legal order as a whole. This consequently has had the effect of minimising the actor status of courts or tribunals of the Member States and the fact that by its very nature preliminary references are *reciprocal*. Unless national courts or tribunals send references, the CJEU does not have a body of cases to choose from, and to use as the raw material for clarifying and expanding the material scope of EU law. This chapter is premised on the idea that the way in which national referring courts and justices formulate questions is important, and that national courts are key actors in shaping EU law. It may be argued that the role of national courts can to some degree be minimised by the way in which the CJEU can reformulate questions contained within a reference to address what it deems to be at the centre of the case at hand.[17] However, this contribution endeavours to elucidate and tease out what role national courts or tribunals play by arguing that even if the CJEU is the more overt actor in driving legal change, it relies upon national courts to refer the body of case law that facilitates this role. A shift in the number or quality of references for example can significantly impact on the speed at which the EU legal order develops. This, consequently, makes national courts or tribunals equally important actors within this process because of its inherent reciprocity.

This chapter argues that national courts must have a degree of fluency in EU law to be able to send this raw material to the CJEU, have the willingness to do so, and that these referred cases and their associated questions must be capable of building upon or expanding the existing case law on an issue. That is to say, the actor status of national courts or tribunals, even at the most basic level, is that they are willing to send the materials the CJEU needs to develop EU law. This is arguably of even greater importance in a modern EU disability context, where the United Nations Convention on the Rights of Persons with Disabilities (CRPD) now enjoys a sub-constitutional status within the EU legal order.[18] This means that EU law must be read as consistent with the Convention's 'social model of disability'[19] as far as practicable, which necessitates that the CJEU clarifies how, and to what degree, this occurs across a diverse field of EU competences – a task that can only be performed quickly via a sufficient body of preliminary references on the matter.

The chapter adopts a socio-legal approach to examine these issues of fluency and capability. This means that it utilises non-legal sources to supplement and enhance its doctrinal analysis of the preliminary reference procedure

[17] Šadl and Wallerman (n 15). See also U Šadl, 'Studying the Role of Legal Actors in EU Law: An Outline' in this volume.

[18] Case C-239/03 *Commission of the European Communities v French Republic* ECLI:EU:C:2004:598.

[19] D Ferri, 'The Conclusion of the UN Convention on the Rights of Persons with Disabilities by the EC/EU: A Constitutional Perspective' in L Waddington and G Quinn (eds), *European Yearbook of Disability Law Vol. 2* (Intersentia 2010) 47–71.

and examination of key judgments in the area. It then applies these, via a case study to Ireland, to focus in on a specific Member State's actor status for the purposes of Article 267 TFEU. Ireland provides an interesting context, as it is both a long-standing member of the EU, having joined in the early 1970s, and also a peripheral state that is often conceptualised via its relationship to the United Kingdom rather than as worthy of study in its own right. Despite arguably strongly benefiting from EU membership, it has been called 'conditionally integrationist',[20] with a historic tendency towards being neglectful and ignorant of the EU institutions[21] – except where it might help the Irish State carve out exceptions to the scope of EU law.[22] Indeed, in terms of direct actions before the CJEU, Fahey notes that 'Ireland has a wealth of litigation initiated against the Commission',[23] suggesting a potential negative relationship in developing the scope of EU law. Consequently, although many Member States arguably seek to maximise the benefits of EU membership whilst minimising the associated 'costs' of the same, Ireland is often far more transparent in acting in its own 'enlightened self-interest'[24] *vis-à-vis* European integration. This means that it offers a potentially more transparent example of a Member State actor.

The chapter is structured as follows. Following on from this brief introduction, section 2 outlines what is required for a preliminary reference, as well as the inherent limitations of the process. Section 3 then details the contribution made by national courts to EU disability law via Article 267 TFEU, and more specifically the rapid expansion of this since the EU acceded to the CRPD. Section 4, leading into the case study of the Irish example, plots out the inherent difficulties or tensions *vis-à-vis* the contribution national courts or tribunals can make via references to the CJEU. It underlines that the *quality* of engagement is key, and that this requires a degree of fluency with EU law, as well as the ability and willingness to do so. Section 5 utilises Ireland as a case study to examine this issue of fluency, highlighting the degree to which Ireland has a historically low engagement with Article 267 TFEU, and that its fluency with even core principles such as 'what is a court or tribunal' as well as more specific areas of EU law can often be considered poor. The chapter then concludes by offering some brief remarks bringing these issues together once more.

[20] D Scott, *Ireland's Contribution to the European Union* (Institute of European Affairs 1994) 3.

[21] E O'Halpin, 'Irish Parliamentary Culture and the EU: Formalities to be Observed' in P Norton (eds), *National Parliaments and the European Union* (Frank Cass 1996) 124.

[22] CE O'Sullivan and C Murphy, 'The "Special Structural Vulnerability" within Migrant Agricultural Work' (2022) 68(2) *Irish Jurist* 50–68.

[23] E Fahey, 'Number Crunching EU Law and the Irish Legal Order' (*Verfassungsblog*, 30 March 2023) available at <https://verfassungsblog.de/number-crunching-eu-law-and-the-irish-legal-order/>.

[24] M McDowell, 18th June 2001, quoted in The Irish Times, 'Divide between EU federalists and what Irish voters want – McDowell' (*The Irish Times*, 19 June 2001) available at <https://www.irishtimes.com/news/divide-between-eu-federalists-and-what-irish-voters-want-mcdowell-1.313829>.

2. The Preliminary Reference Procedure

Article 267 TFEU provides the formal constitutional basis[25] for making a preliminary reference by first outlining that:

> The Court of Justice of the European Union shall have jurisdiction to give preliminary rulings concerning:
>
> (a) the interpretation of the Treaties;
>
> (b) the validity and interpretation of acts of the institutions, bodies, offices or agencies of the Union.

It then goes on to detail the key circumstances required for a preliminary reference to be made as:

> Where such a question is raised before any court or tribunal of a Member State, that court or tribunal may, if it considers that a decision on the question is necessary to enable it to give judgment, request the Court to give a ruling thereon.

This cumulatively means that the key requirements are that: a preliminary reference must be a matter related to EU law, in a case currently pending before the national court; and, perhaps most importantly from the standpoint of this contribution, it must be made by a court or tribunal of a Member State.

The scope of reviewable acts within a preliminary reference and what engages with EU law is intentionally broad, and can include binding acts such as directives and regulations, as well as non-binding measures, for example, recommendations or opinions – the latter being primarily limited to situations in which they produce or demonstrate *legal effect*, i.e. where they are applied as if they are binding and affect someone's legal position.[26] The CJEU is also capable of interpreting its own judgments, to either apply them to new factual circumstances or to qualify the way an element on which they have previously ruled should operate in alternative circumstances.[27] Where the CJEU is expressly limited, is in ruling on matters of purely national law: 'the Court is not entitled … to interpret rules pertaining to national law' as it is 'for the national court, which alone is competent to interpret national law'.[28] Rather, the CJEU provides an interpretation of EU law, which may help the national court determine if a national law is compatible with the same.[29] This means that while the CJEU is limited to merely answering the questions posed to it, and

[25] R Buxbaum, 'Article 177 of the Rome Treaty as a Federalising Device' (1969) 21 *Stanford Law Review* 1041.

[26] Case C-113/75 *Frecassetti v Amministrazione delle finanze dello Stato* ECLI:EU:C:1976:89; Case C-90/76 *S.r.l. Ufficio Henry van Ameyde v S.r.l. Ufficio centrale italiano di assistenza assicurativa automobilisti in circolazione internazionale (UCI)* ECLI:EU:C:1977:101.

[27] Case C-135/77 *Robert Bosch GmbH v Hauptzollamt Hildesheim* ECLI:EU:C:1978:75.

[28] Case C-75/63 *Mrs M.K.H. Hoekstra*, para 2.

[29] Joined Cases C-338/04, C-359/04 and C-360/04 *Placanica*, para 36.

cannot apply them to the specifics of a case,[30] – once there is an interaction between national and EU rules, the Court has a relatively wide remit to determine how the latter will affect national measures once it can be framed from the perspective of the same.'

The second issue of whether it is a matter currently pending before a national court is a clear practical consideration, as it ensures that the CJEU is only called upon to render decisions that will aid in national decisions of a judicial measure,[31] and in a manner which helps the national court to settle the case with the freshly provided interpretation of EU law.[32] This means that the CJEU is not capable 'of delivering advisory opinions on general or hypothetical questions but of assisting in the administration of justice in the member states'.[33] Of course, it also 'cannot empower the [CJEU] to investigate the facts of the case or to criticise the grounds and purpose of the request for interpretation'.[34] This is supported by the fact that this is a kind of cooperative federalism and to do so may impact upon the working relationship between the national and EU courts. The CJEU can, however, reject where the answers to the questions posed are patently obvious or there is no relationship between the facts of the case and the questions posed.[35] Consequently, irrelevant or purely hypothetical questions cannot be answered by the CJEU, and fictitious proceedings that are engineered to receive answers from the CJEU on the interpretation or validity of EU rules may also be rejected.[36] It is also the case that the reference sent must 'define the factual and legislative context of the questions which it is asking or, at the very least, explain the factual circumstances'.[37] This is expanded upon elsewhere in Article 94 of the Rules of Procedure of the CJEU[38] and allows for a preliminary reference to be rejected where these basic components are not included – although as discussed later, in cases such as

[30] Case C-20/64 *SARL Albatros v Société des pétroles et des combustibles liquides (Sopéco)* ECLI:EU:C:1965:8; Joined cases C-28 to 30/62 *Da Costa en Schaake NV, Jacob Meijer NV, Hoechst-Holland NV v Netherlands Inland Revenue Administration* ECLI:EU:C:1963:6.

[31] Case C-96/04 *Standesamt Stadt Niebüll* ECLI:EU:C:2006:254, para 13.

[32] Case C-104/79 *Pasquale Foglia v Mariella Novello* ECLI:EU:C:1980:73, para 11.

[33] C Gray, 'Advisory Opinions and the Court of Justice' (1983) 8 *European Law Review* 24; G Bebr, 'The Existence of a Genuine Dispute: An Indispensable Precondition for the Jurisdiction of the Court under Article 177 EC?' (1980) 17 *Common Market Law Review* 525.

[34] Case C-6/64 *Costa*, para 2; T Tridimas, 'Knocking on Heaven's Door: Fragmentation, Efficiency and Defiance in the Preliminary Reference Procedure' (2003) 40(9) *Common Market Law Review* 21–26.

[35] Case C-126/80 *Maria Salonia v Giorgio Poidomani and Franca Baglieri, née Giglio* ECLI:EU:C:1981:136.

[36] F Shouldice and L O'Brien, 'EU Court Entertained Bogus Case on Welfare Rights' (*EUObserver*, 21 December 2015) available at <https://euobserver.com/investigations/131569>.

[37] Case C-42/07 *Liga Portuguesa de Futebol Profissional, Bwin International Ltd v Departamento de Jogos da Santa Casa da Misericórdia de Lisboa* ECLI:EU:C:2009:519, para 40.

[38] Rules of Procedure of the Court of Justice [2012] OJ L265/1.

Minister for Justice and Equality and the Commissioner of An Garda Síochána v. The Workplace Relations Commission,[39] the Court can be more generous in allowing cases even where these questions are, for example, of questionable construction.

The third paragraph of Article 267 TFEU only imposes an obligation to refer on courts or tribunals with final jurisdiction, or against which there is no right of appeal. Where the answer is 'so obvious as to leave no scope for any reasonable doubt' or where the issue has already been dealt with in a previous judgment of the CJEU, the obligation dissipates.[40] All questions regarding the potential invalidity of EU laws, regardless at which level of court this occurs at, must be referred to the CJEU.[41]

Lastly, the issue of what constitutes a court or tribunal of a Member State for the purposes of making a preliminary reference has been the subject of a great body of case law on the part of the CJEU, and is perhaps one of the most innovative elements of this procedure. Possibly most significantly, the CJEU has been firm in noting that 'the expression 'court or tribunal' is a concept of Community law',[42] and this ultimately means that national definitions of the same are irrelevant. What is instead fundamental to which bodies can make a reference, is the qualities or characteristics it possesses – that is to say, does it operate in practice in line with the attributes of a judicial body. In *Dorsch Consult*,[43] these characteristics were outlined as being: is the body established within law, does it apply rules of law and with full 'force of law', i.e. is it compulsory in its jurisdiction, is it permanent, are its proceedings *inter partes*, and does it have independence in its operation.[44]

This has historically ensured that the broadest number of bodies has been empowered to make references, and by extension, ensured that these can be made earlier, and more frequently without the need to enter the formal courts system of a Member State, which may not occur in all instances if an appeal is not sought or entertained. For example, many professional or administrative bodies have been empowered via this set of criteria and adoption of an EU concept of 'court or tribunal' to send questions to the CJEU that they would otherwise be nationally excluded from doing so. In *Broekmulen*, a Dutch doctor who qualified

[39] Case C-378/17 *Minister for Justice and Equality, The Commissioner of An Garda Síochána v Workplace Relations Commission, notice parties: Ronald Boyle and Others* ECLI:EU:C:2018:979.

[40] Case C-283/81 *Srl CILFIT and Lanificio di Gavardo SpA v Ministry of Health* ECLI:EU:C:1982:335, para 21.

[41] G Bebr, 'The Reinforcement of the Constitutional Review of Community Acts under the EEC Treaty' (1988) 25 *Common Market Law Review* 667.

[42] Case C-24/92 *Pierre Corbiau v Administration des Contributions* ECLI:EU:C:1993:118, para 15.

[43] Case C-54/96 *Dorsch Consult Ingenieurgesellschaft mbH v Bundesbaugesellschaft Berlin mbH* ECLI:EU:C:1997:413.

[44] Case C-53/03 *Synetairismos Farmakopoion Aitolias & Akarnanias (Syfait) and Others v GlaxoSmithKline plc and GlaxoSmithKline AEVE* ECLI:EU:C:2005:333.

as such in Belgium was refused registration as a General Practitioner by the relevant national professional registration body and believed this was a violation of his freedom of movement rights. The CJEU argued that this was a court or tribunal capable of making a reference due in part to the fact that it was a 'professional body acting under a degree of governmental supervision' which 'creates appeal procedures which may affect the exercise of rights granted by [EU] law'.[45]

Few of the conditions set out for what constitutes a court or tribunal for the purposes of making a preliminary reference have been viewed as absolute, and are subject to a degree of flexibility – although the requirement that the dispute be adjudicated by an independent third party is far more inflexible and has invariably meant that appeals bodies at the administrative level are more likely to be empowered by Article 267 TFEU.[46] Similarly, the recent case of *Banco De Santander*[47] has further expanded upon the notion of independence in light of the rule of law crises in several of the Eastern European Member States,[48] although this is not explicitly referenced by the CJEU.[49] This reformulation now mandates that two separate elements of independence be satisfied: internal, meaning that there be a clear degree of impartiality on the part of the decision-maker;[50] and external, which ensures that they are free from institutional constraints and cannot, for example, be removed as retribution, etc.[51] Although covered by the CJEU in the opposite order, it is conceptualised here in this manner because of the way in which the external would impede or exert significant pressure on their impartiality to affect this internal aspect and because, as Bogdanowicz and Taborowski argue, 'the Court [had previously] adopted a very formal approach in relation to the external aspect of independence',[52] making this the issue that appears to be the most refined element. Whilst they appear to argue that this has thus far been of limited effect, and does not substantively alter the previous permissive attitude towards the independence requirement in a material way,[53] the specific impact that this will have in practice is yet to be determined.

[45] Case C-246/80 *C. Broekmeulen v Huisarts Registratie Commissie* ECLI:EU:C:1981:218, para 16; G Bebr, 'Arbitration Tribunals and Article 177 of the EEC Treaty' (1985) 22 *Common Market Law Review* 489.

[46] Case C-24/92 *Pierre Corbiau.*

[47] Case C-274/14 *Banco de Santander* ECLI:EU:C:2020:17.

[48] L Pech and D Kochenov (eds), *Respect for the Rule of Law in the Case Law of the European Court of Justice: A Casebook Overview of Key Judgments since the Portuguese Judges Case* (SIEPS 2021).

[49] Case C-274/14 *Banco de Santander*, para 55.

[50] Ibid para 61.

[51] Ibid paras 57-59.

[52] P Bogdanowicz and M Taborowski, 'The Independence Criterion for National Courts in the Preliminary Reference Procedure After Banco de Santander: Still the Joker in the Deck?' (2023) 60(3) *Common Market Law Review* 770.

[53] Ibid 793.

3. The Role of National Courts in Shaping EU Disability Law

As the introduction underlined, the contribution made by the preliminary reference procedure to the scope and power of EU law is vast. This also extends to fundamental rights protection within the EU legal order. Maas, for example, has emphasised that 'men and women who share the aim of creating European citizens have occupied key institutions' such as the CJEU and nationally, that 'have worked to integrate Europeans not only economically but also socially and politically by conferring upon them European rights'.[54]

It was, indeed, upon a preliminary reference that the CJEU established that fundamental rights are unenumerated but implicit in the general principles of EU law,[55] – and later, allowed for the CJEU to pull fundamental rights from the common constitutional traditions of the Member States.[56] However, Maas also qualified that the way in which early reticence to adopting a human rights based approach to European integration meant that there was an emphasis on economic integration, with rights consequently often being framed as stemming from the more developed economic competences of the EU.[57] This has meant that, particularly in respect of policy areas such as disability, the expansion of rights was often based on employment or economically-focused legislation and utilised the principle of non-discrimination – because these were viewed as 'rule[s] of EU social law of particular importance'.[58] For example, in *Emmett*,[59] it was found that the principle of effectiveness meant that time limits could not be put on challenging a potential discrimination in accessing a disability benefit, or in *Coleman*,[60] the CJEU expanded the scope of Directive 2000/78/EC establishing a general framework for equal treatment in employment and occupation (Employment Equality Directive)[61] to cover discrimination by association in a disability context. This is not to suggest that the scope of these were not of significant importance, merely that the development was often less radical, and it did historically adopt a medicalised conception of disability that held that this was legally distinct from sickness.[62]

[54] W Maas, 'Fifteen Years of European Union Citizenship' (2007) (Paper prepared for the 2007 Meeting of the Canadian Political Science Association) available at <https://cpsa-csp.ca/papers-2007/Maas.pdf>.

[55] Case C-29/69 *Erich Stauder v City of Ulm – Sozialamt* ECLI:EU:C:1969:57.

[56] Case C-11/70 *Internationale Handelsgesellschaft v Einfuhr* ECLI:EU:C:1970:114.

[57] W Maas, 'Introducing European Rights' in W Maas, *Creating European Citizens* (Rowman & Littlefield 2007) 11–28; W Maas, 'The Evolution of EU Citizenship' in S Meunier and K McNamara (eds), *Making History: European Integration and Institutional Change at Fifty* (Oxford University Press 2007).

[58] Case C-429/09 *Günter Fuß v Stadt Halle* ECLI:EU:C:2010:717, para 33.

[59] Case C-208/90 *Emmott v Minister for Social Welfare* ECLI:EU:C:1991:333.

[60] Case C-303/06 *S Coleman v Attridge Law and Steve Law* ECLI:EU:C:2008:415.

[61] Council Directive 2000/78/EC of 27 November 2000 establishing a general framework for equal treatment in employment and occupation (Employment Equality Directive) [2000] OJ L303/16.

[62] Case C-13/05 *Chacón Navas v Eurest Colectividades SA* ECLI:EU:C:2006:456.

As Favalli and Ferri thoughtfully detail, the true power and potential of preliminary references within the disability sphere becomes apparent following the EU's accession to the CRPD.[63] The Employment Equality Directive has not had a clear definition of disability, and recent case law generated via preliminary references has facilitated the CJEU in trying to solve this problem, and to bring it in line with the socio-contextual/human rights-based model of disability contained within the CRPD. In *Ring and Werge*,[64] the CJEU for the first time embraced the CRPD definition of disability.[65] This, in particular, meant that the kinds of cases and material scope of disability began to be questioned in cases involving surrogacy,[66] obesity,[67] and how the duration of an incapacity interacts with this new model of disability being embraced by the CJEU.[68] It even quickly moved outside of the employment context, and began to influence how disability within the Charter of Fundamental Rights (CFR) should be defined.[69]

Certainly, these cases are not without criticism, and the evolution of this issue has been uneven.[70] What is repetitive, true, as Favalli and Ferri note, is that the activism of the CJEU was moving more rapidly than the legislative institutions in attempting to adopt formal reforms.[71] As the authors highlight, despite a proposal in 2008 for a new directive on non-discrimination,[72] by 2016 this still had not incorporated a clear definition of disability in line with the CRPD,[73] and consequently the CJEU had been called in to 'fill the gap'.[74] By 2021, the proposal for this directive remained stalled,[75] and this has meant that the gap on disability remains one which must be filled by the CJEU to a large degree.

The rapid pace of this legal dialogue regarding how to incorporate a Convention-compliant definition of disability within the EU legal order would not

[63] S Favalli and D Ferri, 'Defining Disability in the EU Non-Discrimination Legislation: Judicial Activism and Legislative Restraints' (2016) 22(3) *European Public Law* 5–35.

[64] Joined Cases C-335/11 and C-377/11 *HK Danmark, acting on behalf of Jette Ring v Dansk almennyttigt Boligselskab and HK Danmark, acting on behalf of Lone Skouboe Werge v Dansk Arbejdsgiverforening, acting on behalf of Pro Display A/S* ECLI:EU:C:2013:222.

[65] Joined Cases C-335/11 and C-377/11 *HK Danmark*, para 41.

[66] Case C-363/12 *Z v A Government Department and The Board of Management of a Community School* ECLI:EU:C:2013:604.

[67] Case C-354/13 *FOA acting on behalf of Karsten Kaltoft v KL acting on behalf of the Municipality of Billund* ECLI:EU:C:2014:2463.

[68] Case C-395/15 *Mohamed Daouidi v Bootes Plus SL, Fondo de Garantía Salarial, Ministerio Fiscal* ECLI:EU:C:2016:917.

[69] Case C-356/12 *Wolfgang Glatzel v Freistaat Bayern* ECLI:EU:C:2014:350.

[70] D Ferri, '*Daouidi v Bootes Plus SL* and the Concept of 'Disability' in EU Anti-Discrimination Law' (2019) 10(1) *European Labour Law Journal* 69–84.

[71] Favalli and Ferri (n 63).

[72] European Commission (Commission), 'Proposal for a Council Directive on implementing the principle of equal treatment between persons irrespective of religion or belief, disability, age or sexual orientation' COM(2008) 426 final.

[73] Favalli and Ferri (n 63) 21-22.

[74] Ibid 22.

[75] Commission, 'Union of Equality: Strategy for the Rights of Persons with Disabilities 2021-2030' COM(2021) 101 final 14.

have been possible without the preliminary reference procedure. This was indeed driven by a more direct and pressing concern over what the appropriate definition is. However, many preliminary references have sought to push this even further and iron out more complex points beyond this.

For example, in *Tartu Vangla*[76] an Estonian prison officer was deemed incapable of performing the essential functions of his employment as he required an auditory aid, and had to be assessed under Estonian law without the use of his corrective device. The question therefore became a more technical issue of whether the requirement to assess his acuity without the devices was legitimate and could be reasonably justified.[77] Interestingly however, even in posing this more complex question, the referring court did not appear to frame this based upon the need for reasonable accommodation.[78]

In *Z v. A Government Department*, a reference from the Irish Equality Tribunal sought to clarify which of three different directives a person having a child born via surrogacy would be subject to, and its relationship to disability. Although the Court ultimately found that none of these applied, and the rationale was not without criticism, it posed an important question regarding which legislation would apply in such cases.

Finally, in *Daouidi*, the referring Spanish social court sought to push forward the definition of disability based not just upon the CRPD, but also Article 21(1) CFR – and by extension, to establish how these two different levels of obligation relate to one another. Although Ferri notes that the questions were 'quite convoluted'[79] and the CJEU ultimately side-stepped the question of the CFR's application. The posing of these questions forces the CJEU to contend with issues that it otherwise may not have considered, and stresses the importance of national courts in shaping EU disability law, challenging the scope of the relevant directives.

Even though this journey has been uneven, and the questions referred may sometimes be inexact, it is the reciprocal nature of this dialogue and the willingness of national courts to attempt to grapple with these questions of EU law that reinforces their important status as actors – by posing these questions, they force the CJEU to confront and try to address the same.

4. The Limits of National Courts as Actors

Although the preceding section highlights the significant potential for Member State courts to drive the evolution of fundamental rights, and by extension,

[76] Case C-795/19 *XX v Tartu Vangla* ECLI:EU:C:2021:606.

[77] Case C-795/19 *Tartu Vangla*, para 25.

[78] T Gyulavári, 'Recent CJEU case law on 'reasonable accommodation' at work: towards the recognition of a new discrimination form' (2023) 24 *ERA Forum* 361.

[79] Ferri (n 70) 73.

disability rights at EU level, as this contribution argues, this requires that these same courts *engage* with Article 267 TFEU in a way that is meaningful and poses questions of substance – this requires that these same courts possess an understanding of the mechanics of EU law and refer the best raw material for the CJEU to engage with.

Golub, for example, underlines – from a political science perspective – the importance of looking at the statistical information on preliminary references made by a Member State, as well as considering how they make them to see how that same state's judiciary engages in substance with EU law.[80] This can act as a clear measure of engagement in that it demonstrates willingness among the Member States to send references, reflecting their degree of participation with Article 267 TFEU. For this reason, the degree to which Member State courts or tribunals are empowered to make references by being considered capable of sending questions is also key, as without the ability to engage with the process, they cannot become an actor capable of contributing to the development of EU law. However, statistical analyses are not indicative of *quality* of engagement – this necessitates that the case law referred is also examined, to see if there is a relationship between quantity and quality of references, and the specific kind of contribution national courts make as actors within this reciprocal process.

On this point of quality, Passalacqua articulated certain factors influencing actors and the ways in which they utilise Article 267 TFEU.[81] Although focused on the ways in which legal representatives for plaintiffs can positively utilise EU law, two factors that the author identifies are instructive for this chapter: EU-expertise, and favourable legal structures. The former, focuses on having the legal knowledge necessary to mount a strong case, but when transferred to the national courts, can be taken as the legal fluency necessary to identify where a reference would be advantageous and the formulation of appropriate questions. This fluency in turn points to the weight of the contribution national courts can make as actors, because they are able to identify the most relevant cases, and articulate the strongest questions for the CJEU to answer. Returning to the point on ability, Passalacqua notes the latter involves 'judicial receptivity' to making a reference and this reinforces the importance of a national court's willingness to refer questions.[82]

Cumulatively, therefore, this chapter takes fluency as being the ability and willingness to engage with the preliminary reference process in a substantive way,

[80] J Golub, 'The Politics of Judicial Discretion: Rethinking the Interaction between National Courts and the European Court of Justice' (1996) 19 *West European Politics* 360–385; J Golub, 'British sovereignty and the development of EC environmental policy' (1996) 4(5) *Environmental Politics* 700–728.

[81] V Passalacqua, 'Legal Mobilization via Preliminary Reference: Insights from the Case of Migrant Rights' (2021) 58(3) *Common Market Law Review* 751–776.

[82] Ibid 770.

which provides the CJEU with the strongest material for driving EU law forward. It takes both the number of references made and the individual quality of each, i.e. the quantity and quality, as equally important in assessing the importance of national courts' 'actorness' within the preliminary reference procedure.

Applying these issues to disability law, the issue of fluency is important in the current context, as the core dialogue at present concerns how EU law can be read as CRPD-compliant. This includes an additional layer of complexity, given that this means reconciling EU law with its international obligations, and then applying this to the particular facts of cases before a national court. Member State courts must therefore be able to identify legal lacunae in an evolving, and arguably more complex area. As the preceding section highlights, the lack of a legislative adoption of a Convention-compliant definition means that references seeking clarification on this are contributing to the CJEU's own activism on the issue. It also means that even where questions are vague or somewhat convoluted, as in *Dauoidi*, that the answer can still be instructive. However, the basic raw material must be constructed in a workable manner and sent to the CJEU to allow it to drive forward the legal reasoning on the CRPD and its impact on EU legislative conceptions of disability.

Chalmers, in analysing the areas in which preliminary references tend to be made, found that economic freedoms, VAT and agriculture were by far the most common.[83] This can in part be explained by the fact that these are long established competences of the EU, and national courts are drawn more quickly to note the EU dimension and the possible need to refer, as well as the way in which fields such as immigration and asylum – which feature highly within national judicial review proceedings – were historically cut off from Article 267 TFEU.[84] Although disability can quite easily be captured within the economic freedoms – in part because of the degree to which employment discrimination is often featured within EU disability case law – the statistics collected by the CJEU on its own judicial activity do not classify disability as a field of action in its own right.[85] This also applies to social security case law, which strongly features disability issues as a result of the proportion of persons with disabilities in receipt of such benefits.[86] This means that even if a Member State would appear to be a strong actor in making a higher level of references per year, it does not necessarily capture its contribution to disability law *strictu sensu*.

[83] D Chalmers, 'The Court of Justice and the Constitutional Treaty' (2005) 4 *ICON* 428, 455.

[84] D Chalmers, G Davies and G Monti, *European Union Law* (Cambridge University Press 2010) 157.

[85] Court of Justice of the European Union, 'Statistics Concerning the Judicial Activity of the Court of Justice' (Annual Report, 2022).

[86] European Parliamentary Research Service, 'Employment and disability in the European Union' (2022) PE 651.932 2, 5; Central Statistics Office, 'Income, Employment and Welfare Analysis of People with a Disability 2019' available at <https://www.cso.ie/en/releasesandpublications/fp/fp-iewad/incomeemploymentandwelfareanalysisofpeoplewithadisability2019/incomeandemployment/>.

5. Ireland as a Case Study

As the introduction highlighted, Ireland serves as an important case study for measuring the impact of national courts in enforcing EU law in demonstrating the actor status of Member State courts because of its complex relationship with EU law and the institutions, as well as the limited degree of focus it tends to attract within the broader scholarly literature.

The Irish Superior Courts in particular have a low engagement rate with preliminary references from a historical standpoint, as well as a less than optimal understanding of EU law, including core concepts such as the definition of 'court or tribunal' for the purposes of making a preliminary reference, and which bodies can and cannot disapply national laws in favour of EU law. From a statistical standpoint, Fahey notes that during its first 30 years of EU membership from 1973-2003:

> the total number of preliminary references from the Irish courts at 44 was comparably the lowest in all of the EU back at the time of the study, with the exception of certain states that recently joined the 1995 wave of accessions.[87]

Although she subsequently justifies this low number of referrals in the context of EU law being infrequently utilised, Fahey highlights that 'the rate of refusals of preliminary reference applications appeared to be significant',[88] and rather than consistently growing as Ireland became more embedded within the EU, the number of references made continued to fluctuate but remain low during this period. This can again potentially be explained by a lack of fluency with EU law within the Irish Courts as a whole, including fundamental principles of the same[89] – one that is exacerbated by an emphasis on national constitutional norms ahead of EU constitutional law. For example, as Justice Hogan held in *Plesca v. HSE*:

> so far as EU law is concerned, it is plain that administrative agencies enjoy no power to determine that domestic enactments are incompatible with EU law and that this jurisdiction is reserved to the judicial branch.[90]

This equates disapplication, which is focused on facilitating not only courts but administrative bodies in setting aside national rules which conflict with EU law, as a form of judicial review, which it is not *strictu sensu* as it does not formally invalidate a rule.

Most importantly for the purposes of making a preliminary reference, the Superior Courts in Ireland have consistently adopted a definition of 'courts or tribunals' that is purely national in nature, and does not comply with the case

[87] Fahey (n 23).

[88] Ibid.

[89] For a more detailed discussion of this issue, CE O'Sullivan, 'Ireland's Non-Compliance with the Principle of Supremacy and the Definition of Court or Tribunal for the Purposes of Article 267 TFEU: A Review of the Recent Case Law' (2019) 61 *Irish Jurist* 159–173.

[90] *Plesca v HSE & Ors*, unreported, Hogan J, High Court, 16 February 2011.

law of the CJEU on the matter. The Irish Constitution, via Article 34 of the same, includes a finite number of recognised courts,[91] with the Superior Courts incorporating the High Court, the Court of Appeals and the Supreme Court, who possess the sole power to perform judicial reviews.[92] Anything that falls outside of these recognised courts has a far more limited set of functions it can perform from a national constitutional standpoint. This issue would come to the fore in *Workplace Relations Commission*,[93] which concerned a number of individuals who believed they had been discriminated against based on their age in applying for positions with the Irish police force, *An Garda Síochána*. A component body of the Workplace Relations Commission (WRC) found this to be unlawful discrimination and disapplied the national rule so that the Employment Equality Directive was given its full effect.

This was first appealed to the High Court, who again suggested a clear equivalency between disapplication and judicial review,[94] as well as emphasising the national conception of courts.[95] This was reaffirmed at the Supreme Court who underlined that judicial functions are constitutionally limited.[96] Compounding this matter, is the fact that even though the Supreme Court found this issue to be obvious and that the WRC could not engage in disapplication as it is not a court, it made a preliminary reference asking if it could continue to hear the case. The Czech government, when this reached the Advocate General (AG), argued this was too poorly constructed a question to be dealt with.[97] AG Wahl agreed that the question was poorly formulated, but stressed that the factual information provided and the constitutional context were sufficient to stress the importance and relevance for hearing it[98] – underlining the degree to which both Ireland's fluency with EU law can be questionable, and the latitude that the CJEU has in allowing references even where the questions are imprecise. Similarly, the Grand Chamber operated on the basis of presumed relevance for its admissibility.

Ultimately, the CJEU held that 'the Court has repeatedly held, that duty to disapply national legislation that is contrary to EU law is owed not only by national courts, but also by all organs of the State – including administrative authorities – called upon, within the exercise of their respective powers, to apply EU law'.[99] It also stated in no uncertain terms that the WRC was capable

[91] Article 34.2 Bunreacht na hÉireann.

[92] Articles 34.3.1 and 34.3.2 Bunreacht na hÉireann.

[93] Case C-378/17 *Minister for Justice and Equality, The Commissioner of An Garda Síochána.*

[94] *Minister for Justice Equality & Law Reform & anor v Director of the Equality Tribunal & ors* [2009] IEHC 72, paras 7-8.

[95] *Minister for Justice Equality & Law Reform & anor*, para 7.

[96] *Minister for Justice, Equality and Law Reform and the Commissioner of An Garda Síochána v The Workplace Relations Commission & ors* [2017] IESC 43, para 5.8.

[97] Case C-378/17 *The Minister for Justice and Equality, The Commissioner of An Garda Síochána*, para 27.

[98] Ibid paras 28-32.

[99] Ibid para 38.

of dealing with this matter,[100] although it did not substantively engage with the definition of 'court or tribunal' for the purposes of Article 267 TFEU.

This particular conception of courts as being limited to what is contained within Article 34 of the Irish Constitution reinforces the limited engagement with preliminary references. That is because if it is only the High Court or higher that can conduct a degree of judicial review, then they will be the primary venues for making a preliminary reference as they can contest the legality of such rules, and then legitimately pose these questions to the CJEU. This of course contains a mistaken understanding of what other bodies would be empowered via Article 267 TFEU to make references, but as a matter of constitutional praxis in the national context, helps to explain this historically low level of engagement – a lack of fluency, which leads to a belief that there are fewer venues in which EU law can be raised, and consequently, who is empowered to make a reference. The 2022 report on judicial activity on the part of the CJEU demonstrates that Ireland sent 52 references between 2018 and 2022.[101] This illustrates that it has statistically improved given that it has sent more in this five year period than in the 30 years examined by Fahey. However, the contemporary example of *Workplace Relations Commission* underlines how the ongoing question of fluency may continue to artificially suppress the number of preliminary references submitted by Irish courts. For the purposes of this volume and the particular issue of disability law, this is arguably of greater importance as national courts have been in an ongoing dialogue with the CJEU concerning how to read existing EU law as Convention-compliant post-accession to the CRPD. Although the CJEU has been dealing with a not insignificant number of referrals questioning how, in particular, the social model can be implemented within the EU legal order, a constant supply of cases and well-formulated questions is necessary to ensure that this issue can become more defined and robust. If there is an artificial suppression of the number of referrals from a Member State, there will be less case law to utilise in this learning process for the CJEU, and quite possibly of cases that would benefit from being referred.

A further example in relation to a more specific area of EU law, came in *Voican*.[102] Importantly, for the purposes of this volume, the case dealt with a dependent relative of an EU worker resident in Ireland who was refused access to the national Disability Allowance, a social assistance payment. The Department of Social Protection had refused on the basis that if the applicant was granted the payment, they would no longer be dependent on their economically-active family member and their dependency would transfer to the state – constituting an undue burden on the welfare system. This extremely convoluted interpretation was challenged before the Irish High Court,[103] which highlighted that this issue had been

[100] Ibid para 46.
[101] Court of Justice of the European Union (n 85) 5.
[102] Case C-488/21 *GV v Chief Appeals Officer, Social Welfare Appeals Office, Minister for Employment Affairs and Social Protection, Ireland, Attorney General* ECLI:EU:C:2023:1013.
[103] *Voican v Chief Appeals Officer* [2020] IEHC 258.

resolved almost 35 years previously,[104] and found against the Department.[105] However, on further appeal, the Irish Court of Appeals, despite the availability of the cogently and methodically laid out rationale in the High Court's judgment, deemed it necessary to refer questions to the CJEU asking if this formulation of dependency was correct[106] – with the ultimate answer from the CJEU mirroring the reasoning of the High Court.[107]

Thus, this case firstly demonstrates, much like in *Workplace Relations Commission*, that where references by lower fluency Member State courts are made, the quality of material being provided to the CJEU for the purposes of developing EU law can be lower. *Voican* merely required a restatement of existing precedent – to the extent that even the High Court was clear on the correct interpretation without the need for a reference. Secondly, it potentially points to a more nuanced point: lower fluency is not a uniform issue, as it was in this instance the Court of Appeals that was having difficulty with a more basic point or knowable point of EU law. From a broader EU perspective, this reiterates that the number of references made can be undercut by the quality of these same references – a low referring country can provide an outsized contribution if its level of legal fluency or expertise is more developed, and a specific national court or even specific justices can, via their fluency, become significant actors, even if the broader judicial structures are less significant actors.

The recent *Nano Nagle*[108] judgment also highlights that Ireland can, and often does deal with more complex issues of EU law, and without the need to refer. This case dealt with reasonable accommodations for persons with disabilities and its relationship to the Employment Equality Directive. The Irish Supreme Court ultimately issued a judgment that was able to parse the complex relationship between EU law and the CRPD, underlining that the actor status of national courts is not uniform, and can vary across time, based upon the composition of these courts, and even individual cases.

6. Concluding Remarks

National courts have, of course, made a number of significant contributions to EU law via the preliminary reference procedure. The procedure has been used by the

[104] *Voican*, paras 53 *et seq* placing a particular emphasis on Case C-316/85 *Centre public d'aide sociale de Courcelles v Lebon* ECLI:EU:C:1987:302.

[105] For a more detailed consideration of the High Court judgment, CE O'Sullivan, 'Access to Social Welfare Payments for Dependent Family Members of EU Citizens in Ireland' (2021) 23 *Irish Journal of European Law* 145–161.

[106] Case C-488/21 *Reference for a preliminary ruling from the Court of Appeal (Ireland)* made on 10 August 2021 – *GV v Chief Appeals Officer, Social Welfare Appeals Office, Minister for Employment Affairs and Social Protection, Ireland, Attorney General* [2021] OJ C422/8.

[107] Case C-488/21 *GV*, para 72.

[108] *Nano Nagle v Daly* [2019] IESC 63.

CJEU as a vehicle for expanding the material scope of EU law, and has led to the development of fundamental constitutional principles. However, as this contribution has sought to elucidate, the 'actorness' of Member State courts within the preliminary reference procedure can be difficult to quantify. For example, a statistical analysis of the number of preliminary references made per year by a Member State can reflect on the openness to engage with Article 267 TFEU, but does not reflect upon the *quality* and *substance* of those engagements. Actorness in this area therefore defies straightforward categorisation, and this necessitates a socio-legal or law-in-context approach be adopted to establish a Member State's overall fluency in EU law and its processes. This is also emulated in Šadl's reflections on the complex role of legal actors,[109] where the author comments on the 'ability and ambition of national courts as potentially influential and powerful allies of the Court'.[110] This statement underlines the reciprocal nature of the preliminary reference procedure, and that the actor status of national courts cannot be wholly divorced from that of the CJEU, its AGs and Chambers either.

This becomes even more important when focusing on areas of EU law that are not subject to widespread statistical recording, such as EU disability law. National courts have certainly been important actors in shaping the meaning of disability, and in somewhat extending the scope of the relevant directives in this area. To some degree, this is driven primarily by a need to resolve the dispute before the national court, which can only be achieved with the necessary answers on interpreting EU law. That there remains a lacuna in respect of a readily CRPD-compliant definition of disability within the EU legal order means that this development can even occur in facilitating the CJEU in its ongoing quest to reconcile EU law with the Convention. However, as cases like *Dauoidi* and *Z v. A Government Department* highlight, where a national court even reframes this to touch upon more complex dimensions of the same issue, it can force the CJEU to engage with questions it likely did not consider, or know how to answer. As these kinds of cases, and the evolution of the case law on the CRPD also make clear, this can often be an uneven process – the value is in the *process* of development, and based on the inherent dialogue between different kinds of courts. Their contribution as actors is therefore in their contribution to this process, and the quality of that contribution.

This conflict with regard to the quality of the contribution of national courts or tribunals and their status as actors within the preliminary reference procedure, is evident within the case study of Ireland. A peripheral Member State, that is often typified by its attempts to benefit from membership whilst attempting to strongly maintain its own discretion and reduce down the potential 'costs' of the same, it is a historically low referrer of cases to the CJEU. Although the number it sends has increased, it has demonstrated a reticence to engage in this reciprocal

[109] Šadl (n 17).
[110] Ibid.

dialogue with the Luxembourg court. This is in large part driven by the lower level of fluency in basic principles of EU constitutional law: the *Workplace Relations Commission* case illustrates that the Irish Supreme Court has a fundamental difficulty in distinguishing Article 267 TFEU from a judicial review, and in recognising that what constitutes a court or tribunal for the purposes of making a reference is distinct from the national definition of courts. This likely has the effect of artificially suppressing the number of references made, given that the Supreme Court would dispute the ability of many lower courts to refer. Although a reference was made, it was of low quality, and did not contribute anything to the overall development of EU law.

However, and perhaps most importantly, the Irish example also highlights how a meta or statistical analysis alone, or a focus on specific cases does not adequately consider the overall quality of the contribution made by national courts as actors in this process. The nature of a dialogue is again that it is uneven, and varies. It is also dependent on the specific actors 'speaking' at specific points, and on what topics they speak. In *Voican* for example, the High Court showed a lucid understanding of EU social security rules, and for that reason the case did not necessitate a reference – it was the Court of Appeals that ended up making a low quality reference in response to this, with the CJEU merely having to restate long-standing principles. Turning specifically to EU disability law, in *Z v. A Government Department*, the Equality Tribunal, a lower level specialised venue, was able to question which of three separate directives was applicable, and in *Nano Nagle*, the Supreme Court, having elsewhere shown a lack of fluency on the primacy, was able to demonstrate a more nuanced understanding of the CRPD and its relationship with EU law.

This ultimately underlines that the 'actorness' of national courts is one that is not cleanly generalisable because their contribution is inherently qualitative, and made up by such a large number of concurrent dialogues with different individual justices, on a wide range of topics. Just as the contribution of the CJEU itself on the incorporation of the CRPD within the EU legal order has been significant but uneven and not without criticism, the same can be said for national courts or tribunals as the other actor that they are in direct conversation with.

8

The Role of the European Ombudsman in Protecting and Promoting Disability Rights

DELIA FERRI*

1. Introduction

The European Ombudsman ('the Ombudsman')[1] is an independent and impartial body that holds European Union (EU) institutions and bodies to account and that promotes the right to good administration, which is enshrined in Article 41 of the EU Charter of Fundamental Rights (CFR). Its mandate is primarily defined by Article 228 Treaty on the Functioning of the European Union (TFEU), while Article 43 CFR confers onto '[a]ny citizen of the Union and any natural or legal person residing or having its registered office in a Member State [...] the right to refer to the European Ombudsman cases of maladministration', in line with Articles 20(2)(d) and 24 TFEU. The Ombudsman can receive complaints on maladministration in the activities of the EU institutions, bodies, offices and agencies. Article 228 TFEU also empowers the Ombudsman to conduct inquiries *motu proprio* or on the basis of complaints submitted to them or through a member of the European Parliament (EP). Further, as of 2013, the Ombudsman has been involved in promoting, protecting and monitoring the implementation of the UN Convention on the Rights of Persons with Disabilities (CRPD) as part of the

* The research supporting this chapter has been conducted within the remit of the project 'Protecting the Right to Culture of Persons with Disabilities and Enhancing Cultural Diversity through European Union Law: Exploring New Paths – DANCING'. This project has received funding from the European Research Council (ERC) under the European Union's Horizon 2020 research and innovation programme (Grant Agreement No 864182). This article reflects only the author's views and does not necessarily reflect those of the European Union or the ERC.

[1] This chapter refers interchangeably to the 'European Ombudsman' or simply 'the Ombudsman'. It uses they/them when referring to the office.

EU framework, set up in compliance with Article 33(2) CRPD,[2] in conjunction with the EP, the EU Agency for Fundamental Rights (FRA)[3] and the European Disability Forum (EDF) – the main umbrella organisation of persons with disabilities in Europe.[4]

Since its establishment by the Treaty of Maastricht, the Ombudsman has aimed to provide a 'cheap, flexible and accessible' alternative to judicial proceedings in the review of EU administrative acts and to further the democratic legitimacy of the EU structure.[5] Tsadiras contends that this extra-judicial mechanism 'sought to enhance the protection of citizens' rights and interests' in the EU but, in political terms it 'was employed as a tool to put a smiling face to a largely distant, impersonal, and incomprehensible [EU] structure, sooth the growing uneasiness of the Union citizenry, and sugar the pill of further European integration'.[6] Since its creation, as Vogiatzis asserts, 'the Ombudsman *is* related and *has contributed* to [the] EU's democratisation'.[7] In a similar vein, scholars have increasingly recognised the role of the Ombudsman as an important means of recourse in the event of administrative misconduct and as a source of administrative norms.[8]

When it comes to disability issues, this chapter argues that the Ombudsman has been an efficient 'watchdog', or, as Wille and Bovens put it, 'both an effective fire-watcher and fire-preventer'.[9] It further contends that the European Ombudsman has also contributed to shaping EU disability law and to tracing its boundaries. It does so on the basis of an extensive body of research that blends traditional legal analysis with a systematic document analysis of decisions adopted by the Ombudsman on individual complaints between 1 January 2010, following

[2] C Conte, *The UN Convention on the Rights of Persons with Disabilities and the European Union: The Impact on Law and Governance* (Hart 2022) 123 *et seq*.; A Hoefmans, 'The EU Framework for Monitoring the CRPD' in D Ferri and A Broderick, *Research Handbook on EU Disability Law* (Edward Elgar 2022) 71–88. See *infra* section 2 of this chapter.

[3] GN Toggenburg, 'The Role of the Fundamental Rights Agency in Advancing Disability Rights within the EU' in this volume.

[4] C Coveney, 'The Role of the European Disability Forum and Disability Organisations in Shaping EU Disability Policy' in this volume.

[5] ME de Leeuw, 'The European Ombudsman's Role as a Developer of Norms of Good Administration' (2011) 17(2) *European Public Law* 349–368. See also A Tsadiras, 'Maladministration and Life beyond Legality: The European Ombudsman's Paradigm' (2015) 3 *International Review of Law* 11–28; A Peters, 'The European Ombudsman and the European Constitution' (2005) 42(3) *Common Market Law Review* 697–743; P Magnette, 'Between parliamentary control and the rule of law: The political role of the Ombudsman in the European Union' (2003) 10(5) *Journal of European Public Policy* 677–694; H Hofmann, 'The Developing Role of the European Ombudsman' in H Hofmann and J Ziller, *Accountability in the EU. The Role of the European Ombudsman* (Edward Elgar 2017) 1–27.

[6] A Tsadiras, 'The Ombudsman' in P Craig, *EU Administrative Law* (2nd online edn, Oxford University Press 2012) 739.

[7] N Vogiatzis, *The European Ombudsman and Good Administration in the European Union* (Palgrave Macmillan 2017) 2 (emphasis in the original text).

[8] de Leeuw (n 5). In a similar vein M Hillebrandt and P Leino-Sandberg, 'Administrative and judicial oversight of the trilogues' (2020) 28(1) *Journal of European Public Policy* 53–71.

[9] A Wille and M Bovens, 'Watching EU watchdogs assessing the accountability powers of the European Court of Auditors and the European Ombudsman' (2020) 44(2) *Journal of European Integration* 183–206.

the decision on the conclusion of the CRPD by the EU,[10] and 31 May 2024, aligning with scope of the volume,[11] and of *motu proprio* and strategic inquiries. While presenting a quantitative appraisal of the documents retrieved by virtue of summarising tables, the analysis provided by this chapter is inherently qualitative in that it conceives of document analysis as a method for reviewing or evaluating documents, thereby combining elements of content analysis (that focus on the legal content) and thematic analysis.[12] As highlighted by Šadl in this volume,[13] borrowing 'selectively from social science methodologies' can help the understanding of legal phenomena, and, in this chapter, supports the identification of trends in the Ombudsman's work.

Further to these introductory remarks, this chapter is divided into five sections. Section 2 briefly revisits the main functions and powers of the Ombudsman, providing a bedrock for the subsequent analysis. Section 3 gives a general overview of the extent to which disability issues feature in the Ombudsman's mandate. It further discusses the role of the Ombudsman as part of the EU framework to monitor the CRPD. Section 4 identifies, maps and critically examines complaints related to equal opportunity for people with disabilities, accessibility and, more broadly, disability rights, that the Ombudsman has dealt with since the conclusion of the CRPD by the EU. Section 5 focuses on relevant *motu proprio* inquiries. Section 6 provides some concluding remarks that argue that, by nudging EU institutions towards compliance with the CRPD, the Ombudsman has *de facto* contributed to the development of EU disability law.

2. The Role of the European Ombudsman in the EU Constitutional Framework

The European Ombudsman is appointed by the EP after each election, for the duration of its term of office (five years), and can be reappointed.[14] Prospective candidates, that are independent and possess the required experience, need the backing of at least 40 members of the EP (MEPs) from a minimum of two EU Member States. Independence is considered essential in ensuring citizens' confidence in the office, although scholarship questions the 'symbiotic relationship'[15] between the Ombudsman and the EP. Notably, Article 228(2) TFEU provides that

[10] Council Decision 2010/48/EC concerning the conclusion, by the European Community, of the United Nations Convention on the Rights of Persons with Disabilities [2010] OJ L23/35. While acknowledging that the entry into force of the CRPD for the EU occurred on January 2011, the start date of the timeframe considered in this chapter follows the adoption of the decision on the conclusion of the CRPD.

[11] D Ferri and ES Krolla, 'Introduction: Walking Through the Looking Glass' in this volume.

[12] GA Bowen, 'Document analysis as a qualitative research method' (2009) 9(2) *Qualitative Research Journal* 27–40.

[13] U Šadl, 'Studying the Role of Legal Actors in EU Law: An Outline' in this volume.

[14] Article 228 Treaty on the Functioning of the European Union (TFEU).

[15] A Tsadiras, 'Unravelling Ariadne's Thread: The European Ombudsman's Investigative Powers' (2008) 45 *Common Market Law Review* 757, 759.

the Ombudsman may be dismissed by the Court of Justice of the European Union (CJEU) if they no longer fulfil the conditions required for the performance of their duties or are guilty of serious misconduct.

The European Ombudsman in office at the time of writing, Emily O'Reilly, was first elected in July 2013, re-elected for a five-year mandate in December 2014 and again in December 2019. She has been the third person to take on the office after Nikiforos Diamandouros, who had succeeded Jacob Söderman, the very first office holder who turned 'the abstract ideal of a European Ombudsman […] into a living, breathing, working reality'.[16] After the 2024 European voting, following the settling of a new EP, a new Ombudsman will be elected.

As Emily O'Reilly put it, the role of the Ombudsman is 'fundamentally about the prevention of abuse of power' but also the protection of 'the administration from itself'.[17] In *Internationaler Hilfsfonds eV*, the CJEU highlighted that:

> [c]omplaints to the Ombudsman, on the one hand, make it possible to identify and to seek to eliminate instances of maladministration on behalf of the public interest and, on the other hand, may make it possible to avoid judicial proceedings if the Ombudsman succeeds in resolving the differences between the complainant and the institution concerned.[18]

Its powers are laid out in Article 228 TFEU, which is the principal legal basis delineating the Ombudsman's mandate.[19] The Statute on the Ombudsman, adopted in compliance with Article 228(4) TFEU, complements Treaty provisions and lays out general rules governing the Ombudsman's duties,[20] which are further expounded by the Decision of the European Ombudsman adopting Implementing Provisions.[21]

This section recalls the powers of the Ombudsman, and than briefly examines the type of remedial actions they can enact in instances of maladministration.

2.1. Complaints and Inquiries

As mentioned in the introduction to this chapter, the Ombudsman is empowered to receive complaints from any citizen of the Union or any natural or

[16] Oath Speech of European Ombudsman, Emily O'Reilly, 30 September 2013, available at <https://www.ombudsman.europa.eu/en/speech/en/51922>.

[17] European Ombudsman, 'The Art of the Ombudsman: Navigating Strategic Choices and Principles. Excerpt from Emily O'Reilly's speech at the International Ombudsman Institute conference at The Hague, Netherlands' (*Medium*, 16 May 2024) available at <https://medium.com/@EUombudsman/the-art-of-the-ombudsman-navigating-strategic-choices-and-principles-054e68e1e15f>.

[18] Case C-331/05 *Internationaler Hilfsfonds eV. v Commission* ECLI:EU:C:2007:390, paras 26–27.

[19] PJ Loewenthal, 'Article 228 TFEU' in M Kellerbauer, M Klamert and J Tomkin (eds), *The EU Treaties and the Charter of Fundamental Rights: A Commentary* (Oxford University Press 2020).

[20] Regulation (EU, Euratom) 2021/1163 laying down the regulations and general conditions governing the performance of the Ombudsman's duties (Statute of the European Ombudsman) and repealing Decision 94/262/ECSC, EC, Euratom (Statute) [2021] OJ L253/1.

[21] Decision of the European Ombudsman adopting implementing provisions [2023] OJ C2023/161.

legal person[22] residing or having its registered office in a Member State concerning instances of maladministration in the activities of the EU institutions, bodies, offices or agencies. The CJEU, when acting in its judicial role, does not fall within the scope of the Ombudsman's mandate.[23] The Ombudsman does not have the power to examine complaints of maladministration at the national level, even when national authorities implement EU law. This major limit to its mandate has nonetheless 'prompted creative ways of collaboration between the national and the [European] ombud offices, such as the 'EU queries' scheme',[24] which allows national ombud offices to send a query on EU law to the European Ombudsman.[25] Furthermore, citizens and legal persons may lodge a complaint to the Ombudsman when they consider that the European Commission (Commission) has not properly handled an infringement complaint towards a Member State. In that way, the Ombudsman can oversee the Commission's behaviour, although such control cannot hamper or impinge on the EU executive's discretion. Notably, individual complaints to the Ombudsman may be lodged directly by the person or through a MEP.[26] The latter process is referred to as 'MEP filter', but 'is rarely being used and constitutes an anachronism for a modern ombud office', although its presence is said not to undermine access to the European Ombudsman.[27]

The admissibility of complaints is not dependent upon the complainant proving their personal interest in the subject matter. Further, the complainant does not have to be affected by the alleged maladministration.[28] However, a complaint must be lodged 'within two years of the date on which the facts on which it is based came to the attention of the complainant', and must be preceded by 'appropriate administrative approaches to the Union institution, body, office or agency concerned'.[29] The Ombudsman must terminate consideration of a complaint and declare it inadmissible if the citizen concerned brings a case before European courts based on the same facts.[30]

The Ombudsman can also conduct inquiries for which they find grounds, either on their own initiative or on the basis of complaints submitted to them directly or through a MEP.[31] The Ombudsman can address systemic issues in the

[22] The term 'legal person' has been interpreted quite broadly and encompasses companies, associations, federations and various types of public or private entities including charities and Non-governmental Organisations (NGOs). See Tsadiras (n 6) 743.

[23] Article 43 Charter of Fundamental Rights (CFR); Article 228 TFEU.

[24] N Vogiatzis, 'The Past and Future of the Right to Petition the European Parliament' (2021) 40 *Yearbook of European Law* 82–110.

[25] On EU queries see N Athanasiadou and N Vogiatzis, 'The EU Queries: A Form of Extra-Judicial Preliminary Reference in the Field of Maladministration?' (2021) 22(3) *German Law Journal* 441–465.

[26] Article 2(1) Statute of the European Ombudsman.

[27] Vogiatzis (n 24).

[28] Tsadiras (n 6) 744.

[29] Article 2 Statute of the European Ombudsman.

[30] Article 2(9) Statute of the European Ombudsman. See also D Martin, 'Article 24 TFEU' in Kellerbauer, Klamert and Tomkin (n 19).

[31] Article 3 Statute of the European Ombudsman.

EU's administration without necessarily opening an inquiry, through a range of soft tools referred to as 'initiatives', which in essence entail for the Ombudsman the possibility to seek clarifications about or raise an issue directly with the institution concerned.[32]

Since the advent of the second European Ombudsman, Nikiforos Diamandouros, 'maladministration', which is not explicitly defined in the TFEU, has been broader than mere illegality.[33] It includes the violation of general substantive and procedural administrative law principles, wrongful interpretation or application of EU norms, which constitute an instance of maladministration, but also includes practices that contravene soft law, such as the Code of Good Administrative Behaviour.[34] The Ombudsman's mandate covers different areas, which span from access to documents to ethical issues, and personnel matters. Further, the role of the Ombudsman is also key in ensuring that EU institutions do not violate fundamental rights, including, as discussed in the remainder of this chapter, disability rights.

2.2. Collaboration and Conciliatory Ethos

The Ombudsman's procedures are informed by the principle of sincere cooperation with the view of reaching amicable solutions to complaints. In that connection, EU institutions and bodies (as well as relevant national authorities) must give the Ombudsman all required documents and information and work in cooperation with them.[35] The Ombudsman can also hear officials of EU institutions, bodies, offices and agencies in relation to issues at stake in ongoing inquiries.[36]

As highlighted by Tsadiras, the Ombudsman's remedial powers 'are premised on a conciliatory ethos' and entail a 'friendly solution between the Union administration and the aggrieved complainant'.[37] This means that the Ombudsman endeavours to 'nudge' EU institutions towards implementing fairer administrative practices, but cannot order binding measures. In spite of the lack of any binding effect, recommendations are generally impactful. Kostadinova's systematic analysis shows that EU institutions tend to accept the Ombudsman's

[32] European Ombudsman, 'Strategic initiatives' available at <https://www.ombudsman.europa.eu/en/strategic-issues/strategic-initiatives>.

[33] Hoffman (n 5) 4.

[34] European Commission (Commission), 'Code of Good Administrative Behaviour and complaints' available at <https://commission.europa.eu/about/service-standards-and-principles/ethics-and-good-administration/good-administration/code-good-administrative-behaviour-and-complaints_en>.

[35] Article 4 Statute of the European Ombudsman; Article 4 Decision of the European Ombudsman adopting implementing provisions.

[36] Article 7 Statute of the European Ombudsman.

[37] Tsadiras (n 6) 752.

recommendations.[38] At various junctures, the current Ombudsman O'Reilly has underlined the 'moral suasion' value of these recommendations and placed emphasis on the Ombudsman's 'power', ensuing from:

> their own personality, the power of the quality of the staff in their institution, the power of their investigative tools, the power of the moral authority of the role itself, the power of its alliances with parliament and with civil society, the power of public opinion and the power of the media.[39]

After receiving a complaint, and provided that it is admissible, the Ombudsman opens an inquiry. If a solution is found with the EU institution or body concerned or the proposal for solution advanced by the Ombudsman is accepted by them, the Ombudsman closes the complaint and the matter is settled. If at the end of an inquiry, the Ombudsman ascertains that no maladministration had occurred or no further inquiries are justified, the inquiry shall be closed with a decision.[40] In these cases, the Ombudsman may still suggest improvements regarding issues identified in the course of the inquiry.[41] When the European Ombudsman finds an instance of maladministration, they make a recommendation and refer the matter to the institution, body, office or agency concerned, which has a period of three months to present their views on the recommendation.[42] The closing decision adopted by the Ombudsman sets out definite findings and indicates whether the EU institution or body concerned has accepted recommendations.

At the end of each annual session, the Ombudsman submits a report to the EP on the outcome of their inquiries, which includes an assessment of compliance with the Ombudsman's recommendations, proposals for solutions and suggestions for improvement.[43] Its report to the EP does not produce legal effects *vis-à-vis* third parties and is not binding on the EP.[44] The Ombudsman lacks the power to refer instances of maladministration to the European courts, which is in line with the 'cooperative style of control' that characterises its office.[45] However, the Ombudsman's decisions are subject to judicial review in that both the complainant and the EU institution or body concerned can challenge a finding of the Ombudsman before the EU courts.[46]

[38] P Kostadinova, 'Improving the transparency and accountability of EU institutions: The impact of the Office of the European Ombudsman' (2015) 53(5) *Journal of Common Market Studies* 1–17.

[39] E O'Reilly, 'The Role of the Ombudsman in Modern Parliamentary Democracies' (Keynote, Brussels, 18 November 2015) available at <https://www.ombudsman.europa.eu/en/speech/en/61362>.

[40] Article 6(2) Decision of the European Ombudsman adopting implementing provisions.

[41] Ibid.

[42] Ibid Article 6(3).

[43] Article 4(5) Statute of the European Ombudsman.

[44] Martin (n 30).

[45] C Neuhold and A Năstase, 'Transparency Watchdog: Guarding the Law and Independent from Politics? The Relationship between the European Ombudsman and the European Parliament' (2017) 5(3) *Politics and Governance* 40–50.

[46] Case C-337/15 P, *European Ombudsman v Claire Staelen* ECLI:EU:C:2017:256; Case T-581/16 *Costas Popotas v European Ombudsman* ECLI:EU:T:2018:169.

3. The Role of the European Ombudsman in the Protection and Promotion of Disability Rights

Neither Article 228 TFEU nor the Statute of the European Ombudsman mention disability or the rights of persons with disabilities. The Decision of the European Ombudsman adopting Implementing Provisions is the only legal document governing the Ombudsman's action that includes a reference to disability. In particular, Article 2(1) of this Decision requires the Ombudsman 'to take appropriate measures to assist persons with disabilities to exercise their right to submit a complaint'.[47] This provision tallies with the general principle of non-discrimination provided in the Treaties and in the CFR,[48] and aligns with the right to access to justice enshrined in Article 13 CRPD. It underscores the duty of the Ombudsman not only to comply with accessibility provisions, but also to provide reasonable accommodation, i.e. any 'necessary and appropriate modification and adjustments not imposing a disproportionate or undue burden, where needed in a particular case',[49] to complainants with disabilities. Besides this general commitment, disability has become increasingly visible in the Ombudsman's action and links to their role as part of the EU framework, which in turn is examined in the following subsections.

3.1. Disability in the Ombudsman's Action

The work of the Ombudsman is guided by internal multiannual strategies, which set up objectives to improve the internal accountability of the ombuds office.[50] Up until 2020, these strategies laid out broad goals that tallied with the general mandate of the Treaty.[51] However, the latest Strategy 'Towards 2024', adopted in 2020, included a specific disability goal, which represented an interesting novelty.[52] This Strategy laid out four general overarching objectives – first, to achieve lasting impact on the EU administration; second, to ensure real-life relevance to European citizens; third, to increase citizens' awareness of the Ombudsman's work; and finally, to improve efficiency –, and, under the third objective, it set out the aim to expand the Ombudsman's 'work with the [CRPD] to

[47] Article 2(1) Decision of the European Ombudsman adopting implementing provisions.

[48] Articles 20 and 21 CFR; Article 19 TFEU.

[49] Article 2 CRPD.

[50] These Strategies are published on the website of the European Ombudsman and are available at <https://www.ombudsman.europa.eu/en/publications>.

[51] See eg European Ombudsman, 'Strategy for the mandate' (20 September 2010) available at <https://www.ombudsman.europa.eu/en/publication/en/5330>; European Ombudsman, 'Strategy of the European Ombudsman "Towards 2019"' (16 November 2014) available at <https://www.ombudsman.europa.eu/en/publication/en/58332>.

[52] European Ombudsman, 'European Ombudsman Strategy: 'Towards 2024' – Sustaining Impact' (6 December 2020) available at <https://www.ombudsman.europa.eu/en/strategy/our-strategy/en>.

help the EU administration to become a global leader as an employer of persons with disabilities'.[53] Objectives such as this exemplify the Ombudsman's ambition to promote disability rights, and to be a driver of systemic change in the EU. This commitment supports the Commission's pledge to lead by example in making its own selection, recruitment, employment and retention processes disability inclusive, and in ensuring accessibility of physical premises, publications and digital environments and communications, set out in the Strategy for the Rights of Persons with Disabilities 2021–2030 (Strategy 2021–2030).[54] In fact, this pledge had initially been instigated by the Ombudsman themselves in 2020.[55]

Since 2010, disability issues have become more and more visible in the complaints procedure and in *motu proprio* inquiries. While these are examined later, it is worth noting that a certain mainstreaming of the rights of persons with disabilities is noticeable. For example, in a Decision on how the Authority for European Political Parties and European Political Foundations ensures transparency of information about European political parties and foundations,[56] the Ombudsman took the opportunity to emphasise:

> the importance of providing information in a format that it is accessible for persons with disabilities. In particular, websites and contact forms of the EU administration should be accessible to persons with disabilities, and efforts should be made to increase significantly the availability of 'easy-to-read' information about the EU administration's work.[57]

Further, disability and the work related to the CRPD are afforded a dedicated section in all the most recent annual reports of the Ombudsman,[58] highlighting an increased prioritisation and its important role as part of the EU framework, discussed below.

3.2. The Ombudsman as Part of the EU Framework to Monitor the CRPD

The EU framework was set up to comply with Article 33(2) CRPD, which obliges State Parties to the Convention to 'maintain, strengthen, designate or establish

[53] Ibid.

[54] Commission, 'Union of Equality: Strategy for the Rights of Persons with Disabilities 2021–2030' COM(2021) 101 final.

[55] European Ombudsman, 'Speech of the European Ombudsman at the Workshop on the Protection of the Rights of Persons with Disabilities: The new Disabilities Strategy' (Brussels, 28 October 2020) available at <https://www.ombudsman.europa.eu/en/speech/en/134285>.

[56] Decision in case 1094/2020/DL on how the Authority for European Political Parties and European Political Foundations (APPF) ensures transparency of information about European political parties and foundations; Case 1094/2020/DL, 25 January 2021, available at <https://www.ombudsman.europa.eu/en/decision/en/137333>.

[57] Ibid para 46.

[58] See eg European Ombudsman, 'Annual Report 2023' (18 March 2024) available at <https://www.ombudsman.europa.eu/en/doc/annual-report/en/183636>.

within the State Party, a framework, including one or more independent mechanisms, as appropriate, to promote, protect and monitor implementation of the [CRPD]'. Article 33(2) CRPD also requires this 'framework' to include at least one 'independent mechanism' taking 'into account' the 'Principles relating to the Status of National Institutions for the Promotion and Protection of Human Rights' (known as the Paris Principles),[59] which *inter alia* place emphasis on independence from governmental control. The tasks of the framework are promotion, protection and monitoring, but Article 33(2) is silent on what each of these entails. De Beco suggests that promotion means 'raising awareness of human rights by disseminating materials and organising events' with a view of fostering 'an acceptance of the values underlying [the] CRPD'.[60] This author contends that protection entails the 'handling alleged human rights violations through quasi-judicial powers in order to complement judicial protection' to support persons with disabilities to vindicate their rights,[61] while, in essence, monitoring encompasses an assessment of compliance with the CRPD.[62]

As recalled by Toggenburg in this volume,[63] the Council decision on the conclusion of the CRPD[64] did not engage with the creation of the framework. This was instead laid out in a Commission 'Non-paper'[65] as encompassing, besides the Commission itself, other existing EU institutions and bodies, namely the EP (and, in particular, the Petitions – PETI Committee), the European Ombudsman, and the FRA. Following an endorsement by the Council of the EU (Council), the EU framework became operational in 2013. It was then revised to exclude the Commission from its composition in 2017,[66] following the recommendations of

[59] UN General Assembly, National Institutions for the Promotion and Protection of Human Rights, 85th plenary meeting, 20 December 1993, UN Doc. A/RES/48/134.

[60] G de Beco, 'Article 33(2) of the UN Convention on the Rights of Persons with Disabilities: Another Role for National Human Rights Institutions?' (2011) 29(1) *Netherlands Quarterly of Human Rights* 95. See also Office of the High Commissioner for Human Rights, 'Monitoring the Convention on the Rights of Persons with Disabilities: Guidance for human rights monitors' (2010) Professional Training Series No. 17 (New York and Geneva) available at <https://www.ohchr.org/sites/default/files/Documents/Publications/Disabilities_training_17EN.pdf>.

[61] 'Protection' is also viewed to refer to the cessation and remedy of violations of the CRPD. G de Beco and A Hoefmans, 'National Structures for the Implementation and Monitoring of the UN Convention on the Rights of Persons with Disabilities' in G de Beco (ed), *Article 33 of the UN Convention on the Rights of Persons with Disabilities: National Structures for the Implementation and Monitoring of the Convention* (Brill 2013) 9, 47.

[62] Ibid.

[63] Toggenburg (n 3).

[64] Council Decision 2010/48/EC concerning the conclusion, by the European Community, of the United Nations Convention on the Rights of Persons with Disabilities [2010] OJ L23/35.

[65] Commission, 'Commission Non-Paper on the Setting-Up at EU Level of the Framework Required by Art. 33.2 of the UN Convention on the Rights of Persons with Disabilities' available at <https://ec.europa.eu/social/main.jsp?catId=1138&langId=en>.

[66] Council of the EU (Council), 'Revised EU-level Framework Required by Article 33.2 of the UN Convention on the Rights of Persons with Disabilities' 6170/17 available at <https://data.consilium.europa.eu/doc/document/ST-6170-2017-INIT/en/pdf>.

the UN Committee on the Rights of Persons with Disabilities (CRPD Committee) with a view to guarantee compliance with the Paris Principles and enshrine the independence of the framework.[67] The 'patchwork of entities' forming the EU framework and the constraints of their respective mandates have often been questioned.[68] As yet, however, scant scholarship has discussed the Ombudsman's role and contribution in detail. While Conte considers that the Ombudsman cannot fully engage in the protection tasks attributed to the EU framework and can instead focus primarily on the monitoring of the CRPD,[69] Hoefmans, by contrast, believes that the Ombudsman satisfies all the requirements of Article 33(2) CRPD, in view of its powers and independence.[70]

In fact, within the limits of its constitutional mandate, the Ombudsman has so far fulfilled all of the functions (promotion, protection and monitoring) of the framework *ex* Article 33(2) CRPD. The Ombudsman promotes disability rights and raises awareness in EU institutions. Indeed, as mentioned above, disability has become very visible in the Ombudsman's public engagement and speeches. In several instances, the Ombudsman has highlighted their work to make their own office and procedures disability inclusive, but also to protect disability rights within the limits of their mandate.[71] A notable example of such a promotional role was evident during the recent COVID-19 pandemic, when the Ombudsman asked how the Commission intended to accommodate the needs of staff with disabilities.[72] Based on the Commission's response, taking into account input from organisations of persons with disabilities (OPDs), as well as other EU institutions, and the European Network of Ombudsmen, the Ombudsman published a list of best practices.[73] While the list includes a series of practical tools to accommodate the needs of staff members with disabilities, both in the context of the COVID-19 pandemic and for future emergency situations, it also included a final general exhortation 'to ensure that any response to an emergency situation is compliant with the obligations enshrined in the [CRPD]'.[74] In that connection,

[67] Committee on the Rights of Persons with Disabilities (CRPD Committee), 'Concluding Observations on the initial report of the European Union' (2 October 2015) CRPD/C/EU/1.

[68] Hoefmans (n 2) 80.

[69] Conte (n 2).

[70] Hoefmans (n 2) 81.

[71] Among many others, see the speech pronounced in 2019 in front of the Council of Europe (CoE) European Commission against Racism and Intolerance (ECRI). In this speech, the Ombudsman placed a strong emphasis on their commitment to promoting disability rights. European Ombudsman, 'Exchange of views, Council of Europe European Commission against Racism and Intolerance' (Strasbourg, 4 April 2019) available at <https://www.ombudsman.europa.eu/en/speech/en/112110>.

[72] Letter from the European Ombudsman to the President of the European Commission on how the European Commission accommodates the needs of staff members with disabilities in the context of the COVID-19 emergency; Case SI/2/2020/MMO, 29 June 2021, available at <https://www.ombudsman.europa.eu/en/doc/correspondence/en/128648>.

[73] Decision How the European Commission has accommodated the needs of staff members with disabilities in the context of the COVID-19 emergency, Case SI/2/2020/MMO, 29 June 2021, available at <https://www.ombudsman.europa.eu/en/decision/en/143861>.

[74] Ibid.

the promotional role played by the Ombudsman supports and somewhat blends with its protection and monitoring functions. The former is mostly fulfilled by the handling of individual complaints.[75] The latter is accomplished through a variety of tools: inquiries that follow individual complaints or that are initiated by the Ombudsman *motu proprio*; strategic initiatives; but, also, general cooperation and dialogues with the institutions. By using all of these (soft) tools, the Ombudsman has thus far played an oversight role in the implementation of the Concluding Observations (COs) of the CRPD Committee. For instance, first in 2016,[76] and then in 2018, the Ombudsman followed up[77] on concerns raised by the CRPD Committee regarding European Schools, whereby the CRPD Committee had highlighted that 'not all students with disabilities receive the reasonable accommodation they need to enjoy their right to inclusive quality education in European Schools and that the latter do not comply with the non-rejection clause'.[78] Although European Schools are an inter-governmental body (and not an EU body *strictu sensu*), the Commission sits on the Schools' Management Board and contributes to their financing. Leveraging on this aspect, the Ombudsman sought explanation from the Commission on how they intended to implement the recommendations from the CRPD Committee. In the end, they commended the Commission for some positive developments, albeit highlighting the need for further action.[79] In 2024, the Ombudsman also launched an initiative to clarify the degree to which revised rules governing the Joint Sickness Insurance Scheme (JSIS) for EU staff comply with the CRPD, which followed a dedicated inquiry that is expounded in section 5.

[75] M Priestley, M Raley and G de Beco, 'The protection role of the Committee on Petitions in the context of the implementation of the UN Convention on the Rights of Persons with Disabilities' Study for the PETI Committee, Citizens' Rights and Constitutional Affairs (European Parliament 2016) 18.

[76] United Nations Convention on the Rights of Persons with Disabilities: European Schools, Case SI/1/2016/EA, 5 October 2016, available at <https://www.ombudsman.europa.eu/en/case/en/48406>.

[77] Letter from the European Ombudsman to Commissioner Oettinger concerning the United Nations Convention on the Rights of Persons with Disabilities and the European Schools (SI/4/2018/EA); Case SI/4/2018/EA, 6 June 2019, available at <https://www.ombudsman.europa.eu/en/doc/correspondence/en/113998>.

[78] CRPD Committee (n 67).

[79] These recommendations follow a 2005 inquiry into a number of complaints and the Special Report sent to the European Parliament in 2005. That report had asked the Commission to take the necessary steps to ensure that parents of children with special educational needs who are excluded from the European Schools are not required to contribute to the educational costs of their children. See European Ombudsman, 'Special Report from the European Ombudsman to the European Parliament following the draft recommendation to the European Commission in complaint 1391/2002/JMA' (7 June 2005) available at <https://www.ombudsman.europa.eu/en/special-report/en/385>. Decision of the European Ombudsman on complaint 1391/2002/JMA against the European Commission; Case 1391/2002/JMA, 7 June 2005, available at <https://www.ombudsman.europa.eu/en/decision/en/1775>.

4. Complaints to the European Ombudsman on Disability Issues

As previously highlighted, one of the key powers of the Ombudsman is that of receiving and investigating complaints from individuals and legal persons about maladministration by EU institutions, bodies and agencies. As annual reports show, over the years the Ombudsman has been confronted with several cases related to allowances for children with disabilities of EU staff, disability discrimination, mostly in the form of failure to provide reasonable accommodation, in hiring and selection processes, and, most recently, also with accessibility issues.[80] A systematic search of Ombudsman's decisions adopted on foot of individual complaints between 1 January 2010 and 31 May 2024 allowed the identification of 45 decisions related to disability, which are discussed below after a brief recount of the methods.

4.1. Methods

The systematic search of Ombudsman's decisions adopted on foot of individual complaints was conducted multiple times between September 2023 and the end of May 2024 on the European Ombudsman's official website, using the search form and including the timeframe selected in the date range boxes (1 January 2010 and 31 May 2024) together with the indication of the document type 'decision' and specific key words in the text search box. As mentioned in the introduction to this chapter and in line with the scope of the volume, the initial cut-off date precedes the entry into force of the CRPD, but grossly aligns with the timing of the Concluding Decision, which was adopted on 26 November 2009, and published in the Official Journal on 27 January 2010. The words used in separate searches were: 'disability', 'disabilities', 'CRPD', 'UN Convention'. An additional search was conducted using 'United Nations Convention on the Rights of Persons with Disabilities'. The search deliberately excluded cases opened but not decided upon in this timeframe. However, it is worth mentioning that a few cases concerning disability were commenced in the first half of 2024.[81] Initial results of this search were screened to exclude decisions that were not relevant to the subject matter and *motu proprio* inquiries, which were examined separately. After a general quantitative appraisal to detect overarching trends, explained below, the analysis conducted

[80] See European Ombudsman, 'Annual Reports' available at <https://www.ombudsman.europa.eu/en/our-strategy/annual-reports>.

[81] See eg How the Commission handled a complaint concerning its refusal to grant aid for the costs of education in a disability case, Case 88/2024/ET, opened on 21 February 2024, available at <https://www.ombudsman.europa.eu/en/opening-summary/en/182341>.

was qualitative. The decisions were coded, and such coding was open, unstructured and mostly inductive, although themes developed from codes considered key legal aspects of the Ombudsman's mandate as well as main features of EU disability law. They were then analysed thematically, taking into account Braun and Clark's methods for thematic analysis (TA).[82] TA is particularly helpful in socio-legal research because it offers great flexibility,[83] allowing the identification of themes or patterns in the data that are relevant to understand the contribution of the Ombudsman to the protection and promotion of disability rights and to the 'shaping' of EU disability law.

4.2. Overarching Trends

As mentioned, 45 decisions by the Ombudsman were retrieved. Among those, 44 decisions stemmed from individual complaints alleging maladministration (see Table 1 below), while one was a query from the Finnish Parliamentary Ombudsman that concerned the EU rules on rail passengers' rights and the accessibility of restaurant cars to wheelchair users,[84] upon which the European Ombudsman decided to open a query procedure in order to seek an opinion of the Commission on EU rules on rail passengers' rights. After the Commission provided an exhaustive reply, the query was closed.

Table 8.1 Cases Related to Disability Decided Between 1 January 2010 and 31 May 2024

CASE NUMBER	KEY ISSUE	DECIDED ON	INSTITUTION CONCERNED
1226/2008/OV	Reasonable Accommodation – Reserved parking for member of staff with disabilities	19 Feb 2010	Commission
129/2009/VL	Child allowance for children of staff with severe disabilities	31 May 2010	Council
1953/2008/MF	Child allowance for child of staff with intellectual disability	18 Oct 2010	EP

(continued)

[82] V Clarke and V Braun, 'Thematic Analysis' (2017) 12(3) *The Journal of Positive Psychology* 297–298; V Braun, V Clarke and N Hayfield, "A Starting Point for Your Journey, not a Map': Nikki Hayfield in Conversation with Virginia Braun and Victoria Clarke about Thematic Analysis' (2022) 19(2) *Qualitative Research in Psychology* 424–445; V Braun, *Thematic Analysis: A Practical Guide to Understanding and Doing* (Sage 2021).

[83] V Braun and V Clarke, 'Using thematic analysis in psychology' (2006) 3(2) *Qualitative Research in Psychology* 77–101.

[84] Query from the Finnish Parliamentary Ombudsman concerning the EU rules on rail passengers' rights and the accessibility of restaurant cars to wheelchair users – Q8/2016/EIS; Case Q8/2016/EIS, 24 January 2017, available at <https://www.ombudsman.europa.eu/en/decision/en/76303>.

Table 8.1 ***(Continued)***

CASE NUMBER	KEY ISSUE	DECIDED ON	INSTITUTION CONCERNED
2295/2009/(TN) ELB	Discrimination on the ground of disability in a staff selection procedure	26 Nov 2010	Commission
2954/2008/MF	Reimbursement of medical expenses	15 Dec 2010	Commission
1804/2009/ (JMA)MHZ	Double dependent child allowance	08 Feb 2011	EP
899/2011/TN	Double dependent child allowance for severely disabled child	13 Dec 2011	Commission
1962/2011/ MHZ	EP's failure to implement the friendly solution in 1804/2009/(JMA)MHZ	12 Dec 2012	EP
683/2012/RT	Failure to provide Reasonable Accommodation	23 Jan 2013	Commission
2455/2011/JF	Lack of accessibility of EPSO's website – EPSO lacking a clear policy towards candidates who are visually impaired	04 Feb 2013	European Personnel Selection Office (EPSO)
1235/2011/ MMN	Discrimination on the ground of disability – Failure to offer a permanent position to a person with a disability	04 Apr 2013	Commission
1512/2011/VL	Failure to cover the entirety of the educational costs for the complainant's disabled son	27 Sept 2013	EP
299/2014/TN	Reasonable Accommodation in tests procedures	06 Aug 2014	Commission
2228/2013/TN	Lack of accessibility – Europass CV for persons with visual impairments	02 Dec 2014	European Centre for the Development of Vocational Training (Cedefop)
118/2013/AN	Failure to provide Reasonable Accommodation – Derogation from mobility requirement for staff with daughter with severe disability	22 Apr 2015	EP

(continued)

Table 8.1 ***(Continued)***

CASE NUMBER	KEY ISSUE	DECIDED ON	INSTITUTION CONCERNED
809/2012/JF	Overpayment of child allowances unnoticed by disabled EU official – Recovery process from the Commission	24 Jun 2015	Commission
1019/2014/PHP	CRPD Compliance of Fellowship Programme	03 Nov 2015	Commission
14/2015/JF	Failure to provide Reasonable Accommodation in staff selection process – refusal by the EPSO to give a candidate with a hearing impairment extra time to sit a computer-based test	26 Apr 2016	EPSO
1418/2016/JN 101/2017/JN	EU role in implementation of CRPD by Member States	11 May 2017	Commission
1487/2016/EIS	European Commission response to a complaint alleging that disabled persons are being stigmatised by a pictorial warning used on tobacco products	11 Jul 2017	Commission
1181/2017/JAS	Failure to provide Reasonable Accommodation in staff selection procedures	23 Nov 2017	EPSO
2179/2017/ AMF	Failure to reply to the correspondence Reimbursement of non-medical expenses relating to a disability	08 Feb 2018	Commission
144/2018/TM	Commission failure to reply to a complaint – CRPD Compliance	13 Feb 2018	Commission
1418/2017/NF	Recruitment of Persons with disabilities – Unfairness of the Positive Action Scheme for Persons with Disabilities	23 Mar 2018	EP
296/2017/NF	Invalidity allowance to retired parliamentary assistant	13 Apr 2018	EP

(continued)

Table 8.1 ***(Continued)***

CASE NUMBER	KEY ISSUE	DECIDED ON	INSTITUTION CONCERNED
413/2018/JAP	European Commission handling of an enquiry concerning the use of pictorial warnings on tobacco products	23 Apr 2018	Commission
1279/2017/KT	Discrimination on the grounds of disability – EU Agency withdrawing an offer to extend a staff member's work contract	31 May 2018	European Maritime Safety Agency (EMSA)
52/2018/KT	Discrimination on the grounds of disability in staff selection procedures	18 Mar 2019	European Investment Bank (EIB)
JOINT INQUIRY 1337/2017/EA 1338/2017/EA	Lack of accessibility of the EPSO website	03 Jun 2019	EPSO
1353/2018/KT	Reasonable Accommodation in staff selection processes	02 Jul 2019	EPSO
1274/2019/JAP	Failure to provide Reasonable Accommodation – Failure to accommodate the needs of associations of staff members with a disability to participate remotely in the plenary session of the Management Committee for Sickness Insurance	05 Aug 2019	Commission
633/2019/AMF	Reimbursement of medical expenses – Invalidity rates	29 Aug 2019	Commission
417/2018/JN	Compliance with CRPD – Human rights violations of Care institution in receipt of EU funding	17 Sept 2019	Commission
1035/2018/AP	Failure to provide Reasonable Accommodation –Rejection of a request to work remotely from a staff member with a disability	10 Oct 2019	EP

(continued)

Table 8.1 ***(Continued)***

CASE NUMBER	KEY ISSUE	DECIDED ON	INSTITUTION CONCERNED
1848/2018/KR	Transparency in Terms of Application for Grants – Rejection of an organisation's application in a call for proposals which aimed to establish support for European networks active in the area of rights of persons with disabilities	07 Nov 2019	Commission
1766/2019/JAP	Failure to provide Reasonable Accommodation to a researcher	26 Mar 2020	Research Executive Agency (REA)
2263/2019/VB	Failure to provide Reasonable Accommodation in staff selection process	17 Jun 2020	EPSO
1233/2019/ MMO	Compliance with CRPD – Spending of ESI by Member States	20 Jul 2020	Commission
1015/2020/ MMO	Discrimination on the ground of disability – non-invitation of candidate with a disability	21 Apr 2021	Commission
179/2021/VB	Reasonable Accommodation in application process	8 Nov 2021	EP
607/2022/ABZ	Complaint on how Commission dealt with complaints that Spain breaches EU law in the area of social security by taxing an incapacity pension from another EU Member State	27 Sept 2022	Commission
535/2021/VS	Double dependent child allowance to a staff member with a child with a disability	23 Feb 2023	Commission
423/2023/JN	Discrimnation on the ground of disability in staff competition – lack of consideration of visual impairment	29 Mar 2023	Council
173/2023/VS	Reasonable Accommodation in staff selection procedure	07 Feb 2024	EPSO

Of the 44 complaints, the majority (22) concerned an alleged maladministration by the Commission. This confirms the role of the Ombudsman as primary watchdog over the European executive. The remainder referred to other institutions and agencies, with most of the complaints referring to the EP (9) and the European Personnel Selection Office (EPSO) (7). Only two (2) complaints alleged maladministration on the part of the Council (see Table 2 below).

Table 8.2 Number of Complaints in Relation to Institutions

EU INSTITUTION CONCERNED	NUMBER OF COMPLAINTS
Commission	22
EP	9
Council	2
EPSO	7
EIB	1
REA	1
Cedefop	1
EMSA	1

The number of decisions varies across years, and it is not possible to detect a consistent upward trend, nor a stable increase in the number of decisions adopted. The highest number of decisions (8) was adopted in 2019.

In five (5) instances maladministration was found,[85] while in most instances either no maladministration was ascertained, or the institutions had taken steps to solve the issues at stake, or the case was settled by the institution, or no further inquiries were justified. In most decisions, the unfolding of the case shows collaborative efforts on the part of the Ombudsman and the institution or body concerned to solve the issues or to provide explanations, evidencing the conciliatory ethos discussed above.

[85] Decision of the European Ombudsman closing his inquiry into complaint 1953/2008/MF against the European Parliament, 18 October 2010, available at <https://www.ombudsman.europa.eu/en/decision/en/5377>; Decision of the European Ombudsman closing his inquiry into complaint 2954/2008/MF against the European Commission, 15 December 2010, available at <https://www.ombudsman.europa.eu/en/decision/en/5537>; Decision of the European Ombudsman closing the inquiry into complaint 809/2012/JF against the European Commission, 24 June 2015, available at <https://www.ombudsman.europa.eu/en/decision/en/60354>; Decision in the joint inquiry in cases 1337/2017/EA and 1338/2017/EA on the accessibility for visually impaired candidates of selection procedures to recruit EU civil servants, organised by the European Personnel Selection Office Decision, 3 June 2019, available at <https://www.ombudsman.europa.eu/en/decision/en/114683>; Decision on how the European Personnel Selection Office (EPSO) handled a request for the reasonable accommodation of the needs of a candidate with disabilities in the context of an EU staff selection procedure (case 173/2023/VS), 7 February 2024, available at <https://www.ombudsman.europa.eu/en/decision/en/181763>.

Even in cases where no maladministration was found or no further inquiries are justified, the Ombudsman has often made suggestions or provided remarks to guide the institution concerned and steer it towards a better consideration of disability rights. For example, in relation to a complaint on the failure of the Commission to accommodate the needs of associations of staff members with a disability to participate remotely in a meeting related to sickness insurance, the Ombudsman ascertained that no further inquiries were appropriate.[86] Nonetheless, they did recommend that, in the context of revision to the general provisions on sickness insurance, the Commission 'ensure, by all technical means at its disposal, a meaningful participation of associations of staff members with disabilities in a consultation process'.[87] In a similar vein, in a case concerning images on advertisement of tobacco products that were alleged to stigmatise persons with disabilities, the Ombudsman 'stresses the importance for the EU administration of having regard to citizens' perceptions and […] believes that […] in order to strike the best possible balance between the rights and interests of people with disabilities on the one hand and the public health perspective on the other, consultation with appropriate civil society groups would be particularly helpful'.[88]

The complaints are often nuanced in their claims, but, in essence, 12 concern the alleged failure to provide some form of reasonable accommodation in selection processes or in employment, five refer to some form of alleged discriminatory behaviour in selection or employment, three concern accessibility issues (particularly digital accessibility), while seven complaints concern allowances for children with disabilities of EU staff (with one of those being a complaint following the failure of the institution to implement a friendly solution previously agreed).[89] The remaining complaints regard varied issues, including practices that are at odds with the CRPD. While the protection of rights of individuals with disabilities is at the core of all complaints, albeit in different ways, two cross-cutting and intertwined themes are identifiable: one relates to the role of the Ombudsman in making the EU administration disability inclusive; the other relates to the role of the Ombudsman in promoting compliance with the CRPD. In exercising these roles, the Ombudsman contributes to the interpretation of norms pertaining to EU disability law and supports the development of this field.

[86] Decision of the European Ombudsman in the above complaint on the failure of the European Commission to accommodate the needs of associations of staff members with a disability to participate remotely in the plenary session of the Management Committee for Sickness Insurance, Case 1274/2019/JAP, 5 August 2019, available at <https://www.ombudsman.europa.eu/en/decision/en/117539>.

[87] Ibid.

[88] Decision in case 1487/2016/EIS on the European Commission's response to a complaint alleging that disabled persons are being stigmatised by a picture warning used on tobacco products, 11 July 2017, available at <https://www.ombudsman.europa.eu/en/decision/en/81308>.

[89] Decision of the European Ombudsman closing his inquiry into complaint 1962/2011/MHZ against the European Parliament Case 1962/2011/MHZ, 12 December 2012, available at <https://www.ombudsman.europa.eu/en/decision/en/12420>.

4.3. Making the EU Administration a Leader in Disability Inclusive Employment Practices

Unsurprisingly perhaps, one of the main themes that emerges is that of ensuring disability inclusive practices in employment. This general theme covers a range of complaints related to (failure to provide) reasonable accommodation and (lack of) inclusive practices, including in cases of discrimination of association (in relation to disabled children allowances). In several recent complaints, the Ombudsman highlights the importance for EU institutions and bodies to promote disability inclusive practices, exhorts the 'EU administration, as an equal opportunities employer, [to] make every effort to avoid discrimination, promote diversity and ensure equal access to job opportunities',[90] and provides specific suggestions. For example, in a decision from February 2024, the Ombudsman recommended to the EPSO to 'put in place safeguards to ensure that any pre-agreed reasonable accommodation measures are provided in practice on the day of the tests' and stated that the EPSO 'should have in place a system to follow up on the implementation of reasonable accommodation measures in all cases and irrespective of whether a contractor is involved or EPSO itself provides the measures'.[91] In doing so, the Ombudsman supports the adoption of soft law or best practices that complement existing measures, somewhat enhancing what I have referred to as the hybridity of EU disability law.[92] In some decisions, the Ombudsman goes even further, contributing to the interpretation of the duty to provide reasonable accommodation, and actively shaping EU disability law and its normative content. This is the case, for example, of the decision adopted in relation to an allegedly discriminatory treatment of an applicant in staff selection procedures organised by the European Investment Bank.[93] The Ombudsman ultimately found no maladministration, but, referring to their previous jurisprudence, affirms that the use of assistive technologies is a form of reasonable accommodation in computer-based tests.[94]

[90] See eg Decision on how the European Personnel Selection Office (EPSO) handled a request for the reasonable accommodation of the needs of a candidate with disabilities in the context of an EU staff selection procedure (case 173/2023/VS), decided on 7 February 2024, available at <https://www.ombudsman.europa.eu/en/decision/en/181763> para 15. See also Decision in case 52/2018/KT on the allegedly discriminatory treatment of an applicant in staff selection procedures organised by the European Investment Bank, 18 March 2019, available at <https://www.ombudsman.europa.eu/en/decision/en/111327> para 24.

[91] Ibid.

[92] D Ferri, 'The role of soft law in advancing the rights of persons with disabilities in the EU: A 'hybridity' approach to EU disability law' (2023) 28(4–6) *European Law Journal* 134–153.

[93] Decision in case 52/2018/KT on the allegedly discriminatory treatment of an applicant in staff selection procedures organised by the European Investment Bank, 18 March 2019, available at <https://www.ombudsman.europa.eu/en/decision/en/111327>.

[94] Ibid para 16.

4.4. Nudging Compliance with the CRPD

In various complaints, in particular since 2013, the Ombudsman cited the CRPD and included explicit suggestions to assess compliance with the Convention and to enhance alignment with it. In a case regarding the alleged failure to offer a permanent position to a person with a disability with consequent breach of the principle of equality, the Ombudsman ascertained that no maladministration had occurred.[95] However they did advise that the Commission 'could examine whether its Code of good practice for the employment of people with disabilities is fully compliant with the [CRPD]'.[96] Further, in an inquiry into how the Commission applies the rule under the EU Staff Regulations concerning the granting of a double child allowance for assisting with the care of children with disabilities, the Ombudsman found that using thresholds on the degree of disability, which automatically excludes certain cases from consideration, is at odds with the EU administration's obligations under the CRPD.[97] In that connection, the Ombudsman took the view that the double dependent child allowance serves the purpose of giving effect to the 'right of persons with disabilities to benefit from measures designed to ensure their independence, social and occupational integration and participation in community life is defined in the [CFR] and in the [CRPD]'. It asked the Commission to revise its approach, and the Commission has in fact initiated a process to revise relevant rules.[98]

Another notable example is a complaint raised by OPDs on the lack of effective monitoring of the use of EU funds to build institutions for persons with disabilities (contrary to Article 19 CRPD).[99] According to the complainant, the Commission had failed to launch infringement procedures against Hungary and Portugal that used European Structural and Investment Funds (ESI funds) to construct segregated institutions. In this instance the Ombudsman pledged to agree with the CRPD Committee that continued investment in institutional care hampers the full realisation of the right to live independently and be included in the community.[100] The Ombudsman went further in stating clearly that 'EU funds spent maintaining, or worse still building, institutions cannot but

[95] Decision of the European Ombudsman closing his inquiry into complaint 1235/2011/MMN against the European Commission, 4 April 2013, available at <https://www.ombudsman.europa.eu/en/decision/en/49771>.

[96] Ibid.

[97] Decision concerning the European Commission's refusal to grant a 'double dependent child allowance' to a staff member with a child with a disability (case 535/2021/VS), 23 February 2023, available at <https://www.ombudsman.europa.eu/en/decision/en/166450>.

[98] Ibid.

[99] Decision in case 1233/2019/MMO on how the European Commission ensures that Member State governments spend European Structural and Investment Funds in line with the obligations stemming from the United Nations Convention on the Rights of Persons with Disabilities, 30 July 2020, available at <https://www.ombudsman.europa.eu/en/decision/en/130886>.

[100] Ibid para 30.

obstruct progress on ensuring deinstitutionalisation'.[101] In this way it did interpret the CRPD, albeit arguably aligning with what the CRPD Committee had already stated. Further, while in the end, the Ombudsman acknowledged that the Commission had taken action to address the problems identified and no further inquiries were justified at that stage, they provided specific suggestions – that were eventually followed up upon, developed and teased out in the following *motu proprio* inquiry discussed in the section 5. Among those suggestions, they recommended that the Commission 'should verify, from the outset, projects that receive ESI funds, with a view to preventing and addressing the type of issues that are described in detail in this case. It should seek to suspend funding, when necessary' in an effort to ensure compliance with the CRPD.[102]

5. The European Ombudsman's Strategic Inquiries on Disability Issues

As mentioned earlier, according to Article 3(3) of the Statute of the European Ombudsman, the Ombudsman 'may conduct own-initiative inquiries whenever he or she finds grounds, and in particular in repeated, *systemic or particularly serious* instances of maladministration, in order to address those instances as an issue of public interest'.[103] This provision also empowers the Ombudsman to promote administrative best practices within EU administration. Notably, even before the conclusion of the CRPD, already in 2003, one of the most significant inquiries concerned disability, namely 'the integration of persons with disabilities by the Commission with the purpose of verifying that these citizens were not discriminated against in their relations with the institution'.[104] At that time, the Ombudsman looked at employment of persons with disabilities by all EU institutions and placed emphasis on the duty to provide reasonable accommodation, but also looked at general issues, such as accessibility and inclusion of pupils with disabilities in European Schools, with the latter issue, as mentioned in section 3, addressed again in 2016 by the Ombudsman as member of the EU framework, and in relation to individual complaints.[105] Since 2010, the Ombudsman has conducted three significant strategic inquiries, mostly overseeing the European Commission's behaviour.

[101] Ibid para 31.

[102] Ibid 'Suggestions for improvement'.

[103] Emphasis added.

[104] Integration of people with disabilities: the Commission's actions Case OI/3/2003/JMA, 4 July 2007, available at <https://www.ombudsman.europa.eu/en/case/en/2060>.

[105] United Nations Convention on the Rights of Persons with Disabilities: UN Committee concluding observation about European Schools (Correspondence 25 January 2016) Case SI/1/2016/EA, 5 October 2016, available at <https://www.ombudsman.europa.eu/en/doc/correspondence/en/63440>.

An important strategic inquiry was opened in 2016 in relation to the treatment of EU staff with disabilities under the JSIS.[106] This inquiry follows the CRPD Committee's COs on the EU initial report which *inter alia* found that the JSIS did not comply with the CRPD as it did not cover disability-related health needs and recommended a revision of such a scheme. The inquiry also follows complaints from staff members on disability related expenses. The Ombudsman ascertained that the failure of the Commission to take any timely action to address the CRPD Committee's recommendation amounted to maladministration, and provided specific suggestions. Among those, the Ombudsman recommended the Commission to publish a non-exhaustive list of assistive devices that are reimbursable under the JSIS and to carry out an assessment to identify – in a non-exhaustive way – non-medical needs relating to disabilities. Importantly, the Ombudsman recommended the Commission to review its current rules on reasonable accommodation for staff with disabilities in light of the CRPD, as well as staff training to raise awareness about disability issues. Further, the Commission was recommended to establish regular contacts and consultations with the associations of EU staff members with disabilities. In doing so, as observed above, the Ombudsman supported the adoption of soft law or best practices that complement existing measures, enhancing the hybridity of EU disability law. Notably, while the Commission accepted the recommendations, in February 2024, the Ombudsman launched a new initiative to clarify whether and to what extent new internal rules (General Implementing Provisions) governing the JSIS cover disability-related health needs.[107]

In July 2017, the Ombudsman opened another seminal strategic inquiry seeking information from the Commission about the accessibility of its websites and online tools,[108] taking into account the obligations laid out in the Web Accessibility Directive (WAD).[109] The Ombudsman noted that although the WAD applies to Member States, the EU institutions are encouraged to comply with its requirements. In 2019, the Ombudsman closed their inquiry by commending the Commission 'for taking steps to ensure and enhance the accessibility of its websites and online tools, and for committing to further improvements' including a plan of action on web accessibility. In fact, a Web Accessibility Action

[106] Decision of the European Ombudsman in her strategic inquiry OI/4/2016/EA into how the European Commission treats persons with disabilities under the Joint Sickness Insurance Scheme for EU staff, 4 April 2019, available at <https://www.ombudsman.europa.eu/en/decision/en/112191>.

[107] How the European Commission ensures that the revised rules governing the Joint Sickness Insurance Scheme (JSIS) for EU staff guarantee comprehensive coverage for disability-related health needs (Case SI/2/2024/AML), opened on 16 February 2024, available at <https://www.ombudsman.europa.eu/en/opening-summary/en/182170>.

[108] Decision of the European Ombudsman closing her strategic inquiry OI/6/2017/EA on how the European Commission ensures that persons with disabilities can access its websites, 20 December 2018, available at <https://www.ombudsman.europa.eu/en/decision/en/107967>.

[109] Directive (EU) 2016/2102 of the European Parliament and of the Council of 26 October 2016 on the accessibility of the websites and mobile applications of public sector bodies [2016] OJ L327/1.

Plan 2022–2025 was published by the Commission in early 2023 and it adds to the EU Web Guide.[110]

The most recent inquiry concerned ESI Funds, and more precisely the extent to which the European Commission monitors that Member States use those funds to promote the right of persons with disabilities to independent living and deinstitutionalisation.[111] Such an inquiry follows individual complaints discussed above, and another *motu proprio* inquiry into how the Commission ensured that the CFR was complied with when EU cohesion policy was implemented by Member States, concluded in 2014.[112] In that inquiry the Ombudsman had recommended the Commission to improve monitoring fundamental rights compliance in the use of funding.[113] While taking a more general approach, the Ombudsman had already looked at the use of EU funds in relation to institutionalisation of persons with disabilities, which is at the core of this most recent investigation. This was opened on foot of recommendations by the CRPD Committee and after complaint-based inquiries into EU-funded projects relating to residential institutions, and followed systemic violations that occurred in institutions during the COVID-19 pandemic.[114] The Ombudsman noted that ESI Funds 'should be implemented in a way that promotes the transition from institutional to family-based and community-based care',[115] and looked into whether the Commission applied sanctions in case Member States built new institutions through the use of such funds. In essence, the Ombudsman assessed the implementation of Article 19 CRPD (on independent living) and found that the Commission could provide better guidance about the need to promote deinstitutionalisation through ESI Funds.[116] The Ombudsman also recommended that the Commission improve the monitoring of ESI-funded activities and take a more proactive role to promote deinstitutionalisation.[117] For instance, the Ombudsman highlighted the usefulness of infringement proceedings in seeking to ensure Member States comply with the CRPD. In addition, the Ombudsman recommended the creation of a clear and transparent system

[110] Commission, 'Europa Web Guide' available at <https://commission.europa.eu/resources-partners/europa-web-guide_en>.

[111] How the European Commission monitors EU Structural and Investment funds to ensure they are used to promote the right of persons with disabilities to independent living and inclusion in the community (Case OI/2/2021/MHZ), 27 April 2022, available at <https://www.ombudsman.europa.eu/en/case/en/58464>.

[112] Decision of the European Ombudsman closing her own-initiative inquiry OI/8/2014/AN concerning the European Commission, 11 May 2015, available at <https://www.ombudsman.europa.eu/en/decision/en/59836>.

[113] Ibid.

[114] A Broderick and S Favalli, 'The Transition from Institutional Care to Community Living in the EU: Lessons Learned in the Shadows of the Covid-19 Pandemic' in G Oberleitner *et al.* (eds), *European Yearbook on Human Rights* (Intersentia 2021) 231–258.

[115] Case OI/2/2021/MHZ (n 111) para 3.

[116] Ibid.

[117] Ibid.

to encourage the participation of civil society in monitoring and implementing the ESI funds. This inquiry complements FRA studies on independent living,[118] but explicitly ascertains the failure of the Commission to protect disability rights in this instance. In doing so, the Ombudsman nudges the Commission towards the adoption of soft law guidance to complement hard law, hence supporting a hybridity approach to EU disability law.[119] At the time of writing, a guidance recommending improvements on independent living and inclusion in the community to Member States, promised in the Strategy 2021–2030, and aligning with the Ombudsman's recommendation has not yet been released. It remains to be seen whether it will be released by the new Commission when it takes office.

In these inquiries, the Ombudsman engages directly with CRPD provisions, recalling the recommendations of the CRPD Committee, and nudges EU institutions, namely the Commission, towards better compliance with disability rights. Further, the Ombudsman has encouraged the adoption of soft law and the implementation of best practices in that contribution (albeit indirectly) to the growth of disability law as a field of EU cation.

6. Concluding Remarks

Thus far, and as part of the EU framework, the European Ombudsman has protected disability rights in particular through the individual complaints procedure. The Ombudsman has also contributed to shaping EU disability law by promoting its alignment with the CRPD through the complaints procedure and its own inquiries, but also through its general work and public engagement. The Ombudsman has backed the interpretation of certain concepts, such as reasonable accommodation, or has supported the interpretation of certain rights, such as that to independent living. In most cases, when engaging with disability rights, the Ombudsman has endorsed an interpretation that aligns with the one given by the CRPD Committee. For example, in the inquiry into accessibility, the Ombudsman highlighted that 'web accessibility has become a prerequisite for "full and effective participation in society on an equal basis with others", as required under the [CRPD]' and indicated that the 'failure to ensure online tools and platforms meet the highest standards of web accessibility undermines the rights of persons with disabilities and risks excluding them'.[120]

Hoffman emphasises that O'Reilly has enhanced the role of the Ombudsman as a driver of systemic change in the EU compared with her predecessors.[121]

[118] Toggenburg (n 3).
[119] Ferri (n 92).
[120] Strategic Inquiry OI/6/2017/EA (n 108) para 6.
[121] Hoffman (n 5) 4-5.

This is particularly true for disability, where the European Ombudsman has recommended the revision of certain rules, such as JSIS rules, or stricter approaches to the use of EU funds. This chapter also shows that the Ombudsman has played a role in the framing of EU disability law and has indirectly enhanced its hybridity, by recommending the adoption of soft law to clarify, integrate and support existing rules or to enhance best practices.

On the whole, disability is an area where the work of the Ombudsman has been rather ambitious and shows that the Ombudsman's soft power can have 'a broad reach' and can 'instigate governance and legal reform'.[122]

[122] Wille and Bovens (n 9).

9

The Role of the Fundamental Rights Agency in Advancing Disability Rights within the EU

GABRIEL N TOGGENBURG*

1. Introduction

The European Union Agency of Fundamental Rights (FRA or 'the Agency') is the European Union's (EU) independent centre of expertise in the area of fundamental rights.[1] In a way, the FRA is to the EU what the National Human Rights Institutes (NHRIs) are to the Member States: it is a Human Rights Institution for the EU. In fact, the Agency's Founding Regulation refers to 'the principles relating to the status and functioning of national institutions for the protection and promotion of human rights (the Paris Principles)'.[2] Its role is to advise EU institutions and

* This chapter is written exclusively in a personal capacity. None of the views expressed here can be attributed to the author's employer (i.e. the European Union Agency for Fundamental Rights – FRA).

[1] The genesis and work of the FRA have been discussed extensively in academic literature. Among others see H Entzinger and R Byrne (eds), *Human Rights Law and Evidence Based Policy: the Impact of the Fundamental Rights Agency* (Routledge 2020); GN Toggenburg, 'The European Union Fundamental Rights Agency' in G Oberleitner (ed), *International Human Rights Institutions, Tribunals, and Courts* (Springer 2018) 443–460; A von Bogdandy and J von Bernstorff, 'The EU Fundamental Rights Agency within the European and international human rights architecture: The legal framework and some unsettled issues in a new field of administrative law' (2009) *Common Market Law Review* 1035–1068; O de Schutter, 'The EU Fundamental Rights Agency: genesis and potential' in K Boyle (ed), *New Institutions for Human Rights Protection* (Oxford University Press 2009); P Alston and O de Schutter (eds), *Monitoring Fundamental Rights – The Contribution of the Fundamental Rights Agency* (Oxford University Press 2005). For a reference overview see GN Toggenburg, 'Grundrechteschutz durch Menschenrechtsinstitutionen: Die EU und ihre Grundrechteagentur' in C Grabenwarter (ed), *Enzyklopädie Europarecht Europäischer Grundrechteschutz, Band 2 der Enzyklopädie Europarecht* (Nomos 2021) 1231–1259.

[2] Recital 20 Council Regulation (EC) No 168/2007 of 15 February 2007 establishing a European Union Agency for Fundamental Rights [2007] OJ L53/1; FRA, 'Bringing rights to life: The fundamental rights landscape of the European Union' (Publications Office of the European Union 2012) 27. Note that all but a handful of EU Member States have a National Human Rights Institution (NHRI) fully accredited under the Paris Principles that establish a list of requirements to qualify as an independent NHRI. The accreditation process is carried out by a sub-committee of the Global Alliance

Member States on fundamental rights-related issues when drafting and implementing EU law. Disability rights are part and parcel of the Agency's mandate and work.

This chapter looks at the role of the Agency as laid down in its *de iure* mandate and legal basis as well as how this is reflected in its actual work and *de facto* role. It takes a 'law-in-context' approach. It begins by looking into the mandate of the Agency (section 1), before examining how disability fits within this (section 2) and the Agency's track-record in protecting and promoting disability rights (section 3). The chapter then explores the Agency's role with regard to the United Nations (UN) Convention on the Rights of Persons with Disabilities (CRPD) framework (section 4), before ending with some conclusions on the way ahead (section 5).

2. The Mandate of the Fundamental Rights Agency and Disability Rights

2.1. The FRA Key Mission and its Objectives

According to Article 2 of Council Regulation (EC) No 168/2007 (hereafter 'Founding Regulation'),[3] the Agency's overall objective is to provide assistance and expertise in the field of fundamental rights. In 2005, before the setting up of the FRA, Baroness Ashton[4] highlighted a notable gap in the promotion and protection of fundamental rights in the EU by stating: 'The current position demonstrates that there is not any body that enables the European institutions to get the benefit of advice or assistance when it comes to fundamental rights'.[5] The FRA was and is meant to fill this 'advice-gap'.

The Agency was established as a consultative body. It has neither quasi-judicial functions, nor does it deal with individual violations of rights. Rather, it is a centre of excellence that provides evidence-based advice to key actors at the EU and national level. It is mandated and expected to provide assistance and expertise to the EU and its Member States, be it the administration, the legislature or the judiciary. Thus far, the emphasis is on providing advice to the legislative

of National Human Rights Institutions (GANHRI), called the Sub-Committee on Accreditation. GANHRI, 'Sub-Committee on Accreditation' available at <https://ganhri.org/accreditation/>. The FRA provides an annual update of the situation in the EU. FRA, 'NHRI accreditation status and mandates – update 2024' (6 February 2024) available at <https://staging.fra.europa.eu/en/publication/2024/nhri-accreditation-status-and-mandates-update-2024>.

[3] Council Regulation (EC) No 168/2007 of 15 February 2007 establishing a European Union Agency for Fundamental Rights [2007] OJ L53/1.

[4] Then Parliamentary Under Secretary of State, later High Representative of the Union for Foreign Affairs and Security Policy and First Vice President of the European Commission in the Barroso Commission.

[5] House of Lords European Union Committee, Baroness Ashton, 'Human Rights Protection in Europe: The Fundamental Rights Agency' (HL 2005-06 155).

and administrative branches of government. To date, the Agency has only once provided written evidence and analysis as well as oral input in a hearing before the Court of Justice of the EU (CJEU).[6] Its territorial mandate is limited to the EU Member States and to states that hold an observer status with the Agency, which currently include Albania, North-Macedonia and Serbia.[7]

The key mission of the Agency is to help to ensure that the EU and its Member States are 'fully respecting' fundamental rights. It does so along three dimensions: upstream and downstream the legislative stream as well as beyond the context of an already existing legislative text or proposal. Upon request by the European Parliament (EP), the Council of the EU (Council) and the European Commission (Commission), the Agency may provide legal opinions on legislative drafts discussed at EU level (upstream). For instance, in 2016, the Agency delivered opinions on six different legislative proposals, mainly in the areas of migration and asylum. Secondly, the Agency may provide practical advice to national actors when these are implementing EU legislation. This type of downstream advice can take a plethora of forms, ranging from informal consultation to comparative reports, surveys or very practical 'do's and don'ts'. By way of illustration for the latter category, one can point to FRA guidance in the area of processing Passenger Name Record data[8] or in the context of border controls at the EU's external land borders.[9]

Another very practical form of advice is provided in the Agency's small field presence in the so-called hotspots in Greece.[10] Given that its mandate is determined by the limits of the EU's 'competence' and not by the scope of (already adopted) EU legislation, the Agency may not only be requested to examine proposed EU legislation but is also mandated to issue its own initiative views on 'where legislative improvements [at the EU level] would be most welcome' in order to close eventual protection gaps and to exercise its advice mission as defined in Article 2 of the Founding Regulation.[11] This advice, beyond the context of an already existing legislative text or draft, is relevant also in the context of the CRPD as it allows the Agency to suggest to the EU to become active in an area that is relevant to the CRPD, but not yet (or not sufficiently) covered by EU law and policies.

[6] Case C-817/19 *Ligue des droits humains v Conseil des ministers* ECLI:EU:C:2022:491.

[7] Article 28 Council Regulation (EC) No 168/2007 as amended by Council Regulation (EU) 2022/555 of 5 April 2022 amending Regulation (EC) No 168/2007 establishing a European Union Agency for Fundamental Rights (Founding Regulation) [2022] OJ L108/1.

[8] FRA, 'Fundamental rights considerations for law enforcement when processing Passenger Name Record data' (13 March 2014) available at <https://fra.europa.eu/de/publication/2015/fundamental-rights-considerations-law-enforcement-when-processing-passenger-name#publication-tab-5>.

[9] FRA, 'Border controls and fundamental rights at external land borders' (Publications Office of the European Union 2020).

[10] Hotspots are specifically assigned areas in Greece and Italy where incoming migrants are identified and registered. For the Agency's advice in that regard see FRA, 'Update of the 2016 FRA Opinion on fundamental rights in the hotspots set up in Greece and Italy' (5 March 2019) available at <https://fra.europa.eu/en/publication/2019/update-2016-fra-opinion-fundamental-rights-hotspots-set-greece-and-italy>.

[11] Para 43 European Parliament resolution on promotion and protection of fundamental rights: the role of national and European institutions, including the Fundamental Rights Agency (2005/2007(INI)) [2006] OJ C117/E242.

2.2. The Fundamental Rights Standards to be Used by the FRA

The Agency is required to embed and apply fundamental rights 'as referred in Article 6 of the Treaty on European Union' within its work.[12] This provision lays down that the Charter of Fundamental Rights (CFR) is an integral part of EU primary law and that the EU recognises fundamental rights as general principles of EU law 'as guaranteed by the [European Convention on Human Rights – ECHR] and as they result from the constitutional traditions common to the Member States'. Whereas the ECHR has a particular relevance in the establishment of such general principles of law, the CJEU underlined that also 'international treaties for the protection of human rights on which the Member States have collaborated or of which they are signatories' form important guidelines for the establishment of general principles of EU law.[13] Further, Article 216(2) Treaty on the Functioning of the EU (TFEU) establishes that '[a]greements concluded by the Union are binding upon the institutions of the Union and on its Member States'. Consequently, the Agency is also bound by the CRPD when carrying out its tasks.

As any international instrument concluded by the Union, the CRPD is part of EU law and ranks between primary and secondary law.[14] Since the CRPD entered into force for the EU, relevant EU legislation 'must, as far as possible, be interpreted in a manner consistent with that convention'.[15] In fact, the CJEU has also taken note of the CRPD when interpreting EU primary law, such as the CFR.[16]

This is of relevance for the FRA given that the Founding Regulation specifies that 'the institutions should be able to request opinions on their legislative proposals or positions taken in the course of legislative procedures as far as their compatibility with fundamental rights are concerned'.[17] The Agency must also consider issues of CRPD-compatibility of adopted and draft EU law, in order to fully deliver under the Agency's overall objective to 'provide the relevant Union institutions, bodies, offices and agencies and the Member States when implementing Union law with assistance and expertise relating to fundamental rights in order to support them when they take measures or formulate courses of action within their respective spheres of competence to fully respect fundamental rights'.[18]

[12] Article 3(2) Founding Regulation.

[13] Opinion 2/13 of the Court (Full Court) 18 December 2014 ECLI:EU:C:2014:2454, para 37.

[14] PS Pohjankoski, 'UN Disability Convention through the prism of EU law: Boosting Human Rights but blurring responsibilities?' (2017) 2 *Anti-Discrimination Law Review* 28–43.

[15] Joined Cases C-335/11 *HK Danmark, acting on behalf of Jette Ring v Dansk almennyttigt Boligselskaband* and C-337/11 *HK Danmark, acting on behalf of Lone Skouboe Werge v Dansk Arbejdsgiverforening, acting on behalf of Pro Display A/S, in liquidation* ECLI:EU:C:2013:222, paras 28-32; D Ferri and ES Krolla, 'Introduction: Walking Through the Looking Glass' in this volume.

[16] D Ferri, 'The Unorthodox Relationship between the EU Charter of Fundamental Rights, the UN Convention on the Rights of Persons with Disabilities and Secondary Rights in the Court of Justice Case Law on Disability Discrimination' (2020) 16 *European Constitutional Law Review* 275.

[17] Recital 13 Founding Regulation.

[18] Article 2 Founding Regulation.

2.3. The Tasks and Key Thematic Areas of the FRA

As already signalled in section 2.1., the Agency's mandate is phrased in broad terms. Admittedly, this has not prevented some from reading it in a narrower manner, including, as discussed below, in the context of the CRPD framework.[19] The FRA can deliver its key objective and mission through a wide spectrum of formats and activities. The Agency's regulation lists as its main tasks: a. *data collection*; b. *development of methods and standards* in the context of data collection and data use; c. *scientific research and surveys*; d. *conclusions* and *opinions* on specific thematic topics; e. *annual reports*; f. *thematic reports*; g. *activity reports*; h. promotion of dialogue with *civil society*.[20]

Regarding its substantial mandate, the FRA Founding Regulation is phrased in a theme-neutral manner and does not refer to any specific human rights theme – such as disability. Over the years, however, the Agency has developed a rich reservoir of datasets, reports, tools, networks, working methods, experience and, partly, indicators in the following main areas:

- non-discrimination issues and equality law, including discrimination based on disability;
- racism, xenophobia and related intolerance;
- the integration and social inclusion of Roma;
- issues and themes related to the rights of the child;
- victims of crime and other 'third pillar issues',[21] such as fundamental rights issues in the context of police work or the fight against terrorism;
- fundamental rights aspects of access to justice and judicial cooperation;
- fundamental rights issues linked to the information society and, in particular, respect for private life, the protection of personal data or the implications of Artificial Intelligence;
- migration, borders, asylum and integration of refugees and migrants.

[19] Some of these views are well intended but superseded by institutional practice and the development of the Agency's mandate over time. See eg L Waddington, 'Reflections on the establishment of a framework to promote, protect and monitor the implementation of the UN Convention on the Rights of Persons with Disabilities (Article 33(2) CRPD) by the European Union' (2011) 3 *Maastricht Faculty of Law Working Paper* 8–18.

[20] Article 4(1) Founding Regulation. Emphasis added.

[21] Before the entry into force of the Treaty of Lisbon on 1 December 2009, the area of police and judicial cooperation in criminal matters, the former 'third pillar', was excluded from the mandate of the Agency. Between 1 December 2009 and 27 April 2022, the Agency could become active in these areas upon request. Since the entry into force of the revision of the Agency's Founding Regulation, the Agency is also mandated to deal with 'third pillar issues' on its own motion. Admittedly, the automatic extension of the Agency's mandate to the third pillar was not uncontested, with the Legal Services of the Council and EP arguing against such an automatism and in favour of the necessity of a review of the Founding Regulation, which took place in 2022.

Before the recent revision of the Founding Regulation, the priority themes of the Agency's work were defined every five years in a Council decision – the so-called Multiannual Framework (MAF). Notably, for the purpose of this chapter, the area of disability was covered by all three MAFs under the thematic area of 'discrimination'. The first MAF (2007-2012) referred to 'discrimination based on sex, race or ethnic origin, religion or belief, disability, age or sexual orientation and against persons belonging to minorities and any combination of these grounds (multiple discrimination)'.[22] The second MAF (2013-2017) replaced this formulation with the wording used in Article 21 CFR, which implied the addition of new characteristics (such as 'genetic features' or 'birth') as grounds of discrimination, but also to the deletion of 'multiple discrimination'.[23] The third MAF (2018-2022) added to the formulation: 'or on the grounds of nationality'.[24] The Agency's Management Board had proposed the inclusion of various further horizontal themes to the MAF, including the 'tasks of the Agency under the monitoring framework of the Convention on the Rights of Persons with Disabilities (Article 33 CRPD)' – a proposal that was not picked up by the Council.[25]

2.4. The Independence of the FRA

The MAF has never placed significant restrictions upon the Agency's mandate, nor on its independence. Firstly, the FRA has always been entitled to deal with themes outside the MAF if requested by the EU legislator to do so. Secondly, the MAF areas were phrased in very broad terms. For example, with regard to disability, discrimination is a key entry point, given that the whole purpose of the CRPD is to ensure and promote the full realisation of all human rights and fundamental freedoms for all persons with disabilities without discrimination on the basis of disability.[26] Finally, contrary to some scholarly assessments,[27] the MAF may limit the Agency's autonomy – on *what* topics to deal with – but it has never

[22] Council Decision No 2008/203/EC of 28 February 2008 implementing Regulation (EC) No 168/2007 as regards the adoption of a Multi-annual Framework for the European Union Agency for Fundamental Rights for 2007-2012 [2008] OJ l63/14.

[23] Council Decision No 252/2013/EU of 11 March 2013 establishing a Multiannual Framework for 2013-2017 for the European Union Agency for Fundamental Rights [2013] OJ L79/1.

[24] Council Decision (EU) 2017/2269 of 7 December 2017 establishing a Multiannual Framework for the European Union Agency for Fundamental Rights for 2018-2022 [2017] OJ L326/1.

[25] FRA, 'Opinion of the Management Board of the EU Agency for Fundamental Rights on a new Multi-annual Framework (2018-2022) for the Agency' (12 February 2016) available at <https://fra.europa.eu/sites/default/files/fra_uploads/mb-opinion-maf-2018-2022_en.pdf> 9; FRA, 'Opinion of the Management Board of the EU Agency for Fundamental Rights on a new Multiannual Framework (2023-2027) for the Agency' (24 February 2021) available at <https://fra.europa.eu/en/news/2021/fra-management-board-publishes-opinion-future-agency-work-areas> 13.

[26] Article 4(1) UN Convention on the Rights of Persons with Disabilities (CRPD).

[27] J Dutheil de la Rochere, 'Challenges for the Protection of Fundamental Rights in the EU at the Time of the Entry into Force of the Lisbon Treaty' (2011) 33(6) *Fordham International Law Journal* 1776–1799.

compromised the independence of the Agency to decide on its very own *how* to deal with certain topics, what aspects to choose, what methodology to apply – and most importantly – what conclusions to draw.

In 2022, the revision of the Founding Regulation granted the thematic programming power exclusively to the Agency. The themes of FRA's work are now defined by the FRA Management Board when adopting the Agency's work programme. Quite atypically for an EU agency and indeed underlining its 'exceptional nature, in comparison to other agencies',[28] the approximately 30 members of the Management Board – with the exception of the two members representing the European Commission and the member representing the Council of Europe (CoE) – are entirely independent and act in their expert capacity. They do not represent the states that have nominated them in any way.

Particularly in the context of the CRPD, it is important to underline that the FRA is under a statutory obligation to exercise its mandate in 'complete independence'.[29] This is not without significance as the CJEU has clarified in another context that complementing the concept of 'independence' with the adjective 'complete' implies an independence without 'any direct or indirect external influence'.[30] In the operational text of the Agency's Regulation independent/independence is mentioned 17 times and, as noted earlier in the introduction, the preamble refers to the Paris Principles.

3. The FRA Work on the Rights of Persons with Disabilities

3.1. The FRA Work in the Context of Disability: Quantity, Quality and Policy Impact

Given the vast thematic scope of the Agency's mandate, disability is just one of the FRA's themes. In that sense the Agency is very far from being a 'disability-focused agency'.[31] In fact, given its limited resources,[32] the FRA engagement with disability issues has thus far been, and will likely remain, selective. A look at the Agency's

[28] Council of the EU (Council), 'Proposal for a Council Regulation establishing a European Union Agency for Fundamental Rights' 6166/07 Annex – Declaration on the Procedure for the Appointment of the Director for the Agency.

[29] Article 16 Founding Regulation.

[30] Case C-518/07 *European Commission v Federal Republic of Germany* ECLI:EU:C:2010:125, para 19. The case concerns the context of data protection authorities established under Directive 95/46/EC.

[31] Neither is it the only EU agency that deals with disability. For instance, Eurofound provides expertise on access to social services and their quality for persons with disabilities and chronic diseases, specifically in relation to employment. See eg Eurofound, 'Living conditions and quality of life' available at <https://www.eurofound.europa.eu/en/topic/living-conditions-and-quality-life>.

[32] J Wouters and M Ovádek, 'Exploring the Political Role of the EU Fundamental Rights Agency: Mandate, Resources and Opportunities' in Byrne and Entzinger (n 1).

2024 work programme is telling: the three units of the Agency directly engaged with research and advisory activities are engaged with 33 activities, out of which only three are focused on disability issues. In fact, a look back shows that, whereas the Agency was heavily engaged in the area of disability at its beginning, this was less the case in later years where the Agency often limited itself to disseminating the results of its earlier disability-related research.[33] Lower levels of engagement in the area of disability are likely to result in a lower level of impact on EU law- and policy-making and in less visibility of the FRA as a relevant actor in the field of disability rights.[34]

The fact that the relative importance of disability in the Agency's work varied over the years could have been counterbalanced by the Agency's statutory role in the EU monitoring framework under Article 33 CRPD. This however, only partly materialised given that the EU did not allocate any additional resources to the members of the EU framework, let alone the framework itself. This is especially concerning against the background of the Agency facing increased demands in new thematic areas, such as digitalisation and Artificial Intelligence. It is further confronted with a new trend, namely that of being explicitly tasked with new activities by the EU legislator.[35] An increase in both human rights challenges and in tasks, combined with a continuing stalemate in resources, puts the Agency under considerable pressure to prioritise its workload and priorities.[36] Every assessment of the Agency's work on disability rights and its impact needs to take this overall institutional environment into account.

After its establishment, the FRA moved quite quickly into the area of disability rights. It considered it important to release its first reports on disability issues when the CRPD and its implications for the EU were still a novel issue, following the conclusion of the Convention by the EU.[37] The Agency decided to start with a focus on what the European Court of Human Rights (ECtHR) has described as 'a particularly vulnerable group in society, who have suffered considerable

[33] This can, for instance, be observed in the Agency's activity report for the year 2019.

[34] The Agency's activity report of 2022 provides a break-down of media references in the area of equality by subtheme: whereas 1418 media references deal with sex, sexual orientation and gender, the respective graph identifies only 13 references to people with disabilities. FRA, 'Consolidated Annual Activity Report of the European Union Agency for Fundamental Rights – 2022' (15 June 2023) available at <https://fra.europa.eu/en/publication/2023/consolidated-annual-activity-report-european-union-agency-fundamental-rights-2022> 85.

[35] Article 10 of the new screening regulation tasks the Agency to 'issue general guidance for Member States on the establishment of a monitoring mechanism and its independent functioning' and states that 'Member States may request the Fundamental Rights Agency to support them in developing their independent monitoring mechanism, including the safeguards for independence of such mechanisms, as well as the monitoring methodology and appropriate training schemes'. Regulation (EU) 2024/1356 of 14 May 2024 introducing the screening of third-country nationals at the external borders [2024] OJ L1356/1.

[36] J Morijn and GN Toggenburg, 'The EU's agency for fundamental rights. The past, the present and the future of an atypical "agency"' (*EU Law Live*, 20 January 2024) available at <https://eulawlive.com/weekend-edition/weekend-edition-no170/>.

[37] Council Decision 2010/48/EC concerning the conclusion, by the European Community, of the United Nations Convention on the Rights of Persons with Disabilities [2010] OJ L23/35.

discrimination in the past',[38] namely, persons with intellectual disabilities and persons with mental health issues. While these are two separate groups, both are too often stigmatised and excluded by society. This consideration led the Agency to research on independent living, legal capacity and political participation. Violence against children with disabilities also became a focus of the Agency's work.

Given that, as previously mentioned, the Agency's engagement with disability is and will remain selective, it is important that the quality of FRA's work reaches the highest standards possible and generates sufficient impact to justify the means invested. It is, however, challenging to measure the impact of fundamental rights research and policy advice. Nevertheless, there are some indications that the disability-related work of the FRA has gained considerable relevance in the EU and its institutions, as well as in regional bodies beyond the EU. With regard to the latter, FRA data, for instance, appears to have triggered an exchange of views within the ECtHR. In the case of *Caamaño Valle v. Spain*, the Strasbourg Court stated that '[t]he European Union Agency for Fundamental Rights noted [...] that the right to vote is often linked in national legislation to legal capacity; consequently, people who have been deprived of their legal capacity (either wholly or in part) are prohibited from voting'.[39] The work of FRA was also referred to, for instance, in documents of the Commissioner for Human Rights[40] and the Agency was involved in relevant CoE formats, such as the Ad Hoc Committee of Experts on the Rights of Persons with Disabilities (CAHDPH) – which was set up to prepare the CoE's Disability Strategy for 2017-2023 and support its implementation. The Parliamentary Assembly of the CoE's Committee on Equality and Non-discrimination to a considerable extent also drew on the Agency's research when it adopted a report on the right to political participation of persons with disabilities in 2017.[41]

When it comes to the EU itself, FRA's work provides an evidence base to argue for more protection of disability rights in EU law- and policy-making. For example, FRA data showed that persons with disabilities are also discriminated against in

[38] European Court of Human Rights (ECtHR), *Alajos Kiss v Hungary*, Application No 38832/06, judgment of 20 May 2010, para 42.

[39] ECtHR, *Caamaño Valle v Spain*, Application No 43564/17, judgment of 11 May 2021. Nevertheless, the ECtHR concluded that there was not yet any consensus among the State Parties of an unconditional right of persons with a mental disability to exercise their right to vote. On the role of the ECtHR see S Jovičić, 'ECHR v. UNCRPD: ending restrictions on voting rights of persons with disabilities' (2021) 22 *ERA Forum* 699–715.

[40] Council of Europe (CoE) Commissioner for Human Rights, 'Persons with disabilities must not be denied the right to vote' (22 March 2011) available at <https://rm.coe.int/168071fdfb>; CoE Commissioner for Human Rights, 'Who gets to decide? Right to legal capacity for persons with intellectual and psychosocial disabilities' (20 February 2012) available at <https://rm.coe.int/16806da5c0#P279_27982>.

[41] See the references to FRA data and analysis in paras 1.4., 3.2., 4.2., 4.7. or 8 of the Explanatory Memorandum of the Committee on Equality and Non-Discrimination, 'The political rights of persons with disabilities: a democratic issue' (22 February 2017) Doc 14268 available at <https://pace.coe.int/en/files/23519#trace-3>.

areas beyond employment – where the European Employment Directive applies.[42] In the FRA's large scale Fundamental Rights Survey, 43 per cent of persons with disabilities reported facing difficulties in using everyday services, such as grocery shopping, banking, postal services, primary healthcare and public transport. Persons with disabilities most often face difficulties in accessing public transport services (26 per cent), postal services (25 per cent) and primary healthcare services (23 per cent). Against the background of this data, the Agency argues for the adoption of the Horizontal Equality Directive[43] as this would result in extending protection against discrimination on the grounds of disability to the areas of education, social protection and access to goods and services.[44] While the EU law- and policy-makers do not necessarily follow the Agency's evidence based policy advice, the FRA's work is reflected in EU level deliberations. As is common with policy advice, much of the influence exercised is not visible and not sufficiently documented. However, being an 'embedded' policy consultant allows the FRA to participate in relevant working groups and to provide its assistance and expertise where most relevant.

Reference to FRA documents were provided, for instance in the Council Conclusions on Enhancing Community-Based Support and Care for Independent Living[45] and in different EP documents that ranged from legislative texts to background policy documents.[46] FRA research results informed the aforementioned Council negotiations on Conclusions regarding Deinstitutionalisation at the Employment, Social Policy, Health and Consumer Affairs Council in 2017. The FRA also developed 28 human rights indicators to assess the political participation of persons with disabilities in the EU. This was done in close cooperation with the Commission and the Academic Network of European Disability Experts (ANED), funded by the Commission.

At the same time, the Agency used the EU's structure to amplify the reach of its work. For instance, the Agency presented its first findings of the project on the right to independent living of persons with disabilities in 2017 at a conference on independent living organised by the Estonian Presidency of the Council. During the COVID-19 pandemic, the FRA used its EU-outreach to raise awareness about the especially concerning situation of persons with disabilities highlighting,

[42] Council Directive 2000/78/EC of 27 November 2000 establishing a general framework for equal treatment in employment and occupation [2000] OJ L303/16.

[43] European Commission (Commission), 'Proposal for a Council Directive on implementing the principle of equal treatment between persons irrespective of religion or belief, disability, age or sexual orientation' COM(2008) 426 final.

[44] FRA, 'Equality in the EU. 20 years on from the initial implementation of the equality directives' (30 April 2021) available at <https://fra.europa.eu/en/publication/2021/fra-opinion-eu-equality-20-years-summary>.

[45] Employment, Social Policy, Health and Consumer Affairs Council at its 3569th meeting held on 7 December 2017.

[46] European Parliamentary Research Service, 'Political participation of people with disabilities in the EU' (April 2024) available at <https://www.europarl.europa.eu/RegData/etudes/BRIE/2023/747889/EPRS_BRI(2023)747889_EN.pdf>.

amongst others, the difficulties of children accessing education, both in schools and distance learning and the fact that people with disabilities continued to be under-represented in decision-making concerning responses to the crisis.[47] Equally, the Agency pointed to promising practices in the hope that transnational learning could help to alleviate the situation. It drew attention to the issues at several high-level hearings and forums, including at the third Human Rights Forum 2021, on the rights of people with disabilities, and during an EP hearing on the impact of COVID-19 on institutionalised people.

Just as with the FRA's work in other thematic areas, reports on disability-related issues are also sometimes picked up in national debates and inform the exchanges and policy reforms at that level as well.[48]

3.2. Persons with Mental Health Issues, Non-discrimination and Involuntary Placement

In 2011, the Agency published a report on non-discrimination and persons with mental health issues.[49] The report followed a socio-legal approach which has become the standard FRA methodology. The report covers the legal frameworks in all 27 Member States; in addition, sociological fieldwork was carried out in nine Member States – typically the FRA selects Member States in a way that allows for a mix of geographic, legal and policy backgrounds. The report shows that in the majority of EU Member States non-discrimination legislation uses a definition of disability that can be interpreted to include persons with mental health issues, who can therefore benefit from protection against discrimination on the ground of disability. The report emphasises the importance of reasonable accommodation and underlines that the great majority of Member States' national legislation contains an explicit duty to provide reasonable accommodation to persons with disabilities in the field of employment. However, beyond the field of employment, the legal situation varies considerably.

A report on involuntary placement and involuntary treatment came out in June 2012.[50] It provided a comparative analysis of the Member States' legal

[47] The political institutions took notice of the concerns as expressed by FRA. European Parliament resolution of 13 December 2022 towards equal rights for persons with disabilities (2022/2026(INI)), para 52.

[48] For example, a report by the NHRI of Germany pointed to the results of the FRA report as an argument for reconsidering the legal situation in Germany. Deutsches Institut für Menschenrechte, 'Gleiches Wahlrecht für alle' (October 2011) available at <https://www.institut-fuer-menschenrechte.de/publikationen/detail/gleiches-wahlrecht-fuer-alle>.

[49] FRA, 'The legal protection of persons with mental health problems under non-discrimination law' (25 October 2011) available at <https://fra.europa.eu/en/publication/2011/legal-protection-persons-mental-health-problems-under-non-discrimination-law>.

[50] FRA, 'Involuntary placement and involuntary treatment of persons with mental health problems' (7 June 2012) available at <https://fra.europa.eu/en/publication/2012/involuntary-placement-and-involuntary-treatment-persons-mental-health-problems>.

frameworks[51] but also the actual experiences of persons with mental health issues concerning involuntary placement and involuntary treatment through semi-structured interviews with persons with mental health issues as well as through focus groups with relevant stakeholders. After presenting the relevant UN and CoE standards,[52] the report dives into the national legislative frameworks in the 27 EU Member States before addressing selected questions related to procedural rights in the context of the review and appeal processes. While identifying differences between the national legal frameworks, the interviews pointed to the trauma and fear people associate with compulsory measures. The largely negative personal experiences described in the report underscored the importance of developing legal frameworks that can minimise such outcomes and that are fully in line with the CRPD. The report draws attention to some of the legal reforms that were required at the time and stresses that any meaningful and practicable reform rests on the participation of the persons concerned, including also the service providers, support persons and local officials responsible for implementing the CRPD in their daily work. This focus on a strictly participatory approach has become a consistent feature in the Agency's work in the area of disability, allowing for a bottom-up approach, which is consistent with the CRPD.

3.3. The Right to Independent Living

In June 2012, the Agency came out with a report on independent living.[53] Article 19 CRPD obliges the EU and its Member States to 'recognize the equal right of all persons with disabilities to live in the community, with choices equal to others' and, consequently, to 'take effective and appropriate measures to facilitate full enjoyment by persons with disabilities of this right and their full inclusion and participation in the community'. The Agency focused on two distinct groups, namely persons with mental health issues and persons with intellectual disabilities. For both groups the reports separately examine living arrangements, daily living situation, available support for daily living, participation in the community, and the barriers to inclusion and participation. The report is based on individual semi-structured interviews and focus groups and concludes as follows:

> [a]cross the [EU] the journey towards social inclusion and participation for people with mental health issues and people with intellectual disabilities has begun. There is still

[51] Ibid Annex 2 provides an overview of the criteria used by the 27 Member States for involuntary placement and involuntary treatment.

[52] Note that according to Article 18 of the Committee of Ministers Recommendation Rec(2004)10, a person may be subject to involuntary treatment only if all the following conditions are met: the person has a mental disorder; the person's condition represents a significant risk of serious harm to his or her health or to other persons; no less intrusive means of providing appropriate care are available; the opinion of the person concerned has been taken into consideration.

[53] FRA, 'Choice and control: the right to independent living' (7 June 2012) available at <https://fra.europa.eu/en/publication/2012/choice-and-control-right-independent-living>.

> a long way to go and little time to lose. At stake are deep-seated values of the EU – a commitment to the dignity and autonomy of the person and an equal commitment to citizenship and inclusion.[54]

This statement is preceded by 11 sets of measures that the FRA identifies as key for facilitating progress in helping persons with mental health issues and persons with intellectual disabilities to live more independently within the community.

3.4. Legal Capacity of Persons with Intellectual Disabilities and Mental Health Issues

In July 2013, the Agency published a report on legal capacity.[55] The issue of legal capacity presented a particular challenge at a time when the CRPD was still a new legal obligation for the EU and its Member States. The latter in particular need to harmonise their legal frameworks with CRPD requirements and these efforts have relevance across all areas of life, spanning such diverse issues as signing a contract of employment, deciding whether to have children, and taking decisions regarding healthcare treatment. The report was also published in an easy-to-read version[56] – an approach that applies accessibility to the research itself and thus 'walks the talk'. The data shows, for instance, that, typically, following a decision on legal incapacity, a guardian is appointed and national legislation in all EU Member States allows for an appeal of the decision depriving a person of legal capacity and appointing a guardian. However, in several Member States the person concerned cannot trigger the appeal or actively participate in these proceedings. The report also presents the concrete experiences with the legal situation concerning guardianship and restricted decision-making, thereby applying again the Agency's socio-legal approach. Presenting real-life stories, captured in the findings of the FRA's in-depth qualitative fieldwork research, gives a voice to those who are seldom heard. Moreover, the Agency's socio-legal approach helps to contextualise the legal framework and offers an inside view of how the legal system affects the lives of persons with disabilities. This approach of the FRA allows policymakers to be informed in an encompassing manner, going far beyond the usual policy-paper rooted in desk-based research.

[54] Ibid 70.

[55] FRA, 'Legal capacity of persons with intellectual disabilities and persons with mental health problems' (26 July 2016) available at <https://fra.europa.eu/en/publication/2013/legal-capacity-persons-intellectual-disabilities-and-persons-mental-health>.

[56] FRA, 'Laws about being able to make important decisions for yourself' (20 September 2013) available at <https://fra.europa.eu/en/publication/2013/laws-about-being-able-make-important-decisions-yourself>; FRA, 'Legal capacity of persons with intellectual disabilities and persons with mental health problems – Factsheet' (3 October 2013) available at <https://fra.europa.eu/en/publication/2013/legal-capacity-persons-intellectual-disabilities-and-persons-mental-health-0>.

3.5. The Right to Political Participation

Given that political participation exemplifies the three key principles of the disability strategies grounded in the CRPD – non-discrimination, equality and active inclusion – and that EU law plays a key role in political participation at local and EU level, the Agency soon engaged with political participation of persons with disabilities.

In November 2010 the Agency published a report on political participation of persons with mental health issues and persons with intellectual disabilities.[57] It clusters the 27 EU Member States in three groups, following three different approaches. Firstly, an approach of exclusion: the right to political participation is linked to the legal capacity of the individual so that partial and plenary guardianship leads to an automatic or quasi-automatic exclusion of the right to political participation. At the time of drafting the report this was the approach chosen by 17 Member States – a clear majority position in the EU. Secondly, an intermediate approach (i.e. a case-by-case consideration): in this approach political participation depends on an assessment made of the individual's actual ability to vote, either by a medical practitioner or a judge. The report identified nine Member States that followed this approach. Thirdly, a participatory approach: here persons with mental health issues and persons with intellectual disabilities have full participation in the electoral process without any individual assessments applied. This was the case for ten EU Member States, with Austria, Finland, The Netherlands, Spain and Sweden enshrining the right to full participation also in their national constitutions.

The Agency continued working on this topic by developing, in close cooperation with the Commission and ANED, indicators that followed the UN model of Structure (commitments), Process (efforts) and Outcome (results). This work on indicators later led to the development of an indicator-based guide for independent national monitoring frameworks on how to best fulfil their monitoring responsibility pursuant to Article 33 CRPD.[58] In September 2014, the Agency published a 100-page report that was dedicated to the political participation of persons with disabilities at large.[59] Alongside the developments on the right of persons with disabilities to political participation, the report also shows how the Agency's working methods have developed and refined over the early years of the FRA: the report is based on a sophisticated system of indicators; it covers many

[57] FRA, 'The right to political participation of persons with mental health problems and persons with intellectual disabilities' (8 November 2010) available at <https://fra.europa.eu/en/publication/2010/right-political-participation-persons-mental-health-problems-and-persons>.

[58] FRA, 'Implementing the UN Convention on the Rights of Persons with Disabilities: Human rights indicators' (20 March 2023) available at <https://fra.europa.eu/en/publication/2023/implementing-un-convention-rights-persons-disabilities-human-rights-indicators>.

[59] FRA, 'The right to political participation for persons with disabilities: human rights indicators' (21 May 2014) available at <https://fra.europa.eu/en/publication/2014/right-political-participation-persons-disabilities-human-rights-indicators>.

detailed aspects (such as the question as to whether television programmes that provide instructions for voting and information on candidates have national sign language interpretation); it makes use of disaggregated data provided by existing EU-wide surveys, including the European Quality of Life Survey and European Social Survey alongside the Agency's own datasets; it identifies promising practices (highlighted in blue boxes throughout the report) and replaces the earlier vague 'ways forward' with more detailed 'opinions' that provide recommendations to the EU and its Member States. Finally, the report demonstrates the efforts of the Agency to make its data accessible and to provide ancillary products that provide easier access to the main messages in comparison to the full-fledged research report. Next to the latter, the Agency published a summary report[60] and five infographics on election authorities, parliaments, political parties, support organisations and voting rights for persons with disabilities, which are available in all EU languages (apart from Irish) and can all be accessed online.[61] Moreover, the dataset that populated the indicators as developed by FRA together with ANED was published in an 'interactive data explorer' that allows access to the data and the opportunity to compare countries via tables or maps.[62] Following up on this work, the Agency published a paper on political participation in February 2019 – ahead of the European elections 2019[63] – and repeated this for the 2024 elections with the paper 'Political participation of people with disabilities – new developments', published at the end of May 2024.[64] Compared with the findings of the Agency's first report on the topic, the number of Member States that allow people deprived of legal capacity to vote has increased from 10 to 14 states. The number of Member States that offer limited participation reduced from nine to six states. Finally, the number of Member States that exclude persons with limited legal capacity from voting decreased from 17 to only seven states in 2024, thereby showing the positive effects of continued monitoring and mutual learning.

[60] FRA, 'The right to political participation of persons with disabilities – Summary' (29 April 2014) available at <https://fra.europa.eu/en/publication/2014/right-political-participation-persons-disabilities-summary>.

[61] FRA, 'Political participation indicators infographic – Election authorities' (2014) available at <https://fra.europa.eu/en/publications-and-resources/infographics/political-participation-indicators-infographic-election>; FRA, 'Parliaments – How can you encourage more people with disabilities to vote?' (2014) available at <https://fra.europa.eu/en/publications-and-resources/infographics/parliaments-how-can-you-encourage-more-people-disabilities>; FRA, 'Political parties – the votes of people with disabilities count too; Support organisations – How can you help people with disabilities to vote?' (2014) available at <https://fra.europa.eu/en/publications-and-resources/infographics/political-parties-votes-people-disabilities-count-too>; FRA, 'Voting rights for people with disabilities – What you need to know' (2014) available at <https://fra.europa.eu/en/publications-and-resources/infographics/voting-rights-people-disabilities-what-you-need-know>. All these infographics were published in accessible pdf format on 25 June 2015.

[62] FRA, 'Indicators on the right to political participation of people with disabilities' (2014) available at <https://fra.europa.eu/en/publications-and-resources/data-and-maps/polpar>.

[63] FRA, 'Who will (not) get to vote in the 2019 European Parliament elections?' (26 February 2019) available at <https://fra.europa.eu/en/publication/2019/who-will-not-get-vote-2019-european-parliament-elections>.

[64] FRA, 'Political participation of people with disabilities – new developments' (29 May 2024) available at <https://fra.europa.eu/en/publication/2024/political-participation>.

3.6. Violence against Children/Persons with Disabilities

In December 2015, the Agency published a report on violence against children with disabilities.[65] The report is based on the data collected through the Agency's research network in all EU Member States and deals with evidence of violence against children with disabilities (including hate crimes), the development of legislative and policy instruments, data collection mechanisms, and services to address violence and hostility against children with disabilities. The data collection is complemented by the findings from 132 semi-structured interviews conducted in 13 countries. These interviews focused on the assessment of the relevant legal and policy frameworks, the extent of violence against children with disabilities and how it is addressed in practices and programmes, the situation of diverging risks in different settings and the intersection of disability with other characteristics (such as gender), as well as possible ways forward.

The report concludes with a series of 'opinions' that call, for instance, for an integrated approach that provides all-round support to children with disabilities and their families or the inclusion of disability as a form of bias motivation in criminal law. The Agency also points Member States to the EU Structural and Investment Funds that they should use to support both children with disabilities and their families in the transition from institutional to family-based care.

The Agency's research has fed into the Commission's policy-making and has triggered interest for further work by FRA. In March 2021, the Commission published a new and strengthened Strategy for the Rights of Persons with Disabilities 2021-2030,[66] which highlights the need for improving access to justice and protection, including by 'monitoring of institutions and investigation in case violence, crimes or abuse occurs' and calls on the FRA to examine the situation of persons with disabilities living in institutions with regard to violence, abuse and torture. The Agency has added a project in this regard in its work programme and began its work in 2024. The work programme specifies that the project examines the availability and function of formal complaints procedures, as well as possibilities for persons with disabilities, in particular children, to access informal complaints systems and external complaints services. Moreover, the project examines additional measures, such as proactive monitoring of closed institutions, unannounced visits by independent authorities and other measures.

3.7. Deinstitutionalisation

Article 19 CRPD requires States Parties 'to recognize the equal right of all persons with disabilities to live in the community' and to ensure that they 'have the

[65] FRA, 'Violence against children with disabilities: legislation, policies and programmes in the EU' (2 December 2015) available at <https://fra.europa.eu/en/publication/2015/violence-against-children-disabilities-legislation-policies-and-programmes-eu>. An easy-to-read version is also available.

[66] Commission, 'Union of Equality: Strategy for the Rights of Persons with Disabilities 2021–2030' (Strategy 2021-2030) COM(2021) 101 final.

opportunity to choose their place of residence and where and with whom they live' and 'have access to a range of in-home, residential and other community support services, including personal assistance necessary to support living and inclusion in the community, and to prevent isolation or segregation from the community'. Given the lack of implementation and discussions about how best to realise the transition from institutional to community-based support, the Agency has focused on the topic of deinstitutionalisation.

Between 2014 and 2018, the FRA engaged in a mapping exercise (phase 1), the identification of implementation gaps by applying a dedicated indicator framework (phase 2),[67] and fieldwork allowing for qualitative research in five EU Member States at different stages of the deinstitutionalisation process (phase 3). The Agency made sure to guarantee a participatory approach by including persons with disabilities and their representative organisations throughout the entire process – from the design of the methodology to the review part and an online survey to validate the local-level findings.

Following the already mentioned Structure-Process-Outcome approach, the Agency published, in October 2017, a triptych of reports on commitments and structures,[68] funding and budgeting[69] and outcomes for persons with disabilities.[70]

In terms of commitments (part I), the Agency notes that there is a significant degree of divergence in how EU Member States organise deinstitutionalisation and coordinate the different levels and sectors of government involved in deinstitutionalisation, which presents a major challenge. Most EU Member States have adopted strategies that cover deinstitutionalisation but some strategies lack the adequate funding, clear timeframes and benchmarks, and involvement of organisations of persons with disabilities required to make them effective. In terms of funding (part II), the Agency notes a lack of robust, comparable and timely data on budget allocations for services for persons with disabilities, which impedes evidence-based policy-making and undermines efforts to achieve deinstitutionalisation. Moreover, the report found that many Member States continue to invest considerable resources in institutions for persons with disabilities, which counteracts the goal of independent living under Article 19 CRPD. Coming to the outcome dimension of deinstitutionalisation (part III), the Agency's report

[67] The indicators are based on four components of Article 19 CRPD, namely: cross-cutting issues, living arrangements, support services (for persons with disabilities) and general services (available to the public).

[68] FRA, 'From institutions to community living – Part I: commitments and structures' (12 October 2017) available at <https://fra.europa.eu/en/publication/2017/institutions-community-living-part-i-commitments-and-structures>.

[69] FRA, 'From institutions to community living – Part II: funding and budgeting' (12 October 2017) available at <https://fra.europa.eu/en/publication/2017/institutions-community-living-part-ii-funding-and-budgeting>.

[70] FRA, 'From institutions to community living – Part III: outcomes for persons with disabilities' (12 October 2017) available at <https://fra.europa.eu/en/publication/2017/institutions-community-living-part-iii-outcomes-persons-disabilities>.

found that large numbers of persons with disabilities continue to live in institutions in EU Member States and that persons with disabilities are, on average, less likely to be satisfied with their accommodation in the community than persons without disabilities. For many of those persons who receive help with everyday tasks, this help is not sufficient to meet their needs. All three reports produced opinions that can be accessed together in a summary report published in May 2018.[71] In 2018, the Agency published a report on the drivers and barriers of deinstitutionalisation[72] and five case studies in that regard.[73] The report concludes with a series of recommendations for the Member States. For the EU, the Agency proposes to ensure that the post-2020 funding scheme contains strong fundamental rights guarantees to ensure that the EU fully respects its human and fundamental rights obligations under the CRPD and the CFR. In fact, the revised Common Provision Regulation did indeed enhance the fundamental rights related conditionalities.[74]

3.8. Mainstreaming

To conclude on the Agency's research activities, it is relevant to underline that the rights of persons with disabilities also play a role in FRA activities that are not focused on disability issues. A few examples help concretise this point. In March 2013, the Agency published a report on access to and quality of

[71] There are five opinions on commitments and structures and seven opinions on funding and on outcomes respectively. FRA, 'From institutions to community living: key findings and FRA opinions – Summary' (28 May 2018) available at <https://fra.europa.eu/hr/publication/2018/institutions-community-living-key-findings-and-fra-opinions>.

[72] FRA, 'From institutions to community living for persons with disabilities: perspectives from the ground' (4 December 2018) available at <https://fra.europa.eu/en/publication/2018/institutions-community-living-persons-disabilities-perspectives-ground>.

[73] Each case study deals with one country, ie Bulgaria, Finland, Ireland, Italy and Slovakia; these FRANET reports are available at <https://fra.europa.eu/en/country-data/2018/country-studies-project-right-independent-living-persons-disabilities-case-study>.

[74] Articles 9 and 73, and Annex III Regulation (EU) 2021/1060 of the European Parliament and of the Council of 24 June 2021 laying down common provisions on the European Regional Development Fund, the European Social Fund Plus, the Cohesion Fund, the Just Transition Fund and the European Maritime, Fisheries and Aquaculture Fund and financial rules for those and for the Asylum, Migration and Integration Fund, the Internal Security Fund and the Instrument for Financial Support for Border Management and Visa Policy [2021] OJ L231/159; FRA, 'EU funds: Ensuring compliance with fundamental rights' (19 December 2023) available at <https://fra.europa.eu/ga/publication/2023/eu-funds>. However, the Court of Auditors draws attention to an important shortcoming: the EU funding framework does not provide for a dedicated category of expenditure concerning support for persons with disabilities which implies that no information is available on the extent to which EU funding contributes to improving the situation of persons with disabilities. Court of Auditors, 'Supporting persons with disabilities. Practical impact of EU action is limited' (2023) available at <https://www.eca.europa.eu/ECAPublications/SR-2023-20/SR-2023-20_EN.pdf>.

healthcare.[75] The report deals, amongst other issues, with the concept of intersectional discrimination, such as the sterilisation of women with disabilities, and is therefore by definition of relevance for disability rights. Moreover, the report stresses the relevance of data and states that while data on sex and age are systematically recorded, data on ethnicity and disability are rarely collected, or the samples are not large enough to allow for further disaggregation of the data.[76]

In November 2012, the Agency published a report on hate crimes and the rights of victims.[77] It also deals with disability concluding that the criminal justice systems:

> in most EU Member States fail to recognise crimes motivated by a person's disability as a fully-fledged bias motivation. Persons with disabilities are therefore often unable to seek redress. The offenders may be tried on the basis of, say, grievous bodily harm, leaving the bias that motivated their attack unaddressed.[78]

In fact, in March 2015 the Agency followed up with a focus paper dedicated to people with disabilities who become victims of hate crime.[79] Against the background of disability not being included in EU hate crime legislation and the fact that victims of disability hate crime are often reluctant to report their experiences, the Agency suggests that Member States systematically collect and publish disaggregated data on hate crime against people with disabilities and undertake trust-building measures to encourage reporting by victims with disabilities of bias-motivated or other forms of crime.

Of course, FRA surveys provide interesting findings for the area of disability law and the experiences of persons with disabilities – either because the data can be disaggregated by disability or because the questions directly address disability. For instance, the Fundamental Rights Survey – the first survey to collect comprehensive and comparable data on people's experiences and views of their rights in the EU-27 carried out in 2019 amongst 34,948 respondents – asked about the awareness of a law that forbids discriminating against job applicants because they have a disability. The results vary drastically between the EU Member States: whereas in France 77 per cent of the respondents are aware of such a law, this figure is only 22 per cent in Cyprus (EU average: 59 per cent).[80]

[75] FRA, 'Inequalities and multiple discrimination in access to and quality of healthcare' (4 March 2013) available at <https://fra.europa.eu/en/publication/2013/inequalities-and-multiple-discrimination-access-and-quality-healthcare>.

[76] Ibid 35-37.

[77] FRA, 'Making hate crime visible in the European Union: acknowledging victims' rights' (27 November 2012) available at <https://fra.europa.eu/en/publication/2012/making-hate-crime-visible-european-union-acknowledging-victims-rights>.

[78] Ibid 29.

[79] FRA, 'Equal protection for all victims of hate crime – The case of people with disabilities' (30 March 2015) available at <https://fra.europa.eu/en/publication/2015/equal-protection-all-victims-hate-crime-case-people-disabilities>.

[80] The data are available in the Agency's interactive data explorer available at <https://fra.europa.eu/en/data-and-maps/2021/frs>.

4. The FRA's Role in the EU Framework under Article 33(2) CRPD

4.1. The Framework as Laid Down in the CRPD

Article 33(2) CRPD obliges State Parties to 'maintain, strengthen, designate or establish' a 'framework … to promote, protect and monitor implementation' of the CRPD, in the case of the EU, at the EU level. As noted above, the framework must include at least one 'independent mechanism' taking 'into account' the Paris Principles.

Further guidance on this provision was laid out in the 'Guidelines on independent monitoring frameworks and their participation in the work of the Committee on the Rights of Persons with Disabilities' by the CRPD Committee.[81] These Guidelines state, amongst other points, that there should be a 'broad, inclusive consultation process' before designating any framework; that any monitoring framework is 'independent from the focal points appointed under Article 33(1) of the Convention'; that the mandate of the framework needs to be 'set out in a constitutional or a legislative text'; and that monitoring activities 'include developing a system to assess the impact of the implementation of legislation and policies'. While the guidelines confirm that the parties 'have a margin of appreciation to decide whether or not their independent monitoring framework consists of one or more monitoring mechanisms' they put a lot of emphasis on the key role of NHRIs and appear to express a clear preference for models where the NHRI is the only, or the central, actor in the Article 33(2) framework. In fact, State Parties are 'encouraged to appoint their Paris Principles-compliant national human rights institution as the monitoring framework or the mechanism forming part of the monitoring framework and to equip it with additional and adequate budgetary and skilled human resources'.[82]

The EU, however, chose an alternative path. The Council decision confirming EU accession to the CRPD designated the Commission as the focal point in the sense of Article 33(1) but remained silent on the framework to be established under Article 33(2) CRPD.[83] The Commission 'carefully analysed' the requirements of Article 33(2) and identified five separate existing EU institutions and bodies – the EP's Petitions Committee (PETI Committee), the European Ombudsman (EO), the Commission, the European Disability Forum (EDF) and the FRA – that together would form 'the EU framework'. Designating a framework built on existing bodies rather than creating a new framework, let alone a new institution was in the eyes of the Commission a 'simple, efficient and

[81] The guidelines were attached as Annex to the Committee's revised rules of procedure. CRPD Committee, 'Guidelines on independent monitoring frameworks and their participation in the work of the Committee' (10 October 2016) CRPD/C/1/Rev.1.

[82] Ibid Annex para 17.

[83] Council Decision 2010/48/EC.

practical' arrangement that would maximise synergies while avoiding the imposition of any 'undue administrative and financial burden'. The five components are – so the Commission explained – 'independent of each other and have the freedom to define their activities related to the CRPD within their current mandates and resources'.[84] By 'sharing information and by acting within a coordinated work plan with independent components defined within their own mandates, each of them will be able to maximise the effectiveness of its own relevant activities and to co-ordinate them with the other participants'. Obviously, in such a maybe all-too pragmatic and cost-efficient approach the focus remained on the components of the framework rather than on the framework itself. Based on these considerations, the Commission in 2012 proposed a formal endorsement of the arrangement by the Council through a simplified procedure.[85]

While Article 33 was perceived by observers as one of the most unique and innovative elements of the CRPD from the outset,[86] it is also a provision whose implementation by the EU raised strong and early criticism. It was said that the EU 'avoided establishing an independent mechanism that could unreservedly scrutinize the law and policy-making of the Union' and basically 'failed to designate a CRPD compliant framework'.[87] When reviewing the EU for the first time in 2015, the Committee on the Rights of Persons with Disabilities (CRPD Committee) provided (partial) guidance in that regard by addressing the most obvious shortcoming of the EU's monitoring framework. The CRPD Committee recommended that the Commission be removed from the framework as it cannot serve as the focal point of the EU under Article 33(1) CRPD and simultaneously function as a member of the monitoring framework tasked with monitoring the EU as a State Party. Moreover, the CRPD Committee called on the EU to 'ensure that the framework has adequate resources to perform its functions'.[88] Following up on the CRPD Committee's Concluding Observations (COs) on the EU, the Commission withdrew in 2016 from the monitoring framework and later proposed a revision of the framework that the Council adopted on 16 January 2017.[89] However, no resources were provided to the framework or its members.

[84] Commission, 'Commission Non Paper on the setting-up at EU level of the framework required by Art. 33.2 of the UN Convention on the Rights of Persons with Disabilities' (CFSP/EAS/1072/12) as updated on 31 August 2012 available at <https://ec.europa.eu/social/BlobServlet?docId=14155&langId=en>.

[85] Ibid. The Council agreed to the proposal on 29 October 2012.

[86] A Hoefmans, 'The EU framework for monitoring the CRPD' in D Ferri and A Broderick (eds), *Research Handbook on Disability Law* (Edward Elgar 2020) 71–88; G de Búrca, 'The EU in the Negotiation of the UN Disability Convention' (2010) 35(2) *European Law Review* 174–196. See also D Ferri, 'The Role of the European Ombudsman in Protecting and Promoting Disability Rights' in this volume.

[87] M Birtha, 'A chance to pioneer or a lost opportunity? Monitoring disability rights effectively and independently in the EU in line with Article 33 of the UN CRPD' in L Waddington, G Quinn and E Flynn (eds), *European Yearbook of Disability Law Volume 5* (Intersentia 2015) 73.

[88] CRPD Committee, 'Concluding observations on the initial report of the European Union' (2 October 2015) CRPD/C/EU/CO/1, paras 76 and 77.

[89] Council, 'Revised EU-level framework required by article 33.2 of the UN-Convention on the rights of persons with disabilities' 6170/17 Annex.

In March 2016, the EP requested the FRA for an opinion on the monitoring framework, including the requirements for full compliance with the CRPD, taking into account the specificities of the EU. After consulting with a wide range of stakeholders,[90] the Agency published an opinion in May 2016[91] that recommended additional steps on how the EU should implement Article 33(2) CRPD, including the following: regarding the frameworks' composition, the Agency acknowledges that a multi-component framework composed of existing EU actors can be an appropriate solution while however stressing that to have a Parliament as part of the framework is 'atypical compared to the situation at national level – where no parliaments or parliamentary committees form part of the Member States' Article 33(2) mechanisms' given that parliaments are a 'prominent branch of the public power of any State party and in that sense tasked with the implementation of the CRPD'.[92] Indeed, this appears to be an important point of principle, which is corroborated by the fact that the EP extended its participation in the framework from one Committee (PETI Committee) to three Committees by adding the Committee on Civil Liberties, Justice and Home Affairs (LIBE Committee) and the Committee on Employment and Social Affairs (EMPL Committee), thereby contributing to the challenge of efficiency,[93] next to the issue of independence.

Based on COs of the CRPD Committee and of the Sub-Committee on the Accreditation of National Human Rights Institutions, as well as in light of practices at national level, the Agency has recommended the EU to provide a solid legal basis for the EU framework.[94] This point was also made within scholarship[95] and would indeed help to enhance the transparency, stability and legitimacy of the framework. The current framework is not based on a formal Council decision, but on an Annex-document that was adopted by the Council and never published in the Official Journal. Without any proper legal basis, 'the framework' remains, legally speaking, a fiction. The 'framework' is a *de facto* conglomerate that provides neither a *de iure* mandate, nor any *de facto* avenue to go beyond the sum

[90] The Agency received input from the secretariat of the CRPD Committee, the Regional Office for Europe of the Office of the High Commissioner for Human Rights (OHCHR), the OHCHR Disability and Human Rights Advisor, stakeholders from 24 Member States (including responses from National Liaison Officers in 23 Member States and members of Article 33(2) frameworks in ten Member States).

[91] FRA, 'Opinion concerning requirements under Article 33(2) of the UN Convention on the Rights of Persons with Disabilities within the EU context' (20 May 2016) available at <https://fra.europa.eu/de/publication/2016/fra-opinion-concerning-requirements-under-article-33-2-un-convention-rights>.

[92] Ibid 18; G de Beco, 'Study on the Implementation of Article 33 of the UN Convention on the Rights of Persons with Disabilities in Europe' (UN Office of the High Commissioner on Human Rights 2014).

[93] On 12 December 2013 the Conference of Presidents of the European Parliament entrusted the EMPL and LIBE Committees to participate – next to the PETI Committee as envisaged already in the 2012 Council decision – in the EU framework, thereby conflating the framework with political actors.

[94] FRA (n 91) 19.

[95] Birtha (n 87) 59-60.

of its components given that the legal and political constraints of any of the four – actually six given that the EP is participating with three Committees – members draw the contours of the framework's constraints.

Finally, the Agency is of the opinion that the EU framework should have the possibility to issue opinions on draft EU legislation with relevance to the rights of persons with disabilities and that such independent external expert advice should be available independently from any EU institutions' request.[96] In that sense, the framework should also arguably be more than the sum of its constituent members in terms of legal portfolio. Given that the framework should be based on a legally binding EU act this would not be a problem as the act would design the framework and its powers.

Indeed, other observers have also made the point that the withdrawal of the Commission from the framework does not lead to a situation in which the EU framework would be fully CRPD-compliant and that for the next EU review a more encompassing assessment of the framework should be taken into consideration, which might also imply 'an interesting policy debate about the establishment of a proper EU NHRI'.[97]

4.2. The FRA Role in the Current Framework

The Commission note that formed the basis for the first framework-document adopted by the Council not only identified the (original five) members of the framework but also described how each of them would contribute to the three tasks of 'promotion', 'protection' and 'monitoring' of the Convention 'within the remit of their existing competences'. Looking at the tasks linked to the Agency, it appears that the Agency's mandate was read in a very narrow manner by the Commission. Under none of the three main tasks is the Agency listed with relevant activities, such as the issuing of reports or opinions; the scrutiny of EU legislation (mentioned for EP and EO) or the provision of technical advice to public authorities on the application of the Convention (mentioned for the EO); the measurement of progress or the issuing of a shadow report to the CRPD Committee (mentioned for EDF).[98] Rather, the Agency is reduced to an entity that may collect data. The revised framework document of 2017 similarly follows that spirit by stating: 'The FRA independently collects and analyses data within the limits of its mandate. Providing such data in an independent manner will be its main task in the framework'.[99]

[96] FRA (n 91) 27. The Agency points also to the role of the European Data Protection Supervisor and, indeed, it is remarkable that the EU legislator should receive less external advice on disability than on data protection despite the international obligations the EU has under the CRPD.

[97] Hoefmans (n 86) 82.

[98] In sum, the Commission's table originally identified 18 tasks for the Commission, 13 for the EP and EDF, ten for the EO and only four for FRA.

[99] Council (n 89).

This rather modest task of FRA in the framework is corroborated by the equally modest design of the framework at large which, as outlined above, does not build a new actor with its own legal mandate and political role, but rather constructs a platform that allows the framework members to share information and coordinate activities within the limits of their respective four individual mandates – with one member, the EP, having to coordinate amongst three Committees. In that sense, the Agency's role in the framework could be described as double-bound: the input dimension is limited due to the restrictive role assigned to the Agency in the framework – rooted in the restrictive reading of the Agency's mandate already in the Commissions 'note' – and so is the output dimension, since the framework focuses on coordination rather than on combining mandates in a proactive way to strengthen the framework as a separate actor. Most importantly, none of the four members of the framework, including the FRA, were assigned any additional resources for their role, which inhibits the current framework in enhancing the degree of monitoring of the EU's performance under the CRPD. The UN Special Rapporteur concluded that with the upcoming review 'further developments or refinements are expected [and that a] way needs to be found to make this framework fully functional with a common focus and way of working'.[100]

Since the Commission has left the framework, the FRA has served as its secretariat – sometimes also as its Chair – offering its website to the framework so that the work programmes, the agenda and the minutes of all meetings as well as other resources can be accessed by interested parties. According to the operational provisions adopted by the framework, the role of the secretariat is to 'facilitate the activities of the framework and carry out organisational tasks', which includes the convening, preparing and organising of at least two meetings a year and the coordination between members in preparation for meetings and in the follow-up.[101]

With the Fundamental Rights Report 2016, the Agency started to publish an annual chapter on 'Developments in the implementation of the Convention on the Rights of Persons with Disabilities'. Since then, this chapter has provided evidence and recommendations[102] on the CRPD implementation every year.

5. Concluding Remarks: The Way Forward

The FRA is amongst the smaller EU agencies, both in terms of budget and in terms of staff. Its mandate however, is very broad and extends over all EU fundamental

[100] OHCHR, 'Visit to the European Union, Report of the Special Rapporteur on the rights of persons with disabilities, Gerard Quinn' (28 December 2022) A/HRC/52/32/Add.1 para 68.

[101] FRA, 'EU Framework for the UN Convention on the Rights of Persons with Disabilities' available at <https://fra.europa.eu/en/cooperation/eu-partners/eu-crpd-framework>.

[102] While the main report is only available in English, the so called 'opinions' of the Fundamental Rights Reports were always published as a separate deliverable in all EU languages (apart from Irish).

rights themes falling within the scope of EU law. Disability is just one of many areas that the Agency is active in. Moreover, the EU has increasingly expanded its fundamental rights activities in law- and policy-making, which also increases requests for the FRA to become active in new areas.

Against this background, the Agency has had to be selective in its approach. In the field of disability, the Agency soon after its establishment engaged with a specific set of topics of special relevance to persons with intellectual disabilities and persons with mental health issues. Despite limited resources, the Agency influenced debates in the context of legal capacity, the right to independent living, political participation and the use of EU funds by applying participatory methodologies and by striving for the highest quality in research. Discussions at EU level profited from research findings and from evidence-based policy advice provided by the FRA, which is also reflected in various policy documents. Currently, the Agency is working on violence against persons with disabilities at the request of the Commission, showcasing another link between FRA research and the work of a key EU political actor.

While this chapter acknowledged the relevance and impact of the Agency's work in the area of disability rights, it also stressed the fact that the FRA's resources are limited and its approach will have to remain selective. The fact that the Agency's thematic depth (vertical dimension) will remain limited to a few selected themes could be compensated for by a strong engagement of the Agency in the monitoring framework under Article 33(2) CRPD and across all EU policy areas (horizontal dimension). However, this is not the case at the time of writing this chapter. Thus far, the composition and design of the EU monitoring framework are not convincing. Here, the ongoing second review of the EU by the CRPD Committee might trigger some more innovative thinking providing for an EU monitoring framework that indeed can mobilise all available resources to promote, protect and monitor the implementation of the CRPD.

In order to avoid any impression that the EU aims to avoid a solid monitoring of its own performance, it should lead by example and establish a framework that is as independent and efficient as possible. This would require that all political actors – not only the Commission – withdraw from the core of the framework, which should only consist of EU 'Human Rights Institutions', namely the European Ombudsman and the FRA. These two members of the framework would focus on the two main monitoring dimensions listed in the Council decision establishing the EU monitoring framework: firstly, the area in which Member States have transferred competences to the EU – data collection, structural analysis, legal opinions regarding EU legislation and policy[103] and, secondly, the 'internal'

FRA, 'Fundamental Rights Report 2023 – FRA opinions' (8 June 2023) available at <https://fra.europa.eu/en/publication/2023/fundamental-rights-report-2023-fra-opinions>.

[103] A major criticism of the Court of Auditors *vis-à-vis* the Commission is that it still did not engage to progressively review the relevant EU legislation to the Strategy 2021-2030 against its compliance with the CRPD. Court of Auditors (n 74).

implementation of the Convention by EU institutions themselves – individual complaints and strategic investigations that concern the EU administration and its relation to its employees and citizens, accessibility to EU buildings and information, etc.. Whereas the EO is perfectly placed to deal with the second dimension, as discussed by Ferri in this volume,[104] the Agency is well equipped to deal with the first dimension. The two institutions could also join forces in carrying out accessibility-audits in the EU institutions or rolling out disability surveys etc..[105]

The framework should establish a statutory obligation for the core of the framework – the independent mechanism formed by the EO and the FRA – to systematically consult with organisations of persons with disabilities. Civil society, in particular persons with disabilities and their representative organisations, shall also be involved via a formally established, dedicated Working Group on the Agency's Fundamental Rights Platform.[106] The core of the framework should be complemented by an accompanying board that brings in the EDF, the PETI Committee as well as representatives from the 27 national monitoring frameworks to allow for a permanent coordination between the EU-framework and the national monitoring frameworks. The PETI Committee would bring in the petitions that citizens bring to the attention of the EP in the context of disability and it would make sure that the FRA is requested to issue legal opinions on EU legislative drafts wherever the PETI Committee considers that the draft raises an important potential or challenge from a CRPD perspective. Of course, the EU monitoring framework needs to be equipped with the necessary resources as was requested by the CRPD Committee.

All these steps would do away with the impression that the EU invests more in monitoring the implementation of, for instance, the right to data protection than of disability rights. After all, the CRPD is the first human rights treaty the EU acceded to, thereby creating the expectation that the EU would want to lead by example, including by equipping the EU's Fundamental Rights Agency with the means to fully play its role and satisfy its mission.

[104] D Ferri, 'The Role of the European Ombudsman in Protecting and Promoting Disability Rights' in this volume.

[105] At the end of 2024 FRA and the EO launched a disability survey amongst all EU agencies in order to check and enhance the CRPD awareness in all corners of the EU administration.

[106] Article 12 Founding Regulation. Note that currently over 1000 civil society organisations across the EU participate in the Platform – over 100 of which focus on disability issues. More information available at <https://fra.europa.eu/en/cooperation/civil-society>. M Kjaerum and GN Toggenburg, 'The Fundamental Rights Agency and Civil Society: Reminding the gardeners of their plants' roots' (2012) 2 *European Diversity and Autonomy Papers*.

PART III

The Role of Non-Institutional Actors in Shaping EU Disability Law

10

The Role of the European Disability Forum and Disability Organisations in Shaping EU Disability Policy

CLAUDIA COVENEY

1. Introduction

Building on findings from a research project conducted from 2019 to 2023 on disability advocacy in the European Union (EU), this chapter discusses how civil society organisations, particularly the European Disability Forum (EDF) and its partners, have been able to shape and influence policy in the EU.[1] It pays particular attention to the ways in which the disability rights movement has adapted to shifting forms of EU governance and the expansion of EU disability policy.[2] It looks at how these changes have opened new opportunities and challenges for organisations like EDF and how they have responded to these.

This chapter develops and tests several hypotheses (or 'fragile ideas').[3] First, it discusses the extent to which civil society actors, such as EDF, bring legitimating resources to legal and policy processes – namely specialist knowledge and moral authority. In doing so, the chapter aims to ascertain whether they contribute to the structure of the processes themselves. Second, the chapter tests the hypothesis that to achieve influence in their consultative position, they must employ calculated strategies – relative to other policy actors bringing more material resources.

[1] This research, that analysed tactics and strategies from a series of collective action campaigns run by the European Disability Forum (EDF) and its partner organisations, was conducted as part of the Disability Advocacy Research in Europe (DARE) project, an Innovative Training Network that received funding from the European Union's Horizon 2020 research and innovation programme under the Marie Skłodowska-Curie grant agreement No 814249.

[2] While the volume tends to use 'law' as overarching term, this chapter tends to use 'policy' as an umbrella term, consistent with A Waldschmidt and ES Krolla, 'The Surge of EU Disability Policy: Historical Developments, Current Issues and the Role of Different Actors' in this volume. On the EU governance see A Volpato, 'The Voices and the Choir: The Importance of a Contextual Analysis of EU Actors' Roles' in this volume.

[3] N Emmel, *Sampling and choosing cases in qualitative research: a realist approach* (Sage 2013).

Third, the chapter discusses whether civil society actors, such as EDF, may find more opportunities to exploit and achieve their goals in periods of systemic change – for example during Treaty revisions or elections. In comparison, as structures of governance 'firm up', actors like EDF will face greater challenges in achieving more substantive change. It thus explores the impact of disability advocacy campaigns on EU policy and how organisations have adapted to new structures of governance. The chapter concludes with a discussion of gains made by organisations of persons with disabilities (OPDs) in EU governance landscapes and critical observations of these spaces.

In line with the approach of the volume, in this chapter, I use the term 'persons with disabilities' in keeping with the UN Convention on the Rights of Persons with Disabilities (CRPD) language, and stemming from an understanding that disability arises from the social, political and economic barriers faced by people with impairments.[4] I refer to the 'movement of persons with disabilities' (DPM) when discussing the movement for full emancipation by persons with disabilities and their organisations. I also refer to the 'disability rights movement' (DRM) in some discussions, which is a more accurate description of the movement of OPDs, allied Members of the European Parliament (MEPs), European Commission (Commission) officials and national ministers, service providers and other organisations, whose goal is the realisation of the rights of persons with disabilities enshrined in the CRPD and EU legislation. When discussing 'disability rights' I refer to Vanhala's definition as 'a broad range of protections and entitlements to ensure equality and respect for people with disabilities'.[5] Additionally, the chapter refers to 'social movement organisations' (SMOs) and European 'civil society organisations' (CSOs). The former refers to all organisations within a social movement community, while the latter refers to organisations that utilise formal civil society platforms that are governed by the EU. The crucial distinction made here is that not all SMOs are granted access to formal civil society platforms, and not all CSOs represent social movements.[6]

Further to this introduction, the chapter is divided into five sections followed by concluding remarks. In section 2, I briefly outline the design of the research underpinning the chapter and the methods used, introducing a fundamental pillar guiding the research: the emancipatory disability research paradigm, largely based on Stone and Priestley's seminal text.[7] Section 3 outlines the key features of EDF and the interlinks between EDF and EU institutions. Section 4 more specifically considers the role of EDF in monitoring the implementation of the CRPD within the EU legal order before section 5 looks at the campaign activity of

[4] C Thomas, *Female Forms: Experiencing and Understanding Disability* (Open University Press 1999).

[5] L Vanhala, 'The diffusion of disability rights in Europe' (2015) 37 *Human Rights Quarterly* 831.

[6] D Della Porta, 'Building bridges: Social movements and civil society in times of crisis' (2020) 31(5) *VOLUNTAS: International Journal of Voluntary and Nonprofit Organizations* 938.

[7] E Stone and M Priestley, 'Parasites, pawns and partners: disability research and the role of non-disabled researchers' (1996) *British Journal of Sociology* 699–716.

European OPD networks. In particular, three different campaigns led by EDF are examined as case studies. The case studies use the binary of public and 'inside' strategies employed by interest associations and the impact of institutional factors on these combinations in the European context. In this regard, Beyers' work is useful for its categorisation of influence strategies of voice and access in which 'voice' refers to public engagement activity and 'access' refers to 'inside lobbying'.[8] In this respect, the chapter – as well as the broader research upon which it is based – is underpinned by theories on opportunity structure, which it uses to analyse the case study campaigns: strategic combination (public versus insider), nature of interests (of a campaign) and institutional factors (which bodies of governance are targeted).[9] The chapter closes by offering some concluding remarks.

2. Research Design and Methods

2.1. Emancipatory Disability Research

The research approach is informed by Fraser's critique of civil society.[10] In line with her account, the public sphere has historically been a space where social movements simultaneously face exclusion and opportunities.[11] As noted above, it is also informed by an emancipatory research approach. Such an approach is rooted in the quest of activists to enhance choice for persons with disabilities and that of their organisations in deciding which research they would like to participate in, and, more importantly, give control to relevant OPDs in the design, funding and carrying out of the research. This approach to research has been coined 'emancipatory disability research'.[12] The aim of any research that follows this approach should be to contribute to the demystification and removal of the disabling structures within society.[13] In the case of the research presented here, communication was established prior to the start of the project and input was sought in the design of the research during communication with secretariat members, visits to the secretariat offices and attendance at organisational meetings of EDF.

[8] J Beyers, 'Voice and Access: Political Practices of European Interest Associations' (2004) 5(2) *European Union Politics* 214.

[9] M Plangger, 'Building something beautiful with stones: How regions adapt to, shape and transform the EU opportunity structure' (2018) 28(1) *Regional & Federal Studies* 1–24.

[10] N Fraser, 'Rethinking the Public Sphere: A Contribution to the Critique of Actually Existing Democracy' (1990) 25/26 *Social Text* 56–80.

[11] Ibid.

[12] M Oliver, 'Changing the social relations of research production?' (1992) 7(2) *Disability, Handicap & Society* 101–114; C Barnes and G Mercer, *Implementing the social model of disability: Theory and research* (Disability Press Leeds 2004).

[13] Oliver (n 12).

Further, the chapter is underpinned by a reflexive approach. Reflexivity refers to the investigation of the social relations of inquiry itself.[14] The practice enables examination on the basis of claims to know the social world and an exploration of forms of knowledge.[15]

2.2. Sampling Campaigns for Study

A purposeful sampling strategy was utilised for this research: campaigns coordinated by EDF were considered and were selected on the basis of their relevance to the research questions, the resources available to me as the sole researcher and the density of information within the campaigns.[16] Further, the selection was based on additional factors, alongside the three general criteria mentioned above. Firstly, the level of available information on the campaigns was considered. Additionally, although the campaigns have been selected for their varied approaches and outcomes, some level of comparison between the collective actions was needed to draw conclusions. Therefore, the selected campaigns each target EU-level legislation and feature similarities in certain elements of their approach. Each uses a combination of 'insider' tactics, such as presenting position papers, drafting legislation and lobbying; and 'public-facing' strategies of protest and awareness raising. Outcomes are but one measure of the 'success' of a movement's activity.[17] The wider impact of the campaigns has also been considered – namely how the resultant legislation (where it has appeared) is perceived by activists, and, recalling Staggenborg and Lecomte's[18] prescription of campaign impact on future mobilisations and organisational structures themselves, whether campaigns have had wider implications for the organisation. The list below details the key informants:

- Current executive committee members of EDF
- Ex-executive committee members of EDF
- Presidents of EDF
- Former directors of EDF
- Representatives of full member organisations
- Representatives of associate member organisations
- EU officials linked to policy action associated with the chosen campaigns

[14] T May and B Perry, 'Reflexivity and the Practice of Qualitative Research' in U Flick (ed), *The SAGE Handbook of Qualitative Data Analysis* (Sage 2014) 109–122.

[15] Stone and Priestley (n 7).

[16] MQ Patton, 'Two decades of developments in qualitative inquiry: A personal, experiential perspective' (2002) 1(3) *Qualitative Social Work* 261–283.

[17] D Suh, 'Intricacies of Social Movement Outcome Research and Beyond: "How Can You Tell" Social Movements Prompt Changes?' (2012) 17(4) *Sociological Research Online* 92–102.

[18] S Staggenborg and J Lecomte, 'Social movement campaigns: Mobilization and outcomes in the Montreal women's movement community' (2009) 14(2) *Mobilization: An International Quarterly* 163–180.

Participants were asked at the start of the interview to talk about themselves and their involvement with the DPM. By answering the question 'What brought you to work with EDF? What politicised you with regards to disability rights?' at the opening of the interview they were given the opportunity to expand on their personal history and connection to disability activism and to EDF in particular. Reflecting on the sample of interviewees reveals a bias toward male, Western European respondents. This sample could be described as narrow; it could also be reflective of EDF at certain points in its history. As I was seeking information from specific time periods, one of which was over a decade ago and another that was two decades ago, my focus was on reaching those present for the campaigns. It was outside the scope of the research questions to identify gender and identity imbalances within the organisation at specific times, although this topic is worthy of further study. The sample satisfied a point of 'saturation' with the data.[19] In other words, I closed the data collection when I had a complete picture of the campaign from a range of perspectives. Participants were given the opportunity to review their interview responses after transcription was completed.[20] In total, 21 interviews were conducted between September 2020 and April 2021 on Zoom. Interview data were supported by archival material made available to me from personal archives of activists and EDF, along with policy documents from EU databases. Documentary material clarified the approach of the campaigns – their framing of issues, for example, and the objectives or desired outcomes. It also acted to sift information given by participants in interviews or 'rationalisations'.[21] Meeting minutes and memos revealed the ways in which issues became topics for campaigns and tracked decision making throughout the campaigns. Choices around tactics and strategies made throughout campaigns began to emerge from documentary sources. This aided the interview process by establishing some understanding of the timelines for the campaigns prior to speaking with interviewees.

3. The European Disability Forum

3.1. Key Features of the European Disability Forum

EDF is an umbrella advocacy body that represents the interests of persons with disabilities and their organisations at the European level. This is done both

[19] Emmel (n 3).

[20] An application for approval was submitted to the University of Leeds Ethics Committee in June 2020, and after minor adjustments were made accordingly, I received ethical approval from the Business, Environment and Social Sciences (AREA) Faculty Research Ethics Committee in August 2020.

[21] J Mason, *Analyzing qualitative data* (Routledge 2002).

within EU borders and with regard to its legislation, and beyond. Additionally, EDF continuously monitors and reports on the rights of persons with disabilities across Europe in alignment with the CRPD and regional instruments such as the European Convention on Human Rights. In fact, EDF also works with the Council of Europe and the United Nations. It responds to global crises, such as the COVID-19 pandemic and the invasion of Ukraine, to advocate for persons with disabilities in crisis contexts. It also runs targeted campaigns that are raised by the organisation to address specific issues at EU level.[22] These campaigns employ a range of tactics and strategies to ensure the demands of persons with disabilities and their organisations are on the agenda of the EU institutions. Some employ contentious tactics for visibility, such as public protests; others involve meetings with Member States' representatives and EU officials. EDF receives funding from the Commission, alongside other organisations, to operate in the civil society space to ensure that decision-making concerning persons with disabilities is undertaken with and by persons with disabilities.[23] EDF is enrolled in the transparency register, a database that lists organisations that try to influence the law-making and policy implementation processes of the EU institutions.[24]

The organisation's statutes[25] set out the requirements for 'full members' – that is, member organisations with decision-making status. Full members are either national council OPDs that represent the EU Member States or European disability network OPDs – for example the European Union of the Deaf. EDF has 112 member organisations across Europe. Alongside full member organisations there are 'ordinary' members, defined as 'European Non-Governmental Organisations for disabled people' which also have voting rights; moreover, there are 'observer' and 'associate' members, without voting rights – the former, five national councils of persons with disabilities from European countries outside the EU with candidate status, and the latter, organisations, corporate or non-profit that are committed to promote the aims of EDF with membership in the EU.

EDF's secretariat employs staff to carry out the daily, administrative operations of the organisation and is headed by a director. The earliest iteration of EDF appeared in the HELIOS II pilot programme,[26] launched in 1993. Twelve pre-existing national disability councils from EU Member States, and European non-governmental organisations (NGOs) that were deemed to be representative

[22] For example, the '1Million4Disability' campaign (2008), discussed in this chapter, calling on the Commission to produce a proposal for a non-discrimination directive protecting disabled people. L Waddington, 'The Role of Academics in Shaping EU Disability Law: Some Personal Reflections' in this volume.

[23] EDF, 'Financial Information and Transparency' available at <https://www.edf-feph.org/financial-information-and-transparency/>.

[24] European Commission (Commission), 'Transparency Register' available at <https://www.edf-feph.org/financial-information-and-transparency/>.

[25] EDF, 'Statutes of the European Disability Forum' (Last reviewed by the General Assembly on 25 June 2022) available at <https://www.edf-feph.org/about-us/our-statutes/>.

[26] Council Decision of 25 February 1993 establishing a third Community action programme to assist disabled people (Helios II 1993 to 1996) [1993] OJ L056/30.

and that promoted the interests of persons with disabilities were included in the pilot programme as an internal advisory committee to complement national level actions aimed at equalising opportunities for persons with disabilities and increasing co-ordination between Member States. The presence of OPDs in the second HELIOS programme was a result of lobbying by OPDs including Disabled Peoples' International (DPI). EDF was then formally established in 1996. What started as an internal advisory group within the Commission became an independent civil society organisation, run by its OPD membership and receiving Commission funding along with a number of other civil society organisations. It is significant to note that the Commission chose to establish a new organisation despite the presence of existing European OPDs, such as DPI Europe.

The priority in the early years of EDF was establishing a unified voice of persons with disabilities around Europe to campaign for change. This meant forging alliances between organisations of people with different types of impairments and overcoming national cultural differences. The understanding that a united coalition and voice is necessary for the organisation to influence social change is an oft-cited strategy of the organisation. This remains the approach of EDF although more recently the organisation has increased its focus on specific challenges faced by some groups of persons with disabilities, including refugees, people with intellectual disabilities (to use EDF's wording) and young persons with disabilities. EDF engages with the European institutions through multiple channels, including through the European Economic and Social Committee (EESC) and through direct communications with members of the three institutions of governance, i.e. the European Parliament (EP), the Council of the EU (Council) and the Commission. These are further discussed in section 4.

3.2. The European Disability Forum and 'Opportunity Structures'

EDF represents the interests of persons with disabilities in formal European civil society spaces, such as the EESC, the EU's formal civil society advisory platform of employers' representatives, trade unions, and CSOs.

Further, EDF has regular channels of communication with the Commission, the EP and the Council. As the executive branch of the EU institutions, the Commission proposes and implements EU legislation.[27] EDF monitors these processes and participates via consultations and position papers. Given that the EP represents EU constituents and operates along party lines, committees and intergroups, EDF works with MEPs within parties, committees, and the Disability Intergroup to influence voting directions, parliamentary resolutions and reports

[27] ES Krolla, 'The Role of the European Commission in Shaping EU Disability Law: A Driver with the Brakes Put On?' in this volume.

presenting the EP's position on legislation. As is well known, and discussed earlier in this volume, the Council represents national Member State governments. The 'presidency' of the EU rotates every six months between Member States. EDF works to influence the work programmes of the upcoming presidencies to ensure the theme of disability is maintained.

European advocacy organisations like EDF attempt to capitalise on the opportunity structures of the EU.[28] As mentioned in the introduction, this chapter examines the case of EDF as a representative of the European movement of persons with disabilities to better understand how such opportunity structures function. Governance scholars stress that collective action is needed to address complex problems – this spectrum of actors is required to find solutions that will satisfy the interests of as many stakeholders as possible.[29] The social transformation of the EU from a single economic market into a body politic with unique values and democratic traditions has created new claims-making opportunities for SMOs. This transformation has in part occurred at the behest of pressure applied by activists for inclusion and recognition at a formal level. As a result, the amendments and revisions of the Treaty on European Union (TEU) have gradually introduced both the recognition of social groups facing discrimination and given the EU institutions powers to legislate to protect those groups. The EU level is also touted as a viable alternative for social movements that have not found success at national level.[30] Certain types of SMOs will be more successful in engaging with EU institutions: resource-rich organisations that use conventional methods of civil society.[31] The openness of a political system, windows of opportunity, appropriation of existing organisations and configurations of actors are further important factors.[32]

The concept of 'legal opportunity' can be considered alongside 'political opportunity' for social movements specifically, distinguishing between policy change strategies of protest, litigation and lobbying.[33] Hilson proposes a framework to

[28] A Sturm *et al.*, 'Exercising influence at the European level: Political opportunity structures for disability rights advocacy and the impact of the UN CRPD' in R Halvorsen *et al.* (eds), *The Changing Disability Policy System. Active Citizenship and Disability in Europe Volume 1* (Routledge 2017) 159–176; R Halvorsen *et al.*, 'Changing Opportunities for Active Citizenship in Europe: Understanding the Lived Experiences of Persons with Disabilities' in R Halvorsen *et al.* (eds), *Understanding the Lived Experiences of Persons with Disabilities in Nine Countries: Active Citizenship and Disability in Europe Volume 2* (Routledge 2017) 1–16.

[29] A Van Buuren, F Boons and G Teisman, 'Collaborative problem solving in a complex governance system: Amsterdam airport Schiphol and the challenge to break path dependency' (2012) 29(2) *Systems Research and Behavioral Science* 116–130.

[30] D Imig and S Tarrow, 'Studying contention in an emerging polity' in D Imig and S Tarrow (eds), *Contentious Europeans: Protest and Politics in an Emerging Polity* (Lanham, Rowman & Littlefield 2001) 3–26.

[31] D Della Porta and M Caiani, *Europeanization and social movements* (Oxford University Press 2009).

[32] H Kriesi, 'Role of the political elite in Swiss direct-democratic votes' (2006) 12(5) *Party Politics* 78.

[33] C Hilson, 'New social movements: the role of legal opportunity' (2002) 9(2) *Journal of European Public Policy* 238–255.

connect the three, arguing groups are more likely to utilise protest strategies in cases where political and legal opportunities are low. Organisations operating closely with state bodies will engage in protest activity less than peripheral organisations. Additionally, the armament of a framework like the CRPD impacts the extent to which strategic litigation features as a lobby strategy. As legal frameworks establishing the rights of persons with disabilities have increased in the past 25 years, advocacy organisations and the wider DRM has had more to 'call on' when making its claims upon the state. The following sections consider the impact of such increasing legal frameworks by looking at the campaign activity of European OPD networks.

4. The Role of the European Disability Forum in Monitoring the CRPD

In its first review of the EU as a party to the CRPD in 2014, EDF criticised the European Disability Strategy 2010-2020 (EDS),[34] the main EU policy instrument related to EU disability policy, in its alternative report.[35] The EDS was not a comprehensive framework of implementation, lacking funding and attention to targets such as poverty reduction, social inclusion and employment. The view from civil society was also that the EU CRPD Monitoring Framework, of which EDF was a part, created to implement Article 33 CRPD,[36] did not function effectively – the Commission's involvement in the monitoring setup contradicted the Framework's independence and caused additional problems.[37] The Commission later withdrew from the framework.[38] In its 2022 alternative report to the Committee on the Rights of Persons with Disabilities (CRPD Committee) EDF has called for the review of the EU for firmer monitoring processes, independent of the EU institutions, with permanent representation of OPDs and mechanisms to punish non-compliance.[39]

[34] Commission, 'European Disability Strategy 2010-2020: A Renewed Commitment to a Barrier-Free Europe' COM(2010) 636 final.

[35] EDF, 'Alternative Report on the Implementation of the UN Convention on the Rights of Persons with Disabilities' available at <https://www.archive.equineteurope.org/EDF-Alternative-Report-on-the>.

[36] M Birtha, 'A chance to pioneer or a lost opportunity: monitoring disability rights effectively and independently in the EU in line with Article 33 of the UN CRPD' (2014) 5 *European Yearbook of Disability Law* 43.

[37] Sturm *et al.* (n 28) 172.

[38] Council of the European Union, 'Revised EU-level Framework Required by Article 33.2 of the UN Convention on the Rights of Persons with Disabilities' (2017) 6170/17.

[39] Committee on the Rights of Persons with Disabilities, 'Concluding observations on the initial report of the European Union Addendum Information received from the European Union on follow-up to the concluding observations' (23 November 2017) CRPD/C/EU/CO/1/Add.1.

The current 'Union of Equality: Strategy for the Rights of Persons with Disabilities 2021-2030' (Strategy 2021-2030)[40] created, as one of its flagship initiatives, an additional expert group in 2021, the so-called 'EU Disability Platform'.[41] The Platform consists of EU Member State representatives, civil society organisations including EDF, and the Commission. The Platform was established as a forum where policy developments, experiences and practices could be discussed and exchanged. It also provides a space to work together on initiatives and proposals, and establish cooperation and coordination between the Commission, Member States and stakeholders.

On the whole, EDF plays a prominent role in both the monitoring and implementation of the CRPD at EU level. At the time of writing, EDF's representative is the EU Disability Platform's chair. Questions about the efficacy of the monitoring mechanism remain despite this addition, due to the lack of coordination between institutions and focal points missing in key institutions, bodies and agencies.[42]

EDF has a designated 'seat at the table' in EU policy, both in the CRPD framework and in the Platform. The EU's ratification of the Convention has solidified the EU's commitment to realising the rights and equality of persons with disabilities in the EU. All of these developments have in significant part been due to advocacy and pressure applied by SMOs, including OPDs. EDF plays a unique role as a civil society actor – monitoring and advising on the implementation of the Convention within the EU's monitoring framework. Participation and activation of new institutional venues increases opportunities for organisations representing social movements within formal civil society spaces, such as EDF, to access EU institutions of governance.[43] Such spaces have been designed to increase the inclusiveness of policy- and decision-making, and to foster participatory democratic politics. In turn, some of these spaces have been described as tokenistic due to their informal, non-binding nature. Although developments such as the Disability Platform improve this communication, they still miss the key 'binding' characteristic that would increase their influence. Participation in these forums is based on past learning: spaces that do not produce opportunities are unlikely to be returned to or invested in by civil society actors.[44]

[40] Commission, 'Union of Equality: Strategy for the Rights of Persons with Disabilities 2021-2030' COM(2021) 101 final.

[41] Ibid 24; Commission Decision of 27.10.2021 setting up the group of experts "Disability Platform" COM(2021) 7591 final; Commission, 'Disability Platform' available at <https://ec.europa.eu/transparency/expert-groups-register/screen/expert-groups/consult?lang=en&groupId=3820&fromMembers=true&memberType=4&memberId=97587>.

[42] EDF, 'Alternative report for the second review of the EU by the CRPD Committee' available at <https://www.edf-feph.org/publications/edf-alternative-report-for-the-second-review-of-the-eu-by-the-crpd-committee/>.

[43] M Di Gregorio, 'Gaining access to the state: Political opportunities and agency in forest activism in Indonesia' (2014) 13(3) *Social Movement Studies* 381–398; S Tarrow, 'Inside insurgencies: Politics and violence in an age of civil war' (2007) 5(3) *Perspectives on Politics* 587–600.

[44] Di Gregorio (n 43); M Holdo, 'Cooptation and non-cooptation: elite strategies in response to social protest' (2019) 18(4) *Social Movement Studies* 444–462.

5. The European Disability Forum and its Campaigns

5.1. Preliminary Remarks

EDF maintains a budget line from the Commission, serves as the secretariat for the EP Disability Intergroup, and relies on its contacts within the institutions. Employees of the Commission form a significant portion of the internal allies for the DRM. Secretariat members explained in interviews that the Commission undertakes much of the practical work related to disability and is, as such, an important target for influencing.

The EP has historically been an ally of the organisation, pushing for the funding of EDF as an independent organisation in its early years. The Disability Intergroup, the oldest intergroup in the EP, is an informal alliance of MEPs from all Member States and political parties. It works to promote the interests of persons with disabilities in parliamentary debates. A secretariat member at EDF deals specifically with the EP and the Disability Intergroup to maintain a strong relationship between the organisation and MEPs. According to EDF members, the budget line for the organisation as an independent entity was due to parliamentary pressure.

> Definitely not an initiative of the European Commission itself. Under the first pilot programme we had nothing basically. Other than a bunch of angry persons with disabilities including myself.[45]

As it emerged as an independent organisation in 1996, EDF joined the wider European disability movement in calling for more attention to the rights and status of persons with disabilities in the European Community as a legislating political entity.

The Council requires attention from the organisation as well. The rotational presidencies taken by Member States every six months are important for EDF. Member States vary in their receptivity to the interests of EDF and the organisation gains access under certain presidencies more than others – during the 'Invisible Citizens' campaign (discussed below), the Dutch presidency was notably unreceptive to the demands of the movement.[46] Recent examples of more receptive presidencies include Spain and Belgium.

5.2. The Campaigns: Background, Tactics, Strategies

This section details the background, aims, approach and outcomes of the three case study campaigns to draw out tactics and strategic decisions made by EDF.

[45] Interview with former EDF leader.

[46] On the Dutch presidency's role, see also Waddington (n 22).

Recalling Suh's[47] observations on the opacity of policy change as an indicator of movement success or failure, and the institutional and issue complexity of the EU context[48] it is reiterated here that in the multifaceted web of policy processes, outcomes can be difficult to link to specific actions. 'Outcomes' here, then, refer to the progress of the campaign's pursued policy intervention. In other words, the extent to which the aims of the campaigns eventuated are considered outcomes. The following sub-sections describe the campaigns in their background, aims and approaches.

5.2.1. *The 'Invisible Citizens' Campaign*

The Invisible Citizens campaign began in 1995 and emphasised the lack of access for persons with disabilities to the benefits of European Community (EC) policies and the ways in which this problem could be addressed through reference to disability in the upcoming Treaty amendments. Specifically, the campaign sought to secure a reference to disability in the later so-called Amsterdam Treaty through the inclusion of a non-discrimination clause and a reference to disability mainstreaming with regard to the internal market. The 1996-1997 Intergovernmental Conference (IGC)[49] was determined to address the gaps left by the Maastricht Treaty and to resolve the difficult negotiations that were to take place. It was also being seized on by many groups as an opportunity for legal recognition and protection. Recalling the absence of disability in the Maastricht Treaty, activists were focused on the introduction of compulsory, binding instruments that would commit Member States more firmly to improving the position and status of persons with disabilities in the EU. EDF spent the first year of this campaign in a transition to an independent organisation. The co-ordinating committee attempted to equip the wider campaign membership with strategic know-how and specialised knowledge to lobby their national governments in a tailored fashion. OPDs were given targeted training on 'interactive lobbying skills' according to campaign material.[50] They were encouraged to find their government's position, find their national parliamentarian responsible for European affairs and arrange a meeting. If ignored they were instructed to find relevant civil servants to contact, and to go to the press about being ignored.

Another key element of the campaign involved the mobilisation of human resources: the employment of legal and economic experts to make the case for the demands of the Invisible Citizens. Two legal experts and one economic expert met

[47] Suh (n 17).

[48] R Ackrill, A Kay and N Zahariadis, 'Ambiguity, multiple streams, and EU policy' (2013) 20(6) *Journal of European public policy* 871–887.

[49] European Parliament (EP), 'Amsterdam European Council 16 and 17 June 1997 – Presidency Conclusions' available at <https://www.europarl.europa.eu/summits/ams1_en.htm#:~:text=The%20European%20Council%20meeting%20in,of%20the%20Madrid%20European%20Council>.

[50] EDF, 'IGC working group meeting minutes, relevant Member State contacts and upcoming agendas for Dutch Presidency' (1997).

any issues that were being raised about cost implications of the non-discrimination clause and the undermining of national disability legislation with the suggested additions to the Treaty.

Reports were published by the legal experts: *Disabled Persons' Status in the European Treaties: Invisible Citizens, Report of the Third European Day of Disabled Persons*; and *How can disabled persons achieve equal rights in the European Union?*.[51] The reports responded to the concerns most frequently expressed by statutory authorities at all levels in relation to Treaty revisions. Significantly, they also addressed the economic consequences of Treaty revisions, firmly identifying disabled citizens as consumers and workers in the Union.

A communication to campaign members on 17 March 1997 titled 'The Bomb had dropped – disability is out!' was sent out by a member of the co-ordination group after drafting it together with a legal expert, which included the following excerpt:

> In its comments the Presidency acknowledges that certain delegations wish to mention explicitly handicap, age, social origin and sexual orientation [in the non-discrimination clause]. However, the majority of Member States seems to believe that the concerns of these groups could be addressed in the context of existing policies (such as social policy, education, vocational training, youth and public health). Whilst it is true that a number of disability issues can be addressed … references to these cannot be used:
>
> a. as a legal base for a new European disability programme
> b. to ensure that technical legislation under Article 100a takes account of the needs of persons with disabilities
> c. to introduce Community legislation to prohibit/combat disability discrimination at the European level.

The co-ordination committee created a network to disseminate updates on the goals of the campaign. It also utilised pre-existing networks held by campaign members and allies. This provided access to inside knowledge about the wider negotiations – for example, it suggested approaches for the upcoming Presidency and IGC with Article additions and adjustments around fundamental rights and non-discrimination from meetings between Member State governments. Coalition partnerships with other social groups were also embraced to highlight cross-cutting issues and the general need for a non-discrimination clause. EDF secretariat staff worked on a strategy for common lobby efforts across social rights issues.[52] There was also horizontal coalition work with other members

[51] T Degener and A Begg, 'From Invisible Citizens to Agents of Change: A Short History of the Struggle for the Recognition of the Rights of Persons with Disabilities at the United Nations' in V Della Fina, R Cera and G Palmisano (eds), *The United Nations Convention on the Rights of Persons with Disabilities: A Commentary* (Springer 2017) 2; EDF, 'Invisible Citizens – How Can Disabled Persons in the European Union Achieve Equal Rights as Citizens? Summary of the Legal and Economic Implications of a Non-discrimination Clause in the European Treaties – A Report by the Legal Expert Working Group' (EDF 1996).

[52] EDF, 'IGC coordination group meeting minutes 6 March 1997'.

of the 'Platform of Social NGOs', or Social Platform, a forum established by the network of EU civil society to operate alongside representatives of trade unions and employers and to improve the recognition of social organisations in the EU Treaties.

While the Invisible Citizens campaign pivoted to a disability focus in its final months to secure the inclusion of disability in the non-discrimination clause, the nature of the campaign favoured the formation of alliances with other CSOs. The success of this first campaign in 1997 in the inclusion of disability in Article 13 EC, marked the beginning of legal visibility in EU law for persons with disabilities in the EU. The campaign saw the beginnings of a coalition across the European Community of disability activists and advocates, and a broader coalition of 'social partners', composed of civil society organisations that were advocating for inclusion and recognition in the Treaty of Amsterdam. It changed the 'state of play' for such groups: for persons with disabilities the symbolic achievement of acknowledgement in the Treaty was accompanied by a more concrete change in the form of the so-called Employment Equality Directive[53] that was adopted after the entry into force of the Treaty of Amsterdam. It also secured a non-binding declaration alongside Article 95 EC (ex 100a) providing that '[t]he conference agrees that, in drawing up measures under Article 95, the institutions of the Community shall take account of the needs of persons with a disability'.[54] Campaigns impact the structure of movements themselves by creating new frames, issues, and tactics for subsequent advocacy. The campaign solidified a coalition of civil society voices and resulted in new strategic instruments for future campaigns. Reference to disability in the EU Treaties created a new environment for collective action by the European movement of persons with disabilities. Similarly, a structure for organisations operating within the EU sphere was beginning to emerge: a permanent (often paid) secretariat working for the decision-making membership, consisting of European-wide networks and Member State level organisations.[55] This type of structure would stabilise to the point of becoming an isomorphic organisational trend of 'Europeanisation', as described by Marks and McAdam.[56] Ideologically the groups calling for inclusion under the banner of non-discrimination were united by their call for EU-level competence to legislate to their specific interests, reducing the discrepancies between Member State policies.[57]

[53] Council Directive 2000/78/EC of 27 November 2000 establishing a general framework for equal treatment in employment and occupation [2000] OJ L303/16.

[54] R Whittle, 'Disability Rights after Amsterdam: the way forward' (2000) 1 *European Human Rights Law Review* 33–48.

[55] C Hoskyns, *Integrating gender: Women, law and politics in the European Union* (Verso 1996).

[56] G Marks and D McAdam, 'On the relationship of political opportunities to the form of collective action: the case of the European Union' in D Della Porta, H Kriesi and D Rucht (eds), *Social movements in a globalizing world* (Palgrave Macmillan 1999) 97–111.

[57] J Niessen and I Chopin, 'The Starting Line and the Racial Equality Directive' in J Niessen and I Chopin (eds), *The Development of Legal Instruments to Combat Racism in a Diverse Europe* (Brill Nijhoff 2004) 95–110.

5.2.2. *The '1Million4Disability' Campaign*

With the competence to combat discrimination enshrined in Article 13 EC, the EU adopted the abovementioned Employment Equality Directive, establishing a general framework for equal treatment in employment and occupation, combatting discrimination on grounds, *inter alia*, of disability in the workplace. Prior to which the Race Equality Directive[58] had been adopted. Following these two strong pieces of non-discrimination legislation, EDF continued its calls for protections against discrimination in other aspects of life similar to those enshrined in the Race Equality Directive – working towards a 'Disability Directive'. Ideally, this would extend protection against discrimination beyond the area of employment for persons with disabilities. This second campaign considered here ran throughout 2008, and was an effort by EDF to secure an additional instrument to tackle discrimination at EU level.

In comparison to the Invisible Citizens campaign, the push for a disability non-discrimination directive was a public-facing pursuit that sought to demonstrate popular support for the movement. While the initial campaign again took place in the build-up to a Treaty revision, similar to the Invisible Citizens campaign, the structures of political opportunity were greatly altered: Treaty negotiations this time took place following the failure in two national referenda to approve the Treaty Establishing a Constitution for Europe. The subsequent directive was debated in the context of an unfolding global financial crisis, and subsequent fiscal austerity in Europe.[59]

This collective action was the most significant attempt at mobilisation EDF had undertaken in campaign activity. The utilisation of networks demonstrates the successful mobilisation of social-organisational resources by the campaign.[60]

The Brussels-based secretariat encouraged national councils to adapt the campaign to local conditions. Obtaining signatures from parliamentarians and national leaders also publicised the cause. Others adjusted the wording of the campaign to suit the national political mood:

> I know that in Germany they adapted a bit the campaign, at the beginning … there was ever a reluctance to this non-discrimination issue … it was also difficult to understand for the general public, so they sort of change[d] the question into a barrier free Europe, or something like that, and so they asked if they could change the question.[61]

[58] Council Directive 2000/43/EC of 29 June 2000 implementing the principle of equal treatment between persons irrespective of racial or ethnic origin [2000] OJ L180/22.

[59] S Benedi Lahuerta and A Zbyszewska, 'EU equality law after a decade of austerity: On the Social Pillar and its transformative potential' (2018) 18(2-3) *International Journal of Discrimination and the Law* 163–192.

[60] B Edwards and JD McCarthy, 'Resources and Social Movement Mobilization' in D Snow *et al.* (eds), *The Blackwell Companion to Social Movements* (Blackwell 2004) 116–152.

[61] Interview with Former EDF Director.

The campaign concluded in October 2008 with a demonstration outside the Commission building and a handing over of the 1.4 million signatures to the Commission President. The original aim of the collective action was the proposal of a disability-specific non-discrimination directive. Pressure from other civil society organisations and MEPs led the Commission to instead propose a Horizontal Equality Directive[62] that covered all groups mentioned in Article 13 EC, now Article 19 Treaty on the Functioning of the European Union (TFEU).

The Commission President had agreed to attend the final demonstration of the campaign to officially receive the signatures collected, but sent apologies at the final moment.

Despite a successful campaign and the use of the European Citizens Initiative (ECI), the response from the Commission did not answer the aims of EDF. What was perceived by interviewees as pressure from the Parliament and other CSOs pushed the Commission to propose an integrated non-discrimination directive that covered a range of inequalities. Barriers such as conservative resistance to protection of sexual minorities, European encroachment and cost all stood – and still stand at the time of writing – in the way of this legislation passing. An interviewee expanded on the perceived attitude towards a Horizontal Equality Directive from the Council:

> They didn't want it, and so they swallowed it with love. They didn't want it, but won't tell you, so want clarity on what it actually means within our country or our Member State and, thereby, we have some questions and those questions could be going on and on and on … I'm not sure it is dead but it is not alive.[63]

Concerns were cited in Council discussions: Germany questioned whether the proposal was timely and needed given its cost implications, and Poland, the Netherlands, the United Kingdom, Czech Republic, and Hungary signalled similar concerns.[64] The directive remains with the Council at the time of writing. A 2018 progress report cited outstanding issues that included 'subsidiarity and the division of competences, legal clarity and consistency with other legal acts, budgetary implications and costs, and implementation'.[65] The context in which social movement activity takes place is often an environment that is resistant to systemic change. Institutional forces work to limit change to the smallest amount and social movements are working against this current.[66]

[62] Commission, 'Proposal for a Council Directive on implementing the principle of equal treatment between persons irrespective of religion or belief, disability, age or sexual orientation' COM(2008) 426 final.

[63] Interview with Senior activist, previously EDF executive committee member.

[64] Benedi Lahuerta and Zbyszewska (n 59).

[65] EP, 'Anti-discrimination directive' (Legislative Train Schedule) available at <https://www.europarl.europa.eu/legislative-train/theme-a-new-push-for-european-democracy/file-anti-discrimination-directive>.

[66] V Lowndes, 'Something old, something new, something borrowed … How institutions change (and stay the same) in local governance' (2005) 26(3-4) *Policy Studies* 291–309.

The 1Million4Disability campaign left a mark on EDF. While successful campaigns can revitalise and invigorate a movement community, a failed campaign can create divisions and misunderstandings that carry over into subsequent campaigns and efforts at coalition work. One interviewee recalled the outcome of the campaign in largely negative terms like 'hijacked', 'broken' and 'not alive'. EDF in its alternative reports to the CRPD Committee remains critical of the lack of non-discrimination legislation in the EU that protects persons with disabilities in areas outside of employment.[67] The currently stuck Horizontal Equality Directive blocks additional non-discrimination legislation from being proposed. The failure to secure a disability directive using the non-discrimination clause of the TFEU prompted a pivot to another Treaty Article. The push for a directive based on Article 114 TFEU[68] is the focus of the third case study campaign: the Free Movement campaign.

5.2.3. The Campaign for the European Accessibility Act

The CRPD triggered the adoption of new directives to protect the rights of persons with disabilities, shifting the structures of opportunity for the movement of persons with disabilities. One of those is the European Accessibility Act (EAA).[69]

Notably, establishing common standards for goods and services in the internal market of the EU is a primary goal of the European project. Acknowledging the need for harmonised standards as a means of achieving the internal market, the Commission started issuing mandates for the development of accessibility standards in the fields of information and communication technologies in 1998. Since then, several accessibility standards have been developed at the EU level following standardisation requests by the Commission to the European Standardisation Organisations. Many goods, services and industries in Member States remain inaccessible to consumers with disabilities and by 2011 there was little room for recourse for the breach of standards or indeed to monitor adherence.[70] EDF began its campaign for a European Internal Market Directive, underpinned by European Standards, for the European Union to fulfil its obligations to ensure accessible markets for persons with disabilities in 2011. According to the 'Freedom Guide',[71] an EDF publication setting out the principles behind

[67] EDF, 'Joint statement: "Building an inclusive European Union of Equality"' (25 March 2024) available at <https://www.edf-feph.org/publications/joint-statement-building-an-inclusive-european-union-of-equality/>; EDF (n 42) 13-14.

[68] Article 114 Treaty on the Functioning of the European Union.

[69] Directive (EU) 2019/882 of the European Parliament and of the Council of 17 April 2019 on the accessibility requirements for products and services (European Accessibility Act – EAA) [2019] OJ L151/70.

[70] L Senden, 'The Constitutional Fit of European Standardization Put to the Test' (2017) 44(4) *Legal Issues of Economic Integration* 337–352.

[71] EDF, 'Freedom Guide. Paving the way towards free movement for persons with disabilities' (2011) available at <https://www.edf-feph.org/content/uploads/2022/04/EDF_FreedomGuide.pdf>.

the Free Movement campaign, the primary aim of the campaign was to ensure a 'strong' EAA was produced and implemented. The receptacles of the campaign moved with the legislation through its different stages of policy production.[72] EDF sought to frame the EAA as an advantageous step for industry, stating in its 'Freedom Guide':

> Access is seen mainly as a problem for businesses, rather than a golden opportunity.[73]

The campaign had two strategic 'sides': one publicly facing that called on the institutions to realise the principles of free movement for persons with disabilities in the EU and circulating material to partner organisations to this end. The other side targeted the institutions from an inward-facing position; that is, it targeted Commission officials allied to EDF, following the proposal through Parliament and calling on MEPs to introduce amendments. At Council level the aim was to maintain communication to gauge which Member States were allies and which had reservations to the EAA as well as which were completely opposed. While most previous campaign work by EDF had been under the banners of non-discrimination, following the 'stuck' Horizontal Equality Directive pursued in the 1Million4Disability campaign, EDF looked at other Treaty Articles and the principle of free movement became central to the campaign strategy:

> The achievement of the internal market, in which there are no obstacles to the free movement of goods, persons, services and capital, is a fundamental objective of the European Union. Obstacles to the internal market can come from many sources and, where such obstacles make free movement more difficult, or distort competition, the EU can intervene.[74]

The EP's Internal Market and Consumer Protection Committee (IMCO Committee) compiled a report balancing industry interests against those of consumers (with disabilities). The EP adopted the report in 2017, despite protests outside the Parliament building by EDF and its partners. For the first time the organisation broke party lines of voting and succeeded in adding amendments at the plenary stage in which the Parliament makes its final decisions. Inserting amendments at the final stage of the parliamentary process was unprecedented. In doing so, EDF side-stepped the position taken by the IMCO Committee and succeeded in contributing to an ambitious EP position to the Council. This process involved not only allies of the organisation; it obliged the conservative rapporteur to advocate for a progressive position. The Council was another hurdle for the campaign, being particularly opaque in its decision-making. At this stage, the EAA was weakened in its protection of interests of

[72] See also the discussion by O Bartlett, 'The EU Legislative Institutions and Disability Rights: Uncovering the Factors that Block Progress and Offering Insights for Future Advocacy' in this volume.

[73] EDF (n 71) 67.

[74] L Waddington, 'The European Union and the United Nations Convention on the rights of persons with disabilities: a story of exclusive and shared competences' (2011) 18(4) *Maastricht Journal of European and Comparative Law* 431–453.

consumers with disabilities.[75] While EDF was successful in lobbying MEPs until late stages of the legislative process, the final legislation fell short of movement expectations.[76] EDF has been vocal in its criticism of the Act. Transport services and household appliances are not included in the EAA and the built environment clause is voluntary. The full implementation of the EAA is lengthy – some products and services do not need to meet the requirements of the EAA until 2039 due to the wording of the Act. EDF has raised the possibility of future strategic litigation before the Court of Justice of the European Union to improve accessibility of goods and services based on the EAA. Indeed, the EAA makes individual claims and claims to be raised on behalf of representative organisations possible.[77] This addition to the EAA was secured by EDF to lessen the burden on claimants. The EAA may therefore represent the introduction of a new avenue of lobbying for disability rights in the EU.[78] A notable difference was detected between the position of secretariat staff and EDF membership in interviews about the EAA. An interviewee from an EU-wide OPD network reported their dubiousness about the EAA upon its announcement. Hoping that the outcome would be different to their expectation, they reported:

> I was really hoping that I would turn out to be wrong about the Accessibility Act and had it been a strong act I would have been happy to declare that I was wrong. But I was just thinking … you're putting your hope into something that is just not there – legally, politically, financially, you are not in a position that you can really challenge these companies, and you know, the lack of [a]ccessibility across Europe through EU legislation, because the EU is an economic project.[79]

EDF is now working with its national members on transposing the EAA into national laws. This has been done so far through support resources: EDF has produced a 'transposition toolkit' explaining the process and timeline of EU Member States giving force to the EAA and advising OPDs on what can be done in each phase to strengthen the transposition process.

5.3. Taking Stock of European Disability Forum Presence

In policy landscapes, contextual factors create windows of opportunity for policy entrepreneurs. As discussed above, these windows of opportunity can break through institutional constraints, such as Treaty revisions that redefine the

[75] EDF (n 42).

[76] D Ferri, 'The European Accessibility Act and the Shadow of the "Social Market Economy"' (2020) 5 *European Law Review* 660–680.

[77] Articles 19-22 EAA.

[78] Bartlett (n 72).

[79] Interview with former EDF member.

competence of institutions of governance. They may also allow for novel collective action within the context of a fixed institutional governance landscape.[80] This can be observed in the example of the ECI utilised in the 1Million4Disability campaign. Institutional resistance to new non-discrimination measures remained and prevented the realisation of the legislation despite the technical successes of the campaign. The Free Movement campaign saw the successful passing of the EAA after the EU became a party to the CRPD. The campaign nevertheless faced powerful industry interests that opposed strong accessibility legislation, which impacted the final Act. Evidence from the three case studies indicates that a strategic campaign utilising novel tactics is constrained in an environment of systemic resistance to that campaign's idea.

The relationship between EDF and the EU institutions holds important contextual value for future collective action by the DPM. EDF and its campaign partners in the DPM have made these claims upon the EU institutions to enact meaningful societal change at a variety of levels: the institutions have responded with protection in the sphere of labour and of consumer rights. Movements operating in a late-capitalist era face a system that shapes their principles as much as their activity.[81] Movement organisations face a challenge in where to lay claims; the context under which each campaign took place speaks to the opportunities and constraints of three eras of governance.

6. Concluding Remarks

The horizontal nature of decision-making is highlighted by scholars as a primary feature of governance networks.[82] The corporatist principles of EU governance intentionally include interest groups as consultants or more official decision-making partners in policy processes. This horizontal nature does not imply that resources are equally available or dispersed among actors.[83] Power distribution in a network influences the creation of rules: they may operate to the advantage of some, and to the disadvantage of others.[84] In their summation of the 'network approach', Klijn and Koppenjan posit that despite power and resource imbalances, less powerful actors (like 'citizen organisations') can influence decision-making, by stagnating the decision-making process or by blocking decisions.[85] The trajectory of civil society involvement over the course of the three campaigns speaks

[80] Lowndes (n 66) 291.

[81] N Fraser, *Fortunes of Feminism: From State-Managed Capitalism to Neoliberal Crisis* (Verso 2020).

[82] E-H Klijn and J Koppenjan, 'Governance network theory: past, present and future' (2012) 40(4) *Policy & Politics* 587–606.

[83] J Knight, *Institutions and Social Conflict* (Cambridge University Press 1992).

[84] E-H Klijn and J Koppenjan, 'Public Management and Policy Networks' (2000) 2(2) *Public Management: An International Journal of Research and Theory* 135–158.

[85] Ibid 146.

to the increasing role of networked decision-making pointed to in literature. The Commission's 'consultation regime' is currently 'marked by the role … [of] non-governmental actors or civil society organisations'.[86] In the case of the three campaigns, however, despite the role of CSO participation as consultants, EDF and its campaign partners had to utilise tactics like lobbying and protest outside of their role in the decision-making process to push for the change they sought. The specific nature of non-public actor roles in network governance literature is often neglected. The Free Movement campaign in particular demonstrates the distribution of power between non-governmental organisations, including civil society, and private interests. The description of governance networks as horizontal is not evidenced in the policy processes connected to the campaigns. Power distribution in the network appears to have been a deciding factor in decision-making. Organisations representing stakeholder interests like EDF often find their interests relegated in regular policy processes and must find alternative methods to exert influence, usually via other more powerful actors. The division of decision-making across several 'politico-administrative' institutions is an important dimension of EU governance specifically.[87] Interdependence between these institutions is emphasised: 'no level of activity being superior to the other … therein, a mutual dependency through the intertwining of policy-making activities' exists both across government and non-governmental actors, and across 'vertical' levels of government.[88] The European project of integration is a 'polity creating process' in which influence and authority are shared across multiple levels of government at supranational, national and subnational levels.[89]

Evidence from the three case studies points to Member State representatives as having the highest level of authority in the EU policy process. The Free Movement campaign ushered the EAA through the policy stages: in this case EDF and its campaign partners faced a more hostile parliamentary committee aligned with industry interests of weaker legislation. The campaign coalition broke lines of voting and remained present for the final stages in the Parliament to ensure the Act was not overly weakened as it arrived at the Council. This notoriously opaque stage of the process presented fewer opportunities for the campaign to influence decisions.[90]

[86] C Quittkat and B Finke, 'The EU Commission consultation regime' in B Kohler-Koch, D Bièvre and W Maloney (eds), *Opening EU-governance to civil society: gains and challenges* (CONNEX report series 2008) 183–222.

[87] G Marks, 'Structural policy and multilevel governance in the EC. The Maastricht debates and beyond' in A Cafruny and G Rosenthal (eds), *The State of the European Community* (Longman 1993) 391–409.

[88] P Stephenson, 'Twenty years of multi-level governance: 'Where does it come from? What is it? Where is it going?'' (2013) 20(6) *Journal of European Public Policy* 817–837.

[89] G Marks, L Hooghe and K Blank, 'European Integration from the 1980s: State-Centric v. Multi-level Governance' (1996) 34(3) *Journal of Common Market Studies* 341–378.

[90] M Caiani and P Graziano, 'Europeanisation and social movements: The case of the Stop TTIP campaign' (2018) 57(4) *European Journal of Political Research* 1031–1055.

Notes 'from the field' of governance – that is, empirical observations from the campaigns – demonstrate an increasingly embedded nature of policy networks over their 25-year course. The EU institutions are obligated to seek advisory input from the EESC according to Article 300 TFEU, and Article 13 TEU. Civil society is also referenced in relation to good governance in Article 15 TEU. The EU as a State Party to the CRPD is required to involve civil society 'fully' in monitoring the implementation of legislation as per Article 33(3) CRPD. This is reflected in the chronological course of campaigns. Along this timeline, the increasingly formalised role of CSOs can be charted, from *ad hoc* lobbying in the Invisible Citizens campaign to the use of an instrument designed for registered CSOs to mediate between the European public and the institutions in the 1Million4Disability campaign, to EDF's presence at plenary stages of EP legislative amendments. The findings raise questions about the opportunities for influence CSOs find in these spaces.

EDF and its campaign partners have engaged in novel campaign activity to gain influence in decision-making. Interviewees, particularly those within the secretariat, report an increase in influence since the Invisible Citizens campaign in 1995. Member States have been joined by other institutions of governance with the power to propose policy in EU governance. Interdependence between the institutions is relatively low in the policy process. For civil society and social movements, this adds complexity and challenges advocacy as influence in one area does not necessarily feed into another. While EDF has made impressive gains in its collective action repertoires over its lifetime and has become more institutionally embedded in these processes, it operates in a landscape of governance that separates stages of decision-making by design. Looking ahead, organisations that favour 'insider tactics' are more constrained in activity and issue in their advocacy. Their agendas are highly dependent on those of the EU institutions. What remains to be seen is the rate at which the institutions wish to implement the principles of the CRPD and to realise the rights of persons with disabilities in the EU.

11

The Path is Made by Walking … The Social Partners and Employment Rights under EU Disability Law

MICHAEL DOHERTY

1. Introduction: The Importance of the World of Work

Perhaps nothing shines a light on the extent of societal exclusion of certain groups quite as brightly as a focus on the world of work and the workplace. In contemporary society, work plays a hugely significant role in the life experience, and most adults spend a large proportion of their lives going to, coming from, completing (or sleeping on) the job. Working fulfils for people important financial, but also personal (sense of worth, achievement, dignity, etc.) and social (friendship and romance, for example) needs.[1] However, given the centrality of work to the life experience of so many, obstacles to full participation in the employment sphere clearly have a hugely important effect on those who cannot fully engage. For this reason, 'inclusion' and 'exclusion' from employment have become huge issues for policy-makers, including at European Union (EU) level.[2] When one talks about employment relations law and policy, one must consider the role of social partners, trade unions and employer representative groups, and that is the focus of this chapter.

As we will see in the next section, the social partners have a unique role in EU law-making (a role not granted to other interest groups) as well as a significant policy role. This unique position, combined with the centrality of work and

[1] M Doherty, 'When the Working Day is Through: The End of Work as Identity?' (2009) 23(1) *Work, Employment and Society* 84–101.

[2] As Bell points out, however, it is important to be aware that the concept of 'inclusion' in employment is open to a range of interpretations; while research and policy often equate inclusion to higher rates of employment, 'a balanced perspective on fostering inclusion needs to consider both the number of people finding a job and their treatment within the workplace'. M Bell, 'People with Intellectual Disabilities and Labour Market Inclusion: What Role for EU Labour Law?' (2020) 11(1) *European Labour Law Journal* 3.

working to the life experience of EU citizens, means that any focus on the rights of persons with disabilities needs to take into account the approach taken by these vital, non-institutional actors in shaping EU disability law and policy. It is a truism for those who engage with labour law and policy (as academics and/or practitioners) that when *employment/industrial relations* practice and procedure meet *legal* practice and procedure controversy is rarely far behind.[3] The law, and lawyers, operate (largely) in terms of black and white; industrial relations (IR), and IR practitioners, by contrast, generally operate in the grey. For this reason, this chapter adopts the approach of looking at both 'hard' legal instruments, and 'soft law' strategies and policies in an attempt to piece together an account of the role of the social partners in orienting EU disability law in recent times, and what we can speculate upon for the future. The chapter also takes the approach that the issue of discrimination in employment is not one that can simply be approached as a *legal* problem with a *legal* solution. The focus on the role of key non-institutional actors (the social partners) and on non-legal strategies, approaches, and policies is intended to concentrate attention on the context in which EU disability law exists; the 'social environment' of law.[4] Attention must be given to structural changes in society, beyond legal developments, such as political, economic or cultural changes, and resulting power shifts.[5] As a result, the fluctuating power dynamics that can be observed in relations between the EU institutions, trade unions, and employer organisations, the effects of austerity measures (post-2008), and the demographic make-up of social partner organisations are all issues to be taken into account in the analysis.

The chapter is set out as follows. In the next section, a little more detail is provided on the role of trade union and employer representatives at EU level in law- and policy-making in general, and specifically in the field of disability rights. The chapter then moves on to focus on three elements, which, it is argued, explain the relatively (and disappointingly) limited impact the social partners have had on the promotion of rights of persons with disabilities at work. First, the chapter engages with the crisis (or at least diminution) of social partner legitimacy within the EU law- and policy-making orders themselves. Secondly, the curiously limited role of the social partners in EU-level soft law strategies is considered. Finally, the role of the social partners in enforcing the rights of persons with disabilities is analysed, in the context of recent EU law initiatives in this space, and

[3] At EU level, the voluminous literature that followed the decisions of the Court of Justice of the EU in the 'Laval Quartet' line of jurisprudence is a case in point; among (many, many) others see ACL Davies, 'One Step Forward, Two Steps Back? The Viking and Laval Cases in the ECJ' (2008) 37 *Industrial Law Journal* 126–142; C Kilpatrick, 'Laval's Regulatory Conundrum: Collective Standard-Setting and the Court's New Approach to Posted Workers' (2009) 34 *European Law Review* 844–864.

[4] URMT de Vries and LMA Francot, 'The Legal Method Reconsidered: Contextual Legal Research from an Interdisciplinary Perspective – Towards Developing a New Paradigm' in M Karinka and R Wiesemes (eds), *Exploring Avenues to Interdisciplinary Research: From Cross- to Multi- to Interdisciplinarity* (Nottingham University Press 2008) 167.

[5] P Selznick, 'Law in Context Revisited' (2003) 30(2) *Journal of Law and Society* 177–186.

links the discussion somewhat with the role of national-level social partners. In the concluding section, some reflections on the extent to which the social partners should have a role at all in this area are offered.

2. First Among Equals: The Social Partners and the EU Legal Order

The social partners at EU level are given unique powers under the Treaty on the Functioning of the European Union (TFEU) in terms of the role of European social dialogue under Title X: Social Policy. Articles 152-155 TFEU set out the requirement for mandatory consultation with the social partners by the Commission in all matters in the social policy field; this includes the health and safety of workers, working conditions, integration of persons excluded from the labour market, and the combating of social exclusion.[6] These Articles also provide for the right of the social partners to negotiate agreements and the legal basis for negotiated agreements to become binding EU law.[7] When social partners have reached an agreement, Article 155(2) TFEU provides for two methods of implementation: either the agreement remains autonomous and is implemented in accordance with the procedures and practices specific to national social partners and the Member States, or the signatories to the agreement jointly request the Commission to give *erga omnes* effect to the agreement via turning the agreement into binding EU law by a Council Decision.[8] A number of agreements have been concluded by the social partners as voluntary framework agreements (for example, the 2010 Framework Agreement on Inclusive Labour Markets),[9] as well as framework agreements elevated to binding EU law (for example, the Framework Agreement on Part-time Work implemented as Directive 97/81/EC).[10] Thus, there is potentially an enormous role for the social partners in shaping the legal regulation of crucial aspects of employment relations.

The social partners (at national level) are also given an important explicit role in secondary EU law. Article 13 of the Employment Equality Directive (on 'Social Dialogue') states:[11]

> 1. Member States shall, in accordance with their national traditions and practice, take adequate measures to promote dialogue between the social partners with

[6] Article 153(1)(a), (b), (h) and (j) Treaty on the Functioning of the European Union (TFEU).

[7] For a comprehensive overview of the role of social dialogue in the EU, see B ter Haar and A Kun (eds), *EU Collective Labour Law* (Edward Elgar 2021).

[8] NV Munkolm, 'Social Dialogue in the EU (legal)' in ter Haar and Kun (n 7) 151.

[9] European Trade Union Confederation, 'Framework agreement on inclusive labour markets' available at <https://www.etuc.org/en/framework-agreement-inclusive-labour-markets>.

[10] Council Directive 97/81/EC of 15 December 1997 concerning the Framework Agreement on part-time work concluded by UNICE, CEEP and the ETUC [1998] OJ L14/9.

[11] Council Directive 2000/78/EC establishing a general framework for equal treatment in employment and occupation [2000] OJ L303/16.

a view to fostering equal treatment, including through the monitoring of workplace practices, collective agreements, codes of conduct and through research or exchange of experiences and good practices.

2. Where consistent with their national traditions and practice, Member States shall encourage the social partners, without prejudice to their autonomy, to conclude at the appropriate level agreements laying down anti-discrimination rules in the fields referred to in Article 3 which fall within the scope of collective bargaining. These agreements shall respect the minimum requirements laid down by this Directive and by the relevant national implementing measures.

It is noteworthy that in Article 14 of the Directive ('Dialogue with non-governmental organisations') the requirement placed on Member States is simply to 'encourage dialogue' with 'appropriate' non-governmental organisations (NGOs) that have a legitimate interest in contributing to the fight against discrimination on any of the grounds referred to in Article 1. The contrast is striking and acts to establish a hierarchy amongst non-institutional actors when it comes to combatting discrimination (at least under the Employment Equality Directive). Trade unions and employer organisations are placed front and centre. Elomäki and Kantola, in their important study of the role of the European social partners as *gender equality* actors, point to the 'long-standing struggle between the EU's economic and social goals and the difficult position of gender equality policies and traditional gender equality actors due to the primacy given to economic goals'.[12] The authors note that the social partners (trade unions and employers) are of central importance to this struggle, because, as issues of gender equality became subsumed by economic priorities, 'it became difficult for gender equality actors, such as civil society organizations and gender experts inside and outside EU institutions, to have their voices heard in EU policy-making … shifts in EU economic governance have narrowed the space for civil society to participate in democratic debate'.[13] Here, we could easily replace 'gender equality actors' with 'disability equality actors', and, indeed, we could even argue that the point is more forcefully made in the sphere of disability rights.[14] In essence, the argument is that as NGOs (including those that advocate for disability rights) get squeezed out of the legal/policy debate, the voice of the 'institutional' social partners (trade unions and employers) becomes more important. The chapter further interrogates this point, and some of the implications, below.

Of course, outside of formal law-making powers, the social partners also have a role in the various soft law measures and strategies undertaken by the

[12] A Elomäki and J Kantola, 'European Social Partners as Gender Equality Actors in EU Social and Economic Governance' (2020) 58 *Journal of Common Market Studies* 1001.

[13] Ibid.

[14] This is certainly the case if one engages with the arguments of authors who contend that EU legislation creates a 'hierarchy of discrimination grounds', with sex/gender equality placed above that of equality for persons with disabilities; see eg E Howard, 'The Case for a Considered Hierarchy of Discrimination Grounds in EU Law' (2006) 13(4) *Maastricht Journal of European and Comparative Law* 445–470.

EU in the area of disability rights. The European Pillar of Social Rights (EPSR) politically commits the EU and its Member States to a number of key principles in the employment and social field. Importantly, Principle 17 of the Pillar is clear that persons with disabilities have the right to income support that ensures their living in dignity, services that enable them to participate in the labour market and in society, and a work environment adapted to their needs. Other principles equally seek to protect the rights of persons with disabilities at work and in society, such as Principle 3 (on equal opportunities); Principle 4 (on active support for employment); and Principle 5 (on secure and adaptable employment). The EPSR serves as a 'compass for employment and social policies' in the EU, as set out in one of its key flanking measures, the Strategy for the Rights of Persons with Disabilities 2021-2030 (Strategy 2021-2030).[15] An Employment Package to improve labour market outcomes of persons with disabilities is one of the seven flagship initiatives announced in the Strategy, the preparation of which involved consultations with the social partners.[16] We return to this issue in the following section.

3. The (Non-)Impact of the Social Partners on EU Disability Law

The chapter opened by emphasising the centrality of work to the life experience and noted that exclusion (in various forms) from the world of work can have extremely deleterious effects. In the section above, the central role of the social partners in the making of law and policy at EU level was outlined. Putting these two things together, then, one might expect that trade unions and employers at EU and national level have had a profound effect (one way or another) on the shaping of EU disability law and on the opportunities for participation by persons with disabilities in the employment sphere. This section (spoiler alert ...) outlines some reasons why this simply has not occurred.

3.1. It's So Funny How We Don't Talk Anymore

First, it is necessary to engage in some labour law/industrial relations navel-gazing. It is by no means only in the sphere of employment equality law that social dialogue is in crisis. The situation has moved dramatically from the

[15] European Commission (Commission), 'Union of Equality: Strategy for the Rights of Persons with Disabilities 2021–2030' COM(2021) 101 final.

[16] For full details on the Disability Employment Package, see Commission, 'Disability Employment Package to improve labour market outcomes for persons with disabilities' available at <https://ec.europa.eu/social/main.jsp?catId=1597&langId=en>.

'golden age' of European social dialogue,[17] during the 1990s and early 2000s, where social partner agreements were put into effect as binding directives in key areas of employment regulation (often affecting precarious and marginalised cohorts of workers) such as part-time work,[18] and fixed-term work.[19] One of the success stories of this age was the Social Partner Framework Agreement on parental leave, given legal effect in Directive 96/34.[20] This was updated in 2010, with the social partners producing a revised framework agreement, given legal effect by Directive 2010/18.[21] Skip forward less than a decade, however, and the social partners were unable to conclude a further revised agreement. Thus, Directive 2019/1158,[22] which contains, for the first time in an EU directive on parental leave, an explicit reference to Article 7 of the Convention on the Rights of Persons with Disabilities (CRPD), progressed through the ordinary legislative procedure after the failure of the social partners to agree to 'enter into negotiations with regard to [work-life balance], including with regard to parental leave'.[23] This is not an isolated example, but reflective of a trend in which all significant labour law legislation in recent years has been passed following the failure of the social partners to agree (or, often, even agree to negotiate) to exercise their mandate under Article 154 TFEU.[24] For instance, in June 2022, the European Trade Union Confederation and the main European employer's confederation, BusinessEurope, signed a work programme agreement, including a commitment to update the 2002 Framework Agreement on Telework, and addressing the 'right to disconnect'.[25] The agreement was also signed by SGI Europe (the organisation representing enterprises that carry out services of general interest), and SMEUnited (that represents small- and medium-sized

[17] P Pochet, 'Social Europe: Social Dialogue at the Heart of the Debate' (Policy Brief, 29 January 2024) Jacques Delors Institute available at <https://institutdelors.eu/en/publications/social-europe-social-dialogue-at-the-heart-of-the-debate/>.

[18] Directive 97/81/EC.

[19] Council Directive 1999/70/EC of 28 June 1999 concerning the framework agreement on fixed-term work concluded by ETUC, UNICE and CEEP [1999] OJ L175/43.

[20] Council Directive 96/34/EC of 3 June 1996 on the framework agreement on parental leave concluded by UNICE, CEEP and the ETUC [1996] OJ L145/4.

[21] Council Directive 2010/18/EU of 8 March 2010 implementing the revised Framework Agreement on parental leave concluded by BUSINESSEUROPE, UEAPME, CEEP and ETUC and repealing Directive 96/34/EC [2010] OJ L68/13.

[22] Directive (EU) 2019/1158 of the European Parliament and of the Council of 20 June 2019 on work-life balance for parents and carers and repealing Council Directive 2010/18/EU [2019] OJ L188/79.

[23] Recital 14 Directive (EU) 2019/1158.

[24] There are numerous examples to offer, but particularly contentious legislative measures include Directive (EU) 2022/2041 of the European Parliament and of the Council of 19 October 2022 on adequate minimum wages in the European Union (Adequate Minimum Wages Directive) [2022] OJ L275/33 and Directive (EU) 2019/1152 of the European Parliament and of the Council of 20 June 2019 on transparent and predictable working conditions in the European Union [2019] OJ L186/105.

[25] BusinessEurope, 'European Unions and Employers sign historic deal' (Press Release, 27 June 2022) available at <https://www.businesseurope.eu/publications/european-unions-and-employers-sign-historic-deal>.

enterprises across Europe). After a year of negotiations, however, BusinessEurope and SMEUnited decided to end the talks without agreement.[26]

There are a number of reasons for this inability to find social partner agreement. Trade unions and social dialogue across the EU (and at EU level) were undoubtedly weakened and often sidelined during the 'austerity' years following the financial crash of 2007/08, when the usefulness of social consultation, and the role of collective bargaining, were often dismissed as 'rigidities' that had to be overcome in order to tackle the financial crisis.[27] It is not only the institution of social dialogue that has come under strain, but the actors too. Across Europe, declining trade union membership and collective bargaining coverage can be observed.[28] Moreover, as Keune points out, the particularly low collective bargaining coverage in Central and Eastern European countries means that EU enlargements have resulted in weakening European social dialogue.[29] On the employers' side, although density is often higher than for trade unions, we also see a weakening (mirroring the unions, employer organisation density is particularly low in Central and Eastern European countries), and a 'phenomenon of exit from sectoral employers' organisations', even in countries with a strong tradition of social partnership, like Germany.[30]

We return to the social partners themselves below, but it is also vital to acknowledge the role of the EU institutions in the decline of social dialogue. As Tricart has argued, 'the Commission has, over the past decade, successfully developed a strategy of obstruction to limit the influence of social dialogue'.[31] Two examples are oft-cited.[32] A 2012 social partner agreement on the health and safety of hairdressers, in respect of which the Commission refrained to take further steps to make the agreement legally binding, and the highly contentious Commission decision in 2018 to refuse the social partner *request* to make binding an agreement on the information and consultation of civil servants and employees in public administrations. The latter decision led to a challenge before the EU Courts by the European Federation of Public Service Unions (EPSU).[33] In essence, the challenge

[26] Social Europe, 'Just a matter of time? The 'right to disconnect'' (12 December 2023) available at <https://www.socialeurope.eu/just-a-matter-of-time-the-right-to-disconnect>.

[27] M Doherty, 'W(h)ither Social Europe? Labour Rights in a Social Market Economy' in D Ferri and F Cortese (eds), *The EU Social Market Economy and the Law: Theoretical Perspectives and Practical Challenges for the EU* (Routledge 2018) 87.

[28] K Vandaele, *Bleak Prospects: Mapping Trade Union Membership in Europe Since 2000* (ETUI 2020).

[29] M Keune, 'The Effects of the EU's Assault on Collective Bargaining: Less Governance Capacity and More Inequality' (2015) 21(4) *Transfer: European Review of Labour and Research* 477–483.

[30] Pochet (n 17) 4.

[31] J Tricart, *Legislative Implementation of European Social Partner Agreements: Challenges and Debates* (ETUI 2020) cited in F Dorssemont and P Van Malleghem, 'Sounding the Death Knell for EU Social Dialogue?: The EPSU Judgment as a Turning Point for EU Labour Law' (*Verfassungsblog*, 21 September 2021) available at <https://verfassungsblog.de/sounding-the-death-knell-for-eu-social-dialogue/>.

[32] Dorssemont and Van Malleghem (n 31); ter Haar and Kun (n 7).

[33] Case C-928/19 P *European Federation of Public Service Unions (EPSU), with other parties to the proceedings Jan Willem Goudriaan, and European Commission* ECLI:EU:C:2021:656 (EPSU Appeal); and Case T-310/18 *European Federation of Public Service Unions (EPSU), Jan Goudriaan v the European Commission* ECLI:EU:T:2019:757.

amounted to a clash between two fundamental principles of the EU; on the one hand, the sole right of legislative initiative of the Commission and, on the other, social dialogue (and social partner autonomy) as an essential element of EU social policy, and law-making. Both the General Court and the Court of Justice of the EU (CJEU) rejected EPSU's claims and backed the Commission position. A full analysis of the case is not necessary for this chapter,[34] but it is widely interpreted as a judicial blow to the head of an already on-the-ropes social dialogue process; 'with its judgment, the Court declares war on labour law's claim to be different'.[35] Within this broader context, the outlook for any initiative via the Treaty's social dialogue process in the area of disability law looks distinctly remote. Given this, let us turn to social partner involvement in more general soft law processes in this sphere.

3.2. Softly, softly ... EU Disability Strategies and the Social Partners

A number of important pieces of research were produced in advance of the preparation of the Strategy 2021-2030. One issue of discussion was the legal requirement in Article 13 of Directive 2000/78 (cited earlier) on Member States to take measures to promote dialogue between the social partners, with a view to fostering equal treatment, and to encourage social partners at a national level to conclude collective agreements that lay down non-discrimination rules. These requirements under the Directive can be met by legally binding measures (in Member States with mechanisms for *erga omnes* extension of sectoral collective agreements to all workers, for example), but also by legally non-binding measures that 'foster equal treatment'. Notwithstanding the provisions of the Directive, and wider measures to tackle discrimination against persons with disabilities at work, Eurofound concluded that '[t]he evidence shows that the prevalence of workplace discrimination remains high'.[36] Eurofound pointed to a number of challenges that remain in relation to tackling workplace discrimination, both cross-cutting (i.e. relevant to all the discriminatory grounds under EU law) and specific to discrimination on the grounds of disability.[37] Some that are particularly relevant to this chapter include

[34] Many excellent analyses are available; see eg S Velluti, 'The European Social Dialogue as a Source of EU Legal Acts Following EPSU: Collective Bargaining and Industrial Relations Get Lost in Translation' (2022) 59(3) *Common Market Law Review* 871–888; F Dorssemont, 'Some Observations on the EPSU Case: A Bad Judgment for Democracy and Subsidiarity, Alias a Textbook Example of *Not* Promoting the European Social Dialogue' in A Hartzén, A Iossa and E Karageorgiou (eds), *Law, Solidarity and the Limits of Social Europe. Constitutional Tensions for EU Integration* (Edward Elgar 2022) 43.

[35] Dorssemont and Van Malleghem (n 31).

[36] Eurofound, 'Role of Social Partners in Tackling Discrimination at Work' (Publications Office of the European Union 2020) 33.

[37] Ibid 29 *et seq*..

the following. In terms of cross-cutting challenges, some key aspects identified were: a low awareness of the rights and obligations on the part of employers and workers; a low level of capacity among social partners to implement measures and support discrimination cases (increasingly, since the implementation of austerity measures); and an unwillingness to make complaints/bring discrimination cases (due to fear, *inter alia*, of a lack of financial and practical support to bring cases). In the specific case of disability, key challenges included: lack of knowledge and understanding of the concept of 'reasonable accommodation'; lack of knowledge of different conditions and misconceptions about limitations to the ability to work associated with them; and lack of dissuasive sanctions for employers that do not respect quotas for the employment of persons with disabilities (where such quotas are in place) and the absence of quotas in the private sector. A significant number of these relate to enforcement, to which we return below.

What the report shows is that (along with age discrimination) disability discrimination is most frequently seen to be 'on the radar' of the social partners in the Member States at cross-industry level.[38] Given this, examples of social partner activities in different Member States are provided, and range from social partner involvement in revising legislation, to the provision of additional leave entitlements for workers with disabilities, to joint social partner texts and projects (on awareness-raising, dissemination of best practice, etc.).[39] However, the report also highlights two main reasons for the lack of social partner action in relation to workplace discrimination. First, in many Member States, the issue of disability discrimination is seen as either not a significant issue or one that has already been addressed. Secondly, the social partner organisations either lack the capacity to take action or prioritise other issues that take precedence.[40] The first reason stretches credulity somewhat and points to a need for much greater political direction (from legislators and social partners) at EU and national level. The second reason, around priorities, is one that must be interrogated further (below).

The Eurofound report fed into the review of the Equality Directives, on which the Commission reported in March 2021.[41] The review acknowledged that the general sentiment was that little progress had been made in the fight against discrimination since 2014, and that '[a]wareness-raising and dialogue with social partners and civil society organisations are key for the effective implementation of

[38] Ibid 35.

[39] Ibid 43-45.

[40] Ibid 50.

[41] Commission, 'Report from the Commission to the European Parliament and the Council on the application of Council Directive 2000/43/EC implementing the principle of equal treatment between persons irrespective of racial or ethnic origin ('the Racial Equality Directive') and of Council Directive 2000/78/EC establishing a general framework for equal treatment in employment and occupation ('the Employment Equality Directive')' COM(2021) 139 final. The report was published days after the Strategy 2021-2030; oddly, given the documents were published so close to each other, the latter includes the publication of the report as one of its deliverables under the Strategy 2021-2030. Commission (n 15) 11.

the Directives'.[42] The report acknowledges that organisations such as trade unions and equality bodies can help victims to seek individual redress, especially when they have legal standing under national law, can play an important role in seeking collective redress, and can be important in raising awareness of the rights of citizens under the Equality Directives.[43] Importantly, the report acknowledges that social partners play a crucial role in fighting discrimination and promoting equality and workplace diversity in the workplace. Nonetheless, the report recognises that awareness of the non-discrimination legislation remains low and points, in particular, to challenges in relation to the understanding of, implementation of, and receiving guidance in relation to, the concept of reasonable accommodation.[44] The Commission ultimately commits to continue working with all stakeholders concerned in order to realise the full potential of the Directives; this includes trade unions, employers and their associations, who have important roles to play in their respective spheres of competence.[45]

The Strategy 2021-2030 was published in March 2021. Preceding this, the Commission published an evaluation of the European Disability Strategy 2010-2020 (EDS) in late 2020.[46] The study found that organisations representing persons with disabilities, business organisations and citizens responding to the public consultation tended to consider employment among the worst performing areas of the EDS due to the persisting gaps between persons with disabilities and without disabilities.[47] Stakeholders also considered that, in terms of their engagement in the implementation of the EDS, 'current fora do not always involve stakeholders representing the interests of persons with disabilities in the workforce (such as trade unions and support organisations of workers)'.[48] The report noted that many EU-level stakeholders consulted for the study, however, and especially the umbrella organisations representing persons with disabilities at EU level, agree that the existence of such a strategy at EU level is in itself crucial, as the adoption of a high-level EU policy document explicitly dedicated to disability has helped to place the disability agenda higher among the EU's policy priorities.[49] Clearly, therefore, there is a gap in terms of stakeholder perception between visibility and outcomes.

The first stage in tackling a problem is its identification, and the Commission (as outlined above) had clear evidence of some of the weaknesses around social partner engagement and involvement in the design, but particularly the implementation, of its disability strategies in terms of the world of work. The second

[42] Commission (n 41) 4.
[43] Ibid 7-8, 11.
[44] Ibid 21.
[45] Ibid 26.
[46] Commission, 'Commission Staff Working Document Evaluation of the European Disability Strategy 2010-2020' SWD(2020) 289 final/2.
[47] Ibid 28. On the other hand, however, stakeholders at *EU and Member State level* considered that the EDS had brought positive effects in the field of employment thanks to the improvements in statistical data and awareness raising.
[48] Ibid 43.
[49] Ibid 53.

stage is … Well, the second stage of the Commission's approach, it is argued here, has been to 'repeat the past'.[50]

The Strategy 2021-2030 contains a clear acknowledgement that, for persons with disabilities, participation in employment is the best way to ensure economic autonomy and social inclusion, and pledges that the Commission will continue to support Member States in the implementation of the relevant Employment Guidelines through the European Semester, in developing statistical tools as well as promoting the exchange of best practices in the context of the Social Open Method of Coordination.[51] There are only two explicit references to the social partners in the entire Strategy 2021-2030: a call on Member States to 'strengthen the capacities of employment services for persons with disabilities and enhance work with social partners and organisations of persons with disabilities to that end'; and a commitment to a Commission package to improve labour market outcomes of persons with disabilities, which will seek 'cooperation with', amongst others, the social partners.[52] The first of these hardly quickens the pulse in terms of expected outcomes (given the evidence the Commission itself has presented, discussed above). Indeed, the Commission itself has hardly provided a best practice example here. As part of the Strategy 2021-2030, the Commission pledged to establish the 'Disability Platform'; an expert advisory group composed of high-level representatives of 'established focal points within national administrations for matters relating to the implementation of the Convention' and in which '[e]xperts from EU-level civil society organisations representing persons with disabilities' and 'other relevant civil society organisation' should participate.[53] The membership of the Platform was confirmed in 2021 and does not include any social partner organisations.[54]

The second reference was to a package of measures to be produced by the Commission; the 'Disability Employment Package' was indeed published in 2022, following the involvement of the social partners, notably a hearing with the Commission in May 2022.[55] The Package envisages actions in six key areas

[50] 'She says, "You can't repeat the past." I say, "You can't? What do you mean, you can't? Of course you can." (Bob Dylan, *Summer Days*).

[51] Commission (n 15) 10. It should be noted here, that the experience of organised labour with the European Semester process has, to put it mildly, not been universally positive; see M Dawson, 'New Governance and the Displacement of Social Europe: the Case of the European Semester' (2018) 14(1) *European Constitutional Law Review* 191–209; P Copeland and M Daly, 'Social Europe: From "Add-on" to "Dependence-upon" Economic Integration' in A Crespy and G Menz (eds), *Social Policy and the Euro Crisis* (Palgrave Macmillan 2015) 140; E Achtsioglou and M Doherty, 'There Must Be Some Way Out of Here … The Crisis, Labour Rights and Member States in the Eye of the Storm' (2014) 20 *European Law Journal* 219–240.

[52] Commission (n 15) 11.

[53] Recitals 5 and 6 and Article 4 Commission Decision of 27.10.2021 setting up the group of experts "Disability Platform" COM(2021) 7591 final.

[54] Commission, 'Equality: All members of the new Disability Platform now known' (Press Release, 13 December 2021) available at <https://ec.europa.eu/social/main.jsp?langId=en&catId=1138&furtherNews=yes&newsId=10124>.

[55] Commission (n 16); Commission, 'Union of Equality: Strategy for the Rights of Persons with Disabilities 2021-2030 Joint Commission Services – Disability Platform Paper: Package to Improve Labour Market Outcomes of Persons with Disabilities (Disability Employment Package – "Employment Package")' available at <https://ec.europa.eu/social/main.jsp?catId=1597&langId=en> 2.

(strengthening the capacities of employment and integration services; promoting hiring perspectives through affirmative action; ensuring reasonable accommodation at work; retaining persons with disabilities in employment; securing vocational rehabilitation schemes in case of sickness or accidents; and exploring quality jobs in sheltered employment and pathways to the open labour market). These are obviously areas on which to concentrate, but what is to be the role of the social partners in this employment-focused package? They are to be 'involved' in its implementation, the deliverables of the Package are to be 'shared' with them, and they are to be invited to 'make full use of and help disseminate' these deliverables.[56] Their role, at least as set out in the Package, in other words, is vaguely defined and somewhat peripheral. It is also somewhat inconsistent. To focus on just one – albeit vital – area, the idea of 'reasonable accommodation' at work for person with disabilities; the Commission had noted in its review of the EDS that limited progress on the effective implementation of reasonable accommodation was an issue that had been recurrently reported, and that, under the actions of equality, raising awareness 'among *trade unions* on the concept of reasonable accommodation' was defined as only 'partially implemented'.[57] Yet, the action outlined in the current Package is to prepare guidelines for reasonable accommodation at work addressing *employers only*, and the reasonable accommodation guide published by the Commission in 2023 contains information provided directly by *employers only* at national level;[58] there is not much evidence of a consistent approach to involving both social partners here. As Atanasova points out:[59]

> effective implementation of inclusive employment policies requires proactive and coordinated work by various stakeholders at EU and national level, consistent actions, and awareness and a willingness to act *on the part of business, with the essential support of trade unions*. And although 'equality bodies and disability organisations have filled this gap [providing guidance on reasonable accommodation], their guidance remains largely informal'.[60]

3.3. Enforcement and the Role of Equality Bodies

A consistent failure of the law and policy to tackle discrimination against persons with disabilities in employment has been the lack of adequate enforcement.

[56] Commission (n 55) 2, 8.

[57] Commission (n 46) 84. Emphasis added.

[58] Commission, 'How to Put Reasonable Accommodation into Practice: Guide of Promising Practices' (Publications Office of the European Union 2021) available at <https://op.europa.eu/en/publication-detail/-/publication/2db3faa7-468f-11ec-89db-01aa75ed71a1/language-en>.

[59] A Atanasova, 'Narrowing the Employment Gap for People with Disabilities. The Need for Effective Policy Implementation' (ETUI Policy Brief, 30 January 2024) available at <https://www.etui.org/publications/narrowing-employment-gap-people-disabilities>. Emphasis added.

[60] I Anglmayer, 'Implementation of the Employment Equality Directive in Light of the UN CRPD European Implementation Assessment' (European Parliament 2020) available at <https://op.europa.eu/en/publication-detail/-/publication/de27f169-604d-11eb-8146-01aa75ed71a1/language-en> 49.

As noted above, trade unions can aid in securing individual and collective redress for victims of workplace discrimination, especially when they have legal standing under national law. Employers, and their representative organisations, obviously have a key role in ensuring the law is properly implemented and observed at the workplace. As Bell notes, however, a defining characteristic of EU non-discrimination legislation is the 'considerable weight that it places upon enforcement by *individual* complaints and litigation'.[61] It has been argued that effective enforcement of rights for persons with disabilities is unlikely if there is a reliance on an individual litigation model as opposed to some sort of model of collective redress.[62] Article 9(2) of the Employment Equality Directive allows 'associations, organisations or other legal entities which have, in accordance with the criteria laid down by their national law, a legitimate interest in ensuring that the provisions of this Directive are complied with' to engage on behalf or in support of a complainant, in any judicial and/or administrative procedure provided for the enforcement of obligations under the Directive. The social partners are not specifically mentioned here,[63] but as Olsson notes, given that social dialogue at national level is identified as a way to implement substantive parts of the Directive, and the requirement that it be promoted (Article 13 of the Directive), the social partners should be taken to be included *when relevant in the national context*.[64] The reference here to the national context is important for at least two reasons.

First, the national context very much determines how the issue of non-discrimination is framed. In some Member States, the issue of 'work accommodations' (reasonable accommodation) is characterised as a matter of occupational health and safety, rather than as an expression of a fundamental principle of equality; a mis-categorisation that conceals the social and political character of the accommodation (and that affects who will be the key actors in resolving disputes):

> changes resulting from work accommodations have the potential for wider social transformation. The prerogative to determine how a job is conceptualised and performed has traditionally rested with the employer, but the duty on employers to make work accommodations, if properly implemented, can disrupt this both symbolically and practically.[65]

Secondly, however, and returning specifically to the *narrower* issue of the involvement of social partners in the enforcement of non-discrimination law,

[61] Bell (n 2) 22. Emphasis added.

[62] S Benedi Lahuerti, 'Enforcing EU Equality Law Through Collective Redress: Lagging Behind?' (2018) 55 *Common Market Law Review* 783.

[63] See, by contrast, the corresponding provisions Article 3(2) Directive 2014/54/EU of the European Parliament and of the Council of 16 April 2014 on measures facilitating the exercise of rights conferred on workers in the context of freedom of movement for workers [2014] OJ L128/8.

[64] P Olsson, 'Collective Bargaining and Equal Treatment' in ter Haar and Kun (n 7) 396. Emphasis added.

[65] D Foster, M Masso and L Osila, 'Work Accommodations and Sustainable Working: The Role of Social Partners and Industrial Relations in the Employment of Disabled and Older People in Estonia, Hungary and Poland' (2021) 27(2) *European Journal of Industrial Relations* 153.

there is clearly a divergence in how this operates across the Member States. As Benedi Lahuerti puts it, whilst in theory, EU law creates rights for individuals *and* groups of individuals, which require the existence of effective enforcement mechanisms, in practice, 'through the combined effect of weak secondary law, national procedural competence and the ECJ requirement of minimum – not adequate – judicial protection' these may not really exist.[66] So, for example, while trade unions may initiate collective actions on behalf of workers in some countries (e.g. Spain), trade union 'class actions' are not permitted in other countries (e.g. Ireland).

A consistent focus of the Commission reports discussed above has been on the role of national equality bodies. The Employment Equality Directive does not provide for the creation of an equality body, but most Member States have established bodies that have competence in relation to the scope of the Directive.[67] The Commission notes that there are divergences between equality bodies in terms of their 'powers, structure, leadership, independence, resources and effectiveness', which in turn have led to 'an unequal enforcement of the Directive across Member States, as regards the level and nature of protection and the promotion of equality and awareness-raising among the general public and national institutions'.[68] Following its 2018 Recommendation on standards for equality bodies,[69] the Commission proposed a new Directive on the issue in late 2022.[70] The proposal points out that levels of discrimination remain high, public awareness about and knowledge of discrimination remain limited, and many 'equality bodies are not properly equipped, in terms of powers and resources, to assist victims effectively'.[71] The social partners, including representatives of employers at EU level, were consulted on the proposed legislation. However, the role of the social partners under the proposed Directive was very marginal indeed. Importantly, the explanation of Article 5 of the proposed Directive recognises that the existing protection mechanisms put forward by the Equality Directives are essentially retrospective

[66] Benedi Lahuerti (n 62) 807.

[67] Commission (n 41) 13. The exceptions cited are Spain, Finland, and Portugal.

[68] Ibid.

[69] Commission, 'Commission Recommendation of 22.6.2018 on standards for equality bodies' COM(2018) 3850 final.

[70] Commission, 'Proposal for a Council Directive on standards for equality bodies in the field of equal treatment between persons irrespective of their racial or ethnic origin, equal treatment in the field of employment and occupation between persons irrespective of their religion or belief, disability, age or sexual orientation, equal treatment between women and men in matters of social security and in the access to and supply of goods and services, and deleting Article 13 of Directive 2000/43/EC and Article 12 of Directive 2004/113/EC' COM(2022) 689 final. The final Directive was adopted in summer 2024; Council Directive (EU) 2024/1499 of 7 May 2024 on standards for equality bodies in the field of equal treatment between persons irrespective of their racial or ethnic origin, equal treatment in matters of employment and occupation between persons irrespective of their religion or belief, disability, age or sexual orientation, equal treatment between women and men in matters of social security and in the access to and supply of goods and services, and amending Directives 2000/43/EC and 2004/113/EC [2024] OJ L2024/1499.

[71] Ibid 3.

and individualised and do not include comprehensive preventive mechanisms.[72] However, there was no mention of the role of social partners in relation to the prevention, promotion and awareness strategies to be put in place under Article 5. Article 12 put an obligation on Member States to ensure that equality bodies have appropriate mechanisms in place to cooperate, within their respective fields of competence, with 'relevant public and private entities, including civil society organisations'.

The final Directive was adopted in May 2024. Article 5 now requires communication with 'relevant stakeholders, including the social partners', and the provision on cooperation (now Article 14) includes an explicit reference to the social partners. Moreover, Article 2 now states that the Directive is 'without prejudice' to the rights and prerogatives of the social partners (including with regard to representation in court proceedings), and the important role of the social partners in preventing discrimination is more explicitly recognised in the Recitals (see, particularly, Recitals 23, 26, and 28).

As with the various strategies and packages discussed above, therefore, and notwithstanding the strengthening of provisions from the original proposal, the role of the social partners under the Directive remains rather vague regarding the monitoring and enforcement of non-discrimination law in the workplace. This is very different to the enforcement role of the social partners (and trade unions in particular) in other areas of worker rights, and to the relationship between the social partners and labour inspectorates more generally. Principally, in the sphere of the enforcement of labour rights, what has been termed the 'enforcement of the EU's Social Dimension',[73] it is seen as a policy priority by the EU institutions that Member States ensure the involvement of the social partners in the design and formulation of national labour inspection plans and in the labour inspections themselves.[74] Pecinovsky and Lombardi conclude that 'traditional approaches purely based on the impact of direct inspections, workplace surveillance and civil/criminal penalties may no longer provide sufficient incentives or have a broad enough scope for an effective enforcement of compliance with the EU's Social Dimension'; they note that both the EU and the International Labour Organization have called for a number of changes in labour inspection regulation, including 'increasing collaboration between (labour inspectorates), other institutions and social partners'.[75] If this is true of labour rights enforcement more generally, why not of the specific area of employment discrimination (including against persons with disabilities)? Obviously, equality bodies have a wider remit than just employment-based discrimination, but insofar as they

[72] Ibid 18.

[73] M Hartlapp, 'Enforcing Social Europe through Labour Inspectorates: Changes in Capacity and Cooperation across Europe' (2014) 37(4) *West European Politics* 805–824.

[74] European Parliament Resolution of 14 January 2014 on effective labour inspections as a strategy to improve working conditions in Europe (2013/2112(INI)).

[75] P Pecinovsky and M Lombardi, 'Social Partners, Labour Inspectorates, and the Enforcement of the EU's Social Dimension' in ter Haar and Kun (n 7) 412, 429.

have a key role in relation to the monitoring, prevention, and enforcement of rules against discrimination at work, it is to this question we must turn in the concluding section.

4. Concluding Remarks: Locating the Golden Compass

This chapter takes the position that the social partners have had a relatively limited role in relation to the development of EU disability law, as it pertains to the issue of workplace discrimination. This might be seen as somewhat strange given that issues related to rights at work are, obviously, where the social partners play their principal part in the EU legal order, and that the Employment Equality Directive is really the cornerstone of ('hard') EU disability law. In the preceding sections, some reasons have been suggested as to why the social partners' impact has been limited. First, it was noted that the role of EU social dialogue (under the Treaties) is itself in a state of crisis; the social partners are finding it increasingly difficult to reach autonomous agreements, and the Commission has been accused of being, at best, lukewarm, and at worst, overtly hostile, towards the process in recent years. However, the picture is not entirely bleak. In June 2023, the Council adopted a new Recommendation on strengthening social dialogue in the EU.[76] Although reaction to this has been mixed,[77] it is, at the very least, a recognition by the EU institutions that the social dialogue process needs to be boosted. Additionally, support for sectoral collective bargaining among sectoral social partners at Member State level is a key focus of the Adequate Minimum Wage Directive.[78] Although the focus of debate on the Directive has been very much about the link between collective bargaining and wage levels,[79] more extensive sectoral collective bargaining at Member State level could and should include issues of non-discrimination at work, and the Directive emphasises the role of state public procurement (in Article 9) in supporting collective bargaining between the sectoral social partners; the use of public procurement to support accessibility and the recruitment of workers with disability is an important element of the Strategy 2021-2030.

The Strategy 2021-2030, the Employment Package, and the Directive on Equality Bodies have all been criticised above as giving the social partners a rather peripheral role. However, it *is* the case that the social partners (especially at EU level) were consulted on all of these measures. It is undoubtedly the case that the role of the social partners under the Directive has been strengthened as a result of this

[76] Council Recommendation of 12 June 2023 on strengthening social dialogue in the European Union [2023] OJ C1389/1.

[77] C Degryse, 'Social dialogue: still a fuzzy conversation' (22 February 2023) available at <https://www.socialeurope.eu/social-dialogue-still-a-fuzzy-conversation>.

[78] Adequate Minimum Wages Directive (n 24).

[79] L Ratti, E Brameshuber and V Pietrogiovanni (eds), *The EU Directive on Adequate Minimum Wages. Context, Commentary and Trajectories* (Hart 2024).

consultation. Furthermore, all the measures require some level of involvement of social partners at EU and/or national level; the extent of this, of course, depends on implementation, and the stance adopted by, *inter alia*, the EU institutions, Member State governments, and the equality bodies themselves. Nonetheless, this involvement *could* well turn out to be extensive. At which point, we must turn to an existential question: should the social partners be so involved in this area of regulation at all?

This volume adopts an '*actor-oriented* perspective' in pursuing its goal of extending understanding of how EU disability law has actually been shaped. This chapter has (mostly) focused on the limitations placed on the social partners by other actors; but what of their own agency? A number of criticisms have been levelled at the social partners in their traditional approach to the issue of equality at the workplace. Most literature has focused on the issue of gender equality, but, it is contended here, it applies equally in the sphere of disability rights. First, social partner organisations in Europe, and the negotiation processes between them, have been marked by their overwhelmingly homogenous gender, racial, and age profile (to which we can add an *absence* of persons with disabilities) and a correspondingly 'masculine' culture;[80] when the conflict between capital and labour becomes the key axis of confrontation, equality is often marginalised in negotiations.[81] There are two distinct, but interrelated points here. The first points to the make-up of social partner organisations themselves, traditionally male-dominated, and without representation from various marginalised groups in the workplace, including persons with disabilities.[82] Although this is slowly changing (at least in the field of gender),[83] it remains the case that the make-up of the social partner organisations have traditionally not reflected, particularly in their leadership, the diversity to be found amongst the workforce at large.

The second, following on from this, is that social partner organisations often do not see equality issues as part of their 'core business',[84] and instead focus attention on 'bread and butter' issues of pay, working time, and so on. Some research has suggested that equality commitments are often weaker in employer organisations than in trade unions, citing matters such as attempts by employers to block or water down issues,[85] or the extent to which the issue of workplace

[80] The pejorative phrase sometimes used to describe the historical make-up of trade unions is 'male, pale and stale'.

[81] Elomäki and Kantola (n 12) referring specifically to gender equality, but, as noted, the argument equally applies in the context of disability rights.

[82] T Weber, K Mantouvalou and D Bianchini, 'Social Partners and Gender Equality in Europe' (Eurofound 2014).

[83] European Trade Union Institute, 'ETUC Annual Gender Equality Survey 2019' available at <https://www.etuc.org/en/circular/etuc-annual-gender-equality-survey-2019>.

[84] Eurofound (n 36) 34.

[85] Elomäki and Kantola (n 12), citing R Guerrina and A Masselot, 'Walking into the Footprint of EU Law: Unpacking the Gendered Consequences of Brexit' (2018) 17(2) *Social Politics and Society* 319–330.

discrimination is high on the agenda of sectoral social partners.[86] If this were the case, it would certainly be of concern, given that it is generally accepted that a power imbalance in favour of employers can be observed.[87] Furthermore, this lack of attention to issues of equality at work may be bound up with a wider problem. Olsson points out that the European social dialogue-based directives on fixed-term and part-time work (noted above) have been criticised for including *weaker* non-discrimination principles than the other equal treatment directives.[88] To explain this (at least partly), she quotes Bell's argument that the provisions reveal:

> the absence of a shared vision concerning what equal treatment means within these instruments or why it should be applied to these categories. Whereas anti-discrimination legislation has, to some extent, been anchored in a framework of human rights protection, equal treatment within … labour law lacks this ethical compass.[89]

Given the absence of this compass, should we abandon the social partner journey? The concluding argument here is that we should not; rather we should redouble efforts to find the path to the ultimate destination of dignity and respect for the rights of persons with disabilities in the workplace. Ultimately, the social partners have a common interest in, and probably the best practical means of, promoting a workplace that is free from discrimination. Equal treatment and non-discrimination, both in the workplace and beyond, is one of the 'ideological principles underpinning the work of the trade union movement', and employers have a clear 'business case' to not place barriers to employment that limit access to skills and human capital, to fail to sufficiently reflect the profile of their customers, and to fail to pursue key goals in terms of Environmental, Social, and Governance principles.[90] Where a key problem identified in the effective enjoyment by persons with disabilities of their rights at the workplace is the lack of awareness among employers (of their obligations) and employees (of their rights), there must be a significant role for the social partners at EU, national, and sectoral levels. Where a lack of information and often unfounded fears about the high cost of hiring and retaining people with disabilities in employment (amongst individual employers) and low awareness of the concept of reasonable accommodation (amongst individual employers and workplace employee representatives) are severe impediments to the employment of persons with disabilities, there must be a significant role for the social partners at EU, national, and sectoral levels.[91]

[86] Eurofound (n 36) 34. However, the report highlights that this could be due to the fact that actions are more likely to be implemented at individual employer level, rather than by employer organisations.

[87] M Keune and P Pochet, 'The Revival of Social Europe: Is This Time Different?' (2023) 29(2) *Transfer: European Review of Labour and Research* 173–183.

[88] Olsson (n 64) 409.

[89] M Bell, 'The Principle of Equal Treatment: Widening and Deepening' in P Craig and G de Búrca (eds), *The Evolution of EU Law* (Oxford University Press 2011) 612.

[90] Eurofound (n 36) 33.

[91] Atanasova (n 59).

This will require EU and national legislators to rethink how social partners can be better engaged in the legal and policy processes that seek to protect the rights of persons with disabilities at work; however, it will also require a significant sea-change in the attitudes and approaches of the social partners themselves, and a widening of the conception of 'core' collective bargaining issues to include equality at the workplace for all workers. The workplace is often a microcosm of the society in which it is located; key actors there, just as in society at large, must try harder to locate the 'ethical compass' that guides a path through the looking glass.

12

The Role of Academics in Shaping EU Disability Law: Some Personal Reflections

LISA WADDINGTON*

1. Introduction

My interest in European disability law existed almost before what is now the European Union (EU) actually adopted such law. In 1993, I defended my Ph.D., entitled *More Disabled Than Others – The Employment of Disabled People within the European Community: An Analysis of Existing Measures and Proposals for Reform*, at the European University Institute.[1] Amongst other things, the thesis looked at a variety of soft law instruments, including programmes 'for' or 'to assist' disabled people, as well as a proposal for a Directive on the minimum requirements to improve the mobility and safe transport to work of workers with reduced mobility.[2] However, there was little hard law to discuss and analyse. Instead, I reflected on the kind of legislation the then European Community could adopt, including what seemed like a pipe dream at the time: a European directive prohibiting disability discrimination in the field of employment. I have subsequently, and only half jokingly, described my Ph.D. as a work of fiction, in that, at the time, there was no European disability law to analyse and no academic literature on the topic to study.

More than thirty years on from my defence, the situation has changed significantly. The Treaties, as well as the EU Charter of Fundamental Rights, explicitly refer to disability, and the EU has explicit competence to adopt legislation addressing the needs of persons with disabilities; there is a wide body of both mainstream

* This chapter is dedicated to the memory of Aart Hendriks. Aart was a pioneer in academic research on European and Dutch disability law and his work contributed to the development of EU law in this field.

[1] My PhD was subsequently published as L Waddington, *Disability, Employment and the European Community* (Maklu 1995).

[2] European Commission (Commission), 'Proposal for a Council Directive on Minimum Requirements to Improve the Mobility and the Safe Transport to Work of Workers with Reduced Mobility' COM(90) 588 final.

and disability-specific EU legislation that addresses disability, and that legislation includes a directive prohibiting disability discrimination in the field of employment (Directive 2000/78/EC);[3] there is an ever growing body of case law on disability from the Court of Justice of the European Union (CJEU);[4] the EU is a party to the United Nations Convention on the Rights of Persons with Disabilities (CRPD);[5] and disability law, and European disability law, has attracted the attention of a wide range of scholars, and is the subject of monographs and journal articles. Throughout that time, I have worked as an academic specialising in, *inter alia*, European disability law at Maastricht University, which is located conveniently closely to Brussels and the European institutions and civil society organisations based there. I have also worked with European Organisations of Persons with Disabilities (OPDs), including the European Disability Forum (EDF), the European Commission and representatives of other EU institutions. That work has frequently concerned the development of European disability policy and law. In 2004 I was appointed Professor of European Disability Law, and my Chair was established in cooperation with EDF.

This chapter concerns the role of academics in shaping EU disability law. However, it does not set out to reflect and analyse the role which academics play in general in shaping EU disability law. It is not based on semi-structured interviews or focus groups with academics and EU policy makers reflecting on the contribution of academics to EU disability law. Its goal is simpler and more personal than that – to reflect on my own 30 year plus experience as an academic working with EU policy makers, OPDs and fellow academics on projects and initiatives relevant to EU policy and law, as well as to present information on the experiences of some of the fellow academics who I work with and who were kind enough to discuss their thoughts with me, or provide me with other relevant information.[6] In that sense the chapter discusses EU law and policy in context and recognises the various ways in which academics can influence that law and policy.

I acknowledge that I was first hesitant to write such a contribution, since I prefer to reflect on legal and policy developments in my writing, rather than on my own experiences and that of colleagues and friends. However, I eventually decided to write this chapter after recalling reading and learning from an autoethnographic paper written by Stefan Trömel on the drafting history of the CRPD.[7]

[3] Directive 2000/78/EC of 27 November 2000 establishing a general framework for equal treatment in employment and occupation [2000] OJ L303/16.

[4] B Cortese, 'The Role of the Court of Justice of the European Union in Protecting Disability Rights' in this volume.

[5] Council Decision 2010/48/EC concerning the conclusion, by the European Community, of the United Nations Convention on the Rights of Persons with Disabilities [2010] OJ L23/35.

[6] I am grateful to the following colleagues who discussed their work with me or provided me with relevant information: Dr David Gutiérrez Colominas, Universitat Autònoma de Barcelona; Professor Rune Halvorsen, Oslo Metropolitan University; and Emeritus Professor Mark Priestley, Leeds University.

[7] S Trömel, 'A Personal Perspective on the Drafting History of the United Nations Convention on the Rights of Persons with Disabilities' in G Quinn and L Waddington (eds), *European Yearbook of Disability Law Volume 1* (Intersentia 2009) 115–138.

Stefan had attended all meetings of the Ad Hoc Committee in his capacity as director, and then advisor, to EDF, and his paper provided insights not found elsewhere in the literature. I hope that this chapter will be equally as interesting to some readers.

This chapter is structured as follows. Section 2 discusses the various ways in which academics can contribute to EU (disability) policy making and law in a generic sense. These are explored in more detail in the subsequent sections. Section 3 therefore explores the contribution of academics to EU disability law and policy through working with the European Commission, and in particular through the work of the Academic Network of European Disability experts (ANED) and its successor, the European Disability Expertise network (EDE). Section 4 looks at the contribution of academics to EU law through working with the following European institutions and bodies: the European Parliament (EP), the CJEU and the Member States holding the Presidency of the Council of the EU (Council). Section 5 considers the indirect influence that academics can have on EU disability law and policy through their collaboration with OPDs, including with EDF in particular. Section 6 considers the contribution of academics to EU disability law and policy through EU funded research programmes. In all cases, I do not claim to give a thorough overview of the work and actions of academics in these fields. Instead, I am largely reflecting on my own experience and that of the academics who I have worked with. Section 7 provides some concluding remarks.

2. Academics and 'Points of Entry' to Impact on EU Disability Law and Policy

Two of the core tasks of academics – namely teaching and research – can, at most, influence EU law and policy in very indirect and uncertain ways. It is possible that some of our students will go on to work for an EU institution, Member State government or civil society organisation – and I have indeed been privileged to see some of my students go on to work on EU disability law and policy at the EU or national level – or that our research will be read by legislators and policy-makers, and will influence their action in some way. Bruno De Witte has described the former trend in the following way:

> EU law scholars must necessarily take an interest in the activities of the legal practitioners in the EU institutions in order for their teaching to be relevant. Through their teaching, they diffuse legal knowledge to new generations of jurists and that knowledge will then indirectly affect the work of the EU institutions when some of the students become practitioners in the EU institutions.[8]

[8] B De Witte, 'Editorial Note: How Much Critical Distance in the Academic Study of European Law?' (2022) 18 *Croatian Yearbook of European Law & Policy* X.

However, in addition our work can have 'societal impact' in other ways, including when we collaborate with policy-makers and civil society. In the context of EU disability law and policy, a number of 'entry points' – or areas in which academics can interact with those influencing law and policy – have opened up over the past thirty years.

Firstly, following discussions over a number of years, the European Commission launched a tender for ANED in 2007, and the first network was established in December 2007.[9] This pan-European academic network supported the development of disability policy by collaborating with the Commission's Disability Unit. A network of this nature has continued to exist since then, with a number of short *hiatus* between calls for tenders, and with some changes being made when the network became EDE in 2020. As of 2014, the Commission has also funded the European Network of Legal Experts on Gender Equality and Non-Discrimination. Some work of this network is particularly relevant to disability equality law. Prior to 2014, two networks, one on non-discrimination generally, which included the disability strand,[10] and one on gender equality, existed. Going even further back, to the end of the last century, the Commission funded ground-specific networks, including a network on disability equality. From a disability perspective, the network provides the Commission with independent advice on disability discrimination in light of the Employment Equality Directive.[11] Both the ANED/EDE network and the Non-Discrimination network are funded via 'service contracts' to the Commission, in that the networks provide services tailored to meet the needs of the Commission. The Commission has also funded a number of other service contracts, often to produce reports on disability specific issues, over the years. In general, it is academics who carry out the research under these contracts, although other individuals, such as lawyers and members of human rights organisations, can also be involved. Funding for this kind of work, as well as academic research that is funded, for example, through the EU research funds, are both identified by Bruno De Witte as ways in which academics and (legal) practitioners in the EU institutions engage in 'co-production of EU law knowledge'.[12] I have been privileged to be a member of all the aforementioned networks since they were established.

Secondly, in addition to working with the Commission, academics also work with other EU institutions on disability law and policy issues. This can include providing advice to individual Members of the European Parliament (MEPs) and helping them to draft proposed amendments to legislation; speaking on disability at events organised by the Parliament; and drafting reports for Parliamentary

[9] ANED, 'About us' available at <https://www.disability-europe.net/about-us>.

[10] Established in 2004. European Equality Law Network, 'About us' available at <https://www.equalitylaw.eu/about-us>.

[11] For reasons of space, the work of the European Network of Legal Experts on Gender Equality and Non-Discrimination is not discussed further in this chapter.

[12] De Witte (n 8) VII.

Committees on disability-related issues. The work of academics may also be considered by Advocates General and Judges at the CJEU, although this is not always explicitly acknowledged in their Opinions or judgments. Moreover, Member States holding the Presidency of the EU Council may collaborate with academics when developing their programme or when organising events on disability.

Thirdly, academics can partner with OPDs. They can provide legal and other advice and contribute to documents that call for changes to EU law and policy. This advice can range from an analysis of the competences the EU has to act, to drafting a fully developed proposal for legislation that the OPD can present to legislators and campaign around.

Lastly, research projects funded by the EU under its flagship research fund, currently Horizon Europe, can also relate to disability and have the goal, *inter alia*, of producing recommendations for policy-makers. Such research is generally led and largely carried out by academics, although it can also involve OPDs and individuals with disabilities.

3. The European Commission and Academics – Academic Network of European Disability Experts and European Disability Expertise Network

Academics who worked on disability from a human rights perspective initiated discussions on the establishment of a European academic network on disability as early as 2000. At that stage the network was not envisaged as a tool to support policy-makers, but rather as a research network on disability studies that could also offer a Master programme. In 2000, a number of academics, including Mark Priestley of Leeds University, Jan Šiška of the Charles University in Prague, Geert Van Hove of the University of Ghent and Catherine Barral of the Centre Technique National d'Etudes et de Recherche sur les Handicaps et les Inadaptations in France met in the Belgian town of Blankenberg to discuss setting up such a network.[13]

The possibility of the European Commission funding such a network, with a view to the network providing support for the Commission's work, also arose, and some academics quietly lobbied for this. This did not initially receive support from the Commission's Disability Unit at the time. However, a new Head of the Unit, Johan Ten Geuzendan, was supportive of the idea, and eventually a call for the first ANED was launched in 2007. Mark Priestley had been connecting with academics working on disability from a human rights perspective across the EU over the previous years, and, following the publication of the call, many academics travelled to Leeds to discuss submitting a proposal. A successful application was subsequently made for what became the first iteration of ANED.

[13] For further reflections on these developments, see M Priestley, 'Why We Need to Work Together in the European Year of Disabled People' (2002) 17(7) *Disability & Society* 845.

As a result, since 2007, the Commission's Disability Unit has been supported by successive pan-European networks of academics and experts working on disability. This work was initially carried out by ANED and, since 2020, has been carried out by EDE. The network involves a small team of core/senior researchers and at least one academic or, occasionally, an individual researcher, from each Member State and three states in the European Economic Area (EEA) (Iceland, Liechtenstein and Norway). In the past, some of the countries that have association agreements with the EU (Montenegro, Republic of North Macedonia, Serbia, and Turkey),[14] as well as the United Kingdom,[15] have also been covered by the network. As of 2024, EDE covers the 27 EU Member States and Iceland, Liechtenstein and Norway. In many cases, teams of academic researchers based at a specific university carry out work for the network. In this way, the network has also supported the development of academic expertise on disability at the national level. Academics within the network come from a number of different disciplines including law, sociology, politics, education and the broad area of disability studies. The network also involves EDF and Age Platform Europe in carrying out its work, and representatives of these two bodies collaborate with the team of senior researchers.

The current core research team includes, Stefanos Grammenos of the Centre for European Social and Economic Policy; Professor Tamás Gyulavári of the Pázmány Péter Catholic University, Budapest; Professor Paula Pinto of the University of Lisbon; and myself. Until Brexit (2020), Professor Mark Priestley of the Centre of Disability Studies at Leeds University was the scientific director of the network. Other academics who have been members of the core research team in the past include Professor Anna Lawson of Leeds University and Professor Rannveig Traustádottir of the University of Iceland. Whilst the Commission issues tenders for the managing of the network every three to four years, the same consortium has run the network since its inception, although the individual academics involved has not remained the same.

The network has, amongst other things, provided the Commission with research and evidence to support the implementation of the European Disability Strategies (2010-2020 and 2021-2030) and the CRPD. The network also works on thematic reports every year. This thematic work results in a set of country reports on the specific theme, a report including relevant statistical data, and a synthesis report, which draws on the individual country reports, and includes recommendations, including regarding new policy and legislation, which are directed at various stakeholders, including the Commission. The country reports are based on a template or questionnaire designed by members of the core research team and approved by the Commission. While the core research team suggests themes for these reports, the decision on what to work on is made by the Commission,

[14] Academics from these additional states were only involved in ANED in the second and third funding periods.

[15] Academics from the United Kingdom who reported on the United Kingdom in country reports were involved in ANED until the first funding period after Brexit.

based on its own priorities at the time. For example, following the launch of the European Pillar of Social Rights (Pillar), ANED produced a report that explored how disability rights could be mainstreamed when taking action within the framework of the Pillar,[16] as well as country reports[17] and EU-wide quantitative indicators that relate to persons with disabilities regarding areas covered by the Pillar.[18] Reports addressing an inclusive labour market, the impact of COVID-19, digitalisation and digital transformation, living independently and being included in the community, as well as work on the European Semester were produced during the last EDE contract (2020-2023).

The work of ANED and EDE has impacted on policy-makers in a number of respects. For example, the Commission requested ANED's advice and research to inform its preparation of the European Disability Strategy 2010-2020,[19] and the Commission Staff Working Document that accompanies the Commission's Communication on the Strategy[20] contains 29 references to ANED's work. The aforementioned ANED report on the Pillar is referred to in the latest European Disability Strategy – Union of Equality: Strategy for the Rights of Persons with Disabilities 2021-2030[21] – to evidence that the quality of disability-related services to support independent living provided across and within Member States varies. This finding helped to justify a flagship initiative that involved the development of a specific framework for Social Services of Excellence for persons with disabilities and improving service delivery for persons with disabilities.[22] Four further references to ANED's work were contained in the Strategy.

The networks' work, and particularly the thematic reports, has also been drawn on in the development of key legislative initiatives, not least of all the European Accessibility Act. The Commission Staff Working Document presenting the Impact Assessment which contains a justification for the decision to propose the Act contains 21 references to ANED's research.[23] This research provided evidence

[16] ANED (edited by L Waddington and M Priestley), 'Mainstreaming Disability Rights in the European Pillar of Social Rights – a compendium' (2018) available at <https://www.disability-europe.net/search?searchword=Mainstreaming%20Disability%20Rights%20in%20the%20European%20Pillar%20of%20Social%20Rights%20%E2%80%93%20a%20compendium&searchphrase=all>.

[17] See general and focused country reports via ANED, 'Social Protection – Article 28 CRPD' available at <https://www.disability-europe.net/theme/social-protection?page=2> and <https://www.disability-europe.net/theme/social-protection?page=3>.

[18] ANED, 'Statistical Indicators – Article 31 CRPD' available at <https://www.disability-europe.net/theme/statistical-indicators>.

[19] Commission, 'European Disability Strategy 2010-2020: A Renewed Commitment to a Barrier-Free Europe' COM(2010) 636 final.

[20] Commission, 'Commission Staff Working Document accompanying the Communication from the Commission to the European Parliament, the Council, the European Economic and Social Committee and the Committee of the Regions, European Disability Strategy 2010-2020: A Renewed Commitment to a Barrier-Free Europe COM(2010) 636 final' SEC(2010) 1323 final.

[21] Commission, 'Union of Equality: Strategy for the Rights of Persons with Disabilities 2021-2030' COM(2021) 101 final.

[22] Ibid 8-9.

[23] Commission, 'Commission Staff Working Document, Impact Assessment, Accompanying the document Proposal for a Directive of the European Parliament and of the Council on the approximation of the laws, regulations and administrative provisions of the Member States as regards the accessibility

of how differences in national legal requirements and practices, including on accessibility, constituted a barrier to cross-border trade.[24] In addition the ANED report on *Disability Benefits and Entitlements in European Countries: Mutual Recognition and Exportability of Benefits*,[25] fed into the Commission's work,[26] which resulted in the proposal for a European Disability Card, which was adopted in October 2024.[27]

Network members have also presented findings of the thematic reports at meetings organised by the European institutions. For example, Mark Priestley presented ANED findings on employment and social inclusion at the European Day of Persons with Disabilities and to the European Economic and Social Committee in 2009, while I presented EDE's findings on digitalisation and EU policy at an event organised by MEPs and EDF in 2022.

In addition, ANED and EDE have carried out a number of other important tasks that feed into policy formulation and monitoring. Since the inception of the network, Stefanos Grammenos has had the task of compiling disability-related statistical data using raw material provided by Eurostat. ANED also developed and established the dot.com tool, which provides information on policy and legislation, in terms of action taken to implement the CRPD, across nine broad areas. It covers the obligations set out in the CRPD, as well as relevant legislation and policy in the thirty states coved by EDE.[28] The networks' work has also been used by the Commission to help it to mainstream disability equality in the European Semester process, including the use of annual Country Reports and the recommendations the Commission issues to Member States.[29] The network also

requirements for products and services' SWD(2015) 264 final. Bruno De Witte has noted that there are 'numerous references to academic work and impact assessment reports that accompany new proposals for EU legislation'. De Witte (n 8) IX.

[24] The relevant ANED reports were M Priestley, 'National Accessibility Requirements and Standards for Products and Services in the European Single Market: Overview and Examples' (2013) and A Lawson, 'Maximising the Impact and Effectiveness of Accessibility Measures for Goods and Services: Learning from National Experience, Synthesis Report for the Academic Network of European Disability Experts' (2013) available at <https://ec.europa.eu/social/main.jsp?catId=1540&langId=en>.

[25] L Waddington, 'Disability Benefits and Entitlements in European Countries: Mutual Recognition and Exportability of Benefits. A synthesis of evidence provided by ANED country reports and additional sources' (ANED 2010) available at <https://www.disability-europe.net/downloads/76-aned-2010-task-7-disability-benefits-and-entitlements-report-final-2>.

[26] The report 'Disability Benefits and Entitlements in European Countries: Mutual Recognition and Exportability of Benefits' was referred to when documenting the work that had been undertaken to fulfil a key action of studying the implications of a mutual recognition of disability cards and related entitlements identified in the European Disability Strategy 2010-2020. Commission, 'Staff Working Document, Progress Report on the implementation of the European Disability Strategy (2010-2020)' SWD(2017) 29 final 56. Twenty further references to ANED were made in this report.

[27] Directive (EU) 2024/2841 of the European Parliament and of the Council of 23 October 2024 establishing the European Disability Card and the European Parking Card for persons with disabilities [2024] OJ L2024/2841.

[28] Commission, 'About DOTCOM – The Disability Online Tool of the Commission' available at <https://ec.europa.eu/social/main.jsp?catId=1541&langId=en>.

[29] M Priestley, 'European Semester 2022 Mainstreaming Disability Equality' (European Commission 2022) and the related country reports prepared by EDE available at <https://ec.europa.eu/social/main.jsp?catId=1532&langId=en>.

produces an annotated review of EU law and policy that refers to disability.[30] The review provides a mechanism for monitoring and evaluating EU laws and policies that affect persons with disabilities. It contains summaries and details of laws and policies, and has been updated on a (quasi-)annual basis since 2008. The review has been drawn on by the Commission when reporting to the CRPD Committee on the action taken to implement the CRPD.[31]

It is important to emphasise that the Commission decides on the focus of the work of the network. It does this both by setting out general obligations and expectations in the tenders, which are launched very 3 or 4 years, and by liaising with the team of core researchers when agreeing on the annual work programme and individual tasks. This includes choosing topics for the two or three thematic reports that are written every year by the network. These decisions are made based on the Commission's priorities, including in the context of actions planned in the European Disability Strategy and upcoming legislative proposals. In this way, the work of the network feeds directly into the policy needs of the Commission and is carried out with a view to providing input and relevant information for upcoming legislative proposals. On occasion, this has also resulted in innovative research in fields that have not been the subject of significant analysis in the past, such as the work on how disability assessment is carried out.[32] ANED's work has also provided some of the deliverables listed under the Strategies.[33]

While the reports produced by ANED and EDE are generally published online, they remain the property of the Commission, and the Commission is not under any obligation to publish. The networks are described as independent,[34] but the work involves providing the Commission with services, and the Commission must approve all reports, and usually requests further information and makes comments on the first draft of the reports that it receives. Comments that could be interpreted as being critical of the EU, the Commission or Member States, must be supported by solid evidence. However, the Commission has also given permission for research carried out by members of the network to be developed and published in peer-reviewed journals, subject to the proviso that reference is made to the

[30] ANED, 'EU law and policy' available at <https://www.disability-europe.net/theme/eu-law-and-policy>.

[31] Commission, 'Initial report of States parties due in 2012 European Union' (3 December 2014) CRPD/C/EU/1 point 204.

[32] The relevant synthesis report for this topic is L Waddington, with contributions from M Priestley and R Sainsbury, 'Disability Assessment in European States, 2018' (ANED 2018). In addition, individual country reports were also written on this topic and are available at <https://www.disability-europe.net/country>.

[33] Commission, 'Catalogue of positive actions to encourage the hiring of persons with disabilities and combating stereotypes' (Publications Office of the European Union 2023) available at <https://ec.europa.eu/social/main.jsp?catId=738&langId=en&pubId=8570&furtherPubs=yes>.

[34] 'The aim of EDE is to collect, analyse and provide independent scientific data and information relating to national policies and legislation, linked with provisions at EU level, as well as providing information about the situation of persons with disabilities'. Commission, 'European Disability Expertise' available at <https://ec.europa.eu/social/main.jsp?catId=1532&langId=en>.

funding provided from the Commission for the original research and the inclusion of statements that the views expressed are those of the authors.[35]

Lastly, it is worth considering what the move from ANED to EDE signifies, since it involved more than simply a change of name. ANED was funded under the PROGRESS fund, which was generally used to fund individual projects and studies. ANED existed independently of the Commission and had its own website on which it published reports, following approval of the Commission. The reports were not published by the Commission, and, in that way, there was some distance between the work of ANED and the position of the Commission. As the reports of ANED began to attract more attention from Member States, which were concerned about critical findings, and OPDs, which quoted from ANED findings in their campaigning work, the Commission began to pay greater attention to ensuring the quality of the reports. This can be seen as reflecting the growing impact and significance of ANED's work. With the move from ANED to EDE, the Commission has taken the work of the network 'in house', and the EDE homepage is now found on the website of the Commission and the reports are officially published by the Commission.[36] The required approval for EDE reports – both in terms of acceptance by the Commission and regarding the decision to publish – now involves Commission officials at a more senior level than was the case under ANED. Moreover, the use of the network's work by the Commission is increasing. The move from ANED to EDE therefore arguably reflects the greater impact on European policy-makers that the network is having, and its work is certainly viewed in a more serious light than when ANED was initially established.[37]

4. Academics and Other EU Institutions

4.1. The Role of Academics in Policy Formulations

Academics also collaborate with other EU institutions in policy formulation. For example, I and other academics have worked with individual MEPs, such as Richard Howitt[38] and Kathalijne Buitenweg,[39] to help draft amendments to legislative

[35] M Priestley *et al.*, 'The political participation of disabled people in Europe: rights, accessibility and representation' (2016) 42 *Electoral Studies* 1–9; L Waddington and M Priestley, 'A human rights approach to disability assessment' (2020) 37(1) *Journal of International and Comparative Social Policy* 1–15; M Priestley and S Grammenos, 'How useful are equality indicators? The expressive function of 'stat imperfecta' in disability rights advocacy' (2021) 17(2) *Evidence & Policy* 209–226.

[36] Commission (n 34).

[37] I am grateful to Mark Priestley for discussing the significance of the move from ANED to EDE with me.

[38] Richard Howitt was a British MEP representing the Labour Party from 1994 until 2016 and was Chair of the Disability Intergroup.

[39] Katalijne Buitenweg was a Dutch MEP representing Green-Left from 1999-2003 and rapporteur for the Committee on Civil Liberties, Justice and Home Affairs on the proposal for a Council directive on implementing the principle of equal treatment between persons irrespective of religion or belief,

proposals that address disability equality. A further route for Parliamentarians to draw on academic expertise is through the Disability Intergroup, which brings together MEPs who have an interest in disability,[40] and I have spoken at events organised by the Intergroup in the past. In addition, the Petitions Committee of the EP commissions an annual study (or report) on a disability-related issue that is relevant to their work, as well as holding an annual workshop on the rights of persons with disabilities, at which the issue and related study is discussed with MEPs, as well as representatives from other key EU institutions, such as the Ombudsman and the Disability Unit of the Commission. The Committee established this practice after receiving the recommendation that it continue to hold dedicated hearings to promote disability issues in the first full study which it commissioned. That study concerned the implementation of the CRPD and was written by Mark Priestley, Meredith Raley and Gauthier de Beco.[41] The topics and studies covered since 2020 are the post-2020 European Disability Strategy,[42] the implementation of the 2015 Concluding Observations of the CRPD Committee by the EU,[43] Disability Assessment, Mutual Recognition and the EU Disability Card,[44] and Coping with the Cost-of-Living Crisis.[45]

Academics are also sometimes asked to speak on disability-related issues at events organised by other European institutions, such as the European Economic and Social Committee and the European Committee of the Regions.[46] In addition, Member States that hold the Presidency of the Council regularly organise meetings and conferences on disability as part of their work, and I and other academics have often spoken at these policy forum events.

I am also aware of at least one disability-related case in which a judge at the CJEU spoke to an academic in person before deciding on how to rule in the case. Aside from such anecdotal evidence, there is no way of knowing how often such

disability, age or sexual orientation in 2008. The report proposed amendments to the Commission's proposal. European Parliament, 'Report on the proposal for a Council directive on implementing the principle of equal treatment between persons irrespective of religion or belief, disability, age or sexual orientation' P6_TA(2009)0211.

[40] EDF, 'Disability Intergroup' available at <https://www.edf-feph.org/disability-intergroup/>.

[41] M Priestley, M Raley and G de Beco, 'The Protection Role of the Committee on Petitions in the Context of the Implementation of the UN Convention on the Rights of Persons with Disabilities' Study for the PETI Committee, Policy Department Citizens' Rights and Constitutional Affairs (European Parliament 2016).

[42] L Waddington and A Broderick, 'The Post 2020 European Disability Strategy' Study for the PETI Committee, Policy Department Citizens' Rights and Constitutional Affairs (European Parliament 2020).

[43] JC Smits, 'The Implementation of the 2015 Concluding Observations of the CRPD Committee by the EU' Study for the PETI Committee, Policy Department Citizens' Rights and Constitutional Affairs (European Parliament 2021).

[44] M Priestley, 'Disability Assessment, Mutual Recognition and the EU Disability Card, Progress and Opportunities' Study for the PETI Committee, Policy Department Citizens' Rights and Constitutional Affairs (European Parliament 2022).

[45] M Birthi, E Zólyomi, F Wohlgemuth and S Gjylsheni, 'Targeted measures for persons with disabilities to cope with the cost-of-living crisis' Study for the PETI Committee, Policy Department Citizens' Rights and Constitutional Affairs (European Parliament 2023).

[46] This has also been noted by Bruno De Witte. De Witte (n 8) IX.

interactions involving members of the Court and its Advocates General and academics happen, although such references and contacts are arguably all the more likely when academics have already foreseen the specific legal issues that arise in the case, and have addressed it in light of European (and national) legislation and case law in their writing. However, Bruno De Witte argues that the extensive legal knowledge of jurists at the Court 'diminishes the need to reach out for academic input to find solutions for their daily legal problems'.[47]

4.2. Academics as Law- and Policy-makers within EU Institutions

In addition to the contribution of academics to the work of the European institutions mentioned above, some academics have moved in and out of employment with the European institutions, or maintained an involvement in academia whilst working for the institutions, and have exerted an influence on EU disability law and policy in this way.[48] For example, Miguel Poiares Maduro, as Advocate General to the CJEU, wrote a very influential Opinion in the case of *Coleman*, which concerned alleged discrimination against a worker on the grounds of her association with her disabled son. The Opinion is notable both for its analysis and reflection on the principles underlying non-discrimination and equality legislation, and for its reference to academic literature. He advised the Court to hold that the directive 'protects people who, although not disabled themselves, suffer direct discrimination and/or harassment … because they are associated with a disabled person',[49] and the Court followed this approach in its judgment.[50] Miguel Poiares Maduro has held a number of academic and political appointments and, following his tenure as Advocate General, he became the director of the School of Transnational Governance and professor of law at the European University Institute, and continues to be a part-time professor at the School.[51] Another example of an employee of the EU institutions who has maintained academic links is Álvaro Oliveira who has worked on equality issues, including, at times, disability issues, at the Commission for many years. Álvaro Oliveira is an active member of the Berkeley Center on Comparative Equality and Anti-Discrimination Law,[52]

[47] Ibid.

[48] Ibid VIII.

[49] Opinion of Advocate General Poiares Maduro delivered on 31 January 2008 in Case C-303/06 *S. Coleman* v *Attridge Law and Steve Law* ECLI:EU:C:2008:61, para 25.

[50] Case C-303/06 *S. Coleman v Attridge Law and Steve Law* ECLI:EU:C:2008:415. For a discussion of the judgment and the Advocate General's Opinion see L Waddington, 'Case C-303/06, *S. Coleman* v. *Attridge Law and Steve Law*, Judgment of the Grand Chamber of the Court of Justice of 17 July 2008' (2009) 46(2) *Common Market Law Review* 665–681.

[51] See 'Luis Poiares Pessoa Maduro' available at <https://www.eui.eu/people?id=luis-poiares-pessoa-maduro>.

[52] See 'Berkley Center on Comparative Equality and Anti-Discrimination Law' available at <https://www.law.berkeley.edu/research/berkeley-center-on-comparative-equality-anti-discrimination-law/about-us/membership-list-2/#bb0-last-name-m-r-2/>.

and has regularly published in academic journals.[53] Lastly, Gerard Quinn, who has made a significant contribution to academic research on disability rights, worked as a temporary civil servant at the European Commission on equality and disability policy in the 1990s. Both Miguel Poiares Maduro and Álvaro Oliveira, as well as myself, studied at the European University Institute in the early 1990s.

5. Academics Working with Organisations of Persons with Disabilities, the European Disability Forum and the Disability Movement

OPDs at the European level, including EDF, but also organisations such as the European Network of Independent Living, campaign on important issues that concern, for example, Treaty amendments, proposing new legislation, and amendments to existing legislative proposals. Academics can help OPDs to formulate arguments that can be used to convince policy-makers to support the OPD's position, as well as drafting concrete proposals for legislative amendments.

As discussed by Coveney in this volume, EDF, as the umbrella organisation representing the interests of persons with disabilities in Europe, plays a leading role in coordinating policy work.[54] However, European based OPDs which existed before EDF became an independent organisation in 1996, have also made an important contribution. One of the most important examples of pre-EDF collaboration amongst European level OPDs concerns the *Invisible Citizens* report, and the related discussions and presentations that took place around the European Day of Disabled Persons on 3 December 1995.[55] While today the annual European Day is jointly organised by the Commission and EDF, and, on the whole, does not provide OPDs with a platform for campaigning for new legislation and policy, the event was somewhat different in the 1990s. In those early years of the European Day, the European Commission provided funding for the event, but it was organised wholly by European level OPDs, which had a great deal of freedom in deciding what to address and whom to invite to speak. The event was also not held within a building belonging to the EU institutions, as it is now.

[53] Á Oliveira, M De la Corte-Rodríguez and F Lütz, 'The New Directive on Work-Life Balance: Towards a New Paradigm of Family Care and Equality?' (2020) 45 *European Law Review* 295–323.

[54] C Coveney, 'The Role of the European Disability Forum and Disability Organisations in Shaping EU Disability Policy' in this volume.

[55] For information on the first European Day of Disabled People, which addressed similar issues, see M Priestley, 'We're all Europeans now! The social model of disability and European social policy' in C Barnes and G Mercer (eds), *The Social Model of Disability: Europe and the Majority World* (The Disability Press 2004) 21–23; M Bell and L Waddington, 'The 1996 Intergovernmental Conference and the Prospects of a Non-Discrimination Treaty Article' (1996) 25(4) *Industrial Law Journal* 328; Report of the First European Disabled People's Parliament, 3 December 1993 available at <https://disability-studies.leeds.ac.uk/wp-content/uploads/sites/40/library/DPI-first-European-Disabled-Peoples-parliament.pdf>. The article by Bell and Waddington also contains information on the 1995 and 1996 European Days of Disabled Persons at 328.

The 1995 European Day was jointly organised by Autism-Europe, ERC-WFMH (now Mental Health Europe) and ILSMH-European Association (now Inclusion Europe) and focused on the absence, or 'invisibility', of persons with disabilities in European Community legislation and, in particular, the Treaty which conferred competence on the EU to act. It addressed the need for a Treaty amendment and secondary legislation addressing disability discrimination as well as certain other issues. It explicitly called for an amendment to the non-discrimination clause in Article 6 of the Treaty on European Union (TEU), so that the relevant article referred to discrimination on the ground of disability, as well as the other 'invisible' grounds of race, sexual orientation and religion. Mark Priestly has argued:

> Since the campaign prioritised legal recognition, input was increasingly invited from those with legal expertise (particularly human rights lawyers). So, while the impetus arose from the self-advocacy of disabled people's organisations, grounded in a broadly 'social' approach, developments took an increasingly legalistic turn.[56]

A team of legal academics and practicing lawyers, with and without disabilities, made presentations on the status of persons with disabilities under EU law, and the need for Treaty amendments and further legislation to address disability discrimination, and other issues, over the two-day event in Brussels. Real life examples of disability discrimination were presented, and information on non-discrimination legislation adopted by EU Member States, and by States outside Europe, were discussed. There was a lot of interaction with the representatives of European and national OPDs who attended the event. Looking back on the event now, I realise how exciting, innovative and empowering it was. It also provided the basis for the long campaign to ensure the inclusion of a disability non-discrimination provision in the Amsterdam Treaty, which happened in 1997.

The *Invisible Citizens* report linked to the 1995 European Day was published on 7 December,[57] and had, as its sub-title, *Disabled Persons's Status in the European Treaties*. It had a foreword by Barbara Schmidbauer MEP, who was chair of the Disability Intergroup at the EP, and a preface by Theresia Degener, who was a lecturer and researcher at the Law Faculty of Goethe University Frankfurt at the time. The first chapter, which I wrote, was entitled *Disabled people are invisible in the Treaties – Why the European Treaties should contain a non-discrimination provision*. In a previous draft of the report, the chapter had been entitled *What 'added value' would European action have?*, and was the penultimate chapter of the report. The decision to move the chapter and to change its title was based on the fact that this chapter set out the key goal of the disability movement and contained arguments as to why such a Treaty amendment was necessary. It revealed how discrimination led to many persons with disabilities being denied rights associated

[56] Priestley (n 55) 22.

[57] EDF, 'Disabled Persons' Status in the European Treaties – Invisible Citizens' (European Day of Disabled Persons 1995, 7 December 1995) D/1995/7560/2.

with EU citizenship, including rights concerning free movement of persons; freedom to provide services and freedom to establish themselves in business in another Member State; freedom to receive services and freedom to purchase goods; and the right to vote. It also argued that there would be economic and social benefits of a binding European instrument that prohibited disability discrimination. Lastly, it submitted that a directive would be the most appropriate form for a binding disability non-discrimination instrument.[58]

Other chapters in the report covered real life experiences of disability discrimination experienced by people across Europe (by Colin McKay, Legal and Policy Adviser of ENABLE in Scotland); disability discrimination within the European institutions (by Aart Hendriks and myself); disability non-discrimination measures adopted by the Member States (containing brief reports from legal experts in Germany, Finland, France, the United Kingdom, Ireland, Sweden and Portugal); and international human rights instruments and disability anti-discrimination law in the United States, Australia and Canada (by Gerard Quinn and Aart Hendriks). The final chapter, by Horst Frehe (a German judge) and Theresia Degener, was entitled *The Way Forward*, and contained detailed and very specific proposals for Treaty amendments and their justifications. I and other legal experts also contributed to this chapter.

In retrospect, this event, and the *Invisible Citizens* report,[59] laid the ground for a concerted and effective campaign led by OPDs across Europe to secure important amendments to the Treaties at the Amsterdam Inter-Governmental Conference. Following the adoption of the Amsterdam Treaty, EDF, by now an independent organisation, published a *Guide to the Amsterdam Treaty*, which was written by the Legal Rights Working Group that I chaired. Nicola Bedlington, the Director of EDF at the time, contributed a chapter to the Guide that analysed the campaigning work that had been done. That chapter said the following about the 1995 European Day and the *Invisible Citizens* report:

> This report played a fundamental role in influencing opinions within the institutions, substantiating arguments in favour of a non-discrimination clause with sound legal analysis. The report moreover acted as a vital awareness-raising tool with disabled people's organisations. It rendered EU policy both accessible and relevant to disabled people across the Union, and put them on the centre stage.[60]

Following the publication of the report, and the establishment of EDF as an independent organisation, myself and other legal academics supported the campaign by providing legal and policy arguments in support of a Treaty amendment. A second report, entitled *How can disabled persons in the European Union achieve equal rights as citizens? The legal and economic implications of a non-discrimination*

[58] The chapter also published in an adapted form as L Waddington, 'The European Community and Disability Discrimination: time to address the deficit of powers?' (1997) 12(3) *Disability & Society* 465–479.

[59] EDF (n 57).

[60] EDF, 'Guide to the Amsterdam Treaty' (EDF, March 1996) Chapter 3 A.2.

clause in the Treaty of the European Union, was written to mark the 1996 European Day of Disabled Persons, which was organised by the same three OPDs as had organised the 1995 event. This report was written by a legal and economic expert working group that I chaired, and which also involved Aart Hendriks, Tom McCarthy and John Wall. The report was structured around 14 questions, such as '*What effect would the proposed non-discrimination clause have at the Community level?*'; '*Would a non-discrimination clause breach the principle of subsidiarity?*' and '*What would be the economic consequences of the proposed non-discrimination clause?*'. The report responded to points raised in the Reflection Group report, which defined the agenda for the Intergovernmental Conference. This report made it clear that the vast majority of Member States favoured amending the Treaty so as to include a non-discrimination clause that referred to disability, although there were some concerns regarding 'any disproportionate economic consequences which might derive from such a provision'.[61] At 23 pages, the 1996 report was considerably shorter than the *Invisible Citizens* Report, which exceeded 100 pages. The 1996 report, and the related European Day, supported the campaign to include a disability non-discrimination clause in the EU Treaty, but was not as groundbreaking as the *Invisible Citizens* report, given that it was far more technical in nature.

The work that needed to be carried out to secure the Treaty amendment was not only addressed to governments within the Member States but also to the national disability councils of the Member States. Ensuring that all national councils were on board was vital, as the Treaty could only be amended with the agreement of all Member States. This meant that each national council had to support such a change.

Whilst almost all national disability councils were supportive of such a Treaty amendment from the start, the Danish National Council was somewhat sceptical. The Danish disability movement had a good and cooperative relationship with the Danish government, and the establishment of mandatory disability non-discrimination provisions was not seen as the 'Danish way'. Instead, there was a preference for mainstreaming disability within law and policy. I travelled to Copenhagen as part of a small EDF delegation with the aim of persuading the Danish National Council to support the inclusion of the non-discrimination clause in the Treaty, or at least not to oppose it. This was a friendly meeting at which Danish representatives asked pertinent questions. Ultimately, while the National Council were not convinced of the value of such a clause for people with disabilities in Denmark, they decided to adopt a neutral stance towards their government representatives, and they did not oppose the inclusion of the clause. This was very important for the overall campaign.

[61] Reflection Group's Report (Messina 2 June 1995, Brussels 5 December 1995) available at <https://www.europarl.europa.eu/enlargement/cu/agreements/pdf/reflex1_en.pdf> para 39. Bell and Waddington (n 55) 328.

A further important element of the campaign was the support for national disability councils and staff of OPDs in Brussels to lobby on the Treaty amendment. I collaborated with colleagues in European level OPDs and the Disability Intergroup in the EP to provide training and advice on how to lobby at the national level. Diana Sutton, who was based in Barbara Schmidbauer's Office at the Parliament, and who was the coordinator of the Intergroup, played a key role in organising this training.

One such training took place in Brussels in the first half of 1996. We drafted a quiz that was intended to stimulate discussion between participants, rather than to test knowledge. Examples of questions included in quiz are:

> Which of the following groups are specifically mentioned in the EU Treaty (including in declarations and protocols)?
>
> a) Animals
> b) Disabled people
> c) Workers
> d) Fish
> e) Women
>
> (Answer – all mentioned, except for disabled people)

Another example is:

> What is the view of the following Member States on a non-discrimination clause on the ground of disability?
>
> a) UK – for – against – considering it
> b) Ireland – for – against – considering it
> c) Greece – for – against – considering it
> d) Italy– for – against – considering it
>
> (Answer: UK – against; Ireland – for; Greece – for; Italy – for)

The training also involved a role-playing session in which I and some colleagues from European level OPDs took on the role of sceptical government ministers or civil servants, and representatives of the national OPDs made arguments to convince us to support the Treaty amendment. We provided participants with lobbying tips and the lobbying drew on the reports produced for the European Day events in 1995 and 1996.

In April 1997, shortly before the Inter-Governmental Conference in Amsterdam at which the new Treaty was agreed on, I was part of an EDF delegation that met Michiel Patijn, the Dutch Secretary of State for Europe. We discussed the need for a non-discrimination clause and a number of other provisions in the new Treaty. Securing the support of the Netherlands was vital, as that country held the Presidency of the Council. Other members of the EDF delegation talked about the importance of prohibiting disability discrimination and the need to ensure persons with disabilities were recognised in the Treaties. The minister listened politely but did not really engage with us. I was the last to speak, and presented legal arguments in favour of including a non-discrimination clause in the Treaty, noting how this would extend rights that other EU citizens already had to persons with disabilities. I also discussed the need to include a reference to disability in the internal market provision (Article 100a TEC at the time). The minister, who had a legal training, asked me a number of questions and made sure his assistant made more detailed notes on this part of the discussion. We were successful in making our case in that the minister agreed that EU legislation setting common standards for goods can fail to take into account the needs of consumers with a disability, and he welcomed arguments that favoured including a reference to disability in Article 100a TEC. In fact, the Amsterdam Treaty did not make a disability-related amendment to the internal market provision, which was renumbered Article 95 TEC, but it did insert a non-binding declaration that read:

> The Conference agrees that, in drawing up measures under Article 95 of the Treaty establishing the European Community, the institutions of the Community shall take account of the needs of persons with a disability.

This wording mirrored the proposal that I had drafted for EDF, and which the disability movement had campaigned on.

As is well known, the Amsterdam Treaty also resulted in the inclusion of a non-discrimination clause, in what is now Article 19 TFEU, which provides the EU with the power to adopt legislation to combat discrimination on a variety of grounds, including disability. This led to the adoption in 2000 of the Employment Equality Directive, which prohibited disability discrimination in the field of employment and vocational training, as well as addressing discrimination on the grounds of religion or belief, sexual orientation and age.[62]

In the aftermath of the Amsterdam Treaty and the adoption of the Employment Equality Directive, I continued to have a close relationship with EDF and, at the end of 2004, EDF and Maastricht University collaborated to establish the Chair in European Disability Law to which I was appointed. In the years that followed, I worked closely with EDF, giving oral and written advice and input into policy documents, and often speaking at Board Meetings and Annual General Meetings. EDF secured funding for a capacity building project in the ten new Member States that joined the EU in 2004, and, along with a team involving EDF staff and representatives of EDF member organisations, I spoke at several national seminars which introduced representatives of OPDs in the new Member States to the EU, and EU disability law and policy in particular, and the work of EDF and its members. Between 2003 and 2006, I also coordinated Maastricht's involvement in a project funded by the European Commission to train disability activists in European and national non-discrimination law in

[62] A more in-depth discussion of both the *Invisible Citizens* campaign and the *1Million4Disability* campaigns is provided in C Coveney, 'A History of European Disability Campaigns: Civil society, social movements & opportunities for counterhegemonic change' (2023) Ph.D. thesis, University of Leeds (on file with author). See also C Coveney, 'The Role of the European Disability Forum and Disability Organisations in Shaping EU Disability Policy' in this volume.

which EDF members participated,[63] and a week's training for activists from EDF member organisations was held in Maastricht at the end of March 2004.

However, perhaps the biggest project I was involved in with EDF during this period was drafting a proposal for a directive to combat disability discrimination in fields beyond employment. As noted above, following the coming into force of the Amsterdam Treaty, the EU adopted the Employment Equality Directive. A second directive, the Racial Equality Directive, had also been adopted in the same year, and this had a broader material scope that covered social protection, including social security and healthcare, social advantages, education, and access to goods and services including housing, as well as employment and vocational training.[64] A similarly broad material scope applied to the legislation prohibiting discrimination on the basis of sex/gender. Civil society organisations that represented groups which were covered by the Employment Equality Directive urgently wanted the Commission to propose a new directive, which would extend the material scope of the protection from discrimination for the groups they represented to that found in the Racial Equality Directive. However, the Commission resisted this on the ground that the Member States needed time to transpose the 2000 directives.[65]

In an attempt to put pressure on the Commission to propose a new equality directive that specifically prohibited disability discrimination, EDF launched the 1Million4Disability campaign to collect a million signatures to a petition that called on the Commission to make such a proposal.[66] In doing so, EDF made use of the 'European Citizen's Initiative'[67] established in the Maastricht Treaty.[68] Alongside this initiative, I drafted a proposal for the directive that EDF wanted the Commission to propose, and which EDF intended to present to the institution. This work was done in close consultation with EDF members and the EDF Board. It was a tricky exercise because I had to balance the expectations of EDF members with what the EU was actually able to adopt based on the competences provided for in the Treaties. In that sense, the process was also a capacity building exercise for EDF, in that it involved detailed discussions of EU legal competences and reflections on how to address the legitimate aspirations of EDF members. I worked on the proposal for more than 12 months. In 2007, the proposed directive was submitted to the Commission.[69] As is now well known, in 2008 the Commission

[63] The project was funded under the EC Non-Discrimination Action Programme.

[64] Council Directive 2000/43/EC of 29 June 2000 implementing the principle of equal treatment between persons irrespective of racial or ethnic origin [2000] OJ L180/22.

[65] L Waddington, 'A Disabled Market: Free Movement of Goods and Services in the EU and Disability Accessibility' (2009) 15(5) *European Law Journal* 575–598.

[66] M Priestley, 'In Search of European Disability Policy: Between National and Global' (2007) 1 *Alter Revue européenne de recherche sur le handicap* 67.

[67] Article 11(4) of the Treaty on European Union (TEU) establishes the basic framework for that right, and Article 24(1) of the Treaty on the Functioning of the European Union (TFEU) sets out the general principles for a regulation defining concrete procedures and detailed conditions.

[68] A Davoli, 'European Citizens' Initiative – Factsheet' (European Parliament, October 2023) available at <https://www.europarl.europa.eu/factsheets/en/sheet/149/european-citizens-initiative>.

[69] Coveney (n 61).

did propose a Horizontal Equality Directive, covering disability and the other grounds addressed in the Employment Equality Directive, which went beyond material scope of the latter Directive.[70] There is no evidence that the disability-specific document I drafted for EDF influenced the Commission's proposal. To date, that proposal remains stalled in the Council, and it is currently the legislative proposal, which has remained unadopted for the longest period of time without being withdrawn. EDF continues to advocate for its adoption, although this no longer has the priority which it once had.

EDF's collaboration with academics has changed over the years. In the first decade or so following its establishment as an independent organisation (up until 2006 approximately), EDF worked with a Legal Rights Working Group, which was made up of academics and other individuals with a legal background, such as practitioners. I chaired the Working Group and other members included, at various times, Aart Hendriks (at the time a lecturer in health law at the University of Amsterdam, and now Professor at the University of Leiden), Gerard Quinn (at the time Director of Research at the Irish Law Reform Commission and now Emeritus Professor at the University of Galway) and Shivaun Quinlivan (University of Galway). Other members, who worked as practitioners, included the late Sir John Wall (judge in the UK), Helga Stevens (who later became a MEP) and Angel Ballesteros (a consultant from Spain). The Legal Rights Working Group gave EDF advice on issues relevant to campaigning and, in the first years of EDF, produced policy documents and reports/papers to support campaigns. For example, following the adoption of the Amsterdam Treaty, members of the Legal Rights Working Group wrote a 50 page guide to the new Treaty from a disability perspective.[71] This reflected the dual role of the Legal Rights Working Group, which involved both support for influencing policy, as well as capacity building for EDF members.

EDF now works with academics to a lesser degree than in the past. Arguably this is partly the result of having an expanded in-house staff who have diverse expertise, and because it carries out a lot of work through various committees, which are made up of representatives of its member organisations. At times, it works with legal practitioners who offer their services on a pro bono basis. Occasionally, EDF puts out a small tender for a report and related presentation on a specific topic which relates to its campaigning work, and academics are sometimes awarded these. In 2021, for example, I wrote, on a pro bono basis, a report for EDF on the prohibition of disability discrimination with regard to healthcare in the EU.[72] EDF also collaborates with academics in research projects funded by the European Commission and receives so many invitations for such

[70] Commission, 'Proposal for a Council Directive on implementing the principle of equal treatment between persons irrespective of religion or belief, disability, age or sexual orientation' COM(2008) 426 final.

[71] See Independent Living Institute, 'Guide to the Amsterdam Treaty' available at <https://www.independentliving.org/docs3/edf98.html>.

[72] EDF, 'Our Work on Health Policy' available at <https://www.edf-feph.org/health-policy/>.

collaborations that it has to prioritise and be selective in deciding which partnerships to work with. Many of EDF's members also collaborate with academic teams on such projects to co-produce research which can be of relevance to European policy makers amongst others.

6. Academics and Research Projects Funded by the EU

The EU funds a substantial amount of academic and applied research through its multi-year flagship research funds. The current programme, Horizon Europe, covers the period 2021-2027. Its most recent predecessors were the 7th Framework Programme for Research (FP7) (2007-2013) and Horizon 2020 (2014-2020). While much of the funded research that explicitly addresses the situation of persons with disabilities is medically or technologically oriented, the programmes have also sometimes funded research that embraces a rights-based approach to persons with disabilities.

The calls for tender under these programmes are often rather broad and, unlike ANED and EDE service contracts mentioned above, researchers have a substantial amount of freedom in developing and implementing the projects. In some cases, the calls for tender that result in disability-related research being funded may explicitly focus on persons with disabilities; however, a reference to persons with disabilities may only be made in passing in the call, or no reference may be made at all. Nevertheless, such calls can still result in the funding of research projects that explicitly include a disability dimension. Exerting direct influence on EU law is unlikely to be an explicit goal or 'deliverable' of a funded project. However, projects may influence EU law or policy in some ways in the long term, for example by training individuals who go on to work for the EU institutions or producing academic research which influences policy makers.

I have been involved in two Marie Skłodowska-Curie doctoral training networks that involved EU funding for networks of Early-Stage Researchers (ESRs)/PhD researchers working on disability-related research. Both the Disability Rights Expanding Accessible Markets (DREAM) and the Disability Advocacy Research in Europe (DARE) training networks were coordinated by the University of Galway in Ireland, and the two networks trained almost thirty ESRs in total. The ESRs have gone on to hold academic positions within and outside Europe, to work for civil society organisations in the field of disability, and to work for consultancy organisations based in Brussels. As far as I am aware, none of the ESRs who received training via DREAM or DARE have gone on to work for European institutions or national governments of the Member States, although some of them have collaborated with ANED, EDE and the Network on Gender Equality and Non-Discrimination law.

Another relevant EU-funded research project is European Research Agendas for Disability Equality (EuRADE), which was funded under FP7, and which ran across 2008 and 2009.[73] The project was coordinated by EDF, while Maastricht University and Leeds University were partners. Myself and Mark Priestley were academic Principal Investigators (PIs) on the project. The project built the capacity of European OPDs to participate in the FP7 research programme and other relevant research initiatives. It also enabled EDF and its member organisations to identify and articulate the research priorities of OPDs; provided research knowledge and skills to OPDs; and identified opportunities for larger scale collaboration between OPDs and European research partners in priority areas.

While EuRADE did not aim to influence EU law directly, it did seek to influence the EU policy-makers who determined the priorities for EU funded research, and to ensure greater funding for disability-related research in future calls under FP7. The EuRADE team and participating OPDs gave briefings on the research priorities of persons with disabilities and how disability could be mainstreamed more effectively into EU calls. One briefing was hosted by the European Parliament in Brussels in 2009, and involved contributions from MEPs and European Commission officials who were responsible for FP7 calls in Social Science, and Science in Society, as well as Eurostat. The EuRADE team also published recommendations to the European Commission on how to align EU research and development funding with the social model and human rights-based approach to disability, and how to promote greater participation by OPDs in research. Following the conclusion of EuRADE, the FP7 Social Sciences and Humanities work programme included a call for a disability specific research project based on the social model of disability, which involved funding of 2.5 million euros.

The project that was funded as a result of this disability specific call was 'DISCIT – Making persons with disabilities full citizens'. It was coordinated by Professor Bjørn Hvinden, Bettina Uhrig and Rune Halvorsen of the Norwegian Social Research (NOVA), which was an institute at Oslo and Akershus University College of Applied Sciences. I was a member of the Advisory Board and an expert consultant on the project. The project ran from 2013 until 2016, and involved ten organisations, including six universities, two research institutes and two civil society organisations. It provided new knowledge about disability policies in European countries and identified the actions policy-makers and stakeholders needed to take to enable persons with disabilities to exercise active citizenship and participate fully in society on an equal basis with others. Its work resulted in eight Policy Briefings.[74] While the researchers behind DISCIT carried out research on the project's impact on policy-makers at the end of the project, they found that it was too soon for the project to have had an effective and wide impact on European policies. This research was based on interviews with researchers involved in the

[73] Commission, 'European Research Agendas for Disability Equality – EURADE' available at <https://cordis.europa.eu/project/id/217783/en>.

[74] See DISCIT Final Report – Executive Summary (Oslo, 20 April 2016) available at <https://oda.oslomet.no/oda-xmlui/bitstream/handle/20.500.12199/6499/DISCIT-Final-Report-Executive-Summary-April-2016.pdf?sequence=1&isAllowed=y>.

project. However, they did note that some of the members of the research team had been invited to be part of the High-Level Group on Disability, a committee made up of European and national experts that helped to define the strategies for implementing the CRPD in Europe. They also found that achieving (quick) policy impact required support measures, for example documents based on research findings that are immediately intelligible to policy-makers.

7. Concluding Remarks

The past 30 years has seen the emergence of a cohort of academic researchers working on European disability law and policy. These researchers work in a variety of disciplines and across different European states. This has been stimulated by the development of EU disability law and policy, which has provided the 'subject' for such researchers to work on, as well as by the availability of EU funding, which supports disability-related research. The pan-European academic research network EDE, and its predecessor ANED, have come to play an increasingly important role in the development of EU disability policy, and this is reflected by the Commission taking 'in house' EDE research outputs, which are now published on the Commission's homepage, and the more critical assessment and closer monitoring of EDE's research outputs by the Commission. Moreover, EDE is now used to provide some of the deliverables related to the European Disability Strategy, as well as laying the ground work for some of the European Commission's initiatives and contributing to the EU's reporting process to the CRPD Committee.

At the same time, a wide-ranging and highly professional set of organisations that represent the interests of persons with disabilities, at both a national and European level, has emerged. These parallel developments have facilitated research collaborations in which academics and representatives of OPDs have co-produced research through projects funded through the European Commission and, in some cases, this research has concerned policy issues. Moreover, in the past European OPDs have worked closely with, in particular, legal academics to develop arguments to support lobbying in favour of Treaty amendments and secondary legislation that recognises the rights of persons with disabilities including, significantly, the right to equality and non-discrimination. This has proved a powerful combination, which reached its highpoint in the 1990s during the successful campaign to secure the inclusion of a non-discrimination clause addressing disability in the Amsterdam Treaty. Collaboration between European OPDs and academics in terms of campaigning and lobbying has declined since then as OPDs have acquired more expertise in-house. However, there remains an open dialogue between researchers and OPDs, particularly in terms of collaboration on research projects.

13

The Role of the Committee on the Rights of Persons with Disabilities in Nudging the EU Towards Compliance with the UN Convention on the Rights of Persons with Disabilities

SILVIA FAVALLI

1. Introduction

The adoption of the 2006 United Nations Convention on the Rights of Persons with Disabilities (CRPD or 'the Convention') and the annexed Optional Protocol marked a paradigm shift in the protection of the rights of persons with disabilities worldwide.[1] For the first time, the CRPD recognised persons with disabilities as autonomous rights holders and provided a comprehensive enumeration of all their human rights, without distinguishing or being limited to particular categories of civil or social rights.[2] It was received by the international community with unprecedented enthusiasm, as it attracted a high number of signatories and ratifications within a short period of time. At the time of writing, the CRPD has been ratified by 191 states and signed by 164;[3] the Optional Protocol has been ratified by 94 states and signed by 105.[4] The CRPD was also the first human rights treaty open for signature and ratification by regional integration organisations (RIOs).

[1] The UN Convention on the Rights of Persons with Disabilities (CRPD) was adopted, along with its Optional Protocol, by the UN General Assembly (UNGA) on 13 December 2006; UNGA, UN Convention on the Rights of Persons with Disabilities, 13 December 2006, in force 03 May 2008, UN Doc A/RES/61/106.

[2] Among many others, see I Bantekas, MA Stein and D Anastasiou (eds), *The Convention on the Rights of Persons with Disabilities: A Commentary* (Oxford University Press 2018); A Broderick and D Ferri, *International and European Disability Law and Policy. Text, Cases and Materials* (Cambridge University Press 2019).

[3] Status on 26 June 2024. Data available at <https://treaties.un.org/Pages/ViewDetails.aspx?src=TREATY&mtdsg_no=iv-15&chapter=4&clang=_en>.

[4] Status on 26 June 2024. Data available at <https://treaties.un.org/Pages/ViewDetails.aspx?src=TREATY&mtdsg_no=IV-15-a&chapter=4&clang=_en>.

The Convention entered into force on 3 May 2008. Shortly thereafter, on 3 November 2008, the Committee on the Rights of Persons with Disabilities (CRPD Committee) was elected during the initial Conference of State Parties (COSP) for monitoring and implementing the CRPD.[5] In this capacity, the CRPD Committee examines State Parties' periodic reports on the implementation of the Convention (reporting procedure),[6] adopts views on individual complaints (complaints procedure),[7] and conducts inquiries on systematic breaches of the Convention (inquiry procedure) under the Optional Protocol.[8] It also provides authoritative guidance about the interpretation of the provisions of the Convention through the adoption of General Comments.

Against this background, this contribution purports to investigate the role played by the CRPD Committee in orientating the EU toward more effective compliance with the Convention and in influencing the development of EU disability law. The chapter, which is informed by doctrinal legal methodology, provides a systematic exposition of the activities performed by the CRPD Committee in relation to EU disability law, examines the relationship between the legal actions taken by the EU as a response, explains areas of difficulty and predicts future developments deriving from the normative and doctrinal analysis performed. In particular, it analyses the 'dialogue' between the CRPD Committee and the EU, especially the European Commission (Commission), during the monitoring process to point out the extent to which the recommendations provided by the Committee have contributed to shape recent EU disability law and policy. Moreover, it explores how the authoritative guidance provided by the CRPD Committee on the interpretation of the provisions of the Convention is gradually influencing the application of the CRPD in the EU legal order.

Following this introduction, section 2 provides a brief overview of the CRPD Committee's functions, while section 3 outlines the CRPD Committee's monitoring in relation to the European Union in 2014 and 2023. Section 4 analyses the pivotal role played by the CRPD Committee in the development of critical initiatives by the Commission. More precisely, while section 4.1. evaluates the impact of the CRPD Committee on the EU legal framework acting in its capacity as a monitoring body, section 4.2. addresses the (less evident) influence of the CRPD Committee in the EU legislative process and on the European Ombudsman's decisions and section 5 concludes.

[5] MA Stein and JE Lord, 'Monitoring the Convention on the Rights of Persons with Disabilities: Innovations, Lost Opportunities, and Future Potential' (2010) 32 *Human Rights Law Quarterly* 689, 690.

[6] Article 35 CRPD.

[7] Article 2 Optional Protocol.

[8] Article 6 Optional Protocol.

2. The Committee on the Rights of Persons with Disabilities: An Overview

The CRPD Committee is composed of 18 members 'of high moral standing and recognized competence and experience',[9] who serve in their individual capacity and do not represent State Parties. They are elected from a list of persons nominated by the State Parties from among their nationals at meetings of the COSP. In 2024, for the first time, the EU, acting as a regional integration organisation, presented a candidate: Inmaculada Placencia Porrero. She has been elected as a member of the CRPD Committee during the seventeenth session of the Conference of the State Parties to the Convention that took place from 11 to 13 June 2024. Notably, during the election, geographical distribution, gender and legal systems representation, and involvement of experts with disabilities were taken into due consideration. The CRPD Committee members are elected by State Parties for a four-year term, with the possibility of being re-elected once. They benefit from the facilities, privileges and immunities of experts on mission for the United Nations (UN).

The monitoring and implementing system of the CRPD only partially resembles one of the other core UN human rights treaties.[10] The most distinctive feature is the key role played by non-governmental organisations (NGOs), in particular organisations of persons with disabilities (OPDs), in the work of the CRPD Committee, which can 'invite the specialized agencies and other competent bodies as it may consider appropriate to provide expert advice on the implementation of the Convention in areas falling within the scope of their respective mandates'.[11] This provision enables the CRPD Committee to receive and consider information and shadow reports submitted by civil society organisations, in order to ensure the active involvement of persons with disabilities and their representative organisations during the monitoring process, in accordance with Article 4(3) CRPD.

The CRPD Committee, in its capacity as a monitoring body, receives a detailed report from the State Parties every four years on the measures taken to give effect to its obligations under the Convention and on the progress made in that regard (reporting procedure).[12] Upon an initial examination of the reports, the CRPD Committee provides general recommendations on the reports received; State Parties have the opportunity to respond to such observations.[13] Following such a dialogue, the CRPD Committee adopts its Concluding Observations, which are

[9] Article 34(3) CRPD.
[10] Stein and Lord (n 5) 689.
[11] Article 38 CRPD.
[12] Article 35 CRPD.
[13] Article 36(1) CRPD.

transmitted to the State Party concerned and which are also made public. Under the follow-up procedure, the CRPD Committee can require State Parties to focus on specific issues of concern and to provide written information on the adoption of the measures recommended. Starting from the reports submitted in 2014, the CRPD Committee offered State Parties the possibility to opt for a simplified reporting procedure. Under this procedure, the CRPD Committee prepares a List of Issues prior to the State Party submitting its report, and the answers of the State Party to the list constitute its periodic report.[14]

The CRPD Committee, on foot of the Optional Protocol, acts as a quasi-judicial body when it considers individual communications from or on behalf of a person or group of persons claiming to be victims of a violation of the Convention by a State Party (complaints procedure).[15] The State Party concerned must have recognised the CRPD Committee's competence by ratifying the Optional Protocol, otherwise the communication is not receivable. As a result of this procedure, the CRPD Committee adopts views that contain two categories of recommendations. On the one hand, it requests the State Party to take special measures regarding the victim of the violation under exam. On the other hand, it makes recommendations related to the implementation of the relevant provisions of the CRPD and the prevention of similar violations. When the CRPD Committee receives reliable information that indicates that the rights contained in the Convention are being systematically violated, it shall invite the State Party concerned to submit observations on the information that it has collected regarding the systematic violations alleged (inquiry procedure).[16] This procedure can be launched only against a State Party that, at the time of signature, ratification, or accession of the Optional Protocol, did not declare that it does not recognise the competence of the CRPD Committee.[17] Although the CRPD Committee's decisions under the individual communication and investigation procedures are not legally binding, it seems evident that State Parties intended to grant a certain authority to the CRPD Committee's views when ratifying the Optional Protocol. Hence, with the ratification they expressed their intention to recognise the competence of the treaty body to examine allegations of breaches of the CRPD, to specify its normative content and to promote compliance to the obligations enshrined. Besides, the peer pressure of other State Parties might function as a further deterrent against disregard of the CRPD Committee's findings.[18]

Further, the CRPD Committee, in its capacity as an expert treaty body, provides authoritative guidance about the provisions of the Convention through

[14] Committee on the Rights of Persons with Disabilities (CRPD Committee), 'Report of the CRPD Committee on its tenth session, 2–13 September 2013' CRPD/C/10/2.

[15] Article 2 Optional Protocol.

[16] Article 6 Optional Protocol.

[17] Article 8 Optional Protocol. To date, similar reservations have been deposited by Guinea Bissau and Syrian Arab Republic.

[18] T Stavrinaki, 'Optional Protocol to the Convention on the Rights of Persons with Disabilities' in Bantekas, Stein and Anastasiou (n 2) 1249.

the publication of General Comments. The leading role of expert treaty bodies in interpreting the provisions of human rights treaties emerges both from international practice and legal scholarship.[19] It was also confirmed by the International Court of Justice in relation to the considerable interpretative relevance of the Human Rights Committee.[20] In addition, a pronouncement of an expert treaty body shall be considered relevant in the treaty interpretation under the provisions of the Vienna Convention on the Law of Treaties of 1969 (VCLT).[21] Namely, it might give rise to a subsequent agreement or subsequent practice by parties under Article 31(3)(a) and (b) VCLT, relevant to frame the context of the treaty, or to a subsequent practice under Article 32 VCLT, relevant as a supplementary means of interpretation.[22]

Overall, the CRPD Committee, performing its functions as a monitoring body, a quasi-judicial body and an expert treaty body, plays a key role in orientating the State Parties towards a progressively increasing compliance to the obligations enshrined in the CRPD.

3. The EU under the Scrutiny of the Committee on the Rights of Persons with Disabilities

The Commission signed the CRPD on 30 March 2007. In November 2009, the Council adopted a Decision concerning the conclusion of the CRPD by the former European Community (EC).[23] It approved the CRPD and authorised the deposit, on behalf of the former EC, of the instrument of formal confirmation of the Convention, with the Secretary-General of the United Nations. On 23 December 2010, the former EC concluded the Convention, which came into effect for the EU on 22 January 2011. However, the EU has not yet ratified the Optional Protocol.

[19] Among many others, International Law Association (ILA), 'Final Report on the Impact of Findings of the United Nations Human Rights Treaty Bodies, Report of the Seventy-First Conference' (ILA 2004); G Ulfstein, 'Treaty Bodies and Regimes' in DB Hollis (ed), *The Oxford Guide to Treaties* (Oxford University Press 2012) 440; G Ulfstein, 'Individual Complaints' in H Keller and G Ulfstein (eds), *UN Human Rights Treaty Bodies. Law and Legitimacy* (Cambridge University Press 2012) 92; C Tomuschat, *Human Rights Between Idealism and Realism* (Oxford University Press 2008) 220; HJ Steiner, P Alston and R Goodman, *International Human Rights in Context: Law, Politics and Morals* (Oxford University Press 2008) 215.

[20] Ahmadou Sadio Diallo (*Republic of Guinea v Democratic Republic of the Congo*), Merits, Judgment, ICJ Reports 2010, para 66.

[21] UN Treaty Series, Vienna Convention on the Law of Treaties 1969, 23 May 1969, in force since 27 January 1980, Vol 1155 Nos 18222-18232.

[22] UNGA, 'Report of the International Law Commission, Seventieth Session (30 April–1 June and 2 July–10 August 2018)' Supplement No 10, A/73/10 11, under the topic 'Subsequent agreements and subsequent practice in relation to interpretation of treaties'.

[23] Council Decision of 26 November 2009 concerning the conclusion, by the European Community, of the United Nations Convention on the Rights of Persons with Disabilities [2010] OJ L23/25.

After the ratification, the Convention became an integral part of the EU legal framework. In the hierarchy of norms of EU law, the CRPD is situated below the provisions of the Treaties, but above secondary legislation.[24] As a result, the Court of Justice of the EU (CJEU) must interpret EU secondary legislation in a manner consistent with the Convention.[25]

For the purpose of EU law, the CRPD qualifies as a mixed agreement under Article 216(2) Treaty on the Functioning of the European Union (TFEU), meaning that part of the international agreement falls within the scope of the competences of the EU and part falls within the scope of the powers of the Member States.[26] This reflects the fact that the EU has no power to adopt legislation in some of the areas covered by the Convention and shares powers with the Member States in other ones. In compliance with Article 44(1) CRPD, the EU deposited, along with the instrument of formal confirmation, a Declaration of Competences to declare the extent of its competence with respect to matters governed by the Convention.[27]

3.1. The 2014 EU's First Report

As a party to the Convention, under Article 35 CRPD, the EU is subject to the scrutiny of the CRPD Committee in its capacity as monitoring body.[28] The EU's first report on the implementation of the CRPD was published on

[24] D Ferri, 'The Conclusion of the UN Convention on the Rights of Persons with Disabilities by the EC/EU: A Constitutional Perspective' in L Waddington and G Quinn (eds), *European Yearbook of Disability Law* (Intersentia 2010) 47, 64; D Hosking, 'The Convention on the Rights of Persons with Disabilities and the European Union' in C O'Mahony and G Quinn (eds), *Disability Law and Policy: An Analysis of the UN Convention* (Clarus Press 2017) 448.

[25] The necessity to interpret EU secondary law in a manner consistent with the CRPD is well-established in the CJEU disability case law. See Joined Cases C-335/11 and C-337/11 *HK Danmark, acting on behalf of Jette Ring v Dansk almennyttigt Boligselskab and HK Danmark, acting on behalf of Lone Skouboe Werge v Dansk Arbejdsgiverforening, acting on behalf of Pro Display A/S*, in liquidation ECLI:EU:C:2013:222, paras 29-32; Case C-363/12 *Z v A Government Department and The Board of Management of a Community School* ECLI:EU:C:2014:159, para 72; Case C-354/13 *Kaltoft v Municipality of Billund* ECLI:EU:C:2014:2463, para 29; Case C-356/12 *Wolfgang Glatzel v Freistaat Bayern* ECLI:EU:C:2014:350, para 70; Case C-406/15 *Milkova* ECLI:EU:C:2017:198, para 48; Case C-395/15 *Mohamed Daouidi v Bootes Plus SL, Fondo de Garantía Salarial, Ministerio Fiscal* ECLI:EU:C:2016:917, para 41; Case C-270/16 *Carlos Enrique Ruiz Conejero v Ferroser Servicios Auxiliares SA and Ministerio Fiscal* ECLI:EU:C:2017:788, para 23; Case C-824/19 *TC, UB v Komisia za zashtita ot diskriminatsia VA* ECLI:EU:C:2021:862, para 26. L Waddington, 'The European Union' in L Waddington and AM Lawson (eds), *The UN Convention on the Rights of Persons with Disabilities in Practice: a Comparative Analysis of the Role of Courts* (Oxford University Press 2018) 132.

[26] M Chamon, 'Negotiation, Ratification and Implementation of the CRPD and its Status in the EU Legal Order' in D Ferri and A Broderick (eds), *Research Handbook on EU Disability Law* (Edward Elgar 2020) 52, 56.

[27] Annex II Council Decision of 26 November 2009 concerning the conclusion, by the European Community, of the United Nations Convention on the Rights of Persons with Disabilities [2010] OJ L23/25.

[28] AM Lawson, 'The European Union and CRPD: Complexities, Challenges and Opportunities' in V Della Fina, R Cera and G Palmisano (eds), *The United Nations Convention on the Rights of Persons with Disabilities: A Commentary* (Springer 2017) 61, 66.

5 June 2014.[29] The CRPD Committee subsequently drew up a List of Issues concerning the information contained in the EU's report in April 2015,[30] and the EU responded to those issues in June 2015.[31] At the end of this interinstitutional dialogue, in October 2015, the CRPD Committee issued its Concluding Observations, which highlighted a series of gaps in EU policy and provided numerous recommendations.[32]

The first paragraphs of the report briefly highlight strengths and good practices. In particular, the Committee noted the EU's practice to include the rights of persons with disabilities in the financing of its external actions and to add disability in priority areas relevant to Sustainable Development Goals, and appreciated the EU's commitment to the Sendai Framework for Disaster Risk Reduction 2015-2030.[33]

Overall, the CRPD Committee identified a series of gaps in EU policy and provided forty-two recommendations. First, it called upon the EU to ratify the Optional Protocol to the Convention. Then, in general terms, it urged the EU to conduct a comprehensive review of its legislation and to develop a strategy for the implementation of the Convention, with the allocation of a budget. It also urged a regular update of the Declaration of Competence and of the list of instruments to include recently adopted instruments and instruments that may not specifically refer to persons with disabilities, but that are relevant to persons with disabilities.

In particular, the report recommended the adoption of different legislative acts, such as, *inter alia*, the proposed Horizontal Equality Directive,[34] the (now adopted) European Accessibility Act (EAA),[35] as well as appropriate measures to ensure that persons with disabilities deprived of their legal capacity can exercise their rights. It suggested that the EU strengthens the monitoring of the use of the European Structural and Investment Funds so as to ensure that they are used strictly for the development of projects of deinstitutionalisation and not for the redevelopment or expansion of institutions, and it urged the implementation of the European Mobility Card, to ensure the mobility of persons with disabilities around the EU. The CRPD Committee also encouraged the EU to ratify and implement the Marrakesh Treaty (in force since January 2019).

[29] European Commission (Commission), 'Consideration of reports submitted by States parties under article 35 of the Convention. Initial report of States parties due in 2012. European Union' (3 December 2014) CRPD/C/EU/1.

[30] CRPD Committee, 'List of Issues in relation to the initial report of the European Union' (15 May 2015) CRPD/C/EU/Q/1.

[31] Commission, 'Replies of the European Union to the List of Issues' (8 July 2015) CRPD/C/EU/Q/1/Add.1.

[32] CRPD Committee, 'Concluding Observations on the initial report of the European Union' (2 October 2015) CRPD/C/EU/CO/1.

[33] Ibid para 4.

[34] Commission, 'Proposal for a Council Directive on implementing the principle of equal treatment between persons irrespective of religion or belief, disability, age or sexual orientation' COM(2008) 426 final.

[35] Directive (EU) 2019/882 of the European Parliament and of the Council of 17 April 2019 on the accessibility requirements for products and services (EAA) [2019] OJ L151/70.

Furthermore, the CRPD Committee expressed its concerns regarding the austerity measures adopted by Member States of the EU, which resulted in cuts in social services with adverse effects on the adequate standard of living of persons with disabilities.[36]

3.2. The 2023 EU's Combined Reports

In the Concluding Observations on the EU's first report, the CRPD Committee scheduled the submission of the subsequent combined second and third periodic reports according to the simplified reporting procedure, adopted in September 2013.[37] The purpose of this new mechanism, which must be accepted by the interested contracting party, is to facilitate the reporting process and to provide more targeted and efficient reports. Under this procedure, in March 2022 the CRPD Committee prepared a List of Issues prior to the EU submitting its report;[38] the replies to the list sent in April 2023 constitute the EU's periodic report.[39]

The resulting document is a detailed report of the measures taken by the EU for the implementation of the CRPD, also in relation to the recommendations issued by the CRPD Committee in its previous Concluding Observations. Significantly, in the first part of the document, the EU provides a non-exhaustive list of measures adopted to monitor the timeframe and the allocation of budget for the implementation of the Strategy for the Rights of Persons with Disabilities 2021-2030 (Strategy 2021-2030).[40] Moreover, it clarifies that disability mainstreaming 'takes place during legislative provisions and when preparing new legislative proposals'.[41] As discussed in other chapters, working groups of disability experts participate in the legislative activities of the EU institutions, such as the Inter-Service Group on Disability and the Task Force on Equality in the Commission,[42] the CRPD Network in the European Parliament, and the Human Rights Working Party in the Council.[43]

The report also addresses the role of the EU in ensuring the effective implementation and enforcement of EU legislation relevant to persons with

[36] CRPD Committee (n 32) para 67.

[37] Ibid para 94; CRPD Committee, 'Report of the Committee on the Rights of Persons with Disabilities on its tenth session, 2-13 September 2013' (13 May 2014) CRPD/C/10/2 para 4, Annex IV.

[38] CRPD Committee, 'List of Issues prior to submission of the second and third periodic reports of the European Union' (20 April 2022) CRPD/C/EU/QPR/2-3.

[39] Commission, 'Combined second and third reports submitted by the European Union under article 35 of the Convention, pursuant to the optional reporting procedure, due in 2021' (4 May 2023) CRPD/C/EU/2-3.

[40] Ibid paras 5-20.

[41] Ibid para 4.

[42] ES Krolla, 'The Role of the European Commission in Shaping EU Disability Law: A Driver with the Brakes Put On?' in this volume.

[43] In the European Parliament, the CRPD Network, an Inter-Committee working group has the task of reviewing and screening documents and activities to raise awareness of possible disability-related issues, and to promote a coordinated approach for the political mainstreaming of disability rights

disabilities by Member States. This is mainly composed of directives that leave it to the national authorities of each Member State to determine the form and the methods they use to incorporate the directive into their national law. The Commission monitors the correct transposition of directives through implementation documents and implementation strategies; if Member States fail to transpose the directive, it can launch an infringement procedure. This is the case, for instance, of the infringement procedures launched in April 2023 for delays in the transposition of the European Accessibility Act.[44]

In subsequent sections, the report analyses in a detailed fashion EU law and policy interventions adopted in relation to specific rights (Articles 5-30) and obligations (Articles 31-33) of the Convention. The implementation of every Article of the CRPD is thoroughly discussed, in response to the comprehensive List of Issues of the CRPD Committee. Hence, the document mainly entails reporting on the implementation of the CRPD Committee's recommendations included in the Concluding Observations to the initial report. In this vein, numerous European civil society organisations, organisations of persons with disabilities, independent monitoring mechanisms, national human rights institutions and other stakeholders have contributed to the periodic reporting of the EU[45] and have submitted their reports to the CRPD Committee directly for consideration.[46] Moreover, new developments that have occurred on the protection of persons with disabilities in situations of risk and humanitarian emergencies, such as the impact of the COVID-19 pandemic and the Russian war against Ukraine, have been analysed.

As a result of the monitoring process, the CRPD Committee will adopt Concluding Observations in relation to the EU's combined reports in one of its future sessions. Nonetheless, due to the tight schedule of the CRPD Committee, such a document is not expected to be adopted by the end of 2024.

4. The Committee on the Rights of Persons with Disabilities as a Monitoring Body: Measuring its Impact on EU Disability Law

Significantly, the very first point raised by the CRPD Committee in the 2021 List of Issues refers to the lack of ratification of the Optional Protocol.

and implementation of the Convention. Moreover, in the Council, the Human Rights Working Party supports the Council's decision-making process that deals with all human rights aspects.

[44] In April 2023, the Commission decided to open an infringement procedure by sending letters of formal notice to Denmark (INFR(2023)2014), Estonia (INFR(2023)2013), and Italy (INFR(2023)2015) for failing to fully transpose EU rules on accessibility of products and services for persons with disabilities (EAA).

[45] Commission (n 39) para 1. Krolla (n 42).

[46] The list of information from civil society organisations submitted for consideration to the CRPD Committee are available at <https://tbinternet.ohchr.org/_layouts/15/treatybodyexternal/TBSearch.aspx?Lang=en&CountryID=218&TreatyID=4&DocTypeID=14>.

In 2008, the Commission issued a proposal for a Council Decision on the EU accession to the Optional Protocol.[47] Pursuant to Article 218(8) TFEU, the Council shall act unanimously when the agreement covers a field for which unanimity is required. This is the case of the ratification of the Optional Protocol, as it fits within the scope of Article 19 TFEU, referring to the power of the EU to take action to combat discrimination based, *inter alia*, on disability. Currently, the Council proposal is pending as not all Member States are parties to the Optional Protocol and thus the unanimous consensus required can not yet be achieved. As stated in its Strategy 2021-2030,[48] the Commission will re-examine the EU's ratification of the Protocol on the basis of the progress of accession by Member States to the Optional Protocol.

Despite the fact that the CRPD Committee cannot act in its quasi-judicial functions with regard to the EU, it does play a pivotal role in orientating the EU toward more effective compliance with the Convention acting in its capacities as, respectively, an expert and a monitoring body.

In the context of the monitoring processes performed in 2014 and 2023, the CRPD Committee recommended the adoption or modification of numerous legislative acts to the EU. Considering the 'legislative activism' that has characterised the period between the adoption of the EU's first report in 2014 and the EU's combined reports in 2023, with the adoption of several acts on web accessibility and digital equality, it seems quite evident that the CRPD Committee's activity as a monitoring body has played an important role in supporting the prioritisation of disability policies at the EU level.

Ensuring access to digital information and communication tools, i.e. web accessibility, has been a priority of the EU disability policy agenda for the last two decades.[49] But the most important initiatives follow (at least chronologically) the release of the CRPD Committee's Concluding Observations. The Web Accessibility Directive (WAD)[50] establishes mandatory accessibility requirements for websites and mobile applications of public sector bodies. As recommended by the CRPD Committee in its Concluding Observations to the 2014 initial report of the EU,[51] the WAD is now complemented by the European

[47] Commission, 'Proposal for a Council Decision concerning the conclusion, by the European Community, of the Optional Protocol to the United Nations Convention on the Rights of Persons with Disabilities' COM(2008) 530 final.

[48] Commission, 'Union of Equality: Strategy for the Rights of Persons with Disabilities 2021-2030' (Strategy 2021-2030) COM(2021) 101 final.

[49] D Ferri and S Favalli, 'Web Accessibility for People with Disabilities in the European Union: Paving the Road to Social Inclusion' (2018) 8 *Societies* 40. In relation to the renewed commitment to accessibility in the Strategy 2021-2030, see D Ferri, 'The New Strategy for the Rights of Persons with Disabilities 2021-2030' (*EU Law Live*, 5 March 2021) available at <https://eulawlive.com/op-ed-the-new-strategy-for-the-rights-of-persons-with-disabilities-2021-2030-a-step-forward-in-realising-the-human-rights-model-of-disability-by-delia-ferri/>.

[50] Directive (EU) 2016/2102 of the European Parliament and of the Council of 26 October 2016 on the accessibility of the websites and mobile applications of public sector bodies [2016] OJ L327/1.

[51] CRPD Committee (n 32) para 29.

Accessibility Act (EAA),[52] which regulates the accessibility of key products and services in the internal market, such as computers, smartphones, tablets, TV sets, banking ATMs and services, payment terminals, e-books and e-readers, e-commerce websites, mobile applications and ticketing machines. In addition, the recast European Electronic Communications Code,[53] which sets an EU-level legal framework to coordinate national legislation on electronic communications networks and services, includes measures to ensure equal access and choice of electronic communication services. Further, the amended Audiovisual Media Services Directive,[54] which contains an explicit reference to the CRPD,[55] requires Member States to ensure the accessibility of audiovisual media services.[56] Furthermore, copyright legislation implemented under the Marrakesh Treaty,[57] the so-called Marrakesh Directive and Regulation,[58] was adopted in 2017 to facilitate access to print works, including e-books, in formats adapted for persons who are blind, visually impaired or those who have difficulties reading.[59] Subsequently, in 2018, the EU also ratified the Marrakesh Treaty, as recommended by the CRPD Committee during the first monitoring process.[60]

Moreover, web accessibility and digital equality have also been mainstreamed in the EU policy initiatives adopted to boost Europe's digital transformation of the

[52] EAA. For a critical analysis of the EAA under the lens of the model of 'inclusive equality', see A Broderick, 'The European Accessibility Act: A Paradigm of Inclusive Digital Equality for Persons with Disabilities?' in C Ricci (ed), *Building an Inclusive Digital Society for Persons with Disabilities New Challenges and Future Potentials* (Pavia University Press 2019) 19.

[53] Directive (EU) 2018/1972 of the European Parliament and of the Council of 11 December 2018 establishing the European Electronic Communications Code (Recast) [2018] OJ L321/36.

[54] Directive (EU) 2018/1808 of the European Parliament and of the Council of 14 November 2018 amending Directive 2010/13/EU on the coordination of certain provisions laid down by law, regulation or administrative action in Member States concerning the provision of audiovisual media services (Audiovisual Media Services Directive) in view of changing market realities [2018] OJ L303/69.

[55] Recital 22 Audiovisual Media Services Directive.

[56] Article 7 Audiovisual Media Services Directive.

[57] Marrakesh Treaty to Facilitate Access to Published Works for Persons who are Blind, Visually Impaired, or otherwise Print Disabled [2018] OJ L48/3. In February 2018, the Council adopted Decision (EU) 2018/254 of 15 February 2018 on the conclusion on behalf of the European Union of the Marrakesh Treaty to Facilitate Access to Published Works for Persons who are Blind, Visually Impaired, or otherwise Print Disabled [2018] OJ L48/1 approving the conclusion of the Marrakesh Treaty. As a result, the EU became a party to the Treaty on 1 January 2019.

[58] In 2014, the EU signed the Marrakesh Treaty to facilitate access to Published Works for Persons who are Blind, Visually Impaired, or otherwise Print Disabled, and started the transposition process into EU law. Directive (EU) 2017/1564 on certain permitted uses of certain works and other subject matter protected by copyright and related rights for the benefit of persons who are blind, visually impaired or otherwise print disabled [2017] OJ L242/6 and Regulation (EU) 2017/1563 on the cross-border exchange between EU and non-EU countries of accessible format copies of certain works for the benefit of persons who are blind, visually impaired or otherwise print-disabled [2017] OJ L242/1 have been adopted to facilitate the access to print works, including e-books, in formats adapted for persons who are blind, visually impaired or those who have difficulties reading.

[59] For an in-depth analysis of this topic, see C Sganga, 'Disability in EU Copyright Law' in Ferri and Broderick (n 26) 201.

[60] CRPD Committee (n 32) para 71.

economy and society,[61] as advised by the CRPD Committee.[62] The Digital Services Act,[63] which sets out responsibilities and a system of accountability and transparency for providers of intermediary services, requires the drawing up of codes of conduct at the Union level 'to promote full and effective, equal participation, by improving access to online services that, through their initial design or subsequent adaptation, address the particular needs of persons with disabilities' and 'pursue the objective of ensuring that those services are accessible'.[64] Moreover, the newly adopted Regulation on Artificial Intelligence ('the AI Act'),[65] which constitutes the first attempt to lay down harmonised binding rules on AI ever drafted, also tackles the prevention and mitigation of the adverse outcomes of AI systems on fundamental rights, including the rights of persons with disabilities. The AI Act adopts a layered risk-based approach, as it classifies AI into categories and imposes obligations on AI systems on the basis of their level of potential or intrinsic harm.[66] Accordingly, it prohibits AI harmful practices that are a threat to people's safety and rights because of the unacceptable risk they create. In particular, it expressly bans those AI systems that, *inter alia*, exploit any of the vulnerabilities of a specific group of persons due to their disability.[67] It is recognised that AI systems may exploit vulnerabilities of a person or a specific group of persons due to their disability, intended within the meaning of the EAA,[68] and that the characteristics of persons with disabilities should be duly taken into consideration when implementing AI tools intended to interact with natural persons or to generate content.[69] Nonetheless, the AI Act still presents some criticalities. It does not require any accessibility obligations for the placing in the market of AI systems; it only encourages businesses to adopt codes of conduct in which voluntary accessibility commitments would be included.[70]

[61] Commission, 'Shaping Europe's digital future' COM(2020) 67 final.

[62] CRPD Committee (n 32) para 83.

[63] Regulation (EU) 2022/2065 of the European Parliament and of the Council of 19 October 2022 on a Single Market for Digital Services and amending Directive 2000/31/EC (Digital Services Act) [2022] OJ L277/1. For a critical position on the lack of binding measures to ensure accessibility for persons with disabilities in the Digital Services Act, see the European Disability Forum (EDF), 'Inclusive and Accessible Digital Services and Platforms. Position Paper on the Digital Services Act and the Digital Markets Act' (March 2021) available at <https://www.edf-feph.org/content/uploads/2021/03/DRAFT-EDF-Position-DSA-DMA-2021.pdf>.

[64] Article 47 Digital Services Act.

[65] Regulation (EU) 2024/1689 of the European Parliament and of the Council of 13 June 2024 laying down harmonised rules on artificial intelligence and amending Regulations (EC) No 300/2008, (EU) No 167/2013, (EU) No 168/2013, (EU) 2018/858, (EU) 2018/1139 and (EU) 2019/2144 and Directives 2014/90/EU, (EU) 2016/797 and (EU) 2020/1828 (Artificial Intelligence Act – AI Act) [2024] OJ L2024/1689.

[66] A Zarra, S Favalli and M Ceron, 'Artificial Intelligence and Disability Rights' in A Quintavalla and J Temperman (eds), *Artificial Intelligence and Human Rights* (Oxford University Press 2023) 248, 258.

[67] Article 5(1)(b) AI Act.

[68] Recital 29 AI Act.

[69] Recital 132 AI Act.

[70] Article 131 AI Act. The absence of binding accessibility requirements for AI systems has been fiercely criticised by civil disability representative organisations, which strongly affirm that lack of

Significantly, as noted by Krolla in her chapter, in 2023, the Commission was particularly active in the presentation of legislative proposals related to critical disability issues that emerged from the List of Issues published by the CRPD Committee in 2021, referring to legal capacity and supportive decision-making, access to justice for victims of crimes, and liberty of movements. In fact, it seems likely that the CRPD Committee's monitoring process gave impetus to the finalisation of the proposals.

For instance, in May 2023, the Commission promoted the adoption of uniform rules to address the current gaps and inconsistencies in the legal protection of vulnerable adults who, due to an impairment or insufficiency of their personal faculties, are not in a position to protect their interests in cross-border situations.[71] It presented a proposal for a Regulation on jurisdiction, applicable law, recognition and enforcement of measures and cooperation in matters relating to the protection of adults,[72] along with a proposal for a Council Decision that obliges all Member States to become or remain parties to the 2000 Protection of Adults Convention.[73] This discipline is supposed to partially supersede and complement the 2000 Hague Convention on the International Protection of Adults[74] among Member States[75] and it is composed of private international law norms; it does not affect Member States' national substantive laws concerning the protection of adults. More precisely, it addresses the conflicts of laws issues that are related to the growing cross-border mobility of people in the EU, where vulnerable adults or their representatives may need, for instance, to manage assets or real estate in another country, seek medical care abroad, or relocate to a different EU country. This legislative initiative is even more significant as the regulation of legal capacity regimes is generally considered a matter of national competence, as demonstrated by the high numbers of reservations to Article 12 CRPD.[76] This applies also in the context of EU law, in which the status or legal capacity of natural persons remains an exclusive competence of Member States. Nonetheless, the proposal has been

accessibility can risk the life and well-being of persons with disabilities. EDF, 'EDF position on the European Commission's White Paper on Artificial Intelligence – A European Approach to Excellence and Trust' (9 June 2020) available at <https://www.edf-feph.org/content/uploads/2021/02/edf_position_on_ec_ai_white_paper_06.2020.pdf>.

[71] CRPD Committee (n 38) para 13, point b; Commission (n 39) paras 104-105.

[72] Commission, 'Proposal for a Regulation of the European Parliament and of the Council on jurisdiction, applicable law, recognition and enforcement of measures and cooperation in matters relating to the protection of adults' COM(2023) 280 final.

[73] Commission, 'Proposal for a Council Decision authorising Member States to become or remain parties, in the interest of the European Union, to the Convention of 13 January 2000 on the International Protection of Adults' COM(2023) 281 final.

[74] Hague Conference on Private International Law, 35. Convention on the International Protection of Adults, 13 January 2000, in force since 1 January 2009.

[75] P Franzina, 'Un nuovo diritto internazionale privato della protezione degli adulti: le proposte della Commissione europea e gli sviluppi attesi in Italia' (2023) 59(3) *Rivista di diritto internazionale privato e processuale* 519. For a critical position, see EDF, 'Re: Proposed EU Regulation on the protection of adults. Opinion' available at <https://www.edf-feph.org/content/uploads/2023/11/Legal-Opinion-Vulnerable-Adults.pdf>.

[76] S Favalli, *Disabilità, diritti umani e diritto internazionale* (Giuffrè 2021) 232.

harshly criticised for its inadequacy with the CRPD by the UN Special Rapporteur on the Rights of Persons with Disabilities and the UN Independent Expert on the enjoyment of all human rights by older persons, who published a joint submission addressed to the Commission in August 2023.[77] First, they observed that the conflict of laws norms of the Hague Convention should be 'progressively re-purposed' to boost the transition of State Parties from substitute to supported decision-making regimes. Moreover, they recommended a modification of critical dispositions of the proposed regulation, to facilitate the recognition of substitute decision-making regimes among Member States. In particular, Article 3(3) should reframe the notion of 'power of representation' only to mean supported decision-making. Moreover, Article 21 needs to be deleted, as it allows protection measures of 'placement' in an institution, in clear violation of both Articles 5 and 19 CRPD.

In July 2023, the Commission presented a proposal for a Directive amending the Victims' Rights Directive,[78] which aims at ensuring that victims of crime receive appropriate information, support and protection and can participate in criminal proceedings.[79] Some of the amendments are dedicated to the effective implementation of Article 13 CRPD on the right of equal access to justice for persons with disabilities, referring to 'the needs to ensure accessibility and provide reasonable accommodation so that victims with disability[ies] enjoy their rights as victims on equal basis with others'.[80] This proposal contains specific and cross-cutting provisions on the rights of victims with disabilities to ensure the accessibility of services and protection measures, as well as to guarantee that the means of digital communication are consistent with the requirements set out by the EAA.

Finally, in November 2024, the Union adopted a Directive for the introduction of a European Disability Card and the enhancement of the current European Parking Card for persons with disabilities.[81] This initiative, which is one of the flagship initiatives of the Strategy 2021-2030,[82] aims at enhancing the freedom of movement of persons with disabilities among Member States. The input for a European Disability Card predates the Strategy 2021-2030 and arises from a strong advocacy of OPDs, accompanied by the CRPD Committee's

[77] The UN Special Rapporteur on the rights of persons with disabilities (Gerard Quinn) and the Independent Expert on the enjoyment of all human rights by older persons (Claudia Mahler), 'Joint Submission. The European Commission's proposal for a Regulation and Council Decision governing the Hague Convention on the Protection of Adults' (2 August 2023) available at <https://www.ohchr.org/sites/default/files/documents/issues/disability/olderpersons/Annex-Joint-Submission-Towards-Greater-Coherence-International-Law.pdf>.

[78] Commission, 'Proposal for a Directive of the European Parliament and of the Council amending Directive 2012/29/EU establishing minimum standards on the rights, support and protection of victims of crime, and replacing Council Framework Decision 2001/220/JHA' COM(2023) 424 final.

[79] CRPD Committee (n 38) para 17, point a.

[80] Commission (n 78) Recital 16.

[81] Directive (EU) 2024/2841 of the European Parliament and of the Council of 23 October 2024 establishing the European Disability Card and the European Parking Card for persons with disabilities [2024] OJ L2024/2841.

[82] Commission (n 48) 6.

recommendations.[83] It establishes rules, including a common standardised model, for a European Disability Card as proof of a recognised disability status and the European Parking Card for persons with disabilities, as proof of their recognised right to parking conditions and facilities reserved for persons with disabilities. The objective is to guarantee the mutual recognition of these documents so as to facilitate the exercise by persons with disabilities, when traveling to another Member State, of their rights to receive and benefit from special conditions and preferential treatment offered by private operators or public authorities to access services, activities and facilities. The proposal has been immediately criticised by relevant OPDs as it requires Union citizenship as a prerequisite to be a beneficiary of the cards.[84] As a result, in November 2024, the Union adopted a separate legal act that extended the scope of the proposal to third-country nationals legally residing in the territory of a Member State who do not fall within the scope of the directive, whose disability status has been recognised by that Member State, and who are entitled to move or travel to other Member States under EU law.[85] Notwithstanding the initial criticism, this initiative might trigger and support further soft cooperation and coordination on disability assessment.[86]

5. The Authoritative Guidance of the Committee on the Rights of Persons with Disabilities as an Expert Body: As Dripping Water Hollows Out Stone

As mentioned above, the Convention, as a mixed agreement, is an integral part of the EU legal framework. EU secondary law must, as far as possible, be interpreted in a manner that is consistent with the CRPD. In that regard, the authoritative guidance provided by the CRPD Committee on the interpretation of the provisions of the Convention must duly be taken into account.

5.1. The Influence of the Convention on the Rights of Persons with Disabilities on the EU Legislature

The CRPD Committee's General Comments could be considered as a source of inspiration for the EU legislators for the further implementation of the CRPD in

[83] CRPD Committee (n 32) para 53; CRPD Committee (n 38) para 20, point a.

[84] D Ferri and ES Krolla, 'The European Disability Card … Reloaded' (*EU Law Live*, 23 November 2023) available at <https://eulawlive.com/op-ed-the-european-disability-card-reloaded-by-delia-ferri-and-eva-s-krolla/>.

[85] Directive (EU) 2024/2842 of the European Parliament and of the Council of 23 October 2024 extending Directive (EU) 2024/2841 to third-country nationals legally residing in a Member State [2024] OJ L2024/2842.

[86] D Ferri, 'Analysis of the European Disability Card. The Proposed Directive: Shortcomings, Strengths and Opportunities' Publication for the Committee on Employment and Social Affairs, Policy Department for Economic, Scientific and Quality of Life Policies (European Parliament 2023).

EU law. As a matter of example, in its General Comment No. 6 on equality and non-discrimination,[87] the CRPD Committee expressly recognises multiple and intersectional discrimination as forms of discrimination prohibited under the CRPD. More precisely, it clarifies that multiple discrimination occurs in 'a situation where a person can experience discrimination on two or several grounds, in the sense that discrimination is compounded or aggravated', while intersectional discrimination 'refers to a situation where several grounds operate and interact with each other at the same time in such a way that they are inseparable and thereby expose relevant individuals to unique types of disadvantage and discrimination'.[88] To date, there is not an explicit and binding prohibition of multiple and intersectional discrimination in EU legislation. More precisely, the concept of multiple discrimination is enshrined in Recitals 14 and 3 of, respectively, the Racial Equality Directive[89] and the Employment Equality Directive,[90] but with no reference to intersectional discrimination.

The CRPD Committee reiterated the opportunity to 'recognize multiple and intersectional forms of discrimination faced by persons with disabilities and to provide access to remedies in case of discrimination' in both the 2014 EU's first report on the implementation of the CRPD[91] and the 2022 List of Issues.[92]

Lastly, the 2023 EU's combined reports highlight that the EU has finally adopted an 'intersectional approach in EU equality strategies',[93] as claimed in the Strategy 2021-2030. The latter document promotes an intersectional perspective, with the aim of addressing 'specific barriers faced by persons with disabilities who are at the intersection of identities (gender, racial, ethnic, sexual, religious), or in a difficult socioeconomic or other vulnerable situation'.[94] On the one hand, all EU social surveys have been modified to provide statistical data based on sex, age, disability, and migrant background. On the other hand, several legislative acts expressly refer to intersectionality or discrimination based on several grounds, such as Directive 2024/1385 on combating violence against women and domestic violence,[95] Directive (EU) 2024/1500 on standards for equality bodies in the field of equal treatment and equal opportunities between women and men in matters of

[87] CRPD Committee, 'General Comment No. 6 on equality and non-discrimination' (26 April 2018) CRPD/C/GC/6.

[88] Ibid para 19.

[89] Council Directive 2000/43/EC of 29 June 2000 implementing the principle of equal treatment between persons irrespective of racial or ethnic origin [2000] OJ L180/22.

[90] Council Directive 2000/78/EC of 27 November 2000 establishing a general framework for equal treatment in employment and occupation [2000] OJ L303/16.

[91] CRPD Committee (n 32) para 19. L Waddington, 'The Influence of the UN Convention on the Rights of Persons with Disabilities on EU Non-Discrimination Law' in U Belavusau and K Henrard (eds), *EU Anti-Discrimination Law Beyond Gender* (Hart 2018) 357.

[92] CRPD Committee (n 38) para 6, point c.

[93] Commission (n 39) paras 43, 271.

[94] Commission (n 48) 3.

[95] Directive (EU) 2024/1385 of the European Parliament and of the Council of 14 May 2024 on combating violence against women and domestic violence [2024] OJ L 2024/1385.

employment and occupation,[96] and the Directive (EU) 2023/970 providing rules on pay transparency.[97] The latter directive also provides a definition of intersectional discrimination, which is described as 'discrimination based on a combination of sex and any other ground or grounds of discrimination protected under Directive 2000/43/EC or 2000/78/EC'.[98] This is a significant step forward in the recognition of multiple and intersectional discrimination in the EU legal order, even though it is still limited to a very specific sector of EU non-discrimination law. Hopefully, this will not remain an isolated attempt to recognise the multiple and intersectional dimensions of non-discrimination within the EU, but the starting point to finally affirm this concept in a dedicated legal instrument.[99] Ideally, this will be the long-expected proposed Horizontal Equality Directive,[100] which aims at setting out a framework for the prohibition of discrimination and at establishing a uniform minimum level of protection against discrimination within the EU.

5.2. The Opinions of Advocates General at the Court of Justice

To date, the practice of the CJEU is to look at the wording of the Convention without explicitly considering the interpretation provided by the CRPD Committee. The same consideration applies to almost all the Opinions of the Advocate General concerning the CRPD.

However, it is worth mentioning that Advocate General Rantos, in their Opinion on *HR Rail*,[101] for the first time cited and examined in detail the views adopted by the Committee on an individual complaint in *V.F.C.*,[102] in relation to the concept of 'reasonable accommodation' under the Convention. This is a significant step forward, which hopefully will not remain an isolated case in the future, further deepening the influence of the CRPD Committee on EU disability law.[103]

[96] Directive (EU) 2024/1500 of the European Parliament and of the Council of 14 May 2024 on standards for equality bodies in the field of equal treatment and equal opportunities between women and men in matters of employment and occupation, and amending Directives 2006/54/EC and 2010/41/EU [2024] OJ L2024/1500.

[97] Directive (EU) 2023/970 of the European Parliament and of the Council of 10 May 2023 to strengthen the application of the principle of equal pay for equal work or work of equal value between men and women through pay transparency and enforcement mechanisms [2023] OJ L132/21.

[98] Article 3(2)(e) Directive (EU) 2023/970.

[99] MV Onufrio, 'Intersectional Discrimination in the European Legal Systems: Toward a Common Solution?' (2014) 14 *International Journal of Discrimination and the Law* 126, 136.

[100] Commission (n 34).

[101] Opinion of Advocate General Rantos delivered on 11 November 2021 in Case C-485/20 *HR Rail* ECLI:EU:C:2021:916, paras 70-72.

[102] CRPD Committee, *V.F.C. v Spain* (2 April 2019) CRPD/C/21/D/34/2015.

[103] G de Búrca, 'Questioning the EU's 'principled openness' to international law: an examination of the Court's reception of the Aarhus Convention and the Convention on the rights of persons with disabilities' in M Claes and E Vos (eds), *Making Sense of European Union Law* (Hart 2022) 3.

5.3. Other Bodies: The European Ombudsman

Beside its influence on the EU legislative initiatives, the CRPD Committee's General Comments could also contribute to shape the interpretation and, consequently, push in the direction of a more stringent protection of disability rights by other important ancillary EU bodies. The most remarkable example refers to the jurisprudence of the European Ombudsman, discussed earlier by Ferri in her chapter.[104] In particular the European Ombudsman has engaged with how the Commission monitors EU Structural and Investment (ESI) funds to ensure they are used to promote the right of persons with disabilities to independent living and inclusion in the community.[105] In particular, the CRPD Committee's General Comment No. 5 on living independently and being included in the community[106] has been mentioned by the European Ombudsman as the benchmark for ensuring the implementation of deinstitutionalisation processes throughout the EU.[107]

In its strategic inquiry, the European Ombudsman recommended that the Commission provides clearer guidance for Member States about the need to promote deinstitutionalisation in the context of the use of ESI funds, and made clear that:

> any exceptions to the prohibition on funding institutions should be interpreted narrowly and reflect the comment of the UN Committee that no new 'long term institutions' should be built and that older 'long term care residential institutions' should not be renovated beyond the most urgent measures necessary to safeguard residents' physical safety.[108]

Moreover, the European Ombudsman pointed out that, although Member States are responsible for selecting and implementing projects that receive ESI funds, the Commission has a responsibility to intervene if a project does not comply with the CRPD.[109] As a result, whether or not the CRPD Committee, acting in its capacity as a monitoring body, raises concerns about the compliance of a Member State's activities funded by the EU with the provisions of the CRPD on deinstitutionalisation, the Commission should take a position by raising the matter with the Member State concerned and by imposing financial sanctions.

[104] D Ferri, 'The Role of the European Ombudsman in Protecting and Promoting Disability Rights' in this volume.

[105] European Ombudsman, Case OI/2/2021/MHZ, Decision on the own initiative inquiry into how the European Commission monitors EU Structural and Investment funds to ensure they are used to promote the right of persons with disabilities to independent living and inclusion in the community (27 April 2022), paras 2, 33.

[106] CRPD Committee, 'General Comment No. 5 on living independently and being included in the community' (27 October 2017) CRPD/C/GC/5.

[107] Ferri (n 104).

[108] European Ombudsman (n 105) para 11.

[109] Ibid.

6. Concluding Remarks

This contribution has scrutinised the role played by the CRPD Committee, in its capacity as, respectively, a monitoring body and an expert body, in nudging the EU toward more effective compliance with the Convention. Nonetheless, it is worth clarifying that, for the purposes of this contribution, the term 'nudge' is used in a non-technical sense and does not entail a behavioural approach to law-making.[110] Hence, it does not discuss the application in international law of psychologically informed law-making tools, such as opting out mechanisms, non-binding goals and rankings, designed to improve the acceptance of human rights obligations.[111] Moreover, in the analysis provided, the function of the CRPD Committee acting as a quasi-judicial body is not taken into consideration, as the EU has not yet ratified the Optional Protocol to the Convention and, as a result, it is not subject to the complaints and the inquiry procedures performed under Articles 2 and 6 Optional Protocol.

On the one hand, in performing its activity as a monitoring body, the CRPD Committee orients the developments of EU disability law. During the monitoring processes in 2014 and 2023, the EU and the CRPD Committee engaged in a rich 'interinstitutional dialogue', which resulted in the adoption or modification of numerous EU legislative acts on critical disability issues. In this context, the impact of the CRPD Committee on the development of EU disability law is crystal clear. Most notably, it is possible to draw a parallel between the recommendations provided by the CRPD Committee and the EU disability law initiatives recently promoted or adopted referring to web accessibility and digital equality, legal capacity and supportive decision-making in Member States' legal reforms, access to justice for victims of crimes, and freedom of movement.[112]

On the other hand, acting as an authoritative guidance, the CRPD Committee contributes to the interpretation of the CRPD obligations and, consequently, pushes in the direction of more stringent protection of disability rights across the EU. Its authoritative guidance on the understanding of the provisions of the Convention, even though not immediately evident, must not be underestimated, also in light of the leading role of expert treaty bodies in interpreting the provisions of human rights treaties emerging both from international practice and legal doctrine.[113] In the EU legal order, this occurs in the European Ombudsman's jurisprudence on deinstitutionalisation in the context of the use of ESI funds.[114] Hence, the Ombudsman expressly refers to the CRPD Committee's General

[110] RT Thaler and CR Sunstein, *Nudge: Improving Decisions About Health, Wealth and Happiness* (Yale University Press 2008).

[111] D Russo, 'L'approccio 'nudge' nel diritto internazionale: una nuova frontiera del soft law' (2022) 2 *Osservatorio sulle fonti* 131-144.

[112] See Section 4.1.

[113] See Section 2.

[114] European Ombudsman (n 105).

Comment No. 5 on living independently and being included in the community[115] as the benchmark for ensuring the implementation of deinstitutionalisation processes throughout the EU. Moreover, General Comment No. 6 on equality and non-discrimination[116] has been a source of inspiration for the EU legislators for the gradual recognition of the multiple and intersectional dimensions of non-discrimination in EU law.[117]

Pending the ratification of the Optional Protocol to the Convention, the influence of the CRPD Committee is less evident. However, this limitation does not affect the leading role of the CRPD Committee in guiding the EU towards a more effective implementation of the Convention, as it emerges from the parallel analysis provided above of the activities performed by the CRPD Committee and the EU institutions on critical disability issues and policies.

Hopefully, the historic election of an EU representative to the CRPD Committee will contribute to advancing the dialogue between the EU and the CRPD Committee, as well as to further reinforcing the commitment of the EU towards the implementation of the Convention across the EU.

[115] CRPD Committee (n 106).
[116] CRPD Committee (n 87).
[117] See Section 4.2.

Epilogue

BRUNO DE WITTE

This book offers a broad panorama of the evolution and current state of European Union (EU) disability law. In addition to offering a major contribution to European disability studies, it also offers an interesting contribution to European legal studies more generally, which is the object of these brief concluding reflections.

A first notable characteristic of this book is that it highlights the importance of examining and understanding institutional practices. EU law cannot properly be understood and described without knowledge of those institutional practices; the 'black letter' of EU law remains a dead letter without reflecting in its analysis the various practices that EU institutions develop in shaping and implementing the formal legal rules. The legal roles of the EU political institutions are primarily those of law-making and law-application. They perform these roles and their specific tasks by means of routinised ways of behaviour that we may call institutional practices. The roles of the European Commission, and of the Council of the European Union and European Parliament, are documented in this volume, with Krolla and Bartlett paying special attention, in their respective chapters, to the reasons that explain when and why the Commission takes policy initiatives in the field of disability, and when and why the co-legislators enact disability laws (and also, importantly, when and why they fail to enact such laws).

Furthermore, the scope of this book is not limited to the role of the main EU institutions, both political and judicial, but also encompasses the role of other actors in disability policy. By devoting considerable attention to the role of non-institutional actors, this book builds on a more general trend in EU legal studies, as noted in Volpato's chapter. However, the role of the non-institutional actors is probably stronger in disability policy than in most other EU policies, as it emerges from several contributions that highlight the roles of civil society actors (such as the European Disability Forum) and of academics. The role of the latter has, arguably, been quite meaningful in shaping EU disability law and policy, and is documented by Lisa Waddington, who herself is a scholar who commented on the evolution of EU disability law since its inception but who also, together with other scholars, helped to shape the EU's disability policy. The influence of academic scholars on the evolution of disability law seems to have been more meaningful here than in other fields of EU law.

The book also adopts a strong evolutionary perspective, not only in the chapter by Waldschmidt and Krolla, which identifies four periods of EU disability policy, but also in many other chapters. The book as a whole adopts a perspective that political scientists might call one of historical institutionalism. The evolution of EU disability law and policy is marked by slow processes of incremental change promoted by the institutional and non-institutional actors, both at the European and national level, but these incremental processes have been shaped and modified by some critical junctures. Two of those critical legal events permeate the accounts in the various chapters. The first of them happened in 1999, with the creation, by the Treaty of Amsterdam, of an EU competence to enact legislation to combat discrimination in what is now Article 19 of the Treaty on the Functioning of the European Union, which was followed the next year by the adoption of the Employment Equality Directive 2000/78 prohibiting discrimination on a number of grounds, including disability, in the field of employment. EU disability law made progress here by being embedded in European equality law more generally. The second critical event happened ten years later and was specific to disability law, namely the EU's negotiation and ratification of the UN Convention on the Rights of Persons with Disabilities (CRPD). The wide-ranging legal duties contained in that Convention, combined with the reporting procedure that it set in place and with the intellectual resources that it offered to Non-governmental Organisations, put pressure on the EU to step up its disability policy in the years after 2010. Since then, the EU has amplified the kinds of tools that compose its disability policy. In addition to the adoption of new disability-specific legislation, we have seen the use of a variety of other legal and policy tools: the mainstreaming of disability in EU legislation more generally, the adoption of funding programmes for disability actions both inside and outside the EU, the enactment of soft law measures, of strategies and action plans, the collection of data, and exchanges of best practices involving national and civil society actors, in particular through the European Disability Forum. Not all these components of European disability *policy* are part of EU disability *law*, but by paying attention to the whole range of policy tools, this book underlines its overall message that EU disability law can best be understood by examining and understanding the political and social context within which a wide range of institutional and non-institutional actors operate.

INDEX